SCIENCE AT THE UNIVERSITY OF EDINBURGH

1583 - 1993

D1638333

"To understand a science it is necessary to know its history."

Auguste Comte (1798-1857)   *Positive Philosophy.*

SCIENCE AT THE UNIVERSITY OF EDINBURGH

1583 - 1993

An Illustrated History to Mark the Centenary
of the Faculty of Science and Engineering
1893 - 1993

Ronald M. Birse

The Faculty of Science and Engineering
The University of Edinburgh
1994

First published in hardback and paperback in 1994 by
The University of Edinburgh
Faculty of Science and Engineering
The King's Buildings, West Mains Road
Edinburgh   EH9 3JY   Scotland

British Library Cataloguing-in-Publication Data
A catalogue record for this book is available from the British Library

ISBN 0 9522883 0 3 Hardback
ISBN 0 9522883 1 1 Paperback

Printed by Macdonald Lindsay Pindar plc
Edgefield Road, Loanhead, Midlothian EH20 9SY

FOREWORD

Science at the University of Edinburgh began in 1583 at the same time as the foundation of what was then the Tounis College of Edinburgh. From small beginnings within the Faculties of Arts and Medicine it flourished to the extent that degrees in science were instituted in 1864, and in 1893 a separate Faculty of Science was established. Today the Faculty of Science and Engineering is outstanding in Scotland, within one of the best research Universities in the United Kingdom.

The Faculty now has 3600 undergraduate and 750 postgraduate students, with 325 academic, 375 research, 304 technical and 123 clerical staff. In the last financial year our income from research grants and contracts exceeded £17m, approximately half the total external income of the University. The total financial turnover of the Faculty of Science and Engineering exceeds £40m.

No book has been written, until now, which traces the origins of the various science departments and the development of the Faculty as a whole over the past four hundred years. Histories of the University such as those by Horn and Logan Turner paint a broad picture, the one up to 1889 and the other from 1883 to 1933. More recently *Engineering at Edinburgh University 1673-1983* by R M Birse, *Britain's First Chair of Agriculture at the University of Edinburgh 1790-1990* by I J Fleming and N F Robertson, and a few other publications have covered in more detail some parts of the Faculty's overall scope.

The Centenary of the Faculty in this academic year, 1993-94, has provided a suitable occasion for tracing and documenting our distinguished past. The Faculty Centenary Committee, chaired by myself, decided to commission Ron Birse (a retired member of Civil Engineering staff with a long-standing interest in historical matters) to put pen to paper again and write this account. We are most grateful to him for spending two years of his life in researching and writing this authoritative volume on behalf of the Faculty.

I commend this illustrated history marking the Faculty Centenary as a source of great value, to be read by past, present and future generations of staff and students alike: it will undoubtedly stand the test of time. I believe that within these pages Ron Birse has not only succeeded in capturing professorial profiles and significant events that stand out through the years, but has also been able to offer a view of the future, as seen through his eyes and those of a number of current students. I wish you all a pleasant and informative read.

Professor John Mavor, FRSE
Dean of the Faculty of Science and Engineering
The University of Edinburgh

14 March 1994

ACKNOWLEDGEMENTS

A work such as this clearly owes a great deal to a great many people, and I am pleased to be able to say a public 'thank-you' to all those who have helped me in many different ways. First of all to the Centenary Committee of the Faculty of Science and Engineering, energetically chaired by the Dean, John Mavor, who conceived the idea of a centenary history, and were prepared to give the job to a non-historian. Both as a committee, and as a group of sympathetic individuals, they have done everything possible to ensure the success of the venture. The Centenary Coordinator Fiona Curle helped us all with her cheerful efficiency.

My search for information in primary and secondary sources in the University Library was greatly assisted by Jo Currie in Special Collections and Mike Barfoot in the Medical Archive. Other historical material was provided by Ray Footman and Mike Westcott, and Bryan McLure organised a very useful selective print-out of notable scientists from the alumni database. The Department of Chemistry was able to provide transcripts of 'recollections' recorded some years ago by Arnold Beevers, Neil Campbell and John Cadogan – it is a great pity that there appear to be no other examples of this kind in existence.

Much valuable information was obtained from previous histories of the University by Dalzel, Grant, Horn and Turner; from the history of the Royal Society of Edinburgh by Campbell and Smellie; from *Edinburgh's Place in Scientific Progress* published by the British Association in 1921; and from Brück's history of Astronomy, Fleming and Robertson's history of Agriculture, Fletcher and Brown's history of the Royal Botanic Garden, and Taylor's history of Forestry, in Edinburgh and Edinburgh University. Other sources are acknowledged in the text and listed as references or in the select bibliography.

The first two chapters owe much of their detail to the work of Christine Shepherd, who was also kind enough to read and comment on them, and to the publications of the late Eric Forbes and the History of Medicine and Science Unit. Robert Anderson, Reader in the Department of History, read the first four chapters and pointed out a reassuringly small number of inaccuracies. Most of the chapters were read by John Mavor and Des Truman, who provided some valuable comments and corrections; parts of the draft were read and commented on by Gordon Craig, Ian Hedge and Neil Mackenzie.

From the very start of my work on the book it was obvious that I would need a small army of collaborators to furnish me with information and answer my questions. I am extremely grateful for the willing help of George Alder, Richard Ambler, Peder Aspen, Richard Battersby, Geoffrey Beale, Geoffrey Boulton, Peter Brand, Grahame Bulfield, Peter Dryburgh, Dougal Drysdale, David Edge, Mike Eggar, Elisabet Engdahl, Douglas Falconer, David Finney, Ian Fleming, Ray Footman, Michael Garraway, Jen Gordon, Sheila Gould, Alan Heavens, Jim Howe, Mervyn Jack, Margaret Jackson, Rob Kempton, Ron Kille, Richard Lathe, Eric Lucey, Ben Malcolm, Douglas Malcolm, Elizabeth Marsh,

Joe McGeough, Andrew McKendrick, David Milne, John Morgan, Terry Myers, Bruce Nelson, John Phillips, Colin Pritchard, John Robertson, Stephen Salter, Peter Schofield, Peter Schwarz, Roger Scott, Dick Sillitto, Norman Simmonds, Keith Stenning, Ian Sutherland, Austin Tate, David Wallace, Keith Weston, John Wilkinson, Keith Winton, Peter Wilson, and Mike Yeoman.

Many of those named above took the time to read the last three chapters in draft, and helped me to weed out a few inaccurate statements of fact or opinion. Any remaining errors or omissions are of course the author's sole responsibility.

As well as being almost equally involved in the sustained effort required over the past two years to get the book published on time, my wife Elizabeth has played the major part in assembling and selecting the illustrations, and in compiling the database of almost 600 names from which the most notable alumni were chosen. We have both had to contend with too much material from some sources and too little from others, and it has not been easy to achieve a reasonably balanced picture of the Faculty of Science and Engineering in all its activities.

For assistance with illustrations, both historical and contemporary, we are grateful to Ray Footman and a number of others already mentioned, but especially to the departmental photographers Jeremy Landless, Peter Tuffy and Duncan Waldron. We record our thanks to those who have allowed us to reproduce copyright material, and we hope that the list of illustrations includes all the necessary acknowledgements to sources, but for any that have been inadvertently omitted we trust that our apologies and thanks will be sufficient.

CONTENTS

Chapter 10   **THE FACULTY OF SCIENCE AND ENGINEERING -
               TODAY AND TOMORROW,** 220

LIST OF ILLUSTRATIONS

A – Half-tone illustrations in text

ABBREVIATIONS AND ACRONYMS
(excluding honours and degrees, and standard abbreviations)

*	*see* or *see also*
AB(G)RO	Animal Breeding (and Genetics) Research Organisation
ABRC	Advisory Board of Research Councils
A(F)RC	Agriculture (and Food) Research Council
AI(AI)	Artificial Intelligence (Applications Institute)
BTO	Biology Teaching Organisation
CAD/CAM	Computer-Aided Design/Manufacture
CAST	Centre for Applications Software and Technology
CAT	College of Advanced Technology
CICL	Centre for Industrial Consultancy and Liaison
CVCP	Committee of Vice-Chancellors and Principals
DAP	Distributed Array Processor
DBS	Division of Biological Sciences
DELTA	Developing European Learning through Technological Advance
Dem	Demonstrator
DES	Department of Education and Science
DSIR	Department of Scientific and Industrial Research
DTI(OSO)	Department of Trade and Industry (Offshore Supplies Office)
EMAS	Edinburgh Multi-Access System
EMF	Edinburgh Microfabrication Facility
EPCC	Edinburgh Parallel Computing Centre
ERCC	Edinburgh Regional Computing Centre
ESPRIT	European Strategic Programme for Research and development in Information Technology
ESRC	Economic and Social Research Council
ETTC	Edinburgh Technology Transfer Centre
EUCS	Edinburgh University Computer Service
FAO	Food and Agriculture Organisation
FoM	Faculty of Medicine
FoS	Faculty of Science
FTE	Full-time equivalent
ICAPB	Institute of Cell, Animal and Population Biology
ICMB	Institute of Cell and Molecular Biology
IERM	Institute of Ecology and Resource Management
ILC	Industrial Liaison Committee
IRC	Inter-disciplinary Research Centre
IT	Information Technology
JCMB	James Clerk Maxwell Building
JOULE	Research and Technological Development Programme in the Field of Energy

KB	King's Buildings
Lect	Lecturer
LFCS	Laboratory for Foundations of Computer Science
LSI	Large-Scale Integrated (chip)
MRC	Medical Research Council
NA	Not Applicable
NERC	Natural Environment Research Council
NIMR	National Institute for Medical Research
NMR	Nuclear Magnetic Resonance
NPL	National Physical Laboratory
PCFC	Polytechnics and Colleges Funding Council
PSTI	Petroleum Science and Technology Institute
Publ	Published
R&D	Research and Development
RAE	Research Assessment Exercise
ROE	Royal Observatory, Edinburgh
RSM, RMS	Royal Scottish Museum, now the Royal Museum of Scotland
SEB	Scottish Examination Board
Sen lect	Senior lecturer
SERC	Science and Engineering Research Council
SHEFC	Scottish Higher Education Funding Council (from 1992)
SOED	Scottish Office Education Department
SSRC	Social Sciences Research Council
SRC	Science Research Council (SERC from 1981)
UCCA	Universities Central Council on Admissions
UCL	University College, London
UFC	Universities Funding Council (SHEFC in Scotland from 1992)
UGC	University Grants Committee (UFC from 1989)
UnivEd	UnivEd Technologies Limited
VLSI	Very Large-Scale Integrated (chip)
WWI	World War I
WWII	World War II

INTRODUCTION

Since the title gives only a general indication of the subject matter, some explanation of this work's origin and aims may be of interest. About three years ago it was suggested that a history of the then newly-renamed Faculty of Science and Engineering should be written to mark its centenary in 1993, and almost as soon as I had agreed to undertake the task I began to realise just how much of a challenge it was. To do justice to the long and very unevenly documented history of science in the University of Edinburgh it quickly became obvious that the centenary history would have to span not one century but four, and cover not just a dozen basic scientific disciplines but almost a hundred departments, research centres, units, schools, laboratories, museums, libraries, spin-off companies, associated institutions and so on. Neither a scientist nor a historian by profession, I have not attempted a historiographical treatment of the subject, and I fully appreciate now why there are so few books of this kind on the University Library's shelves.

The institution of a Faculty of Science in the University of Edinburgh was decreed by the Scottish Universities Parliamentary Commissioners in Ordinance No 31, dated 5 June 1893, approved by Order in Council on 23 November 1893 and coming into force on that date. By the same Ordinance, under the Universities (Scotland) Act, 1889, Faculties of Science were created also in the Universities of Glasgow and Aberdeen.

It must not be assumed, however, that the whole realm of science and technology was suddenly brought into being in the Scottish universities by the Parliamentary Commissioners in 1893. In Edinburgh, on the contrary, Chairs of Mathematics, Natural Philosophy, Botany, Chemistry, Natural History, Astronomy and Agriculture had all been established before the end of the eighteenth century. From the very foundation of the University as the Town's College of Edinburgh in 1583, scientific subjects such as mathematics and natural philosophy were taught in the Faculty of Arts, and by the early eighteenth century chemistry and botany were being taught in the Faculty of Medicine. Thirty years before the Faculty of Science was founded the Senatus introduced in the Faculty of Arts the degrees of Bachelor and Doctor of Science, which could be awarded in the mathematical, physical or natural sciences.

So it became the aim of this history to tell the story of science and engineering in the University of Edinburgh wherever, whenever and in whatever guise they have flourished over the past 410 years. The history of engineering at Edinburgh has already been documented, however, in the author's *Engineering at Edinburgh University: a short history, 1673 - 1983*, and accordingly in this volume the development of engineering in the University up to 1983 has been treated more briefly than would otherwise be merited. Some new material has been included, most of it relating to the contributions made by Edinburgh engineers to one or other of the sciences.

Since the centenary of the Faculty of Science and Engineering is the book's *raison d'être* the main emphasis will be on the subjects which are currently part of this Faculty, and in general the medical sciences, such as biochemistry and bacteriology, and the social sciences, such as economics, geography and psychology, are excluded. But life would be intolerably dull if there were no exceptions to the rules, and in these pages there are many individuals, and quite a few departments, straddling some fences and jumping others. The results have generally been so beneficial that, especially in the medical and non-medical biological sciences, many of those long-standing barriers have been breached, and in some cases removed altogether, during the past few years at Edinburgh University.

As originally constituted in 1893, the Faculty of Science consisted of the Professors of eleven subjects; five (in chemistry, natural history, botany, anatomy and physiology) remained primarily members of the Faculty of Medicine, and two (in mathematics and natural philosophy) of the Faculty of Arts, while the remaining four (in astronomy, geology, engineering, and agriculture and rural economy) were transferred, as it were, from the Faculty of Arts to the Faculty of Science. Just over half a century later in 1949, the Faculty of Science consisted of 23 professors and 19 non-professorial members; today the numbers in the Faculty of Science and Engineering have increased to 70 and 201 respectively.

The growth of science at Edinburgh University extends over the whole of its four-hundred-year history, and it is not the purpose of this book to record in detail every change in every degree course, every decision tortuously arrived at in Faculty or Senatus, *ad infinitum*. The intention is to show how the University gained and maintained its place as a front runner in many areas of scientific teaching and research, and to highlight some of the most notable achievements, past and present, of its staff and former students.

With these aims in mind, and with the knowledge that sometimes very complicated changes involving more than one department would have to be described, it was decided that the most appropriate type of historical narrative would be a broad survey of science throughout the whole Faculty (and beyond) within the period of time selected for each chapter, rather than a series of historical accounts of the major subject areas, complete in themselves but involving the reader in a succession of chronological U-turns. Within each chapter, therefore, all the major developments and changes during that period are described in turn, along with the achievements of a few outstanding alumni. At the end of most chapters there is a very limited collection of biographical notes on some of the other notable alumni.

The disadvantage of this format is that the long-term development of most subjects is spread over several chapters, and it is hoped that the chronological summaries in Appendix A will give the reader the necessary bird's-eye view of an otherwise fragmented picture. Some personal details are also to be found in the Appendix, rather than allowing them to interrupt the flow of the main narrative.

I have to end with an apology, however, for the fact that even in a book which is now half as long again as originally envisaged, it has not been possible to include more than a small fraction of the information available to me, which in turn must be only a small fraction of the information still hidden in one archive or another. In particular I regret that only some 135 science alumni could be included out of the more than 600 who presented themselves, as it were, from various historical and biographical sources as being specially worthy of a place. To put the figure of 600 into perspective, a reasonable estimate of the total number, from 1587 to the present day, of Edinburgh University alumni in the non-medical sciences would be of the order of 30,000. The whole book, in fact, represents little more than the tip of an iceberg.

Having to select and condense fairly ruthlessly, while trying not to become seriously indigestible, has also meant that the leading actors have had to be given virtually all the best lines. By that I mean that Edinburgh University's 214 scientific professors, 57 of whom are members of the Faculty today, have all been given a place in the spotlight, while very few of the large and hard-working supporting cast have even been mentioned. Until the end of the nineteenth century, of course, practically all the teaching and research was done by the professors, and even by 1904-05 the University Calendar lists only sixteen lecturers in science subjects, in addition to the nine professors.

Today, however, as the Dean rightly points out in his Foreword, the Faculty of Science and Engineering has a teaching staff of 57 professors supported by 268 'other ranks'; there are 375 research staff supported by 304 technical staff; and the whole complicated machine would grind quickly to a halt without the 123 clerical staff. I very much regret that so few of them can be mentioned by name, and I ask the reader to bear in mind that no scientific research group today can hope to achieve significant results without the help of enthusiastic research assistants and resourceful technicians – nor would the results ever be published without the efforts of the secretarial and clerical staff.

CHAPTER 1

Early science teaching – Aristotelianism for young scholars

The University of Edinburgh was the youngest of Scotland's four ancient universities when it was founded in 1583, and it was the only one to be created at the instigation of a Town Council, though still with the essential support of Church and Crown. The older Universities of St Andrews (1411), Glasgow (1451) and King's College, Aberdeen (1495) were to a large extent the work of strong-minded bishops, and the fact that Edinburgh was not an episcopal see probably explains the absence of a university foundation there in the fifteenth century. Close ties with the Church were not an unmixed blessing, however, and the universities were directly and sometimes seriously affected by the periods of religious turmoil that seized Scotland from time to time before and after the Reformation. Not a few teachers were dismissed for refusing to subscribe to the religion of the day, and religious instruction played an important part in the students' daily lives.

Scotland's three oldest universities had all known times of prosperity in the fifteenth century, but it has to be admitted that by the middle of the sixteenth century they were all in decline. Student intakes were tiny by present-day standards – an average of about thirty at St Andrews and Aberdeen, even fewer at Glasgow, which suffered chronic poverty for more than a century until it was rescued from its moribund state by Andrew Melville and the Burgh Council in 1573.

The principal functions of Scotland's pre-Reformation universities, commonly and more accurately known as colleges until about the end of the eighteenth century, were similar to those of today's secondary schools; most of their first-year students were aged between twelve and fifteen, instruction was by dictated notes and frequent questioning, discipline was strict and corporal punishment commonplace. The prescribed language of teaching, examining and everyday conversation was Latin.

The subjects of study were based on the traditional medieval curriculum, in which grammar, logic, metaphysics and ethics predominated. Students were taken through the whole of the four years' course for a Master's degree by the same regent, who taught all the subjects in turn. The great fount of classical learning on whom much of the regents' teaching would be based was Aristotle, whose scientific and philosophical works, translated into Latin in the middle ages, thus survived as teaching texts for more than two thousand years.

In spite of occasional attempts by one College or another, sometimes under a degree of external pressure, to introduce changes in teaching methods or course content, the

B

situation remained much the same in all the Scottish universities until the end of the seventeenth century.

Edinburgh and the Tounis College

The creation of a university college in Edinburgh had long been looked for by the religious and civic leaders of Scotland's capital, but this is not the place to recount the many set-backs that had to be overcome before they were eventually successful. Horn (1967) tells the story in some detail, and Scotland (1969) paints the broader picture of school and higher education in Scotland from the earliest times.

Rothiemay's map of Edinburgh showing buildings of the Tounis College by 1646.

The Tounis College was founded in 1583 under the general powers granted to Edinburgh Town Council by the Charter of King James VI dated 14 April 1582. The first regent was **Robert Rollock (1555-1598)**, a graduate of St Andrews, where he had been a regent of philosophy since 1580. He moved to Edinburgh in October 1583, and three years later, at the age of 31, he was appointed the first Principal, a further four regents having been added to the teaching staff by that time. Rollock's first class completed their studies in 1587, and he had the satisfaction of capping 47 Masters of Arts that year. From the very first the College was successful in attracting students, not only from Scotland and Ireland

James VI and I. Painting attributed to Cornelius Jansens, c1600

Principal Robert Rollock – detail from an anonymous painting in the Scottish National Portrait Gallery

but also, because of its secular constitution, Puritans from England and Huguenots from France. Within a few years, in fact, Edinburgh had more students than any of the older Scottish universities had ever had.

Thomas Craufurd, the first historian of the University of Edinburgh, gives sixteen score as a fair average of the total number of students in the 1630s, and the number is thought to have reached nearly 500 soon after the Restoration in 1660. An interesting comparison is that the combined total of Oxford and Cambridge students in the early seventeenth century was probably not much more than two thousand, closely supervised academically and morally by their tutors in thirty-two residential colleges.

The four-year Edinburgh MA curriculum adopted more or less the same sequence of studies as the older Scottish foundations, which in turn had followed the example of other European universities such as Paris and Bologna:-

first year	Greek
second year	Logic and Metaphysics
third year	Metaphysics and Ethics
fourth year	Natural Philosophy

In addition to these principal subjects of study, which were taught by the Regents of Philosophy, instruction in Latin was provided by Regents of Humanity for the substantial numbers of unmatriculated students whose proficiency in the language was insufficient to allow them to enter the first year of the MA course. There was also some teaching of mathematics, though at first not so much as a subject in its own right, more as an aid to understanding the lectures in natural philosophy.

As with other distinctions that we would regard as fundamental (between 'university' and 'college' for example), there was no such firm demarcation in the sixteenth and seventeenth centuries between 'regent' and 'professor' as there is in our minds now. Some of the older historians refer to Professors of Humanity, not Regents, and it is a matter of fact that in 1620 the senior Regent of Philosophy was made 'public professor of mathematics', while the second Regent became 'public professor of metaphysics'.

The University has accordingly adopted the uniformitarian view that the following chairs were all instituted in 1583 at the same time as the subjects began to be regularly taught when the Tounis College was founded in that year:-

Humanity (Latin)	Greek
Logic and Metaphysics	Moral Philosophy
Mathematics	Natural Philosophy.

We simply have to bear in mind that, especially before 1708, the chairs were not continuously occupied by professors – a situation that is sadly not unfamiliar to us today.

Aristotelianism and the Scientific Revolution

It would be easy to dismiss the teaching of science in Edinburgh, and in the other Scottish universities for that matter, as of little consequence until after the end of the seventeenth century, but that would be to ignore the general state of scientific knowledge (or more accurately lack of knowledge) at the time.

For example, comparing two aspects of Aristotle's scientific beliefs in more detail, some of his most successful and accurate work was in biology, where he studied and classified more than 500 animal species, dissecting almost fifty of them himself, and arranged them into hierarchies. This led him to believe, more than two thousand years before Darwin, that animal species represented a chain of progressive change; in other words, an evolutionary process. On the other hand, his understanding of the universe as a whole, and the laws governing the behaviour of earthly and heavenly bodies, was wildly inaccurate, but was hardly improved upon until the middle of the sixteenth century. On earth all things were impure and transient, in heaven all was pure and everlasting. 'Natural' motion took place vertically upwards or downwards, horizontal motion was 'unnatural' and required a force to create and sustain it. The heavenly bodies, which had no particular place of rest they were trying to reach, moved in paths that were constant and circular.

Examples of the arbitrary nature of some of Aristotle's judgements are his rejection of the atomism of Democritus, and his acceptance of the four elements of Empedocles, earth, air, fire and water, but restricted to the earth itself. He suggested that the heavens were composed of a fifth element, the aether, and agreed with the Pythagoreans that earth and heaven were subject to two different sets of natural laws. His acceptance of the Pythagorean notion of the earth as a sphere was, however, based on observational evidence of the fact that new stars become visible, and others disappear, as one travels to the north or south. He believed that the heart is the controlling organ in the human body, the brain being employed merely in cooling the blood.

Medieval science, in the universities and among scholars generally, was largely based on Aristotelianism, and confined to book learning and disputation. With the exception of a few outstanding individuals, experimental (as distinct from observational) work in science was almost unknown. Most kinds of experimental work were in any case severely handicapped by the lack of accurate measuring devices, especially in recording short intervals of time. It is hardly surprising in the circumstances that there was more interest in astrology and alchemy than in astronomy and chemistry.

The earliest signs of the coming scientific revolution appeared in Europe in the second half of the fifteenth century, one of the most important contributory inventions (or importations) being that of printing with movable type. Then, almost a century later, the year 1543 saw the publication of two remarkable books which could almost be said to mark that year as the exact beginning of the scientific revolution – Copernicus's *De revolutionibus orbium coelestium* and Vesalius's *De humani corporis fabrica*. A third published in the same year by Peter Ramus was an attack on Aristotelian physics, *Aristotelicae animadversiones*.

These works signalled the beginning of the end of Greek science – Ptolemy's astronomy, Galen's physiology and Aristotle's natural philosophy. But the end of the end didn't come until another hundred years and more had passed.

Seventeenth Century Science in Edinburgh

The most comprehensive study so far of philosophy and science in the Scottish universities in the seventeenth century was undertaken by Christine Shepherd (1975), and parts of this and the following two sections are based on her unpublished thesis, together with a shorter treatment of the same subject by Forbes (1983). Perhaps it should be said at the outset that the regents of philosophy, at Edinburgh as elsewhere, faced several difficulties in attempting to keep their lectures up to date, not the least of which was the fact that over a period of four sessions they had to teach the whole syllabus for the MA degree. Furthermore, when the College first opened there was only one month's holiday in the year, though that was soon extended from mid-July to the end of September, with another week between Christmas and New Year.

Historians such as Horn (1967) tend to dwell on the rigours of student life:- 'in the early days lectures began at six o'clock in winter and five in summer . . . the regents read their lectures at dictation speed, hence lectures were often called 'dictates' . . . each lecture was followed by intensive questioning until the regent was satisfied that it had been thoroughly understood by the whole class . . . afternoon sport (compulsory) was supervised by the regents, after which more lectures and tutorials continued into the evening . . . the senior classes often took part in public debates on Saturdays . . . on Sundays both regents and students attended divine service, after which the students were examined on the sermon, and instructed on the catechisms'.

Looking at the time-table from the regents' point of view, however, it must have required considerable dedication on their part to devote any of their extremely limited free time to academic study and revision of their lectures. Even with the necessary dedication, there was the intellectual problem of deciding who to believe, and consequently what to teach. Throughout the seventeenth century there were always at least two, often three or more, conflicting systems of natural philosophy from which to choose, with no possibility of being certain that any one choice was correct rather than another.

In spite of these difficulties, there is a good deal of evidence that many of the regents did introduce new material into their dictates from time to time, even though it is clear that their lectures on the whole remained strongly influenced by Aristotle and the scholastic tradition. Certainly after the regent system was abolished in 1708 a more radical change could be expected, but Forbes (1983) states that 'the general conclusion derived from an examination of all the available primary sources is therefore that the seventeenth-century Scottish regents (in particular, those in Edinburgh) were more informed about contemporary scientific developments than the nature of the teaching curriculum and reports in standard histories of the universities would suggest'.

Natural Philosophy and Mathematics

One of the Regents of Philosophy from 1626 was **Thomas Crawford** or Crawfurd, who was then appointed the second Professor of Mathematics in 1640. He has left in copies of his dictates in 1653 and 1661, evidence of the strong Aristotelian influence on scientific method in the middle of the seventeenth century. Crawford followed the precepts of Aristotle in teaching that knowledge of natural things would follow from knowledge of principles, and that one should proceed in any scientific investigation from the general to the particular.

The final eclipse of Aristotelianism was initiated by René Descartes (1596-1650) and completed by Isaac Newton (1642-1727). Descartes published his *Discours de la méthode pour bien conduire la raison et chercher la vérité dans les sciences* in 1637, and *Principia philosophiae* in 1644. References to Descartes first appear in student notes in the 1650s, but initially his mechanistic view of the universe, even though God was still accorded his proper place in it, was clearly thought by many of the regents to be dangerously atheistic. By about 1680, however, many of the lecture notes and theses in natural philosophy were entirely Cartesian, although some contained elements of both Aristotle and Descartes as uneasy bed-fellows.

This process of radical change is perhaps best exemplified by **John Wishart**, a

Regent of Philosophy from 1653 whose surviving lecture notes cover the two decades from 1660 to 1680. His earliest lectures were solidly based on Aristotle's works, with only passing references to Descartes and Gassendi; ten years later Aristotle had been replaced by more modern scholastics and by such recent or even contemporary philosophers as Descartes, Leeuwenhoeck, and Robert Boyle. Wishart described experiments by Torricelli and others that appeared to disprove Aristotle's dictum that the existence of a vacuum is impossible, and in his last lecture notes of 1679 he referred to Newton's theory of light which had been published in the *Philosophical Transactions* of 1672, 1675 and 1676.

Newton's *Philosophiae naturalis principia mathematica* was published in the original Latin in 1687, and in an English translation in 1729, two years after his death. This is unquestionably one of the greatest scientific works ever written, and it was widely, though not at first universally, accepted as such. William Whiston's *Memoirs*, quoted by Dalzel (1862), relate how he was 'greatly excited to the study of Sir Isaac Newton's wonderful discoveries in his *Principia* by a paper of Dr. Gregory's when he was Professor in Scotland, wherein he had given the most prodigious commendations to that work, as not only right in all things, but in a manner the effect of a plainly divine genius, and had already caused several of his scholars to 'keep acts', as we call them, upon several branches of the Newtonian Philosophy, while we at Cambridge, poor wretches, were ignominiously studying the fictitious hypotheses of the Cartesian'.

The Dr. Gregory referred to by Whiston is said in the DNB to have been **David Gregory** (1661-1708) who was Professor of Mathematics at Edinburgh, 1683-91; Shepherd (1975), however, considers it more likely that it was his brother **James Gregory** (1666-1742) who was Professor of Mathematics at Edinburgh, 1692-1725. It does not greatly matter which of them it was, for both Gregories were enthusiastic champions of Newton, and between them they effected a considerable improvement in the standard of mathematics teaching in the College of Edinburgh.

The Edinburgh regents in the last decade of the seventeenth century were on the whole somewhat wary of Newtonianism. It is evident that some of them considered Newton's mathematics too difficult for their students, and one suspects that in some cases it was too difficult for them as well. By the turn of the century, however, most of the regents had apparently mastered Newton's ideas (and mathematics) and incorporated them into

James Gregory, 1638-1675

their dictates. It is interesting to note that a copy of Newton's *Principia*, published in 1687, was purchased by Edinburgh University library in 1690, the first of the Scottish university libraries to have one on its shelves.

Shepherd (1975) considered that 'Edinburgh would appear to have been the most progressive of the Scottish universities' in the seventeenth century, a view apparently shared by the first James Gregory when after only four years he left St Andrews for the more congenial Edinburgh chair. Certainly in the second half of the seventeenth century there seems to have been in Edinburgh University a growing awareness of the importance of mathematics to an understanding of contemporary natural philosophy, an awareness which found expression in the appointment of the first Regent-cum-Professor of Mathematics there in 1620, and the first 'specialist' Professor of Mathematics, **James Gregory** (1638-1675), uncle of David and the second James, in 1674.

Cosmology

At the same time as they were attempting, with varying degrees of success, to come to terms with Cartesian and Newtonian natural philosophy, the regents had to consider

Map of the heavens, c1553

whether to accept or reject the cosmological revolution proposed by Nicolas Copernicus (1473-1543), restated in slightly modified form (with elliptical orbits) a century later by Johannes Kepler (1571-1630), and finally brought within the scope of a coherent system of terrestrial and celestial mechanics by Newton himself in the Principia of 1687. The Copernican revolution, with its implied attack on the long-established teaching of the Church, required both insight and courage on the part of its supporters, and it was only towards the end of the seventeenth century that it was being taught by the majority of Scottish university regents. In this particular branch of science it appears that Edinburgh was uncharacteristically conservative in adopting the new heliocentric view of the universe after the rest of the Scottish universities.

The Edinburgh regent **William Tweedie**, for example, acknowledged in his lectures in 1662 that there were different theories about the earth's place in the heavens, but had no hesitation in describing the cosmology of Copernicus as 'an absurd hypothesis'. Another of the regents, **James Pillans**, in 1672 was prepared to allow that the theories of Copernicus and Tycho Brahe were ingenious, but still preferred a modified version of the Ptolemaic system since it did not conflict with what was written in the scriptures.

Several other lecture notes from the 1670s and 1680s attempt a comparison of two or three of the competing cosmologies, and by the end of this period there was a good deal of support for Descartes' vortex theory, in spite of its inability to explain such well-known phenomena as comets. Soon after the appearance of Newton's *Principia* in 1687, however, its obvious superiority to all previous hypotheses led to its adoption by most natural philosophers within the space of the next decade, and even in Edinburgh by the turn of the century there were only a few regents who still clung to the old cosmologies. The conclusion reached by Russell (1974) was that by the beginning of the eighteenth century, scientific teaching in the Scottish universities was 'thoroughly up to date and probably as good as was to be found anywhere in Europe'.

The Edinburgh Physick Gardens

The origins of the teaching of botany in the Town's College are far from straightforward, but they are firmly rooted in the seventeenth century and indeed, if we allow that the Chairs of Mathematics and Natural Philosophy were instituted when the College was founded in 1583, the Chairs of Botany (1676) and Physiology (1685) were the only scientific chairs established in the seventeenth century. Man's interest in botany stretches farther back than recorded history, and one of the prime reasons was his discovery of the healing powers of many types of plant. It was this very practical use of botanical specimens that led directly to the establishment of Edinburgh's physick gardens.

Sir Andrew Balfour, a physician who had studied at St Andrews and in London, began in 1668 to cultivate a small botanic garden in Edinburgh, partly to provide him with the 'simples' of materia medica and partly as a display collection. He was assisted by **Sir Robert Sibbald**, who had graduated in Arts at Edinburgh in 1659, and thereafter studied medicine at Leyden, Paris and Angers. Balfour in his travels had also assembled a large general natural history collection of plants, animals and fossils. Two years later

Old Trinity Hospital with the Physick Garden in the foreground. View of Edinburgh generally.

Balfour and Sibbald established a garden at Holyrood, and quickly assembled a collection of some eight or nine hundred plants. To look after it they obtained the services of the young **James Sutherland**.

In 1675 Sutherland obtained from the Town Council the lease of some land adjoining Trinity Hospital which lay near the stream issuing from the Nor' Loch. Here, with the support of Balfour and Sibbald, he laid out a garden intended primarily to supply the needs of the physicians of Edinburgh. The following year he was appointed intendant of what was then known as the 'Edinburgh Physick Garden' in the grounds of the Trinity Hospital (now the east end of the Waverley Station, in which there is a commemorative plaque). At the same time he was given a salary of twenty pounds per annum by the Edinburgh Town Council, and his post was 'joined with to' the other professions taught in the Town's College.

The Town Council formally created for Sutherland in 1695 a Chair of Botany, with an increase of ten pounds in salary for planting the College garden as well as intending the Physic Garden (the Botanic Garden) and teaching two days a week in the Town's College. In 1699 Sutherland was appointed King's Botanist and Keeper of the Royal Garden at Holyrood to William III, a post he held until 1714. He was also appointed instructor in botany to the apprentices of the Royal College of Surgeons of Edinburgh. By this time he was however neglecting both the College Garden and his teaching duties, and after being censured by the Town Council he resigned from his employment with them in 1706.

The Scientific Gregories

Three Gregories have been mentioned in the course of this chapter, the older James and his two nephews, David and the younger James, all of them occupying the Chair of Mathematics at Edinburgh University before the end of the seventeenth century. The Gregories were a remarkable Aberdeenshire family (the name was originally spelt Gregorie) whose members occupied more than twenty chairs at five universities over a period of almost exactly two hundred years.

The first Professor of Mathematics in the University of Edinburgh who was not at the same time burdened with the duties of regent was **James Gregory** (1638-1675), educated at the Grammar School and Marischal College in Aberdeen. Before he was 24 years of age he had discovered the principle of the reflecting telescope, which he described in his book *Optica Promota*, published in London in 1663. He was sorely frustrated in his attempts to have one built, since even the best glass-grinders could not produce a satisfactory reflector, and it was only with improved glass-grinding techniques that many examples were made in the eighteenth century, some of the finest by James Short who studied at Edinburgh University from 1726 to 1731.

During a three years' sojourn in Padua Gregory published in 1668 a notable treatise on geometry which earned him the Fellowship of the Royal Society. He then returned to Scotland and in 1670 was appointed to the Chair of Mathematics at the University of St

Andrews, moving in 1674 to the same Chair in the University of Edinburgh, where as well as lecturing in mathematics he pursued his interest in astronomy. But ill-luck continued to dog his footsteps, and barely a year after taking up his post in Edinburgh he was showing the satellites of Jupiter to some of his students when he was suddenly struck blind, and within a week he was dead. There was at the time no mathematician not already occupying a snug university chair who could be considered worthy to succeed James Gregory, and the Town Council had little option but to leave the chair vacant for the next eight years.

In 1683 they appointed **David Gregory** (1661-1708), James's nephew, who was then about to graduate with an MA from Edinburgh University, having previously studied also in Aberdeen. David was fortunate in having inherited his uncle's mathematical manuscripts, and both he and his younger brother James became ardent admirers of Isaac Newton, and were certainly among the first to expound his philosophy in their lectures. David Gregory is known to have included the elements of geodesy, optics, mechanics and astronomy in his courses, and he brought the mathematical teaching at Edinburgh into the vanguard of scientific progress.

In 1690 the Parliament of William and Mary appointed a Commission to inquire into the religious and political persuasions of 'the Principalls, Professors, regents, masters and others bearing office in the universities, colledges and schoolls.' Many were deprived of their positions for one reason or another, or even for no reason at all, but in spite of his refusal to subscribe to the Confession of Faith, 'Dr Gregorie, the only truly great man among the Episcopalian professors, was wisely spared'. But it was a time of great anxiety, and when David learned of the resignation of the Savilian Professor of Astronomy in the University of Oxford he determined to apply for the post.

He went immediately to London and succeeded in enlisting the support of Sir Isaac Newton, even though the only other candidate was Edmund Halley who had arranged for the publication of Newton's *Principia* largely at his own expense. Although probably better qualified scientifically, Halley was openly agnostic in his religious views, and had no chance of selection by a committee headed by the Archbishop of Canterbury. David Gregory occupied the Chair at Oxford from 1692 until his death in 1708; Halley was elected Professor of Geometry at Oxford in 1703, and was appointed Astronomer Royal in 1720.

Throughout his life David Gregory wrote some 400 papers, most of which remain in manuscript, on mathematics, natural philosophy and astronomy. He published several important works, including one on optics in which he suggested how achromatic lenses might be made – an idea put into practice by Dollond half a century later. In 1702 his most important treatise appeared, *Astronomiae Physicae et Geometricae Elementa*, in which he presented Newton's scientific philosophy in more readily understandable terms.

The third mathematical Gregory to hold an Edinburgh chair was David's younger brother **James Gregory** (1666-1742), of whom little is known until his name appears among the graduates in Arts at Edinburgh in May 1685. Soon afterwards he was appointed to the Chair of Philosophy at St Andrews, but felt compelled to resign on the accession of William and Mary, and thus for a few years was without any settled work. When David left Edinburgh for Oxford, however, James almost inevitably succeeded him as Professor of Mathematics, occupying the chair from 1692 until his death in 1742, even though ill-health compelled him to give up teaching in 1725.

In those days a Professor occupied his chair, and drew his salary (meagre though it often was) for life, and if through some infirmity he could no longer teach, it was his responsibility to arrange for a substitute to lecture in his place, often as joint Professor, sometimes sharing the salary but more often completely dependent on the class fees paid by the students. Edinburgh was particularly fortunate in the man chosen in 1725 as James Gregory's substitute, for he was one of the finest mathematicians Scotland has produced, Colin McLaurin, one of the subjects of the next chapter.

Physics, Metaphysics and Satan's Invisible World

There could hardly be a more appropriate seventeenth century scholar than **George Sinclair** (c1625-1696) to exemplify the character of the age. The whole realm of knowledge and its utilisation for the benefit of mankind was then the province, and the hall-mark, of the educated man. Details of Sinclair's early life and education are lacking, but it is known that in 1654 he was appointed Regent of Philosophy in the University of Glasgow. He was forced to resign some ten years later for refusing to declare his adherence to the episcopalian church in Scotland, and in 1665 he is noted as one of the regents in Edinburgh's less authoritarian University. It seems probable that he remained in Edinburgh until after the Glorious Revolution of 1688, and was then able to return to his post of regent in Glasgow, where two years later in March 1691 he was appointed Professor of 'Mathematicks and Experimentall Philosophy'.

His not uneventful academic career was, however, completely overshadowed by his other activities. In 1655 he was involved in experiments with a primitive form of diving-bell invented by one Maule of Melgum, which was used with some success near Tobermory on the Isle of Mull, to explore the wreck of the *Florida*, one of the ships of the ill-fated Spanish Armada. Sinclair later described a kind of diving-bell of his own invention, which he called an *Ark*, in his *Hydrostatical Experiments* of 1680. He was one of the first men in Scotland to devote his attention to the study of physics, then held, as he put it, 'of little account'. He made use of the barometer to measure relative heights both above and (in coal mines) below ground, though he based his calculations on the erroneous assumption that the atmosphere is a homogeneous fluid.

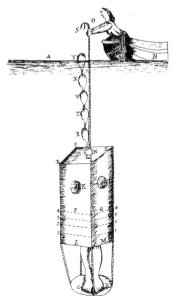

Diving Bell (George Sinclair)

Edinburgh water supply wells at the foot of Victoria Street

On many occasions he was consulted by coal-owners in the Lothians for advice on overcoming difficult geological conditions, and on improving drainage of the lower seams at a time when mechanical pumps or other water-raising devices were not in general use in the coal-fields. He published his observations in a work which, when it was reprinted in 1680, bore the title *Hydrostatical Experiments, with Miscellany Observations, and a relation of an Evil Spirit; also a Discourse concerning Coal*. The 'relation of an Evil Spirit' was an account of the witches of Glenluce, and it was an early manifestation of Sinclair's preoccupation with such metaphysical phenomena.

In 1672 he was asked by the Magistrates of the City of Edinburgh to design and superintend construction of the works for a new water supply from springs some three miles south of the Old Town. This work was successfully accomplished in 1673-76 using lead piping of 3-inch bore, and for his 'attendance and advyce in the matter of the waterworks' Sinclair received £66 13s 4d, and in 1681 a pension of £100 Scots (about £8 sterling) per annum from the Town Council.

He is probably best remembered today for his treatise *Satan's Invisible World Discovered*, published in Edinburgh in 1685, containing more than forty detailed accounts of supposedly demonic happenings both historical and contemporary, in Scotland and abroad. It was frequently reprinted up to 1814 and again in 1871, and was for a long time a constituent part of every cottage library in Scotland.

George Sinclair was a true scholar of the scientific revolution, a man who clearly believed there was nothing, practical or theoretical, physical or metaphysical, sacred or profane, beyond the grasp of his understanding. The last words on him, and perhaps on seventeenth century science in general, can be found in Chambers' *Biographical Dictionary of Eminent Scotsmen* (1853-57):-

"It is curious to find science and superstition so intimately mingled in the life of this extraordinary person. It is hardly possible to censure delusions which seem to have been entertained with so much sincerity, and in company with such a zeal for the propagation of real knowledge".

Some Seventeenth Century Edinburgh University Scientists

CHEYNE, George FRS (1671-1743) studied medicine at EU under Pitcairne, on whose theory of 'mathematical physick' he based some medical works. Published mathematical treatises, and *Philosophical Principles of Natural Religion* (1705) in which he claimed that the observed phenomena of attraction in the universe support belief in a supreme being. [DNB, DSB]

CRAIG, John FRS (d. 1731) a student of David Gregory, and friend of Newton at Cambridge, he wrote three influential mathematical treatises and in 1699 a curious tract *Theologiae Christianae Principia Mathematica* applying probability theory to the gospels. [DNB, DSB]

DRUMMOND, William (1585-1649) 'of Hawthornden' MA, 1605. Poet. Granted 16 (Scottish) patents in 1627 for mainly military appliances including a box-pistol, pikes and battering-rams, telescopes and burning-glasses, and an instrument for measuring wind speed. [DNB]

KEILL, John FRS (1671-1721) MA, 1690. Went with David Gregory to Oxford, where he gave the first lectures on (Newtonian) experimental philosophy at Hart Hall; Savilian Professor of Astronomy, 1712; champion of Newton in protracted dispute with Leibniz over priority in the discovery of the differential calculus. [DNB, DSB]

CHAPTER   2

Eighteenth century science – from Newton to Dalton

In comparing the seventeenth and eighteenth centuries in the history of Edinburgh University, it is a fortunate coincidence that a fundamental change should have occurred in the year 1708. Before that date, in all the Scottish universities, teaching of the whole Arts curriculum had been with few exceptions in the hands of the regents. For a short time in the first half of the seventeenth century the Colleges in Glasgow, St Andrews and Aberdeen introduced teaching by specialist professors, but for no very obvious reason they had all reverted to the old system of regents by 1645. In 1708 Edinburgh was the first of the Scottish Universities to wholly abolish this archaic system, and the advantages were so obvious that gradually the other Scottish Universities did the same, little inclined as they were to follow Edinburgh's example. It was finally discarded by Glasgow in 1727, St Andrews in 1747, and by Marischal and King's Colleges in Aberdeen in 1755 and 1798 respectively.

On 16 June 1708 the Town Council of Edinburgh 'taking to their consideration what may be the most proper methods for advancing of learning in their own Colledge of Edinburgh, . . agreed upon the following articles as an Rule of Teaching in the said Colledge'. The effect of the six articles was to sweep away the regent system and appoint the four senior regents as Professors of Logic and Metaphysics, Ethics and Natural Philosophy, Pneumatics and Moral Philosophy, and Greek. The Regent of Humanity (Latin) became Professor of Humanity, and there were also by that time Chairs of Mathematics, Botany and Medicine. The first six of these chairs constituted what was sometimes spoken of rather grandly by their earlier occupants as a Faculty of Philosophy, and in due course became known as the Faculty of Arts.

It is important to make the distinction between the creation of chairs, which can almost always be exactly dated, and the origin of the faculties, which prior to 1893 seem to have formed like galaxies by a process of mutual attraction, and have to be more or less arbitrarily dated. Another potential source of confusion is that a chair could be, and often was, created in more than one faculty, and the occupants of chairs could independently become members of as many faculties as their teaching commitments dictated. The term 'department', in its current sense, did not even begin to come into use until after the appointment of the first University Lecturers and Assistants to Professors in the late nineteenth century. To avoid administrative confusion, departments could not exist in more than one faculty at a time (even if their Professors did), though transfers occurred quite frequently for a variety of reasons.

There were some incidental consequences of the change introduced by the Town Council in 1708 that they perhaps did not anticipate. Under the regent system all students undertook the same four-year course of studies leading to the degree of Master of Arts, and those who were successful graduated MA at the end of their course. No doubt the intention was that future students would still attend all the necessary lecture courses, and at the end of four years would graduate with an MA degree, but the reality was rather different. Students were now free to attend whatever classes, in whatever order, they wished, the only formalities being payment of the matriculation fee to the College, and the class fees to the Professors. One result of this change was that graduation in Arts became the exception rather than the rule, and remained so until after the passing of the Universities (Scotland) Act, 1858. It was said that in the early nineteenth century it was usually the weaker students who actually graduated; the able ones found it paid them better to get testimonials from their professors! Another result was to increase the already considerable attraction of Edinburgh to students from furth of Scotland, ushering in a century of general prosperity and progress.

Biographical notes on some of the scientists who studied at Edinburgh University in the eighteenth century appear at the end of this chapter, and others are included under the appropriate subject heading. The variety of scientific interests pursued by these men is remarkable, as is the fact that many of them made their mark in one or more of the sciences while continuing to practise medicine. Narrow specialization was not a characteristic of eighteenth century homo sapiens.

The Scientific Revolution continues

It is obvious that in a few paragraphs only the sketchiest outline of the Scientific Revolution during the eighteenth century is possible, but even that will I hope assist the reader to keep the progress of science at Edinburgh University in perspective. Revolution is in any case only a rather dramatic word for change, and another word for change is transition. In this study I have come to regard the eighteenth century as essentially a period of transition between two contrasting approaches to the challenge of understanding and explaining the natural world – from the almost completely erroneous but firmly-held beliefs of the pre-Newtonian philosophers, to the step-by-step accumulation of 'hard' knowledge by the scientists of the nineteenth and early twentieth centuries. It was a change of attitude more than anything else that characterised the Scientific Revolution, a change from philosophical speculation to methodical observation, experiment and conclusion.

In astronomy, as in most other sciences, discoveries went hand in hand with improvements in instruments, observational techniques and mathematical skills. The proper motion of the fixed stars was established; the return of Halley's comet was predicted to within 30 days in 1759; and many countries collaborated in observing the transits of Venus in 1761 and 1769. Towards the end of the eighteenth century the nature and shape of the Milky Way was known, although its size was greatly underestimated; the nebular hypothesis was put forward to explain the origin of the solar system; and the existence of 'black holes' was predicted by Laplace in 1798.

The biological sciences of botany, physiology and zoology were included with meteorology, hydrography, geology and mineralogy under the broad heading of natural history. Botanists devoted much of their time to collecting, studying and classifying large numbers of plants, many of them used by the medical profession for their curative properties, real or imaginary. Linnaeus in 1753 introduced the binary nomenclature of species, but rejected the concept of evolution which was being tentatively advanced at about the same time. The mechanism of reproduction and the differentiation of animal species began to be understood towards the end of the century, pointing the way to Darwin's *Origin of Species* in 1859. Until the second half of the eighteenth century knowledge of the earth and its minerals was almost entirely derived from mining and the exploitation of precious ores. The first systematic study of the earth's crust by Werner led to the Neptunism vs Plutonism controversy around the turn of the century, in which Hutton, Hall and Playfair took leading parts.

One of the most striking examples of a theory that was more or less universally accepted, and staunchly defended by its supporters, in spite of being completely erroneous, was the phlogiston theory advanced by Stahl (after Becher) in 1697. For almost a century it held back the progress of chemistry in both theory and practice, until in 1783 Lavoisier finally disposed of it with incontrovertible experimental evidence. With phlogiston out of the way, chemistry at last began to advance towards an understanding of the laws governing chemical reactions. The crucial atomic theory of John Dalton (1803) ushered in the new chemistry that was to make such rapid strides in the nineteenth century.

Natural philosophy provided another such example in the caloric theory of heat as a kind of fluid, the explanation favoured by many scientists throughout the eighteenth century. Even though some eminent natural philosophers including Newton, Huygens and Hooke regarded heat as a 'mode of motion', and Rumford's observations in 1798 on the boring of cannon cast serious doubt on the caloric theory, it was not until the middle of the nineteenth century that it was finally disproved. Significantly, its demise was largely due to developments in the mathematical approach to thermodynamics, an early example of the increasingly important role of mathematics in science.

Eighteenth Century Science in Edinburgh

The eighteenth century in Edinburgh was a remarkable period in many ways, not the least of them being the flowering of the Scottish Enlightenment, about which more can be found in the next chapter. Just as the Enlightenment was the work of a few men of genius, so most of the science in Edinburgh University in the eighteenth century was the product of a few outstanding men, Professors such as Alston, Hope and Rutherford in Botany; Plummer, Cullen and Black in Chemistry; McLaurin and Playfair in Mathematics; Walker in Natural History; and Robison in Natural Philosophy. The Scottish Enlightenment philosophers such as David Hume, Adam Smith and Adam Ferguson made their impact on the intellectual development of eighteenth century Europe mainly through their

Encyclopaedia Britannica. *Frontispiece to the 3rd edition, 1788. An engraving exemplifying the ideals and inspirations of the Scottish Enlightenment, with art, science and technology shown in a classic setting*

writings, whereas the scientific professors did the same partly through their writings but perhaps even more effectively through the achievements of their students.

Even the philosophers took more than a passing interest in science. David Hume in his *Treatise of Human Nature* (1739) for example, asserted that it was impossible to prove that a scientific law was true. This remained a serious problem for most philosophers and a few scientists until the work of Karl Popper and others in the present century. In the index to the Macmillan *Dictionary of the History of Science* Hume's name is linked to 34 different scientific topics, from Aristotle's theory of cause and Association of ideas to Utilitarianism and Vindication of induction. His ideas are still discussed in almost every new book on the philosophy of science.

Although the Royal Society was founded in London in 1660 there was no scientific society of any consequence in either Oxford or Cambridge, with the result that for almost a century Edinburgh was the only place in Britain with a university *and* a very active intellectual community meeting regularly in various clubs and societies. The Society for the Improvement of Medical Knowledge was instituted in Edinburgh in 1731, and published five volumes of *Medical Essays and Observations* which were translated into several other languages. In 1737 Colin McLaurin proposed that its scope should be broadened to include literature and philosophy, and its name was changed to the Edinburgh Society for improving Arts and Sciences and Particularly Natural Knowledge or, more briefly, the Philosophical Society of Edinburgh. Its *Essays and Observations, Physical and Literary* appeared in three volumes between 1754 and 1771. In the later 1770s the Philosophical Society became much less active, and some of the professors at the University, many of whom were also members of the Society, resolved to form a more effective society, which in 1783 emerged as the Royal Society of Edinburgh.

Moreover, before the end of the eighteenth century a number of other societies had been founded, including the Academy of Physics, the Royal Medical and Royal Physical Societies, the Chirurgo-Physical Society, the Natural History Society of Edinburgh, the Edinburgh University Chemical Society and the Agricultural Society of Edinburgh. Small wonder that in 1789 Thomas Jefferson, writing from Paris to Dugald Stewart, said that so far as science was concerned 'no place in the world can pretend to a competition with Edinburgh'.

Mathematics

The first eighteenth century Edinburgh Professor of Mathematics, James Gregory, has already been introduced as one of the mathematical Gregories. He seems to have been an able teacher, but did not otherwise add to the reputation of the Gregory family. It is interesting to record that the Town Council, in appointing him to the chair in 1692, described mathematics as ' . . for the accomplishment and education of youth, and particularly in the art of Navigation (the great ornament of any Kingdom or commonwealth).' By 1725 Gregory was in poor health and no longer able to teach, and it was on the recommendation of Sir Isaac Newton that Colin McLaurin, then Professor at

Marischal College in Aberdeen, was invited to be 'associated' with Gregory in the Edinburgh chair. This of course meant that he would have no salary until Gregory's death, and Newton offered to contribute £20 per annum to McLaurin until then, '. . if I live so long'.

So **Colin McLaurin** joined Gregory in 1725, and on the latter's death in 1742 became the sixth Professor of Mathematics, '. . the one mathematician of the first rank trained in Great Britain in the eighteenth century', according to the DNB. He had graduated from the University of Glasgow at the age of fifteen, and at nineteen was elected to the Chair of Mathematics at Marischal College after a competitive examination lasting ten days. In Edinburgh he became the life and soul of the University, and was instrumental in broadening the scope of the Society for the Improvement of Medical Knowledge so that it became the Philosophical Society, and eventually in 1783 the Royal Society of Edinburgh.

The detailed syllabus of his mathematics lectures was published in the *Scots Magazine* in 1741. The first course included vulgar and decimal arithmetic, six books of Euclid, plane trigonometry, the use of logarithms, surveying, fortification and other practical parts, the elements of algebra, and a lecture on geography once a fortnight. The second course consisted of algebra, the theory and mensuration of solids, spherical trigonometry, the doctrine of the sphere, dialling (construction and use of sun-dials) and other practical parts, conic sections, with the theory of gunnery; and the elements of astronomy and optics. In the third course he began with perspective, then dealt more fully with astronomy and optics; he lectured on Newton's *Principia* and explained the direct and inverse methods of fluxions. He also gave a separate course of experimental philosophy, in which ' . . at proper hours of the night he described the constellations and showed the planets by telescopes of various kinds'. All that, incidentally, within the confines of the winter session which at that time extended from the beginning of November to the end of April.

His early work *Geometrica Organica* of 1720 established his reputation, and in 1742 his best-known work, *A Treatise of Fluxions*, provided a geometrical interpretation of Newton's calculus, as well as solving a large number of problems in geometry, statics and gravitational attraction. It was translated into French in 1749, and subsequently praised by Lagrange. In 1745 McLaurin applied some of the 'practical parts' of his lectures to fortifying the city of Edinburgh against the advancing Jacobite army, supervising and assisting in the work himself. All to no avail, however; when a short time later the city fell into the hands of the rebels without a shot being fired he was forced to flee into England, and after his return a few months later the privations he had suffered resulted in his death in June 1746. Alexander Carlyle wrote of him: – ' . . he was the clearest and most agreeable lecturer on that abstract science that ever I heard'.

The seventh Professor was **Matthew Stewart**, who had been trained as a mathematician mainly under Robert Simson at Glasgow University, although he had also studied under McLaurin at Edinburgh in 1741-42. Simson was Professor of Mathematics for fifty years from 1711, and among his many other students were Colin McLaurin and John Robison. He was essentially a classical geometer with a strong prejudice against algebra, and his influence is said to have held back the development of analytical mathematics in

John Playfair, Professor of Mathematics, 1785-1805 and Professor of Natural Philosophy, 1805-1819. Painting by Sir Henry Raeburn

Scotland for most of the eighteenth century. Matthew Stewart in particular followed Simson's teaching, and it was his constant aim to reduce to the level of ordinary geometry problems that were supposed to require the higher calculus.

The next notable occupant of the Mathematics Chair, **John Playfair**, was from 1785 to 1805 'associated' with Adam Ferguson as Professor of Mathematics, although in reality the latter had been allowed to retire in 1785. Playfair was educated at St Andrews and, having been unsuccessful in his early efforts to enter the academic world, spent ten years as a parish minister before coming to Edinburgh. He was possessed of great scientific erudition, and was disturbed to find that most English mathematicians in the second half of the eighteenth century believed that what Newton had written was 'the last word' on mechanical philosophy. Playfair was sufficiently detached to realise that the *Principia*, though certainly epoch-making in concept, was mathematically quite primitive, and that practically all the subsequent advances in analytical mathematics had been made in France. He took every opportunity, therefore, in his writings and his teaching, to make these advances known, and to show that further progress in mechanical philosophy would require more than an unquestioning belief in Newton's God-like powers.

One of Playfair's students was **Sir James Ivory** FRS (1765-1842), who studied with his friend John Leslie at St Andrews and, after 1784, at Edinburgh with the original intention of entering the ministry, though neither of them did. Ivory became Professor of Mathematics at the Royal Military College from 1805 until ill-health forced his retirement in 1819, but he continued his work in applied mathematics and published a large number of papers on the theory of attraction and atmospheric refraction. His study of the gravitational attraction of ellipsoids such as the earth extended the work of McLaurin and Laplace and brought him international recognition.

Natural Philosophy

The first Professor of Natural Philosophy, **Sir Robert Stewart**, had been a Regent since

1703, and was appointed to the chair when that system was abolished by the Town Council in 1708. The *Scots Magazine* of 1741, already referred to in connection with McLaurin, gave details of Stewart's syllabus in natural philosophy, together with a list of relevant text-books: –   Keill's *Introductio ad veram Physicam*; mechanics from several authors; hydrostatics and pneumatics from his own manuscript; David Gregory's *Optics* and *Astronomy*; Sir Isaac Newton's *Of Colours* and the *Principia*; the eye and the phenomena of vision; microscopes and telescopes; astronomical observations, both ancient and modern; and exhibitions of experiments in mechanics, hydrostatics, pneumatics and optics.

By 1742 Stewart was '. . a very old man worn out with age', and his son **John Stewart** was 'associated' with him in carrying out the duties of the chair. In 1759 **Adam Ferguson** was appointed, '. . not as by any means a tried specialist, but as a man of versatile talent, capable of learning almost anything, and therefore capable of learning Natural Philosophy so as to be able to teach it'. Three months after being appointed he was ready to begin his lectures, which were said to have given universal satisfaction by rendering the subject popular and attractive. In 1764 the Town Council sanctioned a redistribution of some chairs which resulted in Ferguson taking over the Chair of Moral Philosophy, in which at last he found his true vocation.

The Chair of Natural Philosophy was then occupied by **James Russell**, of whom virtually nothing is known, until 1774 when the Town Council, pressed strongly by Principal Robertson and Professors Cullen and Black, appointed **John Robison** to succeed him. Educated at Glasgow from his twelfth to his nineteenth year, he was then made assistant to the Professor of Natural Philosophy, but was judged too young and inexperienced to get the Chair when it fell vacant. It was during his studies in Glasgow, in about 1758, that he made the acquaintance of James Watt, and the two men became close friends and associates, sharing their thoughts on such radical ideas as the use of the separate condenser to improve the performance of the steam engine.

At the time of his appointment to the Edinburgh chair Robison was Professor of Mathematics at Cronstadt in Russia. In Edinburgh his lectures embraced the sciences of mechanics, hydrodynamics,

John Robison, Professor of Natural Philosophy, 1774-1805. Painting by Sir Henry Raeburn, c1798

astronomy and optics, together with electricity and magnetism. Unfortunately they were difficult to follow, being delivered with great rapidity, and with very few experimental demonstrations, so he never became a 'popular' lecturer in the style of Black or Hope. His writings, however, were numerous and influential, including a large selection of articles for the third edition of the *Encyclopædia Britannica* (1793-1801), an edition of Black's *Lectures on Chemistry* in 1803, and his own *Elements of Mechanical Philosophy* of which only the first volume had appeared before his death in 1805. He was a founder member of the Royal Society of Edinburgh, and acted as its first General Secretary from 1783 to 1798.

Botany

Before resuming the story of botany in the University it would be appropriate to introduce a very early eighteenth-century Edinburgh graduate who subsequently devoted much of his time to botany and other sciences. **Cadwallader Colden** (1688-1776) was born in Ireland of Scottish parents who sent him to Edinburgh University, where he graduated MA in 1705. After studying medicine in London he emigrated to America in 1710 and for the next few years practised medicine in Pennsylvania. He was appointed in 1720-21 to a number of administrative offices in the City of New York, and thereafter was able to devote more time to his various scientific pursuits, proving himself to be '. . one of the most versatile men of learning in the colonies'. In addition to medical and historical works he collected and classified the flora of Orange County, NY, sending specimens and a detailed report to Linnaeus who published it approvingly in 1749, and named the *Coldenia* for him in 1753. He wrote papers on philosophy, psychology, mathematics and the natural sciences, including his *Explication of the First Causes of Action in Matter* (1745, revised 1751), an unsuccessful attempt to explain the nature of the force of gravity. He was lieutenant governor of New York from 1761 to 1775.

The early history of the Physick Gardens in Edinburgh has been told in chapter one, and there were further complications in the first quarter of the eighteenth century. In 1712 **George Preston** succeeded his brother **Charles** as College Professor of Botany, Intendant of the College Garden and the Botanic Garden at the Trinity Hospital, and Instructor in Botany to the apprentices of the Royal College of Surgeons in Edinburgh. In 1716 **Charles Alston** received a commission from King George I appointing him King's Botanist, third Regius Professor of Botany and Materia Medica, and Overseer of the Royal Physick Garden at Holyrood. This highly unsatisfactory duplication continued until George Preston resigned in 1738, and **Charles Alston** was appointed the fourth College Professor of Botany and Materia Medica, in the Faculty of Medicine.

Thus was established the tradition continued without a break for the next two hundred years, combining the posts of King's Botanist in Scotland with the Chair of Botany in the University of Edinburgh. Alston had studied medicine in Glasgow and under Boerhaave at Leyden, and in Edinburgh he was a distinguished occupant of both posts. He disagreed with Linnaeus on one point concerning the fertilisation of plants, and was proved correct. His total opposition to the system of classification proposed by

Linnaeus was, however, a case of swimming against the tide. He initiated the physiological approach to botany, continued by his successor John Hope, which for almost a century was characteristic of the Edinburgh school of botanists. He produced a number of notable botanical works, including a *Materia Medica* published posthumously in 1770 by his friend and successor John Hope, which was said to have been the best in Europe up to that time.

One of Alston's frequent correspondents was **Dr John Fothergill** FRS (1712-1780) who graduated MD at Edinburgh in 1736 and practised as a physician in London from 1740. He maintained at Upton in Essex one of the finest botanical gardens in Europe, and supplied Alston with all the information that came his way on matters of materia medica. Linnaeus named the genus *Fothergilla* for him, but of Linnaeus himself Fothergill wrote:– 'I did not take it well that Linnaeus had made no mention of the Physic Garden at Edinburgh in his *Fundamenta Botanica* tho' he had taken notice of some that deserved less'.

Mention should also be made here of **Erasmus Darwin** (1731-1802) who after graduating BA from St John's College Cambridge in 1754 came to Edinburgh to study medicine. He must have been an exceptionally diligent student, for in 1755 he was awarded the degree of MB at Cambridge, and finally left Edinburgh in 1756 to set himself up in practice as a physician. He became a founder member of the Lunar Society in Birmingham and is remembered for his scientific writings, many of which appeared in verse form. His early poems were mainly on botanical subjects, and he was a supporter of the system of classification introduced by Linnaeus. In his last book, *Zoonomia* (1794-96), he advanced the theory that evolutionary changes are directly due to environmental influences, a proposal similar to that put forward by Lamarck some 15 years later. He was the grandfather of Charles Robert Darwin who also studied medicine at Edinburgh, 1825-27; in passing, it may be remarked that in all seven members of the Darwin family studied medicine at Edinburgh between 1754 and 1840.

In 1760 **John Hope** became the fifth Professor of Botany and Materia Medica in the University of Edinburgh, and the following year he was appointed King's

Professor John Hope visiting the Physic Garden. From Kay's Old Edinburgh Portraits, 1786

C

DANIEL RUTHERFORD, M.D. F.L.S.
Professor of Botany in the University of Edinburgh.

Botanist in Scotland and Superintendent of the Royal Garden. Finding the site of the Physic Garden in the grounds of the Trinity Hospital quite unsuitable for the purpose, he established in 1763 the New Botanic Garden, supported by a permanent endowment from the Crown, on a five-acre site in Leith Walk (now Haddington Place), to which the collections in the Trinity Hospital and Holyrood Gardens were transferred. Unlike Alston, Hope was an enthusiastic admirer of Linnaeus, and in the new garden '. . the plants were arranged according to the Linnaean system, suitable hot-houses were erected, and a pond was established for the growth of aquatic plants'.

Until 1768 he followed the established practice of teaching materia medica in winter and botany in summer, but in that year he persuaded the University to separate the two subjects. Dr Francis Home was appointed (without salary) to the new Regius Chair of Materia Medica, and Hope became the Regius Professor of Medicine and Botany. Practical demonstrations and experiments supplemented his lectures, and students were encouraged to study the flora of Scotland in the field. There is no doubt, in fact, that Hope and his students were the first thorough investigators of the flora of Scotland, and from his notebooks it is clear that they had collected a significant number of Scottish plants long before they were claimed as 'discoveries' by other botanists. He was, like Alston before him, a pioneering plant physiologist, and it was a great loss to the science of botany that he died suddenly while engaged in the writing of a botanical treatise, and it was never published.

From Hope's many students perhaps one may be cited as typical of those who made their name abroad. **William Roxburgh** FLS FRSE (1751-1815) graduated MD in 1776 and served as a surgeon with the East India Company before undertaking a survey which led to the publication in three volumes of his *Plants of the Coast of Coromandel*. In 1793 he was appointed Superintendent of the Calcutta Botanic Garden and in 20 years increased the number of species represented from 300 to 3500. He also embarked on further botanical studies which enabled him to complete the manuscripts of his *Flora Indica* and *Hortus Bengalensis* by the time he was forced in 1813 to retire owing to ill-health. Both works were published posthumously to great critical acclaim.

Hope was succeeded in 1786 by **Daniel Rutherford**, the sixth Regius Professor of Medicine and Botany. His MD thesis in 1772 *De aere fixo dicto aut Mephitico* had clearly established the distinction between carbon dioxide and nitrogen, though he did not give the latter a name. He is usually regarded as the prime discoverer of nitrogen, in spite of the fact that the same discovery was made independently in the same year by Priestley, Scheele and Cavendish. After this auspicious start to his career he did not achieve the same distinction in the Chair of Medicine and Botany; by training and inclination he was more a chemist than a botanist, and most of the collecting of botanical specimens was done by a succession of head gardeners.

The most celebrated botanist to study under Daniel Rutherford was **Robert Brown** FRS (1773-1858) who graduated MD in 1795. His interest in botany was encouraged by

Daniel Rutherford, Professor of Botany
Edinburgh from beyond the Nor' Loch

John Walker the Professor of Natural History, and his first botanical paper was published in 1791. He spent a short period as a military surgeon and was then appointed naturalist on an expedition to survey the coast of Australia (1801-6), from which he brought back and catalogued more than 1,700 new plant species. After four years as librarian of the Linnean Society he was made curator of Sir Joseph Banks' splendid library and natural history collections; when they were transferred to the British Museum in 1827 he became keeper of the botanical collection there. Of his many important contributions to the botanical literature his name is best remembered by his discovery in 1827 of the 'Brownian movement' of pollen grains suspended in water. This was the first evidence for atomism arising from observation rather than speculation, but it was not explained until Clerk Maxwell and others developed the kinetic theory of gases later in the nineteenth century.

Chemistry

In December 1713, largely on the initiative of Principal Carstares, a Chair of Physick and Chymistry was instituted by the Edinburgh Town Council. In its minutes the Council explained that the appointment was made '. . particularly considering that through the want of professors of physick and chymistry in this Kingdome the youth who have applyed themselves to study have been necessitat to travel and remain abroad a considerable time for their education to the great prejudice of the nation by the necessary charges occasioned thereby'. **James Crawford** was appointed the first Professor, but with no salary, a condition that was applied to many of the Edinburgh medical and scientific chairs. He had graduated MD at King's College, Aberdeen, in 1708 without examination because he had been awarded the same degree in 1707 at Leyden. It is interesting to note that a Chair of Chemistry was founded in 1703 at Cambridge, but not until exactly a century later at Oxford.

Between 1718 and 1725 Crawford acted as principal examiner in medicine for twelve external candidates for the MD degree of the University of Edinburgh – there were no internal candidates until the founding of the Faculty of Medicine in 1726. During his tenure of the chair Crawford gave only one course of lectures in medicine, and in chemistry from 1713 to 1726 he gave only three or four full courses of lectures. Surviving lecture notes show that he attempted to convey the principles upon which the science of chemistry was then based, but he was severely limited in what he could do by lack of space and equipment.

Andrew Plummer and **John Innes**, together with John Rutherford and Andrew St Clair, were the four Professors initially appointed in the Faculty of Medicine. Up to the year 1733 when Innes died, all four were nominally involved in the teaching of chemistry, but almost certainly Plummer and Innes more than the others. The course was advertised as: – "On Chymistry, being a Complete Course, according to the Method of the celebrated Herman Boerhaave, at Leyden . . ." The four Professors formed a business partnership, of which Plummer was the executive secretary, to regulate their private practices, their teaching of the medical students, and their running of the pharmaceutical laboratory which combined instruction of the students with the sale of medicines to other medical men and apothecaries.

In order to have a ready supply of medicinal plants, they acquired rent-free use of the College Physick Garden and made considerable improvements to it. The sale of medicines must have been substantial because in 1732 a new impression of 500 copies of the Catalogue was printed. Plummer was a knowledgeable and industrious chemist, but a poor lecturer; however, from the records, there can be little doubt that he was the organisation man of the Medical Faculty. The number of medical graduates rose from only one in 1726 to 17 in 1755. He was successful, too, in his private practice as a physician, and he invented Plummer's Pills, a concoction of antimony and mercury, '. . popular(!) for nearly a century'. [Donovan, 1975]

Among his students were John Roebuck, James Hutton and James Keir, whose subsequent careers are fairly typical of the substantial proportion of students who entered the medical school but did not make the practice of medicine their life's work. Roebuck and Keir both made their names in the embryonic chemical industry, but of the three there can be no doubt that it was **James Hutton** FRSE (1726-1797) who made the greatest contribution to the progress of science in the eighteenth and early nineteenth centuries. He was the only surviving son of a wealthy Edinburgh merchant who died while James was young, and from whom he inherited two farms in the Scottish borders.

His remarkably varied career followed university studies extending over nine years, beginning at Edinburgh from 1740 to 1743. He was then apprenticed to a lawyer who, finding his office fast deteriorating into a chemical laboratory, swiftly set young Hutton at liberty again. Medicine seemed at the time a more attractive profession, and after further studies at Edinburgh and Paris he proceeded to Leyden where he graduated MD in 1749. Soon after his return to Edinburgh he gave up the idea of practising medicine and spent most of the next twenty years farming in England and Scotland, constantly experimenting with crops, soils, fertilisers, farm implements and methods of drainage, and at the same time observing the face of the land and speculating on the forces that had formed it.

James Hutton and John Clerk on the Salisbury Crags, Edinburgh. Detail of sketch showing the examination of an exposure where the underlying sandstone has been broken by an intrusive sill of teschenite

His ever-increasing interest in geology led him in 1764 to join his friend George Clerk Maxwell (great-grandfather of James Clerk Maxwell) on a tour of the Scottish Highlands, which provided him with many new examples for his studies. In 1768 he let his farm and settled in Edinburgh, devoting the rest of his life to scientific investigations and sociable converse with his many friends, who included William Robertson, Adam Ferguson, Adam Smith, Joseph Black, James Watt, Sir James Hall and John Playfair.

Hutton was one of the Founding Fellows of the Royal Society of Edinburgh in 1783, and two years later he read his paper on *The Theory of the Earth* which was published in the first volume of the Society's *Proceedings* in 1788. The principal conclusion of his thirty years of study and contemplation was that the surface of the earth is constantly being worn away, and subsequently renewed, by natural processes which are still at work, in much the same way as they have been throughout past geological ages. The phenomena associated with volcanic activity convinced him that the earth, from a geological point of view, was essentially a machine fired by heat, and he concluded that, '. . with respect to human observation, this world has neither a beginning nor an end'.

Not surprisingly Hutton's uniformitarian views met with fierce opposition, and he was accused of impiety and atheism both by the Church and by the majority of conservative geologists, many of whom were followers of Abraham Werner (1749-1817) and his Neptunist school. After the publication of his paper Hutton undertook six further geological excursions which provided him with even stronger evidence in support of his theory, and in 1795 he published an expanded version in two volumes, *Theory of the Earth with Proofs and Illustrations*.

Unfortunately, by that time he was a sick man, and in contrast to his original paper the book is difficult to read and understand. It did little if anything to popularise his views, and it was not until after his death that his genius began to be recognised, when his friend and disciple, John Playfair, published in 1802 his *Illustrations of the Huttonian Theory of the Earth*, which according to Archibald Geikie '. . for luminous treatment and graceful diction stands still without a rival in English geological literature'.

Experimental proof of some of Hutton's intuitive conclusions was provided by the work of **Sir James Hall** PresRSE (1761-1832), the Father of Experimental Geology, who studied at Edinburgh from 1781 to 1783. Twenty years later he was able to reproduce in the laboratory such fundamental geological processes as the crystallisation of lavas and whinstones at different rates of cooling, the transformation of limestone into marble at high temperature and pressure, and the heating of calcium carbonate without dissociation when subjected to high pressure. A wider acceptance of Hutton's theories, and his status as the Father of Scientific Geology, followed the publication by Charles Lyell in 1830-33 of *The Principles of Geology: being an Attempt to Explain the Former Changes of the Earth's Surface by reference to Causes now in Operation*. Only after Charles Darwin's *Origin of Species* appeared in 1859 was the link between biological and geological evolution finally made clear, though not without another rearguard action being mounted by the traditionalists.

To return now to the progress of chemistry at Edinburgh University, in 1755

William Cullen was appointed joint Professor of Chemistry with Plummer until the latter's death a year later. He served an apprenticeship with a surgeon in Glasgow, studied medicine for two years at the University of Edinburgh, and in 1740, in his thirtieth year, graduated MD from the University of Glasgow – even though there was no effective School of Medicine there at the time. He was given permission to lecture in the University on the theory and practice of physic, chemistry and botany, and in 1751 he was appointed Professor of Medicine. Four years later when Plummer could no longer lecture Cullen was a candidate for his chair, along with Francis Home (who got the Chair of Materia Medica in 1768) and Joseph Black. After Cullen was appointed to the Edinburgh chair, Black succeeded him in the Chair of Medicine at Glasgow.

Cullen wrote very little on chemistry and made no noteworthy discoveries. His reputation is based on his teaching in which he employed a variety of skills, none of them innovations, but which had never before been so effectively brought together by the one man.

> 'The importance of Cullen to our purpose is that he broke with Boerhaave's teaching and in fact founded a new teaching tradition which was to bring forth considerable fruit of its own. He assigned a prominent place to industrial chemistry, and – most revolutionary – lecturing in English, not Latin, turned the attention of his pupils to the improvement of arts and manufactures, and developed a teaching laboratory. Although he almost discovered the phenomenon of latent heat, it was left to Cullen's gifted pupil and successor Joseph Black to achieve this and, with elegant experiments, to further the work so well begun.'
> [Emmerson (1973), 68]

He was certainly a pioneer in giving his students the opportunity to do voluntary practical work in the laboratory – though he complained that few of them did so. Cullen occupied the Chair of Chemistry until 1766, then he was successively Professor of the Institutes of Medicine (Physiology) and of the Practice of Medicine until his retirement in 1789. The numbers in his chemistry classes rose steadily from 17 in his first year to 145 in his last; during his 11 years as Professor he had 40 American students, many of whom sent their own most promising students to Edinburgh in future years.   [Horn, 69-70]

In 1766 **Joseph Black** was appointed the fourth Professor of Chemistry. He was for three years Cullen's assistant in Glasgow, then in 1752 came to the University of Edinburgh where he graduated MD in 1754. Two years later he published his classic paper, based on his graduation thesis, *De Humore Acido a Cibis Orto et Magnesia Alba* (On the Acid Humours arising from Food, and Magnesia Alba). In it he described the experiments on 'Magnesia Alba' (a basic magnesium carbonate) which resulted in his discovery of the gas he called 'fixed air' or carbon dioxide. This was a pioneering work in quantitative chemistry, acknowledged as such by Lavoisier in a letter to Black in 1789.

In the same year (1756) he was appointed Professor of Anatomy and Botany, and lecturer in chemistry, in the University of Glasgow; the following year he was made

C*

Joseph Black, Professor of Chemistry and Medicine (1766-1799).

Professor of Medicine. During his time in Glasgow he carried out a series of experiments from which he deduced the existence of *latent heat*, and derived other properties of water and steam. He met James Watt, who in 1757 was appointed Mathematical Instrument Maker to the University, and the two men became close friends, corresponding regularly on all manner of scientific subjects even after Black moved to Edinburgh and Watt to Birmingham. John Robison had graduated MA at Glasgow in 1756 and shortly afterwards was introduced to Watt and through him to Black, joining their discussions on the phenomena associated with latent heat and specific heat, and their application to the Newcomen/Watt steam engine.

Black was an admirable teacher and excelled in the use of practical demonstrations in the course of his lectures. When he was appointed to the Edinburgh chair in 1766 it is said that many of his Glasgow students followed him there. In Edinburgh he became more involved in teaching, and instead of pursuing further research in chemistry he took an increasing interest in the rapidly developing local chemical industries, to the extent of becoming financially involved with some of them.

In the beginning of the year 1785 a Chemical Society was formed in the University of Edinburgh. A 'List of Members of the Chemical Society' drawn up by Black in 1785 was rediscovered in 1935 by Prof Kendall, and of the 59 names on the list, 53 were members of Black's class between 1783 and 1787. This antedates the Chemical Society of Philadelphia founded in 1792, previously regarded as the oldest chemical society in the world. Even more remarkably, in 1947 the first volume of the manuscript *Proceedings* of the Society was identified in the Library of the Royal Irish Academy, whose members graciously agreed to return the volume to Edinburgh. It is thought to be the oldest surviving journal of a purely chemical character, antedating by five years the *Annales de Chimie* founded in Paris in 1790.

In the 1790s the average number of students in Black's chemistry class was over 200, so although his chair, like most of the others in medicine and the sciences, was unsalaried he had a good income from the class fees of three guineas per student. Morrell (1983) lists on p 49 '. . some of his British students (who) were so inspired by him that they followed him as university teachers of chemistry, the best known being Thomas C Hope

(Edinburgh), Thomas Thomson (Glasgow), Thomas Beddoes (Oxford), Smithson Tennant (Cambridge), and Thomas Garnett (Andersonian Institution, Glasgow).'

Another very eminent scientist who attended Black's lectures while studying medicine at Edinburgh was **Thomas Young** FRS (1773-1829), who was that rare phenomenon, an infant prodigy who matured into an adult prodigy. His interest in the physiology of perception led him to restate Huygens' wave theory of light in 1801, although there was then no new evidence to support it. His own diffraction experiments soon provided the necessary proof, and also enabled him to calculate the wavelength of visible light. He was the first to suggest that combinations of three primary colours could produce the whole range of colours in the visible spectrum, now known as the Young-Helmholtz three-colour theory. He also proposed in 1807 that heat might be a wave vibration similar to that of light, though again this was not generally accepted at the time. Experiments on the elastic properties of materials resulted in his discovery of the relationship between stress and strain known as Young's modulus, which he defined originally in terms that were almost impossible to understand. His *Course of Lectures on Natural Philosophy and the Mechanical Arts* (1807) was published in a second edition in 1845, revised by Philip Kelland, Professor of Mathematics at Edinburgh University.

Natural History

According to Grant (1884), in the year 1770 a **Dr Robert Ramsay** presented to the Town Council a Commission from George III, dated 13 March 1767, appointing him Regius Professor of Natural History and Keeper of the Museum in the University of Edinburgh, with a salary of £70 per annum. Strangely, no explanation for this appointment 'out of the blue', as it were, seems to have survived. All that is known of Ramsay is that he was a medical graduate of the University (MB, 1757; MD, 1758) and a Fellow of the Royal College of Physicians of Edinburgh (1761). The Town Council admitted him as Professor on condition that he conformed to their regulations and delivered to their clerk an inventory of the curiosities in the University. Another peculiarity of the Chair of Natural History is that according to the Edinburgh Evidence (1826) it was at different times said to belong to the Faculty of Arts and the Faculty of Medicine.

There was, wrote Grant (1884), '. . some sort of a Museum for Ramsay to be Keeper of, but it was so meagre as to be useless for teaching purposes. Partly perhaps from this cause, but probably also from want of zeal, Ramsay hardly attempted lecturing. For more than eight years he treated the Chair as a sinecure.' The University's collection of natural history specimens had been accumulated originally by Sir Andrew Balfour and Sir Robert Sibbald [*Botany, 1668] and presented to the University shortly after the former's death in 1694. Ramsay seems to have done little or nothing to care for this once extensive collection, though it is only fair to add that it had already greatly deteriorated by the time it became his responsibility.

On the death of Ramsay in 1779 the **Rev John Walker** was appointed to the Chair. Having studied for the ministry at Edinburgh he was then the parish minister in the

Church of Scotland at Moffat, and had acquired a considerable reputation as a more or less self-taught naturalist. It appears that he was also something of an opportunist, for he managed successfully to combine the duties of a parish minister (latterly at Colinton on the outskirts of Edinburgh) with those of a University Professor. He also took a leading part in the establishment of the Royal Society of Edinburgh in 1783, not so much as a desirable academic and learned society, more as a defence against the threatened encroachment of the Society of Antiquaries into his subject area.

Although natural history was at first devoted mainly to the biological subjects required by medical students, it is known that Walker's lecture courses included meteorology, hydrography, geology, mineralogy, botany and zoology. By the time he succeeded to the Chair, most of the remains of the Balfour/Sibbald collection had to be thrown out, but he assembled a fresh collection with which to illustrate his lectures. Unfortunately, after his death it was removed by his family who considered it to have been his personal property. His lecture notes in the University library show the originality of his ideas on botany and geology, and he perhaps deserves greater recognition in these areas than has been accorded to him up to now. One of the best-known of his students was (Sir) James Hall.

During his life-time he contributed some valuable papers to the Royal Society of Edinburgh and the Highland Society, and after his death his friend Charles Stewart published his *Economical History of the Hebrides* in 2 vols (1808) and his *Essays on Natural History and Rural Economy* (1812). He occupied the chair until his death in December 1803.

Some Notable Eighteenth Century Edinburgh University Scientists

BARTON, Benjamin (1766-1815) born in Pennsylvania, studied medicine at Edinburgh, London and Göttingen (MD, 1789). An influential teacher at the University of Pennsylvania, he wrote the first botanical textbook published in the United States, *Elements of Botany* (1803), and numerous papers on medicine, natural history and physical geography. [DSB, DAB]

BAYES, Thomas FRS (1701?-1761) studied at the University and the associated Theological College in Edinburgh. From 1731 until he retired in 1752 he was minister at the Presbyterian meeting-house in Tunbridge Wells. His fame rests on his posthumously-published paper *An Essay towards Solving a Problem in the Doctrine of Chances* (1764), the first attempt to establish foundations for statistical inference. [DNB, DSB]

BIRKBECK, George (1776-1841) graduated MD at Edinburgh in 1799, and succeeded Dr Garnett as Professor of Natural Philosophy at the Andersonian Institution. In 1800 he began courses of lectures for working men, and these 'mechanics' classes' became in 1823 the Glasgow Mechanics' Institute. He was instrumental in founding a similar

Institute in London in 1824; it was later named the Birkbeck Institution. [*see* HORNER, Leonard] [DNB]

BLAGDEN, Sir Charles FRS (1748-1820) MD, 1768. From about 1782 to 1789 he acted as assistant to Henry Cavendish and was drawn into the so-called 'water controversy' involving Cavendish, Watt and Lavoisier. From 1784 he was secretary of the Royal Society. He discovered *Blagden's Law* relating to the freezing point of solutions in 1788. [DNB, DSB]

BRISBANE, Sir Thomas MakDougall FRS PresRSE (1773-1860) studied at Edinburgh, then in 1789 enlisted in the British Army, rising to the rank of general in 1841. In pursuit of his interest in astronomy he erected an observatory at his Scottish home, another near Sydney when he was Governor of New South Wales (1821-25), and a third at Makerstoun on his return to Scotland. He catalogued in Australia 7385 stars, and at Makerstoun in 1841 he established the first geomagnetic observatory in Scotland. [DNB, DSB, CSBD]

DAWSON, John (1734-1820) is said to have taught himself mathematics while herding sheep in the Yorkshire dales. As soon as he had saved £100 he walked to Edinburgh, where he studied medicine and mathematics until his money ran out, and he was forced to trudge home again. He subsequently obtained a medical diploma in London, and practised in Sedbergh, where he became a renowned teacher of mathematics. [DNB]

DICKSON, Adam (1721-1776) took his MA degree and studied for the ministry at Edinburgh. He was minister at Duns in Berwickshire, 1750-70, and, like his father before him, was also a successful farmer. He published a useful *Treatise on Agriculture* in two volumes, 1762 and 1770, particularly adapted to the practice of farming in Scotland. [DNB]

GARNETT, Thomas (1766-1802) was articled at the age of 15 to 'the celebrated John Dawson of Sedbergh', matriculated at Edinburgh in 1785 'possessed of exceptional scientific knowledge', and graduated MD in 1788. Some eight years later he became Professor of Natural Philosophy at the Andersonian Institution in Glasgow, and in 1799 was appointed to a similar post at the Royal Institution in London. [DNB, DSB]

KEIR, James FRS (1735-1820) studied medicine at Edinburgh, but did not graduate. He joined the Army but resigned his commission in 1768 and settled in West Bromwich, devoting himself to chemistry and geology. As a member of the Lunar Society in Birmingham he met Boulton and Watt, but declined the offer of a partnership with them 'on account of the financial risk'. In about 1780 he founded the Tipton alkali works, often regarded as marking the genesis of scientific chemical manufacture in Britain. [DNB, DSB, CSBD]

MACCULLOCH, John FRS (1773-1835) MD, 1793. Appointed by the Government in 1811 to conduct a mineralogical survey of Scotland which resulted in the posthumous publication of the first large-scale geological map of Scotland (1836) with an accompanying Memoir. Also published in 1819 *A Description of the Western Isles of*

Scotland. [DNB, DSB, CSBD]

MENZIES, Archibald FLS (1754-1842) one of John Hope's gardeners, was encouraged by him to study medicine at Edinburgh. He then joined the Royal Navy and in 1786 was appointed surgeon-naturalist on a three-year round-the-world voyage of exploration. On his return the Government appointed him naturalist on the *Discovery* during its round-the-world voyage, 1790-95. He brought back from Chile the *Araucaria* or monkey-puzzle tree. [DNB, CSBD]

MITCHELL, John FRS (1711-1768) was born in Virginia, graduated MA at Edinburgh in 1729, and subsequently obtained a medical qualification. He practised from 1735 to 1746 in Virginia, at the same time pursuing his interest in botany. He then moved to London where he published in 1755 a large-scale *Map of the British and French Dominions in North America*, known as 'the most important map in American history'. [DNB, DAB, WAB]

PEARSON, George FRS (1751-1828) MD, 1773. A careful and ingenious experimenter in chemistry and electricity, he is best remembered for his paper *On the Nature of Gas Produced by Passing an Electric Discharge through Water*, 1797. [DNB, DSB]

RENNIE, John FRS FRSE (1761-1821) served an apprenticeship as a millwright, and studied at Edinburgh for three years, 1780-83. He became an outstanding civil engineer, noted for his scientific approach to problems involving aerodynamics (windmills), hydraulics (canals and watermills), wave action (docks and harbours), theory of structures, mechanics and strength of materials (bridges, mill buildings and machinery etc). [DNB, CSBD]

ROEBUCK, John FRS FRSE (1718-1794) studied medicine at Edinburgh, graduated MD at Leyden, 1742. Practised in Birmingham, but within a few years had turned to the manufacture of sulphuric acid by a new process of his own invention, at Prestonpans near Edinburgh. He was a better chemist than a businessman, however, and he failed in his attempt to give Watt the backing later provided by Boulton. [DNB, DSB, CSBD]

ROGET, Peter FRS (1779-1869) commenced his studies at Edinburgh at the age of 14 and five years later graduated MD. In addition to a distinguished career as a physician, he gave courses of public lectures in animal physiology, invented a log-log slide rule, and attempted unsuccessfully to construct a calculating machine. He is best known, however, as the author of *Roget's Thesaurus of English Words and Phrases* (1852) still in print today. [DNB]

RUSH, Benjamin (1745-1813) born near Philadelphia, completed his medical studies at Edinburgh (MD, 1768). Returning to Philadelphia, he began to practise medicine, and in 1769 became the first Professor of Chemistry in the College there. He wrote the first American textbook on chemistry, *A Syllabus of a Course of Lectures on Chemistry* (1770). In 1791 he joined the medical school of the University of Pennsylvania. [DAB, DSB, WAB]

SHORT, James FRS (1710-1768) began his studies at Edinburgh in 1726 intending to enter the ministry, but abandoned that career, it is said after attending the lectures of

McLaurin, who in 1732 encouraged him to learn by trial and error the difficult craft of making mirrors for reflecting telescopes. Within a few years of moving to London in 1738 he achieved fame as the finest maker of these instruments in Europe. [DNB, DSB, CSBD]

SMELLIE, William FSAS (1740-1795) attended some classes at the University while working as a printer's apprentice. In 1765 he founded his own firm which later became the University printers, and in 1768-71 he took a large part in the writing and printing of the first edition of the *Encyclopædia Britannica*. He was a candidate for the Edinburgh Chair of Natural History in 1779 when the Rev John Walker was appointed. [DNB, CSBD, BDES]

SMITH, Sir James Edward FRS (1759-1828) studied mdicine at Edinburgh (1781-83), London and Leyden (MD, 1786). Interested in botany, he purchased for £1000 in 1784 the entire collections of Linnaeus, and in 1788 founded and was elected first President of the Linnean Society. He published a number of important botanical works. [DNB, DSB]

THOMSON, Thomas FRS (1773-1852) studied at St Andrews before embarking on the medical course at Edinburgh (MD, 1799), where he was inspired by Joseph Black to devote his life to chemistry. He opened a school of chemistry in Edinburgh (1800-11), and in 1818 became Regius Professor of Chemistry at Glasgow University. In both places he established teaching laboratories which were the first of their kind in Britain. [DNB, DSB, CSBD]

TOULMIN, George (1754-1817) studied medicine at Edinburgh (MD, 1779). Few details of his subsequent career are known, but in 1780 he published *The Antiquity and Duration of the World*, which anticipated in a general way Hutton's *Theory of the Earth* (1788). [DSB]

WELLS, William FRS (1757-1817) born of Scottish parents in South Carolina, studied medicine at Edinburgh (MD, 1780) as well as London and Leyden. He settled in London from 1784 and began to publish papers on medical and scientific subjects. His *Essay on Dew* (1814) was the first to describe the exact process of the formation of dew, and he was considered by Darwin to have outlined the principle of natural selection in a paper on human skin colour and climate read to the Royal Society in 1813. [DNB, DSB, *Origin of Species* (1859)]

CHAPTER   3

The Scottish Enlightenment . . . and the Scottish Achievement

The latter part of the eighteenth century has been described by some Scottish historians as a Golden Age, a period when the printer William Smellie reported a remark made by 'Mr Amyat, King's Chemist, a most sensible and agreeable English gentleman', who spent a couple of years in Edinburgh:– "Here I stand at what is called the Cross of Edinburgh, and can, in a few minutes, take fifty men of genius and learning by the hand." But of course, what else could 'a most sensible and agreeable English gentleman' have said? On the other hand, could it be that amongst the undoubted exaggeration there is a great truth here, could it be that the Scottish Enlightenment did fire a torch that, for more than a few decades, illumined the whole of the European cultural scene? To find the answer we must digress for a few pages and examine the roles played by Edinburgh and its University, and by all Scottish 'men of genius and learning', in the development of science and technology in eighteenth century Europe.

A Hotbed of Genius

The Scottish writer Tobias Smollett (who studied medicine at Glasgow University and got his MD in 1750 from Marischal College, Aberdeen), in his last and finest work *Humphrey Clinker* (1771), committed to paper the penetrating statement:– 'Edinburgh is a hotbed of genius'. It was not a phrase that stuck to Edinburgh in the same way as 'Auld Reekie' or 'Athens of the North', but it gained fresh currency in 1986 when an exhibition was held in Edinburgh, and a very well illustrated book was published, both with the title *A Hotbed of Genius: the Scottish Enlightenment, 1730-90* (Daiches et al, 1986). In the preface to the book the point is made that in Scotland '. . there were great intellectual, artistic and technical advances in the eighteenth century. This period, now generally referred to as *The Scottish Enlightenment*, was at its most remarkable between about 1730 and 1790 and made Scotland briefly the cultural leader of Europe'.

The authors took the view that no single date can be said to mark the beginning or the end of the Scottish Enlightenment, that the goal of much of the scientific work in Scotland was explicitly practical, and the notion of *improvement* was everywhere apparent. They concluded that it is no longer possible to be at the forefront of several disciplines as most learned men were then – '. . the Scottish Enlightenment, it is generally held, did not survive the death of its great men'. In short, the reader of *A Hotbed of Genius*, or indeed most of the other publications on the subject, will be left with the impression that the Scottish Enlightenment was something like an intellectual nova, flaring up brilliantly for a few decades before diminishing again to a barely distinguishable point of light. I hope to be able to show, without introducing more than a few relevant facts and figures, that nothing could be farther from the truth.

Havelock Ellis, in his *Study of British Genius* (1927), took a sample of 1030 individuals from the *Dictionary of National Biography* (DNB), and discovered that in the fields of science and soldiering, Scotland's production of outstanding men was very much higher in relation to its population than that of the other British nations. Of the 120 scientists in the sample, England could claim 90 (75%) and Scotland 24 (20%).

Another quantitative study, using a wide variety of sources, was made by Clement and Robertson in *Scotland's Scientific Heritage* (1961), based on their selection of 230 eminent Scottish scientists, engineers and inventors whom they christened 'Scottish Savants'. Using their Fig 1, which records the number of Scottish savants born in each decade from 1550 to 1900, it is possible to estimate (assuming an average working life of 40 years) the number of savants *active* in each decade. The number active per million of the population (NPMP) in each half-century decade from 1650 to 1900 is shown in Table 2.1.

A similar exercise can be conducted with the aid of Chambers *Scottish Biographical Dictionary*, 1992 (CSBD), using the Subject Lists to select the relevant categories of scientists and technologists and distribute them in decades of activity. With different criteria for inclusion the total number of names is 430, and each individual was assigned to a number of decades corresponding to his working life-span. The resulting figures for NPMP are included in Table 2.1 [Birse [CSBD] (1993)], together with an extract of the comparable figures relating to Scotland from Table 2.4 [Birse [Table 2.4] (1989)]. Allowing for the variation in the numbers and sources of the samples, the three sets of figures are not dissimilar.

These figures for NPMP, the number of eminent scientists and technologists active per million population in each decade, confirm that there was indeed a great upsurge of intellectual activity in Scotland early in the eighteenth century, but they show equally clearly that, far from dying away before the end of that century, it continued to increase until the middle of the next, and in the two most recent sets of data, was still at a high level at the beginning of the twentieth century.

There is one subject category in Chambers, however, in which the number of savants active showed a six-times increase between 1720 and 1750, followed by a decrease to one-third between 1770 and 1790. The subject? Philosophy – and it should be noted that the actual numbers were one, six and two individuals respectively. So the Scottish Enlightenment really did happen between about 1730 and 1790, but mainly through the publication of a few seminal works by a handful of outstanding men. Most of them – philosophers David Hume, Adam Ferguson and Dugald Stewart, historian William Robertson and preacher Hugh Blair – had studied or taught at Edinburgh University.

Only in a very limited sense was the Scottish Enlightenment a short-lived burst of intellectual creativity. In most of the established sciences, and quite spectacularly in engineering, a period of sustained growth began in the first half of the eighteenth century and continued for more than a hundred years. The pioneering studies of William Cullen

Table 2.1 NUMBER OF SCOTTISH SAVANTS ACTIVE PER MILLION
POPULATION (NPMP) IN EACH HALF-CENTURY DECADE

	1650 to 1660	1700 to 1710	1750 to 1760	1800 to 1810	1850 to 1860	1900 to 1910	Total in Sample
Clement and Robertson (1961)	7.5	3	19	30	20	6	194
Birse [Table 2.4] (1989)	3.8	7.0	18.4	35.3	40.3	22.2	319
Birse [CSBD] (1993)	4	15	31	47	45	29	430
Scottish population in millions	0.8	1.0	1.25	1.5	3.0	4.5	

and Joseph Black in chemistry, James Hutton and Sir James Hall in geology, Sir John
Hope in botany, the Rev John Walker in natural history, John Robison in natural
philosophy and its practical applications, and the works of Scottish engineers such as
James Watt, William Murdock, Thomas Telford, John Rennie, William Symington and
Robert Stevenson, were only the beginning of what might appropriately be called the
Scottish Achievement.

Edinburgh University and the Scottish Achievement

Two other questions must therefore be asked, and answered, before we move on to the
nineteenth century. The Scottish Enlightenment is now well documented, and it is beyond
doubt that Edinburgh University took a leading role in it: but how did Edinburgh
compare with other universities in the provision of education for scientists and
technologists in the eighteenth century? And secondly, now that we have introduced the
notion of the Scottish Achievement, what evidence can we find of an especially noteworthy Scottish contribution to the progress of science and technology in Europe between
about 1740 and 1865?

Using data from the *Dictionary of National Biography* (DNB), Hans (1951) compared the
educational careers of 680 scientists of the seventeenth and eighteenth centuries. The
numbers of those who studied at different universities are shown in Table 2.2, from
which the exceptional record of Edinburgh University in the eighteenth century is
apparent. It has also been pointed out by Morrell (1971) that in Hans' much larger
sample, also from the DNB, of 3500 men eminent in all walks of life in the eighteenth
century, out of Edinburgh's 343 alumni no fewer than 152 were English.

Table 2.2 [abridged from Hans (1951) Table IV, p 32]
UNIVERSITY EDUCATION OF 680 SCIENTISTS OF THE SEVENTEENTH AND
EIGHTEENTH CENTURIES BY AGE GROUPS

When	None	Oxford	Cam-	Edin-	University attended: Other	Leyden	Other	Total
1600-45	16	29	24	**1**	2	5	3	80
1646-65	12	15	4	**1**	2	5	1	40
1666-85	23	12	13	**4**	4	5	5	66
1686-1705	30	9	20	**3**	6	9	5	82
1706-25	31	13	17	**10**	6	11	2	90
1726-45	51	14	23	**26**	5	4	5	128
1746-65	40	17	14	**25**	7	2	1	106
1766-85	45	7	11	**15**	8	2	-	88
Total in 17th cent	51	56	41	**6**	8	15	9	186
Total in 18th cent	197	60	85	**79**	32	28	13	494
GRAND TOTAL	248	116	126	**85**	40	43	22	680

Number of DNB scientists who were Fellows of the Royal Society - 539
Percentage of DNB scientists who attended university - 63.5%

A more recent study by Davies (1982) made use of data from the *Dictionary of Scientific Biography* (DSB), which includes information on more than 5,000 scientists who died before 1974. It is international in scope, but Dr Davies based his analysis exclusively on the entries relating to British scientists, 829 in number. The place of birth or, if more relevant, the parental home was noted for the 743 individuals for whom that information was given, the total for England being 514 (69.2%), and for Scotland 153 (20.6%). Details of the universities attended by the DSB scientists are given in Table 2.3. All those who attended more than one institution were credited as halves to each. Of the total of 84 scientists counted at Edinburgh University, $22^{1/}_{2}$ of the credits arose from scientists born in England, and a further four were born overseas.

Table 2.3 [adapted from Davies (1982) Table 5, p 12]
HIGHER EDUCATION OF 829 BRITISH DSB SCIENTISTS UP TO 1974

Institution of Higher Education:	Date founded:	Number attending:	Percentage attending:
St Andrews University	1411	$5^{1}/_{2}$	0.7
Glasgow University	1451	$25^{1}/_{2}$	3.1
Aberdeen University	1495	16	1.9
Edinburgh University	1583	84	10.1
Strathclyde University	1964	2	0.2
Total Scottish Universities		133	16
Oxford University	c1150	$108^{1}/_{2}$	13.1
Cambridge University	c1200	$190^{1}/_{2}$	23.0
London University	1826:1836	$58^{1}/_{2}$	7.1
Manchester University	1851:1903	18	2.2
Birmingham University	1880:1900	5	0.6
Total English Universities		$380^{1}/_{2}$	45.9
London Medical Schools		17	2.1
Trinity College Dublin	1591	19	2.3
Other Institutions		15	1.8
Total All Institutions		$564^{1}/_{2}$	68.2
No Institution recorded		264	31.8
GRAND TOTAL		829	100

Science and Technology in Western Europe

Having put Edinburgh in her place, as it were, it remains for us to take a brief overview of the growth of science and technology in Western Europe from 1600 to 1900. In an unpublished paper [Birse (1989)] read at a Symposium on the History of Technology, Science and Society 1750-1914, I indulged in a prosopographical analysis of a sample of 3299 scientists and technologists from 15 countries of Western Europe. The sample was derived from 24 assorted sources, all international in their coverage of science and/or technology, including works of biography, history and chronology. The numbers of eminent scientists (NES) and technologists (NET) in the UK, and for all ten selected countries the combined total (NEST) and the NEST per million population (NPMP) are given in Table 2.4.

The sample totals in the last column relate to the whole time-span of the original analysis, 1400 to 1920. The most significant figures are the numbers of scientists and technologists active in each decade per million population (NPMP), and it is clear from the table and in Fig 2.1 that Scotland's record is truly extraordinary. From another graph in the original paper it can be seen that in Scotland it was the biological (including medical) sciences that led the expansion from about 1650, followed by the physical sciences from 1720 and technology from 1760. The total of 319 eminent Scottish scientists and engineers in this sample includes 179 (56%) who studied at a university; of that number, 98 (55%) studied at Edinburgh University, and a further 31 were members of staff who had not previously been students.

One important factor that has undoubtedly helped to obscure Scotland's pre-eminence is the very high proportion of her most talented men who 'emigrated', by which is meant either settled abroad (including in England) or spent most or all of their working lives abroad – from 1750 to 1914 the percentages of Scottish scientists and engineers who did so were 65% and 71% respectively. Among the other countries of Western Europe, with the exception of those who emigrated to the United States, relatively few nationals of one country worked for more than a few years in another – Scotland's large-scale and long-term export of talent in science and technology was quite unprecedented.

When comparing Scotland with much more populous countries such as England, France and Germany, it was at first suspected that a comparison per million population might unduly favour smaller countries in general. The data reproduced here, however, for Switzerland, Sweden and Denmark as well as Scotland, show no sign of any significant overall bias, either towards or away from the smaller countries. It is worth noting also that in actual numbers of scientists and technologists, Scotland maintained from about 1750 to 1860 an output that was never less than three-quarters that of Germany, whose population was more than ten times greater.

Table 2.4 [abridged from Birse (1989)]
SCIENTISTS AND TECHNOLOGISTS IN TEN COUNTRIES OF WESTERN EUROPE
1600-1900

Country:	Decade starting–	1600	1650	1700	1750	1800	1850	1900	Sample TOTAL
England	NES	14	23	34	34	52	135	162	
and	NET	5	8	10	32	51	240	188	
Wales	NEST	19	31	44	66	103	375	350	1088
	NPMP	4.5	6.2	7.7	11.0	11.1	20.8	10.6	
Scotland	NES	2	2	5	20	29	54	46	
	NET	-	1	2	3	24	67	54	
	NEST	2	3	7	23	53	121	100	319
	NPMP	**2.9**	**3.8**	**7.0**	**18.4**	**35.3**	**40.3**	**22.2**	
Ireland	NEST	-	3	2	2	5	27	23	60
	NPMP	-	1.7	0.8	0.7	1.0	4.2	5.1	
France	NEST	9	25	25	60	112	138	129	546
	NPMP	0.5	1.2	1.1	2.5	3.9	3.8	3.1	
Holland	NEST	8	7	6	4	2	6	21	84
	NPMP	5.3	3.5	3.0	2.0	1.0	2.0	4.0	
Germany	NEST	12	10	12	22	59	168	228	628
	NPMP	1.0	0.9	0.9	1.5	3.3	6.2	5.3	
Switzerland	NEST	4	1	5	11	14	23	36	110
	NPMP	4.0	1.0	4.0	7.3	8.0	9.2	11.1	
Sweden	NEST	-	2	2	8	7	9	21	68
	NPMP	-	1.6	1.3	4.0	2.8	2.6	4.2	
Italy	NEST	22	17	17	14	16	15	25	195
	NPMP	1.8	1.5	1.3	0.9	0.8	0.6	0.7	
Denmark	NEST	4	4	1	1	3	8	17	47
	NPMP	5.7	5.3	1.3	1.1	3.0	5.3	6.8	
Western	NES	58	72	91	145	252	516	646	2131
Europe–	NET	24	32	35	69	129	395	364	1168
Totals &	NEST	82	104	126	214	381	911	1010	3299
Mean	NPMP	1.21	1.51	1.62	2.4	3.4	5.9	4.6	

One final anticipated concern about the figures for Scotland was that there might be an unduly high proportion of engineers in the totals for 1800 to 1900. Comparison with England and Wales for the same decades shows that, particularly in 1850, Scotland produced a significantly higher percentage of scientists (45%) than England and Wales (36%). The figures for the five leading countries in Table 2.4 have been plotted in Fig 2.1, where it can readily be seen that for more than two centuries Scotland was producing more scientists and technologists per head of population than any other country, large or small, in Western Europe – or, indeed, anywhere else in the world including the United States, whose NPMP did not reach double figures at any time up to the end of the nineteenth century.

Fig 2.1
NUMBERS OF SCIENTISTS AND TECHNOLOGISTS ACTIVE IN
EACH HALF-CENTURY DECADE PER MILLION POPULATION

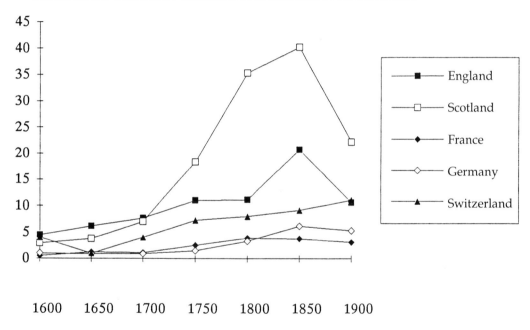

Conclusions
There seems to be no doubt that a remarkable outburst of scientific and technological activity in Scotland began, slowly at first, in the second half of the seventeenth century, gathering momentum throughout the eighteenth century to reach a peak in about 1850, then declining to perhaps half that level by the start of the twentieth century. Philosophy and science led the way, much of it centred in Edinburgh University and its assembly of distinguished professors. Engineering and other industrial applications of science followed from about 1750. The Scottish Enlightenment in philosophy and some of the sciences was thus only the first phase of a much greater phenomenon, the Scottish Achievement. The Enlightenment, concentrated almost entirely in Edinburgh and easily identifiable as the product of a handful of outstanding men, has overshadowed the

widely dispersed but collectively even more impressive Achievement, the work of several hundred Scottish scientists and engineers, many of them (almost one-third) educated at Edinburgh University, and most of them (about two-thirds) 'emigrating' to England or even farther afield.

It is not easy to find an explanation for these events, and it is certainly hard to believe what many historians of Scotland tell us, that it was all due to the beneficial effects of the Union of 1707. Would that really have persuaded young men to study natural philosophy instead of moral philosophy, geology instead of pneumatology? I prefer to think that the turning-point came one year after the Union, when in 1708 the regenting system was swept away in Edinburgh University. Consider the effect on the students, who were no longer constrained for four years to scribble down the dictates of one man on mainly philosophical subjects, intended as a suitable prelude to further studies in divinity or law. Within a few years they were able to pick and choose between courses given by famous professors vying with each other to attract students (and income!) by making sure that their lectures were interesting, and covered the applications as well as the principles of their subjects.

There were limits, of course, to this heady new *lernfreiheit*, since all but a few students had to equip themselves to earn a living when, and in many cases even before, they completed their studies. Opportunities in science were very limited, so in the eighteenth century a good deal of what we would now call research was accomplished by scientific amateurs whose profession was actually that of doctor or minister, or who had private means to sustain them. Engineering, on the other hand, though it was never a profession on the same level as the law or medicine, was the driving force behind the industrial revolution, and a young man with a mechanical bent, who took the trouble to study mathematics, chemistry and natural philosophy, could look forward to a challenging and rewarding career.

This was nothing less than a revolution in higher education, initiated in the University of Edinburgh in 1708, spreading to three of the other Scottish universities within the next half-century, and without any counterpart in England until the stifling duopoly of Oxford and Cambridge was finally ended in 1826. Looked at from that viewpoint, the otherwise hardly credible comparisons in this chapter become almost a natural consequence.

CHAPTER   4

Science in the Faculties of Arts and Medicine 1800 - 1893

After reading the previous chapter it will come as no surprise that although the pace of scientific advance in Europe was fairly constant for most of the seventeenth century – some ten to twenty major discoveries per decade, in the non-medical sciences and technology – a dramatic change then took place. By the middle of the eighteenth century the figure had risen to about fifty, and by the end of that century to about a hundred. Throughout the nineteenth century the rate of increase stayed much the same, so that by 1900 roughly two hundred major discoveries were being recorded world-wide in each decade. Although much harder to assess in a contemporary context, probably not more than four hundred major discoveries are being made in a decade today.

This is not the same exponential rate of increase as de Solla Price and others have charted for the growth of science in terms of numbers of scientists and scientific publications, or national expenditure on scientific research. The explanation for the much lower rate of increase in scientific *knowledge*, lies of course in the increasing difficulty and complexity of what scientists are still trying to discover. No longer does one scientist working for one year equal one discovery, no longer is one discovery in a hundred a major discovery. Today, one scientist working for three or four years should equal one PhD, usually a very minor discovery, and it could take as many as ten or even a hundred PhDs five or ten years to make a major discovery, only to have it disproved the next day, or the next year, by a similar team working on the same problem elsewhere.

Nineteenth Century Science

Whatever we take major discoveries to mean, I have no doubt that even to attempt a discursive overview of nineteenth century science in the manner of the first two chapters would be very unwise. However, it may be helpful to list briefly some reminders of the most notable scientific and technological advances (and retreats!) in the decades 1800-1810, 1850-1860 and 1900-1910.

A - astronomy	B - biology, botany	C - chemistry	G - earth sciences
M - mathematics	Mt - meteorology	P - physics	T - technology

1800	P/T	Volta invented the voltaic pile - the first 'battery'
	C	Priestley, still unconvinced by Lavoisier's experiments in 1786, published his *Doctrine of Phlogiston Established and the Composition of Water Refuted*.
		T Watt retired, having built about 500 of his beam engines with the help of Matthew Boulton and William Murdock

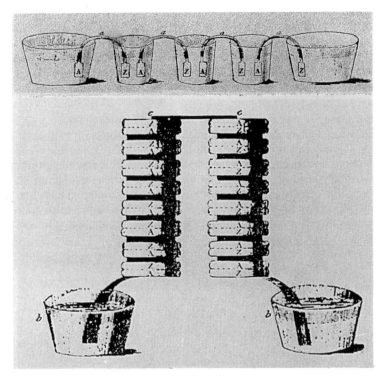

*Voltaic Pile. a) Crown
of cups. b) Pile*

1800/1	P	Herschel and Ritter detected infrared and ultraviolet radiation
1801	M	Gauss's *Disquisitiones arithmeticae* on number theory
	G	Haüy's 4-vol *Traité de minéralogie* (crystallography)
	A	Piazzi discovered the first asteroid *Ceres* – then lost it!
1802	G	Playfair's *Illustrations of the Huttonian Theory of the Earth* led to its more general acceptance
1803	C	Dalton proposed his atomic theory, further extended in his *New System of Chemical Philosophy*, 1808-27
	P	Young proved the wave nature of light using interference
1804	Mt	Gay-Lussac and Biot made scientific observations during balloon ascents to heights of up to 7,000m
1805	T	Jacquard 'programmed' looms by using sets of cards with punched holes – forerunners of computer punched cards
1806	M	Legendre described the method of least squares, which Gauss had discovered in 1794 but not published
1807	C	Davy isolated potassium and sodium by electrolysis
1808	C	Davy wrongly concluded that sulphur is *not* an element
1809	A	Gauss's *Theoria Motus Corporum Coelestium*

	B	Lamarck's *Philosophie zoologique* included a theory of evolution by inheritance of acquired characteristics
1850	P	Clausius first stated the second law of thermodynamics
	T	Robert Stephenson's Royal Border Bridge completed the east coast railway line from London to Edinburgh
1851	P	Kelvin proposed -273°C as zero on the absolute (later Kelvin) scale of temperature
1852	C	Frankland on 'combining power' (valency) of elements
1853	M	Hamilton introduced quaternions
1855	Mt	Ferrel's explanation of global atmospheric circulation
1856	T	Bessemer's converter used for the manufacture of steel
	C/T	Perkin manufactured the first synthetic dye, mauveine
	B/T	Pasteur heated wine to 55°C to avoid excessive fermentation – 'pasteurization'
1857	A	Bond calculated stellar magnitudes from photographs
	G	Owen's *Key to the Geology of the Globe* postulated continental drift, but his theory was neglected thereafter for several decades
1858	C	Kekulé on bonding of carbon compounds
1858/9	C/P	Clausius and Clerk Maxwell on kinetic theory of gases
	B	Wallace and Darwin's theories of natural selection
1859	C/A	Kirchhoff and Bunsen's spectroscope enabled them to identify some of the elements present in the sun
1900	B	Mendel's 1865 paper on hybridization was rediscovered and its importance recognised by (among others) . . .
	B	de Vries, who himself discovered the existence of large, discontinuous variations or 'mutations' in offspring
	G	Oldham identified primary and secondary seismic waves
	M	Pearson's chi-square test of goodness of fit
	P	Planck's quantum theory and blackbody radiation formula
1900s	M	Russell, Poincaré, Whitehead, Zermelo and Brouwer debated the mathematics of sets and logical paradoxes
1901	B	Takamine isolated and purified the hormone adrenaline
	T	Marconi made the first transatlantic radio transmission
1902	C	Lewis explained valency in terms of transfer of electrons
1903	A/T	Tsiolkovsky's *Exploration of Cosmic Space by means of Reaction Devices* — a prospect realised more than fifty years later
1903/4	T	Wright Brothers made the first powered, controlled and sustained man-carrying flights at Kitty Hawk
1904	T	Parsons built steam turbo-alternators with an output of 3·5MW
1905	P	Rutherford and Soddy's theory of nuclear transmutation

D

	P	Einstein on the particle-wave duality of light (photons)
	P	Einstein's special theory of relativity, and the most wonderfully concise formula $E=mc^2$
1906	A	Lowell's *Mars and its Canals* asserted that they were evidence of intelligent life on the planet
1907	B	Pavlov's work on conditioned reflexes in dogs
1908	B	Garrod's *Inborn Errors of Metabolism* developed the idea of genetically induced disease
	Mt	Arrhenius described the action of the 'greenhouse effect'
1909	C/T	Baekeland produced the first commercial plastic *bakelite*.

Perhaps the most striking overall contrast is between Priestley's head-in-the-sand defence of phlogiston in 1800, and Planck's quantum theory and Einstein's theory of relativity a hundred years later. On the other hand, there is a remarkable similarity between Priestley in 1800 and Lowell in 1906. Even Sir Humphry Davy got it wrong in 1808, but Tsiolkovsky got it right in 1903 – except that he was 54 years too soon. Gauss was one of the few still writing scientific works in Latin in the early nineteenth century, and some of the others were Edinburgh University students, whose graduation theses prior to 1833 had to be submitted in Latin.

James Watt in the late eighteenth century was building beam engines of about 15 horse-power, which he had carefully calculated to be the power of fifteen horses. He would have been surprised to find that a century later his name was attached to a unit of power related not to horses but to two eminent scientists. He might have been even more surprised to learn that Parsons' steam turbine of 1904 developed more power than three hundred of his beam engines – and, without boiler and condenser, didn't take up as much space as one of them.

An exciting century, the nineteenth, full of discoveries in science and progress in technology; a challenge to the universities to produce the men who would lead the country forward.

The University of Edinburgh and the Royal Commissions

At the beginning of the nineteenth century the French Revolution and the Napoleonic Wars had an impact on Edinburgh University in several ways. Britain was effectively cut off from the rest of Europe for a whole generation, and many English tourists who would have spent a holiday on the continent ventured north to Scotland instead. English students too came north, and the total number of students at Edinburgh University doubled within less than twenty years, from one to two thousand, the number of professors being at that time thirty. The wars led to a greatly increased demand for artillery officers, military engineers, doctors and surgeons, and Regius Chairs in Clinical Surgery, Military Surgery and Forensic Medicine were endowed by the government in rapid succession. Lectures on navigation, gunnery and fortifications had for many years formed part of the lecture courses in mathematics and natural philosophy.

Another consequence of the wars was inflation, and even with a much larger student population the University was forced to double the matriculation fee in 1806, and two years later all class fees were increased by one guinea to three or four guineas. At the same time the government was looking for additional sources of revenue, and in 1808 a tax was proposed on matriculation and graduation. As a result matriculation became compulsory, each Edinburgh MD paid £10 stamp duty on his diploma, and the Collector of Taxes even tried to levy male servant's duty on all the janitors employed by the professors to open and shut their classroom doors.

One situation on which the outside world and its troubles didn't seem to have much effect was the perennial power struggle between the University of Edinburgh and its nominal masters, the Town Council. Added to that was the internecine strife among the professors, dependent still on class fees for much of their remuneration, and ready at all times to object fiercely to any proposal or manoeuvre that might result in students deserting their class for that of a colleague. By the 1820s the situation was so serious that Robert Peel, then Home Secretary, set

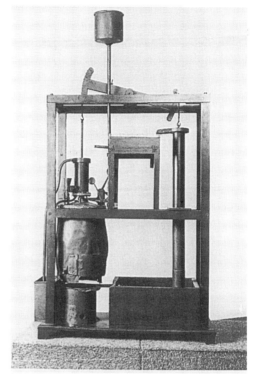

Model of Newcomen Steam Engine.
While repairing this engine, Watt concluded that it would be more efficient to cool the steam in a separate condenser instead of in the cylinder itself. This innovation was the basis of his fame and fortune

up in 1826 a Royal Commission on the Universities of Scotland. Its report to Parliament was published in 1831, but there was strong opposition to some of its proposals, and although the Whigs were then in power, for the next quarter of a century nothing was done to implement its recommendations.

The most useful outcome of the Commission's deliberations was the vast amount of 'Evidence, Oral and Documentary' it accumulated on the state of the Scottish universities in the 1820s and earlier; published eventually in 1837, the volume relating to Edinburgh University alone ran to more than 900 foolscap pages. In the Edinburgh Evidence it was stated that the Winter Session began on the last Wednesday of October, and ended on the last day of April; the Summer Session began on the first day of May, and ended on the last day of July. Most classes were held only during the Winter Session of six months; Natural History was one of the few non-medical classes held in summer (3 months) as well as winter (5 months). At that time the average age at entry to Edinburgh University was about fourteen and a half.

Not only in Scotland was there growing dissatisfaction with the state of university education. A telling comment was made by Louis Simond in his *Journal of a Tour and Residence in Great Britain 1810-11*, **i**, 375-6 — 'The two great universities, Oxford and Cambridge, repose themselves under the shade of their laurels, while Edinburgh cultivates hers.' The first signs of a radical change, in an area of education far removed from the universities, were the mechanics' institutes founded in Edinburgh by Leonard Horner in 1821, and in Glasgow and London by George Birkbeck in 1823 and 1824. They were so successful in filling an obvious gap in the education system that by 1850 there were some 700 of them throughout the UK.

At the same time the English higher education scene was transformed by the founding of University College (1828) and King's College (1831) in London, the University of Durham in 1832, and the University of London as a degree-giving institution in 1836. Mainly because of chronic under-funding, however, the new universities in London and Durham were not immediately successful. Durham had 82 students in 1840, only 51 in 1860. At UCL the founders had hoped for 2000 students, but that number was not reached for 80 years. Nevertheless, the combined effect of these and other factors brought the number of students at Edinburgh below a thousand in 1842, though after that there was a fairly steady increase to about three thousand by the end of the century.

The government did at length act on the report of its own 1826 Royal Commission, and the resulting Universities (Scotland) Act, 1858, although resented for various reasons by the other Scottish universities, was warmly welcomed at Edinburgh. It put an end after many years to the frequent disputes between the Tounis College and the Town Council, by curtailing the powers of the Town Council in the appointment of the Principal and Professors, transferring them to a panel of seven curators, four nominated by the Town Council and three by the University Court. In all the Scottish universities it established the University Court and the General Council, their membership and powers, and also provided for the election of a Chancellor by the members of the General Council.

What the 1858 Act and the subsequent ordinances of its commissioners achieved was confined mainly to administrative matters, and particularly to the union of the two colleges into the University of Aberdeen. Though given the power to regulate courses, the commissioners seem to have fought shy of doing this in other than minor ways, and their powers of distributing any Treasury grants that might be allocated to them were limited to very specific purposes such as the payment of pensions to retired professors, the endowment of new professorships, and the reimbursement of their own expenses. It was, in effect, a very half-hearted Act, and as a result it all had to be done again thirty years later.

The agitation for a more radical reform of Scottish university education continued through the 1860s, and eventually another Royal Commission on the Universities of Scotland was appointed in 1876. One of its most important remits from our point of view was to rationalise the regulations in the Scottish universities for the granting of degrees in science. Its Report, presented to Parliament in February 1878, proposed the institution of Faculties of Science in the four Scottish universities, and favoured greater specialisation in the arts curriculum, with the abandonment of the long-standing Scottish emphasis on philosophy as the backbone of all courses whether literary or scientific.

When the Government bill based on the 1878 Report was published five years later it incorporated a number of controversial proposals, none more so than that relating to the future financing of the Scottish universities. Ever since the Act of Union they had received modest annual grants from the Treasury, but the bill made provision for an annual grant of £40,000 (or, at the discretion of the Treasury, a single lump sum payment of $33^{1}/_{3}$ times the annual grant) to be 'deemed to be in full discharge of all claims, past, present, and future, of the said Universities.' This became known as the 'finality clause', and when the Treasury indicated that it was indeed contemplating the virtual disestablishment of the Scottish universities there was an immediate chorus of outraged protest.

In the meantime Lyon Playfair had resigned his Edinburgh Chair of Chemistry in 1868 on being elected MP for the Universities of Edinburgh and St Andrews, and by 1886, as Liberal MP for South Leeds and vice-president of council, he was a parliamentarian of considerable influence. Playfair and other MPs were joined by many outside Parliament in opposition to the successive bills introduced by the Government almost every year from 1883 to 1888, until in 1889 a sufficiently amended bill, without the 'finality clause', became the Universities (Scotland) Act, 1889. Three years later the Scottish universities received a further Parliamentary grant under the Education and Local Taxation Account (Scotland) Act, 1892.

Annual Grant under:	All Scottish Universities:	Edinburgh University:
The 1889 Act	£42,000	£15,120
The 1892 Act	30,000	10,800

These sums remained unchanged for more than twenty years, and it was not until the Standing Committee which became known as the University Grants Committee was set up in 1919 that the Scottish universities were funded in common with those of the rest of the United Kingdom. To allow meaningful comparisons of the value of money over a time-scale of several centuries, estimated figures, derived in part from Burnett (1969), are given in Table 4.1 of the comparable purchasing power of £1 in September 1993.

The Universities (Scotland) Act, 1889, 'An Act for the Better Administration and Endowment of the Universities of Scotland', was passed on 30 August 1889 and came into operation on 1 January 1890. It specified increased powers for the University Courts and Senates, and appointed a body of Commissioners who were given very comprehensive powers to inquire further into the existing state of the Scottish Universities, and thereafter to make such ordinances 'as shall to them seem expedient' to regulate almost every aspect of the Universities' administration, staffing, teaching and examining.

On 5 June 1893 in Ordinance No 31 – Glasgow, Aberdeen, and Edinburgh, No 1, under the said Act, the Commissioners specified the Composition of the Faculties and the Institution of Faculties of Science in the three Universities. They were also given the

Table 4.1 PURCHASING POWER OF ONE POUND

	£		£
1700	85.5	1910	50.8
1750	80.4	1920	19.5
1790	58.0	1930	39.6
1800	32.2	1940	32.1
1810	30.2	1950	16.0
1820	37.3	1955	12.7
1830	44.1	1960	11.3
1840	39.3	1965	9.6
1850	52.1	1970	7.7
1860	38.4	1975	4.2
1870	40.7	1980	2.1
1880	43.1	1985	1.5
1890	53.3	1990	1.1
1900	50.8	1993 (Sept)	1.0

power 'to enable each University to admit women to graduation in one or more faculties, and to provide for their instruction'. In Ordinance No 18 – General, No 9, in February 1892, the Commissioners made *Regulations for the Graduation of Women and for their instruction in the Universities*. The year 1893 was thus notable in Edinburgh University not only for the founding of the Faculty of Science but also as the year in which the first eight women were admitted to graduation in Arts. They had already completed their studies as members of the Edinburgh Ladies Education Association, attending classes taken by the University professors and lecturers, and had been awarded University Certificates in Arts.

Science in the University of Edinburgh

Although, in common with the other Scottish universities, Edinburgh had no Faculty of Science until the last decade of the nineteenth century, the sciences flourished in the Faculties of Arts and Medicine under a succession of outstanding professors, thirty-six in all, of whom fifteen were Fellows of the Royal Society of London, and all but three of the remainder were Fellows of the Royal Society of Edinburgh. The names that immediately come to mind include Thomas Henderson in Astronomy; the two Balfours, father and son, in Botany; Hope, Lyon Playfair and Crum Brown in Chemistry; Fleeming Jenkin in Engineering; the brothers Geikie in Geology; Chrystal in Mathematics; Jameson and Wyville Thomson in Natural History; Playfair, Leslie, J D Forbes and P G Tait in Natural Philosophy. The professors and their most eminent pupils have a place in this chapter under the appropriate subject heading.

Principal Sir David Brewster, from the Tercentenary Photographic Album, 1883, of the University of Edinburgh

The Principal of Edinburgh University from 1859 to 1868 was **Sir David Brewster** FRS PresRSE (1781-1868), an Edinburgh MA at the age of nineteen, a past-President of the British Association and a renowned figure in the world of scientific optics. He had been passed over in 1833 in favour of J D Forbes for the Edinburgh Chair of Natural Philosophy, but it may have been no more than a coincidence that in 1859 Forbes left Edinburgh to become the Principal at St Andrews. Another nineteenth century 'statesman of science' was at that time also in Edinburgh University. Since 1858 the Professor of Chemistry had been Lyon Playfair, previously secretary for science to the government's Department of Science and Art, who had publicly expressed his great concern that Britain was falling behind the rest of Europe in scientific education and research. No doubt he found Brewster sympathetic to his views.

In February 1863 Playfair proposed in the Senate 'That a committee be appointed to consider the best means by which a Degree in Science may be initiated in this University.' A year later the Committee reported, and its proposals were generally accepted. Only John Goodsir, the Professor of Anatomy, dissented in a lengthy speech, at the end of which he said:– "Degrees of this kind, in spite of every precaution, would tend to diminish the value put upon a general mental culture, would indicate mere scientific attainment, and not necessarily indicate scientific ability. Finally – I dissent from the proposal because I see in it the commencement of a process which will convert this University into a mere degree-giving institution . . ."

D*

Grant (1884) notes that the decision to establish degrees in science was taken by the Senate without reference to the Court, the Chancellor, or the Privy Council.

The new Degrees of Bachelor of Science and Doctor of Science were first offered in the academic year 1864-65, in the following three sections of Pure Science:-

SECTION A — Physical and Natural Science
    (a)   The Mathematical Sciences
        Higher Mathematics   Natural Philosophy
    (b)   The Physical Experimental Sciences
        Chemistry   Experimental Philosophy
    (c)   The Natural Sciences
        Zoology   Botany
        Physiology   Geology

SECTION B — Mental Science
    (a) Logic and Metaphysics
    (b) Moral Philosophy and Political Economy

SECTION C — Philology
    (a) The Latin and Greek Languages
    (b) The Semitic Languages
    (c) The Sanskrit Language, and Comparative Philology.

Administration of the new degrees was undertaken by a Science Degrees Committee, presided over by two Conveners, Alex Crum Brown, Professor of Chemistry and John Hutton Balfour, Professor of Botany and Dean of the Faculty of Medicine. After it had been in existence for a few years the status of the Committee was expressed thus in the University Calendar:– 'FACULTIES – The University contains four Faculties and a Science Degrees Committee. Each Faculty is presided over by a Dean, and the Science Degrees Committee by two Conveners.' So the Science Degrees Committee of 1864 was almost a Faculty of Science in embryo, albeit a Faculty without departments.

Nor, at first, did it have many students – the first two BSc degrees were awarded in 1866, and the total number of BSc degrees in any year did not reach double figures until 1876, and then it was mainly because of the popularity of the newly-instituted degree in Public Health. The Committee assumed responsibility in due course for the BSc and DSc degrees in Engineering (from 1868) and Public Health (from 1875), and the BSc in Agriculture (from 1886). It was decided that only DSc degrees would be awarded in Mental Science and Philology.

One of the most telling indications of the extent to which British science and industry had fallen behind the rest of Europe within the space of less than two decades, was provided by the 1867 Paris Exhibition. In contrast to the Great Exhibition of 1851 when Britain's manufacturers carried off a large majority of the awards, 1867 in Paris was a national disgrace. Lyon Playfair, who at the time was still Professor of Chemistry at Edinburgh, wrote a strong criticism of the British exhibits which led to the setting up of a Select Committee on Scientific Instruction. When its report was published the Government appointed in 1870 a Royal Commission on Scientific Instruction and the Advancement of Science, headed by the Duke of Devonshire.

In Edinburgh, as a result, a Science Instruction Committee was appointed by the Senatus, to prepare a 'statement as to scientific instruction and the means available for the advancement of science in the University of Edinburgh, with suggestions for the improvement of the same'. In February 1871 its report was sent to the Royal Commission. Meanwhile, in November 1870, a Sub-Committee of the Science Instruction Committee was appointed to 'enquire into the propriety' of forming a Faculty or Department of Science. The 1870 Royal Commission was a very wide-ranging inquiry which took evidence over a period of three years from a total of 169 professors and others representing all the universities and colleges in England, Scotland and Ireland, as well as the national scientific museums and other institutions.

The picture presented to it of the science teaching in the University of Edinburgh around 1870 is of what might fairly be called a modest triumph over adversity. One after another Professors Crum Brown, P G Tait, Archibald Geikie, Wyville Thomson and Fleeming Jenkin told of the problems and frustrations caused by lack of sufficient classroom and laboratory space, lack of sufficient funding to pay for class assistants, apparatus and specimens, books and periodicals, and lack of sufficient time for study and research. Without the benefit of their frank answers to the questions put by the Commissioners, especially on the subject of practical instruction, we might well have accepted the information in the 1869/70 Edinburgh University Calendar at face value.

The Calendar informs us that there were Museums of Natural History (in the adjacent Museum of Science and Art), Botany (at the Royal Botanic Garden), and Natural Philosophy (among others). There were laboratories for the courses in Chemistry and Natural Philosophy, where 'it is hoped that, with the valuable collection of apparatus in the Museum, results of real use to science may be obtained.' For Engineering students there were drawing classes and a fortnight's practical surveying; and there were courses in Practical Astronomy and Agriculture. But the Professors complained that the Natural History and Mineralogy collections (prior to 1854 the property of the University) in the Museum of Science and Art were not displayed in a manner suitable for teaching; that there was no suitable space to store the instruments in the Natural Philosophy collection; that the Chemistry laboratory could accommodate only 12 students at any one time, and the Natural Philosophy laboratory about the same; that the course in Practical Astronomy was almost completely in abeyance; and that no space whatever could be found for a laboratory in the essentially practical subject of Agriculture.

At that time the funds applied annually to scientific instruction at Edinburgh amounted to £5573 out of the University's total income of just over £20,000. The Parliamentary Grants to Edinburgh and Glasgow in 1869/70 amounted to £2500 and £1408 respectively. The scope of 'scientific instruction' under the remit of the Royal

Commission included all the pure and applied sciences, the medical sciences, and music, but not mathematics. The number of students recorded as attending science classes at Edinburgh University in 1869-70 varied greatly between different subjects:–

Natural Philosophy	185	Chemistry	232
Agriculture	27	Engineering	26
Practical Astronomy	1	Geology	43
Natural History	189	Botany	283

One outcome of the 1870 Royal Commission's report was that the Government accepted the need for an expansion of scientific instruction in the universities, and the need for additional funding by Parliament to enable the universities to undertake it. The effects were felt by the Scottish universities as their Parliamentary Grants increased to the following totals over the ten years ending in March 1883:–

	1873-83:	plus special grants in aid:
Aberdeen	£65,821	——-
Edinburgh	85,906	£80,000
Glasgow	66,182	20,000
St Andrews	38,111	——-

Edinburgh was not alone, of course, in the move towards science in the second half of the nineteenth century. In 1846 William Thomson (later Lord Kelvin) became Professor of Natural Philosophy at Glasgow, and soon afterwards established the first laboratory for the teaching of physics. In 1873 Glasgow University's first BSc degrees were conferred, and in 1876 in St Andrews University the BSc degree was instituted and a special science committee established. Cambridge University established the world-famous Cavendish (Physical) Laboratory in 1871, followed by the Clarendon at Oxford in 1872.

The published list of *Graduates of the University of Edinburgh, 1859 to 1888* includes the following totals of science degrees conferred from 1866 to 1888:–

	DSc	BSc
Mental Sciences	11	NA
Philology	6	NA
Mathematical Sciences	2	22
Physical Experimental Sciences	21	44
Natural Sciences	12	53
Engineering	1	38
Public Health	12	66
Agriculture	-	1
Totals:	**65**	**224**

The total number of degrees (including science degrees) conferred in the same period of 23 years was 8557, the annual number having increased fairly steadily from 153 in 1866 to 617 in 1888.

The Faculty of Arts

At the beginning of the nineteenth century the only scientific chair that had been added to those of Mathematics and Natural Philosophy was the Chair of Agriculture in 1790. Prior to that date occasional short courses of lectures on the subject had been given by the Edinburgh professors William Cullen and John Walker. In 1855 a Regius Chair of Technology [*Engineering] was instituted, only to be abolished on the death of the incumbent, George Wilson, four years later. The Regius Chair of Engineering took its place in 1868, substantially endowed by Sir David Baxter of Dundee, with a contribution from the Treasury to the Professor's salary. Finally in 1871 the Regius Chair of Geology was generously endowed by Sir Roderick Impey Murchison.

In 1825, somewhat belatedly, it was prescribed that candidates for the degree of Master of Arts must have attended a university during four regular sessions, and in that time must have attended the classes of Humanity, Greek, Mathematics, Logic, Rhetoric, Moral and Natural Philosophy. From session 1862/3 graduating MA in the Department of Natural Science with Honours in Chemistry, Botany, Zoology or Geology became possible, though very few students did so – only three in the next ten years!

In the 1870s it was still only a small minority of students that finally graduated in Arts. From a total number of about 700 students in the Faculty only some 40 to 50 graduated MA each year, with another half dozen taking honours in Classics, Philosophy, Mathematics or Natural Science. The average age at entry was beginning to rise from about fifteen (before 1860) to seventeen or eighteen by around 1900.

From 1890 to 1912 **Prof George Chrystal** (Mathematics) was Dean of the Faculty of Arts, and from 1925 to 1928 the Faculty elected its last scientific Dean in the person of **Prof Edmund Whittaker** (Mathematics). The Faculty of Arts seems to have been quite ready to take science under its wing towards the end of the nineteenth century: in the Calendars of the 1860s and '70s it was described as 'The Faculty of Arts, or of Literature and Philosophy', but by the 1880s it was 'The Faculty of Arts (or of Literature, Science, and Philosophy).'

The Faculty of Medicine

Throughout the nineteenth century the 'scientific' subjects of Botany, Chemistry and Natural History continued to be taught in the Faculty of Medicine. The story of the origins of *Public Health in the Faculty of Law and its development in Science and Medicine is told in this chapter.

The evidence given to the 1870 Royal Commission by the professors of science concerning overcrowding in the Old College made frequent reference to the 'new medical building' proposed for a site in Teviot Place. It was anticipated that the removal of the entire Medical School (including the Department of Chemistry) to the new building would provide at least in the short term adequate accommodation for the other departments remaining in the Old College. The new building was completed shortly after the University celebrated its tercentenary in April 1884, and for the next twenty years there was a programme of refurbishment and reallocation of space in the Old College.

Medical School buildings

Agriculture

The extraordinary life-story of Sir William Johnstone Pulteney (1729-1805), who endowed the Chair of Agriculture in Edinburgh University in 1790, has been told by Ian Fleming and Noel Robertson in their book *Britain's First Chair of Agriculture at the University of Edinburgh, 1790-1990*. Born William Johnstone, he studied law at Edinburgh and became an advocate in 1757, but moved to London three years later on his marriage to Frances Pulteney, heiress to the Earl of Bath. He became at once a very wealthy man, and graciously added her name to his – it was said that at his death he was the richest commoner in the land. He was probably the first private individual to endow a Chair in any Scottish University, and his gift of £1250 was equivalent to about one half of Edinburgh University's annual income at that time.

The new Professorship was advertised in 1789 and it is known that it was drawn to the attention of Robert Burns, but there is no record of how many applications were received. John Walker, the Professor of Natural History, was anxious to secure the Chair,

Sir William Pulteney, by Thomas Gainsborough.
MP for Shrewsbury and founder of the First Chair of Agriculture in Britain at Edinburgh University.

but was not successful, and in 1790 **Andrew Coventry** was installed as the first Professor. He had graduated MD at Edinburgh in 1783 but is not known to have practised medicine – indeed he seems to have been always more interested in agriculture. After his installation he delivered courses of lectures (as many as 140 in one academic year) on Agriculture and Rural Economy. In the Edinburgh Evidence (1826) Coventry stated 'I have generally wished the students to have attended chemistry, botany, natural history, and mechanical or natural philosophy *before* coming to the class for agriculture . . '

David Low, who had studied under Coventry in 1805, succeeded him in 1831; he established a museum of agriculture in Old College, and published in 1834 *Elements of Practical Agriculture* which was translated into French and German, and in 1842 'a splendid work' in two volumes *The Breeds of Domesticated Animals of the British Islands*.

In 1854 **John Wilson** was appointed the third Professor, coming to Edinburgh from his post as Principal of the Royal Agricultural College, Cirencester. After ten years as professor, teaching the whole course single-handedly, he still had a salary of only £50 per annum, but in 1869 it was increased to £350 per annum. Wilson became Secretary of the Senatus in 1868, and supported the establishment of a Division of Applied Science, to include Agriculture, Engineering and Veterinary Surgery; there was much opposition within the University, however, and although details appeared in the 1869-70 Calendar the proposal was never put into effect.

The fourth Professor in 1885 was **Robert Wallace**, also from Cirencester. In his studies at Edinburgh he attended the lectures of John Wilson and won the Class Medal in 1878. He rapidly built up a group of specialist extra-mural lecturers (County Organisers), and persuaded the Senatus in 1886 to institute a BSc degree in Agriculture, administered by the Science Degrees Committee. He also initiated courses in colonial and tropical agriculture – 'a man bursting with ideas for the development of agricultural education', in the words of Noel Robertson. He wrote *Farm Livestock of Great Britain* (1885, 4edn 1907) which was a classic work in its day. In 1890 a Steven Lectureship in Agricultural and Forest Entomology was endowed, and two years later the Edinburgh Incorporated School of Agriculture was formed by Wallace in association with the extra-mural teachers.

Astronomy

From the foundation of the Tounis College in 1583 Astronomy was studied as part of both Mathematics and Natural Philosophy in the four-year courses given by the Regents in Philosophy. After Chairs of Mathematics (1674) and Natural Philosophy (1708) had been established, there was from time to time some disagreement between their occupants as to whose prerogative it was to teach astronomy. John Leslie stated in the Edinburgh Evidence (1826) that in the 1740s 'Professor Maclaurin made great exertions to have an Observatory erected within the College. He raised some money by subscription, and the Town granted a heap of old stones, to the value of about £20; the building was to have commenced in 1746, when that illustrious Professor died.' The continuing efforts on the part of Thomas Short and others to get an observatory built in Edinburgh are told in Hermann Brück's *Story of Astronomy in Edinburgh* (1983).

Short telescope (Gregorian type)

In 1785 the Regius Chair of Practical Astronomy was instituted in the Faculty of Arts; **Robert Blair**, a graduate of Edinburgh in medicine, was installed as first Professor, but refused to lecture on the grounds that he had neither observatory nor instruments at his disposal. Instead he embarked on a lengthy series of experiments with the aim of developing an improved type of achromatic refracting telescope lens, but his compound lenses were too complicated to be used in practice. Blair died after a long illness in 1828, and three years later the Royal Commission on the Scottish Universities recommended that the chair should not be filled 'until a suitable observatory, attached to the University, could be provided'.

The observatory erected on the Calton Hill (1818-24) by the Astronomical Institution of Edinburgh (which had become the Royal Observatory of King George IV in 1822) was made over to the University in 1834 'for their unlimited use', on condition that

The Old Observatory on Calton Hill,
1792

The New Observatory on Calton Hill,
1824—by Playfair

the Government would appoint a Principal Observer, to be known as the Astronomer Royal for Scotland, whose post would be combined with the Regius Professor of Astronomy. **Thomas Henderson** was accordingly appointed to the joint position in 1834. Somewhat improbably Thomas Carlyle was also a candidate, on the strength of his having been a student of mathematics under John Leslie some twenty years before. Henderson accomplished a great deal of observational work as Astronomer Royal, but did not find time to institute a course of lectures in astronomy in the University.

In 1846 **Charles Piazzi Smyth** became the second Astronomer Royal for Scotland and third Regius Professor of Astronomy. Born at Naples in 1819, the second son of Admiral William Henry Smyth, the Italian astronomer Giuseppe Piazzi was his godfather. As his first priority in Edinburgh, over the next four years he completed the reduction of Henderson's observations and their publication as the *Edinburgh Astronomical Observations*. He then embarked on the first lectures ever delivered by the Professor of Practical Astronomy in the University, sixty-five years after the Chair had been founded.

In his Annual Report for 1852 Smyth proposed for the first time a mountain observatory, suggesting the peak of Tenerife as a suitable location. Four years later observations were carried out during a summer camp on Mt Teide in Tenerife, with very promising results published in further volumes of the *Edinburgh Astronomical Observations*. A permanent out-station of the Royal Observatory in the Canary Islands was eventually built in the 1980s.

Smyth was elected a Fellow of the Royal Society in 1857, and a few years later began his investigation into the metrological properties of the Great Pyramid. He became increasingly fanatical in his attempt to unravel the pyramid's mysteries, and in 1867/68 published his conclusions in the three volumes of *Life and Work at the Great Pyramid*. The work excited great popular interest and at the same time a good deal of opposition – Smyth resigned from the Royal Society in 1874 because he was not permitted to present his paper on the design of the Great Pyramid. The continuing fascination of the pyramids even today is shown by the fact that *The Great Pyramid: its secrets and mysteries revealed* by

'Piazzi Smyth' was reprinted in America as recently as 1990.

In 1872 a difference of opinion arose between Smyth and the University of Edinburgh over his position and duties as Professor of Practical Astronomy; by this time his teaching had become minimal, partly because of a lack of financial and material support from the University, partly because he found the intellectual level of the students to be much lower than he had expected. In a Statement presented to the Royal Commission on Scientific Instruction in 1870, the point was made that since Astronomy was not required for graduation in any of the Faculties, the number of students was always very small – to be precise, only one in session 1869-70.

Smyth retired in 1888, leaving the Royal Observatory on the Calton Hill in a poor state due to chronic underfunding. Poor viewing conditions in the middle of 'Auld Reekie' were a factor in its neglect. The Royal Commission of 1889 on the Scottish Universities recommended that the observatory on the Calton Hill should be handed over to the University – public outcry resulted in the Earl of Crawford offering his astronomical instruments and outstanding collection of scientific and astronomical books to the nation on condition the Government built and maintained a new Royal Observatory.

In 1889 **Ralph Copeland** was appointed the third Astronomer Royal for Scotland and fourth Regius Professor of Astronomy. He divided his time conscientiously between the two posts, giving regular courses of 80 lectures and practical sessions at intermediate level, and offering an advanced course when there was sufficient demand for it. The course in Practical Astronomy given by Professor Copeland included lectures and instruction in the use of portable and fixed astronomical instruments. 'In the practical lessons the requirements of the scientific traveller will be kept specially in view.'

Botany

Robert Graham became in 1820 the seventh Regius Professor of Medicine and Botany; he had been apprenticed to a surgeon in Edinburgh in 1804 and graduated MD in 1808. He was appointed in 1818 to the first Regius Chair of Botany in the University of Glasgow, but in Edinburgh he was, like his predecessors, obliged to concern himself, at least nominally, with the teaching of medicine as well as botany. One of his first tasks (1822-24) was to move the Botanical Garden yet again, this time to its present site at Inverleith, involving the transplanting of large numbers of mature trees and shrubs.

Graham's success as a teacher may be judged from the number of students in his 1828/29 class – 280. On his annual summer botanical expeditions, with a few students and friends, he would regularly cover twenty miles in a day – occasionally as many as fifty miles. With his wide-ranging botanical knowledge he prepared a comprehensive *Flora of Great Britain*, which unfortunately he did not live to publish. By 1845 he was no longer able to conduct his classes, and he arranged in May for Dr Joseph Hooker to deputise – by August he was dead. Hooker clearly hoped – indeed, expected – to succeed him, but another candidate came forward, and the Town Council voted 23 to 10 against Hooker, who went on to become one of the most celebrated of British botanists.

So **John Hutton Balfour** became the eighth Regius Professor of Medicine and Botany, again from the Chair of Botany in the University of Glasgow. An Edinburgh MD of 1832, he was for many years Dean of the Faculty of Medicine and Secretary to the Royal Society of Edinburgh. His teaching efforts were concentrated in botany, however, and his title of Professor of Medicine became a nominal one. An alternative 'title' of 'Woody Fibre' was apparently bestowed on him by his students. He introduced practical laboratory work in which extensive use was made of the microscope, and he placed an increased emphasis on field work. Like Graham before him he led his students on botanising expeditions, one of which led to 'the celebrated battle of Glen Tilt in 1847' (Horn, 1967, p 143), when the Duke of Atholl and his gamekeepers sought to bar the way to Prof Balfour and some of his students.

As an illustration of the teaching commitment involved in a practical subject such as botany in the second half of the nineteenth century, in the summer of 1878 the lectures and demonstrations in the Botanic Garden were attended by a total of 412 students of medicine, science and pharmacy as well as other subjects. Lectures were given at 8 am Monday to Friday, from the beginning of May to the end of July. Competitive exam-inations were held every month, on the basis of which First and Second Class Honours Certificates were awarded. Demonstrations and practical classes were held on weekdays at 9 am, and 'Saturdays are occupied with excursions and demonstrations in the fields.' The number of fresh specimens of plants used was more than forty-seven thousand. There was also an excursion for eight or ten days at the beginning of August.

John Hutton Balfour published a *Manual of Botany* (1849) and a *Class Book of Botany* (1852), as well as a number of botanico-religious books including *Phyto-Theology* (1851) and *Plants of the Bible* (1857). When he retired in 1879 there was considerable support for his son Isaac Bayley Balfour, then only 26 years old, to succeed him, but he had to wait a further nine years for that honour.

On this occasion when the Chair was advertised it was decided that it was time to drop the 'Medicine and' from the title, so in 1880 **Alexander Dickson** became the ninth Regius Professor of Botany and Regius Keeper of the Royal Botanic Garden, yet again from Glasgow. He too graduated in medicine at Edinburgh, and before moving to Glasgow in 1868 had been Professor of Botany at Dublin. During his time in the Chair a new large lecture hall was brought into use at the Garden, seating more than 500 students. Dickson was primarily a research botanist, and in only seven years published upwards of fifty papers. He died suddenly at the age of 51 on 30th December 1887 while engaged in a curling match on his estate at Hartree in the Scottish borders.

After his death the chair was strongly canvassed by **Patrick Geddes** (1854-1932), who had been Dickson's demonstrator since 1880 and was also lecturer in zoology at the time. He was unsuccessful, but in 1889 was appointed Professor of Botany in University College, Dundee. He later turned to sociology, civics and town planning, and after 1924 settled in Montpellier where he established an unofficial 'Scots College'. Among his many publications were *The Evolution of Sex* (one of several he wrote with Edinburgh graduate J Arthur Thomson, 1889), *Chapters in Modern Botany* (1893) and *Cities in*

Evolution (1915 repr 1949, 1968 etc). He was knighted in 1932.

When Dickson was appointed in 1880 to the Chair in Edinburgh **Isaac Bayley Balfour** succeeded to his Chair in Glasgow, then in 1884 moved to Oxford as Sherardian Professor of Botany, with a Fellowship at Magdalen and an MA degree as bonuses. He still had no hesitation in returning to Edinburgh in 1888 as the tenth Regius Professor of Botany. He had graduated DSc with first-class honours in Botany in 1875 – the first student awarded a DSc in Botany by the University of Edinburgh. In the year of his appointment Balfour strongly, and successfully, resisted the proposal in the Universities (Scotland) Bill, 1888 that the Botanic Garden be transferred to the University of Edinburgh. It was instead vested, by the Act of the following year, in the Commissioners of Her Majesty's Works and Public Buildings, and was made more accessible to the public – even, very controversially, on Sundays, but only after the hours of public worship.

Chemistry

In 1795 **Thomas C Hope** was appointed the fifth Professor of Chemistry and Chemical Pharmacy conjointly with Joseph Black, who was then in declining health. In session 1796-7 they shared the course of lectures almost equally, but from October 1797 Hope was effectively the sole Professor of Chemistry in the University. He had graduated MD at Edinburgh in 1787, and was thereafter successively Professor of Chemistry and Assistant Professor of Medicine at Glasgow until 1795. Hope's first research, carried out from 1791 to 1793 while he was in Glasgow, was on a mineral from Strontian in Argyllshire. He prepared several compounds of what he believed was a new element, but strontium was not isolated until Humphry Davy's work in 1808. His only other significant research was on the temperature at which the maximum density of water occurs; his results published in 1805 gave a value of between 39.5° and 40.0°F (the value accepted today is 39.2°F).

He was an excellent lecturer and became the most popular teacher of chemistry in Britain. Attendance at his lectures increased from 293 in 1799 to a peak of 559 in 1823 then gradually declined to 118 in 1842. His success was due to clarity of expression and the use of numerous well-contrived demonstrations. It was also due to the fact that he received no salary as such, and was dependent for remuneration on class fées, out of which he had first to pay all the class expenses. Unlike not a few eminent professors of his time he was particularly diligent in keeping his lectures up to date, and it has been said that he was the first in Britain to expound the ideas of Lavoisier, and later to base his teaching on Dalton's atomic theory.

In 1823 he somewhat reluctantly introduced what proved to be a popular laboratory course in practical chemistry and pharmacy, conducted by his assistant. But it was considered by some to be less than adequate, and in the Edinburgh Evidence (1826) it was stated by Dr Brewster that he thought a regular laboratory should be established, 'as there is at all the foreign universities, where young men can receive practical instruction in the analysis of minerals, which now forms one of the most important branches of chemistry.'

It was, however, customary at the time for students to supplement the lectures at the University by attending some of the many well-established lecture and laboratory courses run by independent teachers, many of them licensed by the University. It is believed that the first chemical laboratory in Britain for the practical instruction of students was set up in Edinburgh in 1800 by the Edinburgh graduate Thomas Thomson (MD, 1799), who in 1818 became Regius Professor of Chemistry at Glasgow and proceeded to set up another teaching laboratory there.

In 1843 Hope resigned somewhat unexpectedly, and Thomas Traill, the Professor of Medical Jurisprudence, lectured in session 1843-44.

William Gregory (MD, 1828) was appointed in 1844 the sixth Professor of Chemistry; he was selected from a total of nine applicants (one of them Lyon Playfair, appointed to the chair in 1858), the first time there had been such an open competition. It was also the first time that the appointment was to the Chair of Chemistry only – previously it had been, nominally, Medicine and Chemistry. The Professor of Chemistry remained a member of the Faculty of Medicine until the appointment of James Kendall in 1928.

As a lecturer Gregory was clear, simple and precise; his memory was so good that he lectured without notes. He published *Outlines of Chemistry* as a class text-book in 1845. As a scientist he was competent but not distinguished – 53 of his papers are listed in the catalogue of the Royal Society. His most significant discoveries were in the field of analgesics such as opium and morphine, essential pain-killers in the days before chloroform (1831) and ether (1841), and increasingly useful after the development of hypodermic injection in 1855.

In 1858 **Lyon Playfair** became the seventh Professor of Chemistry. He had already accomplished much in public life, but in his autobiography he declared – "Once more I succeeded in breaking away from public life to enjoy the quiet of an academic office. The Chair of Chemistry in the University of Edinburgh has always been the chief ambition of scientific chemists". Ten years later, however, he was elected as the first MP for the Universities of St Andrews and Edinburgh; he resigned his Chair in 1869 and spent the rest of his life in politics.

The Universities (Scotland) Act, 1858 established the post of Assistant to some of the Professors, as distinct from the assistants which professors had up till then employed and paid out of their own pockets. The first Assistants were appointed in 1862. By 1876 the Professor of Chemistry had two such Assistants; one helped with lecture demonstrations, the other ran the practical class. He also employed privately one other assistant and three servants.

After the introduction of the BSc and DSc degrees in 1864/65 the number of students taking degrees in science was at first very low, and the Chemistry course of about 100 lectures continued to be designed primarily for the students of medicine, usually about 200 in number. In addition to the lectures, there was a practical course of about 60 hours,

Professor Alexander Crum Brown—chemistry and chemical pharmacy

and tutorial work which Playfair had introduced.

Alexander Crum Brown succeeded Lyon Playfair in 1869 as the eighth Professor of Chemistry. He had entered the University of Edinburgh in 1854 as an arts student, graduating MA in 1858, then transferred to medicine and graduated MD in 1861. For the next two years he studied chemistry in Germany, under Bunsen at Heidelberg and Kolbe at Marburg. In 1863 he was licensed as an extra-academical lecturer in chemistry by the University of Edinburgh. Students were few and he had ample time for research, so he was well supported by the time he applied for the Chair, even though one of the other candidates was William Perkin (1838-1907), the pioneer of synthetic dyestuffs.

It was in his MD thesis of 1861, *On the Theory of Chemical Combination*, that his most significant and lasting contribution to chemistry was made. He proposed a new system of illustrating chemical formulae graphically, using lines joining the chemical symbols to represent the valency, with parallel lines for a double bond, in accordance with the new theories of Frankland and Kekulé. It was essentially the system still in use today, and it made the visualisation of the bonding between atoms in a molecule both simple and rational. It transformed the teaching of organic chemistry, especially in the hands of Frankland, and it became known, rather unfairly, as 'Frankland's notation'.

In 1874 planning began for the building of the new Medical School in Teviot Place, and the nine Professors, including Crum Brown, were asked to specify their requirements. Ten years later in 1884 the chemistry rooms in the Old College were handed over to zoology, and the Department of Chemistry occupied the north-west corner of the new buildings, where it had two lecture rooms, seating 400 and 120 students, and a practical chemistry classroom (laboratory) with about 100 places. Crum Brown, on opening the spacious new accommodation, is quoted as saying:– "A golden cage, but will the birds sing?".

Engineering

Fifteen years after the first Chair of Engineering in the UK had been endowed by the government in the University of Glasgow, a Regius Chair of Technology was instituted in 1855 in the Faculty of Arts at Edinburgh University, the holder also to be Director of the proposed Industrial Museum of Scotland in Edinburgh. **George Wilson** FRSE (1818-1859) was appointed to the combined post; he had studied medicine at Edinburgh but then turned to chemistry which he taught as an extra-mural lecturer to the Royal College of Surgeons and other institutions. He must have been an unexpected choice, since he is described in the DNB as a 'chemist and religious writer'; and certainly it was mainly on the fringes of chemical technology that his chosen syllabus seemed to lie.

Even at the time of his appointment he was not a fit man, but his lectures quickly became popular, and he published a useful series of papers on the subject of colour-blindness. However, when Wilson died in 1859 at the early age of 41 the government, supported by the Senate, promptly abolished the Chair and appointed a civil servant from the Department of Science and Art as the new Director of the Museum.

Professor Fleeming Jenkin—engineering

Sir David Brewster, the Principal at the time, was anxious to see engineering satisfactorily instituted in Edinburgh, and he lived just long enough to know that it would be, with the aid of an endowment of £5000 from the Dundee industrialist Sir David Baxter, and an equivalent contribution to the Professor's salary of £200 per annum from the Treasury. In 1868 the Regius Chair of Engineering was founded in the Faculty of Arts, and **Henry Charles Fleeming Jenkin** was appointed, from the Chair of Engineering at University College, London. It is interesting to note that the other outstanding candidate for the chair was W J McQuorn Rankine, an Edinburgh student himself, who had been the Regius Professor of Civil Engineering and Mechanics at Glasgow since 1855.

Fleeming (pronounced as 'Fleming', so we are informed by his one-time student Robert Louis Stevenson, who wrote an affectionate *Memoir* of him) Jenkin brought to the Edinburgh Chair a notable combination of scientific knowledge, practical experience and business acumen. Within a few years he had established a successful engineering course, though it has to be said that in common with other departments in the University there were many more students than graduates. His reputation rested principally on his work, in close collaboration with Kelvin, on long-distance undersea telegraphy, and on the committee which drew up the proposals for methods of electrical measurement, subsequently ratified as international electrical standards.

Recently, however, his work in two entirely different fields has been subjected to critical reassessment after an interval of well over a hundred years. In June 1867 Jenkin published in the *North British Review* a criticism of Darwin's *Origin of Species* extending to almost fifty pages; it was willingly and publicly accepted by Darwin at the time, though the later work of Mendel and others has shown Jenkin's objections to be largely, but by no means entirely, invalid. Stephen Jay Gould, in *Bully for Brontosaurus* (1991) Chap 23 'Fleeming Jenkin Revisited', presents a fascinating account of his discovery of the Scottish engineer's influence on Darwin, who wrote to Joseph Hooker:– 'Fleeming Jenkin has given me much trouble, but has been of more real use to me than any other essay or review.'

Gould also passes on to us, in a postscript to chapter 23, references to two essays on economics published by Jenkin in 1868 and 1870. The second of these, *The Graphic Representation of the Laws of Supply and Demand, and their Application to Labour*, shows that Jenkin was 'the first British economist to draw and clearly understand supply and demand curves.' The great economist J A Schumpeter regarded Jenkin as . . 'an economist of major importance, whose main papers . . . form an obvious stepping-stone between J S Mill and Marshall.' In Fleeming Jenkin's collected *Papers, Literary, Scientific etc* (ed Colvin and Ewing, 2 vols, 1887) there are in fact five papers on economics extending to a total of 154 pages.

One last example of Fleeming Jenkin's versatility must suffice. A paper by Jenkin and J A Ewing (who as Sir Alfred Ewing became the Principal of Edinburgh University in 1916) was published in the *Trans of the Royal Socy of Edinburgh* (1878) on their experiments with a vowel synthesizer designed by Prof Crum Brown of the Department of Chemistry, based on the phonograph which had been invented by Edison earlier in the same year.

Many of Fleeming Jenkin's most notable students were included in *Engineering at Edinburgh University* (Birse, 1983), but one who must now be added is **Alan A Campbell Swinton** FRS (1863-1930). He was the son of the Professor of Civil Law at Edinburgh, and at the age of 15 succeeded in linking two houses some distance apart by telephone, only two years after its invention by **Alexander Graham Bell**, another Edinburgh University student. Although it is not mentioned either in the DNB or his own autobiography, the University's records show that Swinton attended the classes of Natural Philosophy and Engineering at Edinburgh in the winter term of 1881-82, before taking up an apprenticeship with Sir William Armstrong at Elswick near Newcastle – for which his father had paid a premium of six hundred guineas. For Armstrong's ship-building firm he devised a new method of insulating electric cables by sheathing them in lead.

Swinton later established himself as a consulting engineer in London, where he produced some of the first medical x-ray photographs in January 1896, within a few days of Roentgen's announcement of his discovery. Among his many speculations on possible future developments in science and engineering was a method of 'distant electric vision' using cathode-ray tubes for transmission and reception. In a letter to *Nature* in 1908 he outlined in principle for the first time the system of television in use today. He made no attempt to put his ideas into practice, however, and it was left to Zworykin and Farnsworth to demonstrate a practical system in 1927.

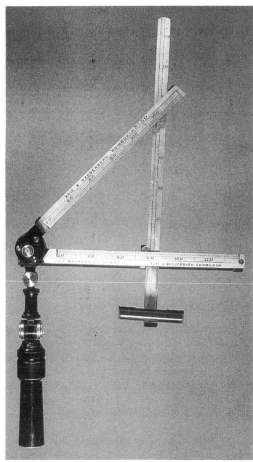

The Mackenzie Dendrometer, patented by D F Mackenzie, was exhibited at the 1884 Exhibition and was awarded a silver medal. It was presented to the Department of Forestry and Natural Resources in 1968 by the Mackenzie family.
Manufactured by Adie & Wedderburn, Edinburgh.

George Armstrong became in 1885 the second Regius Professor of Engineering. A graduate of Cambridge University, he spent a few years in railway engineering and in 1871 was appointed the first Professor of Engineering in McGill University, Montreal, returning to Britain in 1876 to become the first Professor of Engineering at the Yorkshire College in Leeds. Under his supervision in 1889 the Fulton Engineering Laboratory was established, 'to provide systematic instruction in experimental methods . . and to familiarise students with the strength and other physical properties of the chief materials used by engineers.'

Forestry

At the inaugural meeting in 1854 of the Scottish Arboricultural Society (now the Royal Scottish Forestry Society) it was pointed out that there was a great need for education in forestry at university level in Scotland. This need was underlined when the Society organised an International Forestry Exhibition in Edinburgh in 1884, and efforts were made to generate the necessary finance.

In 1889 **William Somerville** was appointed to the new University Lectureship in Forestry, to give a course of one hundred lectures for which the fee was three guineas. There was no salary attached to the post, and he had to survive on the class fees, and grants totalling £200 per annum. Himself an Edinburgh graduate (BSc, 1887), he resigned in 1891 to accept the Chair of Agriculture at Durham College of Science, moved to Cambridge in 1899 and to the Board of Agriculture in 1901. From 1906 to 1925 he was Sibthorpian Professor of Rural Economy at Oxford. The University of Edinburgh was the first British university to institute regular courses of lectures in Forestry.

Lt Col Fred Bailey RE was appointed rather hastily in 1891 to succeed Somerville as Lecturer, but proved to be a good choice. He faced many difficulties, and at first had no accommodation of any kind. Eventually he had to make the best of two underground cellars in a corner of the Old College.

Geology

[For antecedents *see* Natural History]

In 1871 the Murchison Chair of Geology was instituted in the Faculty of Arts, and **Archibald Geikie** was appointed the first Regius Professor of Geology. He was at the time Director of the Geological Survey of Scotland, and for the next 11 years combined the two posts. In 1882 he was appointed Director General of the Geological Survey in London, and was succeeded by his younger brother. He was one of the outstanding geologists of his day as well as a fluent and prolific writer of geological memoirs, textbooks and biographical works, such as *Scenery of Scotland* (1865), *Text-book of Geology* (1882), and *Founders of Geology* (lectures delivered at Johns Hopkins University, 1897). His manner was inclined to be rather stern, but he gave unstintingly of his time to the many scientific societies with which he was associated.

James Geikie succeeded his brother in 1882 as the second Regius Professor of Geology. Both James and his eldest brother Archibald were born and educated in Edinburgh and attended some classes at the University, but did not graduate. The Chair was now (by order of big brother Archibald!) separate from the Directorship of the Geological Survey of Scotland, and James had been forced in effect to choose one or the other. He was a more convivial character than his brother, and from time to time confessed that he was 'pining for his old Survey chums'. He was chiefly noted for his work on the Quaternary and his book *The Great Ice Age* (1874) became a classic, as did his student text-books *Outlines of Geology* (1886) and *Structural and*

Professor James Geikie—geology

Field Geology for Students (1905). In 1900 he contributed to the debate then raging on the age of the earth, putting forward the view that Kelvin's estimate of 20 to 40 million years was much too short to account for such geological processes as the folding of the Alps.

Mathematics

John Leslie was appointed in 1805 the tenth Professor of Mathematics, in spite of opposition ostensibly based on his espousal of David Hume's atheistic theory of causation. He studied at the Universities of St Andrews and Edinburgh without graduating at either. Leslie and Rumford, in the opinion of Cardwell (1971), were the two pioneers of a new science of heat in the first decade of the nineteenth century. Leslie published his famous *Experimental enquiry into the nature and propagation of heat* in 1804, at a time when the nature of heat was still the subject of much speculation. He favoured the hypothesis that light and heat are different manifestations of one and the same thing, and he investigated the properties of heat radiation in respect of straight line propagation, reflection, refraction, diffraction and interference. He invented the wet- and dry-bulb hygrometer, discovered the theory of its action, and used it as a sensitive 'difference thermometer' in his experiments. Like John Playfair, Leslie also moved from Mathematics to Natural Philosophy, succeeding Playfair in 1819.

William Wallace then became the eleventh Professor of Mathematics, Charles Babbage being the only other notable contender. He had attended classes at Edinburgh University while apprenticed to a book-binder in the city. He was also Observer (1822-34) at the Astronomical Institution's observatory on the Calton Hill, the erection of which he had actively promoted. He proposed in 1823 to include Astronomy in his Mathematics course, but was prevented by the usual chorus of objections. He was almost entirely self-taught as a mathematician, with a strong practical bent – he was the inventor of the pantograph and the eidograph. An outstanding teacher, in the Edinburgh Evidence (1826) he estimated the total number of students attending his three mathematics classes as an average of 188 over the previous six years. He stated the ages of his students as from 13-14 upwards. In addition to many mathematical papers he contributed to the *Edinburgh Encyclopædia* and the *Encyclopædia Britannica*, and wrote *Geometrical Theorems and Analytical Formulae* (1839).

When Wallace retired in 1838 a sharp division appeared between those who, like him, adhered to the traditional Scottish mathematical philosophy, and those such as J D Forbes, recently appointed at the age of only 24 to the Chair of Natural Philosophy, who maintained that the students' knowledge of mathematics in the Scottish universities was in general extremely low. Forbes, soon after his appointment in 1833, went so far as to beg Whewell at Cambridge to produce a simplified version of his well-known text-book on mechanics, for the use of students whose mathematical knowledge was very limited. This he duly did, by removing some of the more advanced sections and publishing them as a separate volume of analytical statics.

So in 1838 Forbes seized the opportunity to support as a candidate for the chair of

E

mathematics a Cambridge don, an Anglican clergyman with no Scottish connections, a senior wrangler and first Smith's prizeman with an excellent reputation both as a mathematician and a tutor. The Rev Philip Kelland could be guaranteed to bring a breath of fresh air into the Edinburgh mathematical scene. The traditionalists were outraged on all counts, and quickly selected as their candidate Duncan Gregory, the last of the academic Gregories, then also at Cambridge – but a mere fifth wrangler. How the supporters of each candidate tried to influence the Town Council in its choice is entertainingly told by Davie (1964), who deals with the contest and its wider implications for Scottish university education in much more detail than is possible here.

The result was a narrow majority for the **Rev Philip Kelland** as the twelfth Professor of Mathematics – 'the first Englishman with an entirely English education admitted to a chair in the University'. He contributed many papers on pure mathematics to the Royal Societies of London and Edinburgh, one of the most important being his *Memoir on the limits of our knowledge respecting the theory of parallels*, on non-Euclidean geometry. As well as mathematical text-books he wrote *How to Improve the Scottish Universities* (1855) and *The Scottish School System suited to the People* (1870).

Kelland's successor in 1879 as the thirteenth Professor of Mathematics was **George Chrystal**. Educated at Aberdeen and then at Cambridge, where he studied experimental physics under Clerk Maxwell, he graduated BA in 1875 as second wrangler and Smith's prizeman. Appointed to the Chair of Mathematics at St Andrews in 1877 he moved to Edinburgh two years later. His text-book on *Algebra* for secondary schools was a standard work for many years, and he contributed many articles to the *Encyclopædia Britannica*. He did much valuable work on oscillations (seiches) in Scottish lochs, for which he was awarded the Royal Medal of the Royal Society in 1911.

Meteorology

Meteorology as a subject in its own right, as it were, dates back only to 1944, when James Paton was appointed Lecturer in Meteorology in the Department of Natural Philosophy. In the Edinburgh Evidence of 1826, however, Prof Jameson of Natural History described how the subject of meteorology was treated from different points of view by the Professors of Chemistry, Natural Philosophy and Natural History. In an appendix to the Evidence Prof Jameson gives a very detailed syllabus (pages 115-8) of the whole natural history course, beginning with:– 'I. METEOROLOGY. 1. General Observations on the Atmosphere; 2. Atmospheric Meteors (in the old sense of any atmospheric phenomenon) – (a) Aqueous meteors eg dew, clouds, rain etc (b) Luminous meteors eg rainbow, aurora borealis, fire-balls, the stones that fall from the heavens etc (c) Winds in general eg force, velocity, hurricanes etc (d) The subterranean and submarine atmospheres (e) Prognostications of the weather from phenomena of the atmosphere, animals, plants and minerals (f) Climate in general, and its effects on animals, especially the human race.

It should also be noted that the University had a close association with the Scottish Meteorological Society (1855-1921), and after it merged with the Royal Meteorological

Society, with that society's Scottish Branch. For instance, six Edinburgh professors were serving on the Council of the Scottish Meteorological Society at the turn of the century.

Robert Jameson, Professor of Natural History

Natural History

In 1804 **Robert Jameson** was appointed the third Professor of Natural History. He had studied under his predecessor John Walker, and also with A G Werner at the Bergakademie in Freiberg (1800-02); for most of his life he strongly supported Werner's neptunist geological theories in opposition to Hutton's, but in the end he admitted that he had been wrong in his views. As a teacher his reputation still suffers from the well-known remarks of Charles Darwin in his autobiography:– 'During my second year (1826) at Edinburgh I attended Jameson's lectures on geology and zoology, but they were incredibly dull. The whole effect they produced on me was the determination never to read a book on geology or in any way to study the science . . .' However, Darwin was only sixteen when he went up to Edinburgh, and he was equally critical of the two years he spent subsequently at Cambridge, so maybe the fault lay more in him than in Jameson.

The volumes already written on **Charles Robert Darwin** (1809-1882) are so numerous that to add even a few paragraphs would be pointless. It will be more relevant to the purpose of this work to draw attention to some of the other Edinburgh University scientists who influenced Darwin at various points in his career. The lecture-demonstrations of Prof T C Hope in chemistry he did enjoy, especially as Hope made a point of disagreeing with Jameson's neptunist geology. He was elected to the Plinian Society and introduced to a wide range of radical ideas, and he began to collect specimens of sea-creatures on walks along the shores of the Firth of Forth. One man in particular had a strong influence on him at that time; **Robert Edmond Grant** (1793-1874) was sixteen years older and had qualified as a doctor at Edinburgh University (MD, 1814) before devoting himself to the study of marine life and becoming an expert on sponges.

Grant was a freethinker who believed with Lamarck that man had somehow evolved from the lower animals, which had in turn evolved from . . etc, etc. Evolution was anathema to the Church and the establishment generally, but Grant's enthusiasm for sea-slugs and his rejection of an uncritical belief in the Creation struck a chord in the young Charles Darwin and influenced his whole subsequent career. Grant was appointed in 1827 the Professor of Comparative Anatomy and Zoology at University College, London, but Darwin felt obliged in later life to distance himself from a man he considered to be a radical extremist.

In the later editions of *The Origin of Species* (first published in 1859) Darwin chronicled the earlier writers who put forward, sometimes rather obscurely, similar evolutionary ideas. Two of them studied at Edinburgh University; the first was **William Wells** (MD, 1780) who was noticed at the end of chapter 2. The second, **Patrick Matthew** (1790-1874), studied for two or three years and became a successful farmer and fruit-grower in Perthshire. He published in 1831 *Naval Timber and Arboriculture*, which contained in an appendix a brief statement of his views on evolution, including the use of the phrase 'natural process of selection.' Darwin, understandably enough, had not seen the passage in question, but when it was brought to his notice he freely admitted that Matthew's view on the origin of species was '. . precisely the same as that . . (of) Mr Wallace and myself.'

Four other men with Edinburgh University connections were closely involved with Darwin before and after the publication of *The Origin of Species*. The first was **Hewett Cottrell Watson** (1804-1881) who studied natural history at Edinburgh from 1828 to 1832. He contributed an article 'On the Theory of Progressive Development' to *The Phytologist* in 1845 and undertook extensive phytogeographical studies which were drawn upon by Darwin. He is referred to at several places in the *Origin*, once as '. . Mr H C Watson, to whom I lie under deep obligation for assistance of all kinds'. Two other naturalists who assisted Darwin during the long period of gestation of the *Origin* were **Sir Joseph Dalton Hooker** FRS (1817-1911) and **Edward Forbes**. It is very difficult now to imagine the mental anguish suffered by Darwin as he worked on his manuscript for two decades, discussing it hesitantly with Watson, Hooker, Forbes and a few other close friends, not daring to publish it while the anti-evolutionists were in such a militant mood.

Finally in 1859 *The Origin of Species* was published and, as expected, Darwin had to face a barrage of criticism as well as praise. His most enthusiastic champion was **Thomas H Huxley** (1825-1895), who though always a close friend had at first disagreed with Darwin's early evolutionary sketches. In the end he was completely converted to a belief in the principle of evolution, though not in every last detail in the pages of the *Origin*. Huxley and Hooker were tireless in their defence of the sensitive and often ailing Darwin.

To return now to Jameson, there is no doubt that he was well thought of as a man and as a teacher, and he was by no means alone in his advocacy of Werner's views. During his fifty years in the Chair he had many distinguished pupils, among them Ami Boué, Necker de Saussure, J D Forbes, Edward Forbes, W H Fitton, Robert Harkness, Lord Greenock, Sir Charles Wyville Thomson and Sir William Logan. He inspired in all of them, and in many others, a lifelong interest in the subjects of his lectures. By all accounts he was a respected and influential, if unexciting, teacher, who put considerable emphasis on demonstrations and field trips. The syllabus of his course of lectures on Natural History embraced 'general and particular details and views in Meteorology, Hydrography, Mineralogy, Geology, Botany and Zoology.'

The Museum of Natural History at Edinburgh University. An engraving by W H Lizars.

Once settled in the Chair he set about the task of building up another natural history collection, for the benefit of his students and the general public. He compiled a 'Set of Instructions for Collectors', and sent copies to ministers and public servants abroad in the hope that they would collect specimens and send them back to the University. Eventually he amassed some 74,000 specimens of plants, animals and minerals from all parts of the world, and in 1812 this second great collection was given the title 'The Royal Museum of the University of Edinburgh'. In 1854, the year of his death, the Government agreed to his proposal that the collection should be made available to the nation in a new museum, and it was transferred to what is now known as the Royal Museum of Scotland in Chambers Street when it was completed in 1856.

It has to be admitted, however, that he turned the museum collection to his own advantage in every possible way. He allowed his students free entry and charged all others; he arranged the geological exhibits to support his Wernerian tenets; and he kept hidden any specimens which he conceived to be anti-Wernerian. In the Edinburgh Evidence (1826) Sir George S Mackenzie of Coul, Bt stated that he '. . presented to the College Museum (which was in the charge of Professor Jameson) in 1810-11, an important collection of geological specimens from Iceland. It supported the Huttonian theory, to which Professor Jameson was strongly opposed, and it was never acknowledged, labelled, catalogued or displayed'.

Edward Forbes was appointed in 1854 the fourth Professor of Natural History, but died six months after taking up his appointment. He was an outstanding naturalist who had been Palaeontologist to H M Geological Survey (1845-54), and also a pioneer in oceanography.

In 1855 **George Allman** succeeded Forbes as the fifth Professor of Natural History.

Educated at Belfast, Dublin and Oxford, he was a first-class research naturalist who produced beautifully illustrated monographs on fresh-water polyzoa (1856) and gymnoblastic hydroids (1871-2), and studies of the hydroids collected by the *Challenger* expedition. He was President of the Linnean Society, 1874-83, and Gold Medallist, 1896. Consequent on the transfer of the Department's collection of museum specimens to the new Museum of Science and Art, Prof Allman was appointed Regius Keeper of the Natural History Department of the Museum. Even at the time of Allman's appointment it was known to be likely that geology would be separated from natural history, but it did not happen for another 16 years, after his retirement in 1870.

Charles Wyville Thomson then became the sixth Professor of Natural History. At 16 he was studying under Jameson, at 23 he was Professor of Mineralogy and Geology at Belfast, and he was 40 when he was appointed to the Chair at Edinburgh. In 1871 the Regius Chair of *Geology was endowed by Sir Roderick Murchison in the Faculty of Arts, and under Archibald Geikie the subject at last became independent of natural history.

The condition of the natural history collection in the RSM was by now a source of friction with the museum staff, who complained that the University Professors didn't put enough effort into caring for it. The final break came when one evening the RSM was holding a reception for a large number of Edinburgh dignitaries.

The alcoholic refreshments for the guests were stored in the enclosed bridge which

HMS Challenger at sea

joins the Museum with the Old College, built to facilitate the access of students and staff to the natural history collection. As it happened the Natural History students were holding a party of their own that day on the University side of the bridge, and being in possession of a key some of them decided to cross the bridge into the Museum.

On finding the totally unexpected treasure trove, however, they went no further but carried their booty back to the party, where every last drop was duly drunk, leaving the Museum's guests totally without refreshment! Thereafter a strong padlock was fixed to the door at the University end of the bridge, and the University was denied access to the natural history collection.

In December 1872 Thomson set off on the *Challenger* expedition, jointly organised by the Admiralty, the Royal Society and the University of Edinburgh, which in four years circumnavigated the globe and brought back a huge number of samples and specimens of many kinds. While Thomson was away from the Department the classes in Natural History were in the care of **Julius Carus** in 1873 and 1874, and of **Thomas H Huxley** in 1875 and 1876. Prof James Ritchie, in a fascinating article 'A Natural History Interlude' in the *University of Edinburgh Journal*, **10** (1939-40), 206-212, commented that 'the ill wind that promised trouble blew fair for Edinburgh, since it brought to the Chair of Natural History, as birds of passage, two of the best known zoologists of Europe.'

On the successful completion of the expedition a *Challenger* office was established in Queen Street with Wyville Thomson, now knighted, as Director. Gradually the fifty massive volumes of Reports were published, a task only completed after his death in 1882 by John Murray.

James Cossar Ewart was appointed the seventh Professor of Natural History. He had graduated in medicine at Edinburgh University in 1874 and in 1878 was appointed Professor of Natural History in the University of Aberdeen before moving to Edinburgh in 1882. He was born in Penicuik and later carried out there the extensive work on the genetics of horses and sheep ('The Penycuik Experiments') for which he is best known. He may be regarded as the first animal breeder in Britain after Darwin who carried out experiments with the objective of *understanding* the process rather than merely improving the stock. He is said to have been the first to introduce regular practical classes in the teaching of zoology, and it was in his time that specialist lecturers became more widely used. He was a quiet, reserved man, and his students found his lectures rather rambling until he began to describe his own research, when in Crew's words – 'he seemed to glow with infectious excitement.'

Natural Philosophy

In 1805 **John Playfair** was appointed the sixth Professor of Natural Philosophy, having been Professor of *Mathematics for the previous twenty years, in which chair he had done much of his best work. He is perhaps best known today for his *Illustrations of the Huttonian Theory of the Earth* (1802). He also published Vols I and II (of the projected three volumes) of his *Outlines of Natural Philosophy* (1812, 1814), '. . being Heads of

E*

Lectures delivered in the University of Edinburgh'. At the end of Vol II 'Astronomy' he wrote:– 'Thus it is found, that the laws of motion, and the general properties of matter, are the same in the Heavens and on the Earth; . . (and) are all explained by *one principle*, — That of the mutual Gravitation of all Bodies . . . Gravitation, nevertheless, is not conceived by us as a property essential to matter: there may be many other laws equally possible . . . Is there, then, any physical cause, yet more general, into which Gravitation may be resolved; or is it an ultimate fact, beyond which our knowledge cannot extend?'

Sir John Leslie, the seventh Professor of Natural Philosophy, had also previously been Professor of Mathematics, from 1805 to 1819. In 1823 he published the first volume of his *Elements of Natural Philosophy*, but the work was never completed. In the Edinburgh Evidence (1826) Leslie stated that the Professor of Natural Philosophy distributed his course under twelve heads:-

1. Somatology, or the general properties of bodies;
2. Statics, or the conditions of equilibrium;
3. Phoronomics, or the laws of motion;
4. Physical Astronomy;
5. Mechanics;
6. Hydrostatics;
7. Hydrodynamics;
8. Pneumatics;
9. Photonomics, or the doctrine of light;
10. Pyronomics, or the properties of heat;
11. Magnetism;
12. Electricity.

Leslie was asked 'Do you exhibit many experiments in your class?' and replied 'I dare say I exhibit near a thousand every session . . . by means of an operator, whom I trained to the business, and whom I direct by a sign when each experiment is to be performed'.

The evidence of David Brewster, on the other hand, was that in his experience by far the greater proportion of the students of natural philosophy were quite unable to understand the lectures, because of their lack of knowledge of mathematics. It was his view that the standard of mathematical knowledge among university students generally in Scotland was extremely low. Leslie gave the numbers of students attending his classes over the previous few years as an average of 160 in the winter session, and 40 in the summer.

James D Forbes, appointed the eighth Professor of Natural Philosophy in 1833, was a delicate child, partly self-educated, but at the age of 17 he began to contribute articles anonymously to Brewster's *Journal of Science*. He entered Edinburgh University to study law but was soon diverted towards the physical sciences. He was elected FRSE in his 21st year, and when Leslie died he was chosen, in competition with Brewster himself, to succeed him. He continued Leslie's experiments on radiant heat, showing that it could be polarised in the same way as visible light (for which he received the Rumford Medal of the Royal Society), and making the first quantitative measurements of thermal conductivity. He was one of the first to make scientific studies of the motion of glaciers, publishing *Theory of Glaciers* (1859). He resigned his chair in the same year, to become the Principal of St Andrews University.

Among the candidates for the Chair were two of Forbes's former students, James Clerk Maxwell and his life-long friend P G Tait, who had both gone on to take the Cambridge Maths Tripos with great success, and were then occupying the Chairs of Natural Philosophy in Marischal College, Aberdeen and Queen's College, Belfast. It is difficult even nów, with hindsight, to decide who should have got the Edinburgh Chair in 1860, and the same hindsight tells us that had he got it, Clerk Maxwell would probably not have stayed in Edinburgh any longer than he did in King's College, London – a mere four years.

Peter G Tait, who became the ninth Professor of Natural Philosophy in 1860, graduated as senior wrangler at Cambridge in 1852 (Maxwell was second wrangler in 1854). Tait wrote on quaternions, thermodynamics and the kinetic theory of gases, and with his son and other golfing friends studied the aerodynamics of the flight of spheres such as golf balls. He was the first to prove scientifically the importance of underspin to the distance carried by a golf ball. In 1861 he conceived the idea of writing a comprehensive treatise on natural philosophy, and was pleased to get an offer of collaboration from William Thomson in Glasgow. The first volume of *A Treatise on Natural Philosophy* by T and T (Thomson and Tait) appeared in 1867, and a much enlarged second edition in two parts in 1879 and 1883, but the intended further volumes were unfortunately never published. Tait was awarded the Royal Medal of the Royal Society in 1886, but declined to put his name forward for election as a Fellow.

Practical teaching in the Department of Natural Philosophy began in 1868 when Tait obtained a small grant from the University Court for equipment, and the use of an attic room in the Old College as a laboratory. From 1884, after the removal of the Anatomy Department to the new Medical Buildings in Teviot Place, more space became available, though still only in the attics and cellars. Practical work in Natural Philosophy was not required for graduation, so that only those students who were particularly interested would make a habit of attending.

A Lectureship in Applied Mathematics was instituted by the University Court in 1892, and Cargill G Knott FRS (1856-1922) was appointed; he had been Professor of Physics at the Imperial University of Japan, 1883-91. The advanced science course on Applied Mathematics, of fifty lectures, was adapted for engineering students, and more than half a century later was renamed Mathematical Physics. Knott was also put in charge of the recently established teaching laboratories.

Public Health

In 1820 William Pulteney Alison was appointed the second Professor of Medical Jurisprudence in the Faculty of Law, in which Faculty the Chair remained for more than

College Wynd—dereliction in late 19th century

fifty years until it became the Chair of Forensic Medicine in the Faculty of Medicine, the Professor being also a member of the Faculty of Law. His lectures included a number of topics dealing with the hygiene of individuals and communities under the somewhat strange title of *Medical Police*. He strongly supported the movement for Scottish Poor Law Reform, and the improvement of insanitary conditions which undermined the health of the people.

Sir Henry Duncan Littlejohn was appointed in 1862 Edinburgh's first Medical Officer of Health. His 1865 Report on the City was soon followed by far-reaching housing improvements and other public works, with the result that cholera and typhus disappeared from Edinburgh sooner than from any other city or large town in Britain.

In 1875 Edinburgh University introduced new postgraduate science degrees in Public Health, the first of their kind in the UK. In the University Calendar under *Graduation in Science*, Section C - Public Health it was stated that in consequence of the importance of the subject '. . Science Degrees of BSc and DSc in the Department of Public Health have been instituted . . . candidates must be graduates in Medicine . .' The subjects of examination for the degree of BSc in Public Health were chemistry (including practical chemistry in the laboratory), physics, sanitary law, vital statistics, medicine and practical sanitation. This postgraduate course was quite separate from the undergraduate lectures in Medical Jurisprudence.

Veterinary Science

1869-70 The Edinburgh University *Calendar* (p 143-4), in the section *Graduation in Science*, Division II - Applied Science, C - Veterinary Surgery, states 'the University of Edinburgh have instituted a degree in Veterinary Surgery, open to qualified Students of all the Veterinary Schools in Great Britain . . .' Successful candidates were awarded the degree of Master of Veterinary Surgery, CVM.

From Chairs to Departments

In most of the science subjects in the University a distinct transition took place in the second half of the nineteenth century from a Chair and little else, to the beginnings of a Department. In Natural Philosophy for example, in P G Tait's time practical classes under the control of assistants began in the Old College in 1868 and this activity was extended in 1884. At about the same time the laboratories began to be used for 'investigations' by a few of the best 'pupils', hand-picked by the Professor. But for most of the nineteenth century scientific investigation was still the preserve of the gifted (and determined) individual – research laboratories as we know them today were only beginning to appear towards the end of the century in Britain's universities, and in the first two decades of the twentieth century in some of the largest industrial firms.

In the University *Calendar* 1869/70 under 'Assistants to Professors' are listed two in Chemistry and one each in Botany and Natural History in the Faculty of Medicine, and one each in Mathematics and Natural Philosophy in the Faculty of Arts. Salaries of Assistants varied from £25 to £100 per annum. In the *Calendar* for 1889/90 nine University Lecturers are listed, none of them in the non-medical sciences, and there are Assistants to Professors in Mathematics, Natural Philosophy, Agriculture, Engineering and Geology in the Faculty of Arts, and in Chemistry (4), Botany (several) and Natural History (3) in the Faculty of Medicine.

Some Notable Nineteenth Century Edinburgh University Scientists
(A selection from a large number of notable Edinburgh University scientists and engineers)

ANDREWS, Thomas FRS, Hon FRSE (1813-1885) Studied chemistry at Glasgow and Paris, medicine at Dublin and Edinburgh (MD, 1835); Prof of Chemistry at Belfast, 1849. He was a brilliant experimentalist who showed that ozone is an allotropic form of oxygen, and that gases cannot be liquified by pressure alone above their critical temperature. [DNB, DSB]

BOUÉ, Ami (1794-1881) Studied medicine at Edinburgh (MD, 1817), but abandoned it for geology. Published geological studies on Scotland, 1820 and Germany, 1822 and 1829; attempted to synthesize geological knowledge in *Essai de carte géologique du globe terrestre*, 1845. [DSB]

DAUBENY, Charles FRS (1795-1867) Studied at Oxford (BA, 1814), and medicine at Edinburgh, 1815-18; MD, 1821 at Oxford. Prof of Chemistry at Oxford, 1822-55; also Prof of Botany 1834, and of Rural Economy, 1840. Publ *A Description of Active and Extinct Volcanoes*, 1826 and an *Introduction to the Atomic Theory*, 1831. [DNB, DSB]

DEWAR, Sir James FRS, FRSE (1842-1923) Studied arts and chemistry at Edinburgh from 1859 and became assistant to Lyon Playfair; in 1875 left Edinburgh for Cambridge when elected to the Jacksonian Chair of Natural Experimental Philosophy. Famous for his work on the liquefaction of gases. Publ *New Researches on Liquid Air*, 1898. [DNB, DSB]

FITTON, William FRS (1780-1861) Studied at Dublin (BA, 1799), geology at Edinburgh (1808), and medicine at Cambridge (MD, 1816). Practised in London, but after marrying 'a lady of ample fortune' in 1820 devoted himself to geology; Pres of Geol Soc, 1828, Wollaston Medallist, 1852. [DNB, DSB]

FYFE, Andrew (1792-1861) Studied medicine at Edinburgh (MD, 1814); assistant to Prof T C Hope; lectured privately in Edinburgh on chemistry and pharmacy. Publ *Elements of Chemistry*, 2 vols, 1827. Prof of Chemistry at Aberdeen, 1844-61. A specialist in inflammable substances, he often acted as an expert witness in that subject area. [DNB]

GRAHAM, Thomas FRS, FRSE (1805-1869) Studied at Glasgow (MA, 1824); and at Edinburgh under Hope and Leslie. Prof of Chemistry in Anderson's College, Glasgow, 1830; and at University College, London, 1837-55. Master of the Mint, 1855.

Discovered Graham's Law, 1829, and studied diffusion of liquids – 'father of colloid chemistry'. [DNB, DSB]

HORNER, Leonard   FRS PresGS   (1785-1864) Studied chemistry and geology at Edinburgh from 1802; founded The Edinburgh School of Arts for the Instruction of Mechanics, 1821, the first Mechanics' Institute in the UK. Commissioner to inquire into employment of children in factories, 1833; chief inspector under the Factories Act, 1833-56. [DNB, DSB]

JENKIN, Charles   FRS   (1865-1940)   son of Fleeming Jenkin, studied engineering at Edinburgh and maths at Cambridge; first Prof of Engineering Science at Oxford 1908-29. [DNB]

LOGAN, Sir William   FRS   (1798-1875)   born in Montreal; studied 1814-17 at Edinburgh High School and Univ, under Jameson and others; engaged in mining ventures in Wales; after 1838 turned to geology and became the first Director of the Geological Survey of Canada, 1842-70. Prepared the still valuable *Report on the Geology of Canada*, 1863. [DNB, DSB]

MASSON, Sir David   FRS   (1858-1937)   Studied at Edinburgh (MA, 1877; BSc-Phys, 1880; DSc-Chem, 1884); research fellow in chemistry, 1882-6. Prof of Chemistry at Melbourne, 1886-1923. Publ valuable papers in theoretical physical chemistry, and took a leading part in the formation of the Council for Scientific and Industrial Research, 1926. [DNB]

McINTOSH, William   FRS   (1838-1931) Studied medicine at Edinburgh (MD-Gold medal, 1860); Prof of Natural History / Zoology, at St Andrews, where he established the first marine zoological laboratory in the UK. [DNB, DSB]

MURRAY, Sir John   FRS   (1841-1914)   born in Ontario, studied medicine and science at Edinburgh (1864-5, 1868-72). Worked closely with Sir C W Thomson on the "Challenger" expedition 1872-6, sampling and analysing sea-bed deposits. Afterwards edited the greater part of the fifty volumes of scientific reports, 1880-95. [DNB, DSB, CSBD]

NECKER de Saussure, Louis-Albert   (1786-1861) Studied at the Academy of Geneva, and at Edinburgh under Robert Jameson and others; made the first geological map of the whole of Scotland, 1808; published notable studies of birds and of meteorological optics. [DSB, CSBD]

NICHOLSON, Henry   FRSE   (1844-1899)   Studied zoology at Göttingen (PhD), and medicine and natural science at Edinburgh (BSc, 1866; DSc, MB, MS, 1867; MD, 1869); awarded Gold Medal for thesis *On the Geology of Cumberland*. Prof of Natural History at Toronto, Biology at Durham, and Natural History at St Andrews and Aberdeen. [DNB]

O'SHAUGHNESSY, Sir William   FRS   (1809-1889) Studied medicine at Edinburgh (MD, 1830). In the service of the East India Company rose to Surgeon-major in 1861, and was also Prof of Chemistry in the Medical College, Calcutta. In 1852 as a result of successful experiments was appointed Director-General of Telegraphs in India. [DNB]

PERCY, John FRS, FGS (1836-1889) Studied medicine in Paris and at Edinburgh (MD, 1838), but did not practise. Became a pioneer of metallurgy as a scientific subject. Invented in 1848 a method of extracting silver from its ores, later extended to other important metallurgical processes. Lect, 1851, later Prof of Metallurgy in Royal School of Mines, London. [DNB]

RAY, Prafulla (1861-1944) Studied chemistry at Edinburgh (DSc, 1887); taught and researched at the Presidency College and the Univ College of Science and Technology, Calcutta. Founded the Bengal Chemical and Pharmaceutical Works and other industries in India. Publ *The History of Hindu Chemistry*, 1902-08. [DSB]

SANG, Edward FRSE (1805-1890) Studied mathematics at Edinburgh – 'one of the most brilliant students' of Wallace and Leslie. He was the first to explain the theory of the Nicol prism (1829) in a paper sent to the Royal Society of Edinburgh in 1837; it was found in a drawer by Tait in 1891 and publ in the *Proc RSE*. [BA, RSE]

STEPHENS, Henry FRSE (1795-1874) Studied agriculture at Edinburgh, and during tour of Europe, 1818-19. Restored and improved a run-down 300 acre farm in Forfarshire; after ten years returned to Edinburgh. Wrote *The Book of the Farm* (3 vols. 1842-4) of which there were many reprints and translations, and other works on agriculture. [DNB]

TURNER, Edward FRS, FRSE (1798-1837) Born in Jamaica; studied medicine at Edinburgh (MD, 1819), and chemistry and mineralogy at Göttingen. First Prof of Chemistry at Univ College, London, 1828-37. Publ *Elements of Chemistry*, 1827. [DNB]

WRIGHT, R Ramsay FZS, FRSC (1852-1933) Studied arts and natural science at Edinburgh (MA, 1871; BSc, 1873); assistant to Prof of Nat Hist at Edinburgh, 1873; Prof, first of Natural History at Toronto Univ College, 1874, then of Biology at Univ of Toronto, 1887-1912; Vice-President, Univ of Toronto, 1901-12. [WWW]

CHAPTER 5

The Faculty of Science, 1893 - 1920

Within the relatively short compass of this chapter we leave the nineteenth century behind, so at this point it is worth summarising some of the most significant changes that took place in that eventful hundred years. Two changes occurred gradually throughout the whole of the nineteenth century, so that their effect at any one time was hardly apparent, but over a hundred years it was very considerable. The first was the improvement and refinement of *experimental procedures*, and the development of more sensitive and accurate observing and measuring instruments, together with better techniques for evaluation of the results. The second of the gradual changes was a two-way process, where on the one hand the inventions of scientists and technologists had an increasing *impact in homes, offices, factories* and elsewhere, but on the other hand the scientists and technologists themselves developed a *jargon-language* that was increasingly foreign to non-scientists. In other words, the division between the two cultures became a real barrier to communication and understanding.

Two further changes took place, or rather accelerated quite dramatically in terms of *rate* of change, towards the end of the nineteenth century. The first of these was a greatly increased *specialization* in research, and the beginning of the progressive division and sub-division of the major branches of science which is still going on. The second was the rapidly increasing involvement of *government* in the funding of the universities, with a consequent increasing influence on their affairs, and a somewhat slower increase in collaboration with, and funding by, industry and commerce.

Since the beginning of regular government funding of the universities (which until 1920 included all British and Irish universities and colleges with the exception of Oxford and Cambridge) the total amount of their grant had increased dramatically, administered by a succession of committees:–

		£ per annum
Ad Hoc Committees -	1889-90	15,000
	1900-01	25,000
University Colleges Committee -	1905-06	100,000
Advisory Committee on University Grants -	1914-15	149,000
University Grants Committee -	1919-20	450,000
plus an additional grant of about		300,000
and a non-recurrent grant of about		220,000

Another important and long-lasting influence on the universities was the Government's belated recognition in 1915-16 that the war effort was being hampered by a shortage of doctors and surgeons, scientists and engineers, partly because a system of deferment for studies in these subjects was almost non-existent. Even university scientists engaged on war work had to appear before military tribunals before being allowed to continue – sometimes they were actually given a false medical certificate as the only 'official' exemption from military service. In fact, mismanagement of qualified manpower in WWI was as bad as the general bungling that almost lost us the war.

In the longer term, however, the universities did benefit from the realisation by the public as well as the authorities that qualified men and women were vital to the country's victory in war and prosperity in peace. The Government in particular accepted that the universities could not expand laboratory-based teaching and research without a much greater level of financial assistance. In 1915, therefore, the Department of Scientific and Industrial Research (DSIR) was formed as a committee of the Privy Council. It was the principal source of government research grants to the universities for the next half century.

The University of Edinburgh

In the Introduction to the *History of the University of Edinburgh, 1883-1933* edited by A Logan Turner (1933) it is stated that in 1884 there were 39 professors, 3 lecturers and 26 assistants, a total of 68 teachers for 3374 students giving a student-staff ratio of just under fifty. In 1933 there were 59 professors, 9 readers, 148 lecturers and 99 assistants, a total of 315 teachers for 4163 students giving a student-staff ratio of just over 13.

In 1895 the Commissioners made regulations in Ordinance No 61 for the encouragement of special study and research, and for the appointment of Research Fellows; and in Ordinance No 62, for higher degrees in arts and science. The degrees thus introduced were the DSc in science, the DPhil in philosophy and the DLitt in literature. Although it has not been possible within the confines of this volume even to list all of the large number of scientists on whom Edinburgh University has conferred honorary degrees, an exception ought to be made for just one.

Eleanor Anne Ormerod LLD, FMetSoc (1828-1901) was taught at home by her mother, aided her brother William in his botanical work, and in 1852 began to teach herself entomology. In 1868 she assisted the Royal Horticultural Society to form an economic entomology collection; from 1877 to 1900 she published *Annual Reports of Observations of Injurious Insects* through correspondence with observers in many countries of the world; in 1878 she was the first woman to be elected Fellow of the (now Royal) Meteorological Society; and from 1882 to 1892 she was consulting entomologist to the Royal Agricultural Society of England. Among other works she published *A Textbook of Agricultural Entomology* (1892), and on 14 April 1900 she became the first woman to receive an honorary LLD from the University of Edinburgh.

From 1901 the Scottish universities and their students enjoyed the benefits of Andrew Carnegie's generosity in setting up the Carnegie Trust with the sum of ten million dollars (£2m). With the assistance of the Trust Edinburgh was able to undertake some much-needed building work, including the provision of better laboratory accommodation for Engineering and Natural Philosophy. In 1906 these two departments moved to the buildings in High School Yards formerly occupied by the old Infirmary.

The year 1908 saw the introduction of a series of reforms, one of which was that the duration of the university session was laid down as a minimum of three terms totalling at least 25 weeks. Science tended to adopt about 30 weeks. In 1913 inclusive fees were instituted in the Faculties of Arts, Science and Law; ten guineas per session for the MA degree, twenty guineas per session for the BSc degree in Pure Science. By this time most students were aiming for a degree, usually an ordinary MA or BSc.

Shortly before the outbreak of WWI the continuing overcrowding in the Old College was again (temporarily, as always) relieved by the removal of Mathematics to Chambers Street, and Agriculture and Forestry to a new building at 10 George Square. Soon after the war there was a general demand for better organisation of postgraduate research, and as part of that process the new degree of PhD was instituted in 1919, to be awarded in any Faculty for a thesis submitted after a prescribed period of research carried out under supervision. At the same time, to avoid confusion, the DPhil in Mental Philosophy was discontinued.

The effects of WWI and its aftermath on the numbers of matriculated students are shown in the following table:–

	Total:	Faculty of Science:
1912-13	3352	434
1913-14	3282	428
1914-15	2415	249
1915-16	1811	147
1916-17	1887	156
1917-18	2083	155
1918-19	3554	678
1919-20	4643	1033
1920-21	4886	1086
1925-26	3953	671
1930-31	4437	678
1935-36	3895	590

The Faculty of Arts

When the Faculty of Science was founded in 1893 the Chairs of Agriculture and Rural Economy, Astronomy, Engineering and Geology, which had been instituted in the Faculty of Arts, were transferred to the Faculty of Science. The Chairs and Departments of Mathematics and Natural Philosophy remained in the Faculty of Arts until 1966, when they were transferred to the Faculty of Science; the Professors of these subjects have been since 1893 members of both Faculties.

Consequent on the foundation of the Faculty of Science, the Faculty of Arts divided itself into four sections, confusingly called Departments, as follows:-

I	Language and Literature	III	Science
II	Mental Philosophy	IV	History and Law.

Under 'Department of Science' in the Edinburgh University Calendar, 1904-05, the Faculty of Arts listed classes in Mathematics, Natural Philosophy including Applied Mathematics, Astronomy (FoS), Chemistry (FoM), Zoology (FoM&FoS), Botany (FoM&FoS), and Geology (FoS).

One of the first substantial endowments of funds for research in the University was the sum of £20,000 from the Trustees of the Earl of Moray in 1895. The income amounted to about £600 per annum, and all graduates and other members of the University were entitled to apply for assistance in carrying out their research.

In 1900 **Chrystal Macmillan** BSc (1882-1937) graduated MA with Honours (Philosophy ii, Mathematics and Natural Philosophy i) in the Faculty of Arts. She was the first woman to address the House of Lords (1908) in appealing, unsuccessfully, for the right of women graduates to vote in a Parliamentary election. She was called to the Bar in 1924 but never practised, immersing herself instead in campaigns for such causes as women's suffrage and pacifism.

The Faculty of Medicine

When the Faculty of Science was founded in 1893 the Chairs of Chemistry, Natural History, Botany, Anatomy and Physiology remained in the Faculty of Medicine, and the Professors of these subjects became members also of the Faculty of Science. New chairs were established in the period up to 1920 jointly in the Faculties of Medicine and Science in Public Health (1898), Bacteriology (1913) and Chemistry in Relation to Medicine (1919), later renamed Biochemistry.

The Faculty of Science

In 1893 Faculties of Science were instituted in the Universities of Aberdeen, Edinburgh and Glasgow under the terms of Ordinance No 31 of the Universities (Scotland) Act, 1889; St Andrews followed four years later. The Ordinance was made by the Commissioners on 5 June, and approved by Order in Council of Queen Victoria on 23 November 1893. In the University of Edinburgh the following eleven Professors constituted the original Faculty of Science:-

Mathematics (A)	Natural Philosophy (A)
Astronomy	Chemistry (M)
Natural History (M)	Botany (M)
Anatomy (M)	Physiology (M)
Geology	Engineering
Agriculture and Rural Economy.	

   (A) Primarily a member of the Faculty of Arts.
   (M) Primarily a member of the Faculty of Medicine.

Lectures in Forestry were included in the programme of the Faculty of Science from its inception, but the degree of BSc in Forestry was instituted only in 1906, and the chair in 1920.

Prof James Geikie (Geology) was elected in 1893 the first Dean of the Faculty of Science, and was re-elected annually until he retired in 1914. The Faculty admitted about 160 students in 1893-94, but numbers did not exceed 200 until session 1902-03. By 1910 the first Adviser (Director of Studies) had been appointed.

In 1896 it was agreed between the University and the Treasury that, because of its association with the Royal Botanic Garden, the Chair of Botany should be transferred to the Crown, and in exchange the Chair of Natural History was transferred from the Crown to the University.

On 4 July 1913 **Bertha Chandler** (Mrs C Norman Kemp), MA, BSc, was awarded the degree of DSc for her thesis:- *The Theory and Practice of Vegetative Propagation in the Flowering Plants*. She was the first woman to be awarded the degree of DSc by the University of Edinburgh.

In 1914 **Prof Sir Thomas Hudson Beare** (Engineering) was elected Dean of the Faculty of Science, and he continued to be re-elected annually until his death in 1940.

Agriculture

In 1893 **Robert Wallace**, the Professor of Agriculture and Rural Economy since 1885, became a member of the newly-instituted Faculty of Science. At the end of the nineteenth century agriculture in Britain was suffering from the effects of the industrial revolution at home, the mechanisation of farming in North America, and the repeal of the Corn Laws in 1846. Wallace and others could see that agricultural practices had to be improved, through more and better education at all levels, and the introduction of advisory services for the farming community.

The Board of Agriculture gave official recognition to Edinburgh as a teaching centre and in 1894 the Joint Administrative Board on Agriculture was formed, with

Model of reaper designed by Rev. Patrick Bell

representatives from the University and the Highland and Agricultural Society. Additional members were co-opted from some County Councils, but Wallace was not invited to become a member until January 1901. In the meantime the Edinburgh School of Rural Economy (ESRE) was established in 1895; it provided a two-year course for day students, as well as evening and extension teaching.

Eventually in 1901 the Edinburgh and East of Scotland College of Agriculture was formed, in which the ESRE merged. Wallace was soon fully involved in the development of new courses and in pressing for better accommodation and the purchase of an experimental farm. In 1904 agricultural teaching moved to 13 George Square and ten years later a new building was completed just before the outbreak of WWI for the Departments of Agriculture and Forestry at 10 George Square.

Wallace paid many visits to countries such as India, South Africa, Canada and the United States, Australia and New Zealand; he had a great ability to assimilate information rapidly, writing a comprehensive account of Indian agriculture after his first visit lasting only six weeks, for example. His reputation led to the growth of the Edinburgh School of Agriculture as a centre of training in tropical and sub-tropical agriculture.

Astronomy

In 1893 **Ralph Copeland**, Professor of Astronomy since 1889, became a member of the newly-instituted Faculty of Science, and at about the same time the word 'Practical' was formally dropped from his title. He urged on the University the desirability of a Chair of Applied Mathematics, but the Tait Chair of Mathematical Physics was not instituted until 1922. Copeland included an optical laboratory for undergraduate teaching in the new Royal Observatory Edinburgh (ROE) on Blackford Hill which was completed in 1894. Brück (1983) notes that from the time women were first admitted to University classes in 1892 there have always been women students of astronomy.

Frank Dyson became the fourth Astronomer Royal for Scotland and fifth Regius Professor of Astronomy in 1905. He came from the Royal Observatory at Greenwich, where he was Chief Assistant, and returned there in 1910 as Astronomer Royal. His interests and skills lay in positional astronomy and the observation of eclipses, but he also gave courses of sixty lectures on astronomy at the University, supplemented by twenty practical sessions at the ROE.

In 1910 Dyson was succeeded by **Ralph Sampson** as the fifth Astronomer Royal for Scotland and sixth Regius Professor of Astronomy. Previously Professor of Mathematics and Director of the Observatory at Durham University, in 27 years he took astronomy in Edinburgh to new heights of teaching and research. He was a great scholar and a remarkable pioneer; under his leadership the ROE moved into the very newest fields of astronomy such as photoelectric stellar photometry. Sampson continued Dyson's course in Intermediate Astronomy and also offered an advanced course to which he reserved the right of admission – a good knowledge of mathematics and optics was stipulated.

The Royal Observatory on Blackford Hill, 1967

Botany

In 1893 **Isaac Bayley Balfour**, Regius Professor of Botany since 1888, became a member of the newly-instituted Faculty of Science, though his Chair was still based, as it were, in the Faculty of Medicine. He had to build up a new and greatly expanded Department of Botany – a task which occupied him for almost thirty years. Previous holders of the Chair had concentrated on the teaching of medical students, and Balfour was the first to offer separate courses for students taking ordinary and honours BSc degrees in science. He also extended the range of subjects covered by the department, which entailed the appointment of Lecturers in Plant Physiology, and Mycology and Bacteriology.

Balfour, with a few others, encouraged a new attitude to botany in Britain, more in line with enlightened teaching on the continent, with the emphasis on living rather than dead plants. He continued the practice of his father in making field excursions an important part of his teaching of the subject. He was an authority on the plants of the Himalayas and western China, interested in forestry as well as horticulture, and he made Edinburgh a leading centre of teaching and research in taxonomy.

Chemistry

In 1893 **Alex Crum Brown**, Professor of Chemistry since 1869, became a member of the newly-instituted Faculty of Science, though his Chair also was still based in the Faculty of Medicine.

The two-year curriculum for the BSc degree was extended to three years, to include passes in a minimum of seven courses. The appointment of Lecturers was regularised; in 1894 Leonard Dobbin who had been an Assistant since 1880 was appointed the first Lecturer in Chemistry. The Professors no longer received class fees from the students, but were appointed with regular salaries – Chemistry was fixed at £1400 per annum, but Crum Brown was paid £1828 in line with what he had been receiving under the class-fee system.

Further much-needed laboratory space was made available in 1903 by adding a floor above the existing laboratories in the Medical School in Teviot Place. When Crum Brown retired in 1908 the academic staff of the Department of Chemistry consisted of the professor, three lecturers and four assistants.

James Walker became in 1908 the ninth Professor of Chemistry. He had been privately employed by Crum Brown as an assistant in 1889-92, and since 1894 had been Professor of Chemistry in University College, Dundee. By this time the chemistry laboratories had (again) become hopelessly inadequate, and the few research students were crowded into odd corners. Even Walker's most persistent agitation could get no more than the use of a wooden shed and the nearby basement of the Physics building in Drummond Street. Plans for a new building for the Department of Chemistry in High School Yards were abandoned on the outbreak of WWI.

During the war in 1915 there was a serious shortage of explosives, and Walker began production of TNT in a disused chemical factory, employing staff, graduates and students of the Department. It was so successful that it gained further contracts and had to move to larger factory premises at Craigleith quarry, where manufacture continued until the end of the war, by which time it held the record for efficiency of production in the whole of the UK.

In 1919 a Chair of Chemistry in Relation to Medicine was founded in the Faculty of Medicine to relieve the Department of Chemistry of the burden of teaching large numbers of medical students. Soon after this the Chair of Chemistry was transferred from the Faculty of Medicine to the Faculty of Science, at about the same time as the Department of Chemistry moved to the King's Buildings site.

Engineering

In 1893 **George Armstrong**, Regius Professor of Engineering since 1885, became a member of the newly-instituted Faculty of Science. After his death **Thomas Hudson Beare** was appointed in 1901 the third Regius Professor of Engineering. Born in Australia, he went to University College, London (UCL) in 1880 on the South Australian Scholarship. He was Professor of Engineering at the Heriot-Watt College, Edinburgh in

Sir Thomas Hudson Beare, Regius Professor of Engineering, 1901-1940

1887, and at UCL in 1889. Unsurprisingly, it was under Hudson Beare that the collaboration was initiated in 1902 with the Heriot-Watt College, which provided courses for Edinburgh University engineering students in mechanical and electrical engineering. The College by this time possessed well-equipped laboratories for instruction in these subjects.

The Department moved in 1906 from the Old College to High School Yards, along with the Department of Natural Philosophy, into two reconstructed buildings previously part of the old Royal Infirmary and the City Hospital for Infectious Diseases; at this time the average number of students graduating each year in Engineering was about fifteen. From 1912 there was a reciprocal arrangement with the Heriot-Watt College which allowed its students to obtain Edinburgh University BSc degrees in civil, mechanical or electrical engineering. Collaboration between the University and the College continued until the latter became the Heriot-Watt University in 1966.

Forestry

When the Faculty of Science was instituted in 1893 **Lt-Col Fred Bailey** had been Lecturer in Forestry for two years and he was not eligible to be a member of the Faculty – it was not until 1919 that a certain number of non-professorial staff could be elected. Notwithstanding the absence of a Chair, in 1906 the University Court took the unusual step of publishing Ordinance No 6 Regulations for the Degree of Bachelor of Science in Forestry. Two years later two additional University Lectureships were instituted, in Forest Entomology and Forest Botany.

In 1910 **Edward Stebbing** was appointed from eight candidates for the post of Lecturer in Forestry. He had joined the Indian Forest Service at the age of 23 after training at the Royal Indian Engineering College at Coopers Hill in Berkshire. Like Bailey, he believed that the Forestry student "should be shown in the woods what he is told in the lecture room". The first Forestry graduate was James Lyford Pike in March 1911; the following year he was appointed First Assistant, and the year after, Lecturer. For most of the 1914-18 war he ran the Department more or less single-handedly, but of course there was only a small number of students in those years. He was promoted Reader in 1939 and, having helped the Department through another war, retired at the age of 70 in 1947.

The new Agriculture and Forestry Building at 10 George Square was completed just at the start of WWI, so the Department was better able to cope with the post-war 'bulge' in student numbers. In 1919 Dorothy G Downie became the first woman to graduate in Forestry, and she later became a Lecturer in Forest Botany at the University of Aberdeen. That same year the Chair of Forestry was endowed, largely through the fund-raising efforts of the Royal Scottish Forestry Society and the Royal Highland and Agricultural Society over many years, with the assistance of the Development Commissioners. In 1920 Edward Stebbing was elevated to the Chair, and the degree of MA was conferred on him.

Geology

In 1893 **James Geikie**, Regius Professor of Geology since 1882, became a member of the newly-instituted Faculty of Science. He did much to encourage micrographic petrography, appointing in 1895 John Flett as the first Lecturer in Petrology in the Department. **Sir John Flett** KBE, FRS FRSE (1869-1947) graduated BSc and MA with Honours in Natural Science in 1892, and went on to take the degrees of MB and CM in 1894, and DSc in 1900. The following year he joined the Geological Survey, in which he became Assistant Director for Scotland in 1911 and Director for Great Britain, 1920-35. He was personally involved in the preparation of about thirty Geological Memoirs, and in 1917 he wrote a biography of James Geikie. He published in 1937 *The First Hundred Years of the Geological Survey of Great Britain.*

Geikie was elected in 1893 the first Dean of the Faculty, a position he occupied until he retired in 1914, when he was succeeded by **Thomas Jehu** as the third Regius Professor of Geology. He had been a student of Geikie, gaining the class medal in 1894, and started his research on glacial deposits in Wales. While in the Edinburgh Chair he and some of his colleagues investigated the rocks along the Highland Boundary Fault, but he is not now remembered as a particularly notable geologist.

He did, however, see the Department through WWI and the great influx of students when it ended. Laboratory facilities were stretched to such an extent that some war-time wooden huts were utilised for a time, but even then the practical classes had to be duplicated owing to the shortage of up-to-date equipment for the new experimental techniques in petrology then coming into use.

Mathematics

In 1893 **George Chrystal**, Professor of Mathematics since 1879, became a member of the newly-instituted Faculty of Science, but he and the Department remained primarily in the Faculty of Arts until 1966. In 1903 a University Lectureship in Technical Mathematics was instituted, the first holder of the post being Dr E M Horsburgh. The course was intended for students of engineering, chemistry and other applied sciences. It must be remembered that Technical Mathematics was exactly what the title suggests, whereas Applied Mathematics was more accurately designated Mathematical Physics, as it was in fact renamed more than half a century later.

Edmund Whittaker was appointed the fourteenth Professor of Mathematics in 1912. A graduate of Trinity College Cambridge, he was Professor of Astronomy in Dublin from 1906 to 1912. Two years later, when the Department moved out of the Old College into the Mathematical Institute in Chambers Street (formerly a Church of Scotland Training College), he established the first mathematical laboratory for numerical computation. His research interests spanned many areas of mathematics, physics and astronomy, including numerical analysis, dynamics and electromagnetic theory, relativity and quantum theory. He was a much respected and highly effective teacher, and his text-books remained standard works for many years:– *A Course of Modern Analysis* (1902), *Treatise on Analytical Dynamics* (1904) and *Calculus of Observations* (with G Robinson, 1924). His *History of the Theories of Aether and Electricity* (1910, rev 1951-53) is the definitive account of the history of electromagnetism.

Natural Philosophy

In 1893 **Peter G Tait**, Professor of Natural Philosophy since 1860, became a member of the newly-instituted Faculty of Science, but he and the Department remained primarily in the Faculty of Arts until 1966.

James MacGregor succeeded him as the tenth Professor of Natural Philosophy in 1901; he was born in Halifax, Nova Scotia and studied at the Universities of Edinburgh

(under Tait) and Leipzig (under Gustav Wiedemann). While Professor of Physics at Dalhousie University, 1879-1901, he spent several summer vacations back in Edinburgh working with his old professor. One of MacGregor's competitors for the chair was Ernest Rutherford, later Lord Rutherford. MacGregor undertook the task of reorganising the Department and moving it from the Old College to High School Yards, where new laboratories for teaching and research were opened in October 1906.

In 1913 **Charles Barkla** was appointed the eleventh Professor of Natural Philosophy, having held the chair of Physics at King's College London since 1909. In 1904 he had established that x-rays were transverse waves, by showing that they could be partially polarised. He later discovered the two kinds of more and less penetrating secondary radiation produced when x-rays are absorbed by matter, which he called K and L radiation respectively. His research into x-rays leading to his discovery of the secondary x-radiation characteristics of elements gained him the **Nobel Prize for Physics** in 1917. After about 1916, however, he

Sketch of Professor Barkla

devoted a great deal of his own and his research students' time to a dogged pursuit of the J-phenomenon (Wynne, 1977), of which only he and a few of his students ever claimed to have found experimental evidence.

One of the Department's students in session 1913-14 was **Igor Evgenievich Tamm** (1895-1971) who spent only that one year in Edinburgh but thereafter is said to have spoken English with a marked Scottish accent! After his return to Russia he received his PhD from the University of Moscow in 1918. From 1934 he was head of the theoretical department of the Lebedev Physical Institute of the Soviet Academy of Sciences, and in 1958 he was one of the first three Russians (the others being Cherenkov and Frank) to be awarded jointly the **Nobel Prize for Physics**, for their discovery of the Cherenkov effect.

Public Health

The foundation of the Chair of Public Health is said to have been directly inspired by Louis Pasteur, who attended the Tercentenary celebrations of the University in 1884. His visit to Edinburgh stimulated Alexander Bruce, a partner in the firm of William Younger and Company, to initiate a fund for the endowment of a Chair of Public Health, to which John Usher made a substantial contribution. In 1893/94 in Ordinance No 35 – Edinburgh No 9, the Commissioners made new Regulations for the Degrees of BSc and DSc in Public Health, and in 1898 the Bruce and John Usher Chair of Public Health was instituted in the Faculties of Medicine and Science, the first chair in this subject in Britain.

Charles Hunter Stewart was appointed the first Professor of Public Health. He had been for some time previously assistant to the Professor of Medical Jurisprudence Sir Douglas Maclagan, whose courses included lectures and laboratory experiments in Public Health. Stewart developed a course of thirty lectures in Public Health for medical students, and assumed responsibility for the BSc and DSc degree courses in Public Health which had originally been instituted in 1875 in the Faculty of Science. The subjects of examination were Laboratory Work, Physics, Geology, Epidemiology, Sanitation, and Sanitary Law and Vital Statistics. The Professor of Engineering gave a special course, theoretical and practical, in Sanitary Engineering and Building Construction. Between 1877 and 1900 thirty-four DSc degrees were awarded in Public Health.

Through the further generosity of Sir John Usher the University was able to build the John Usher Institute of Public Health in Warrender Park Road, formally opened in 1903. A Department of Public Health was created in the Faculty of Science at about the same time. In 1919 a twelve-month postgraduate Diploma course in Public Health was instituted, including much the same range of subjects, in the Faculty of Medicine. The Diploma quickly superseded the more lengthy and taxing BSc and DSc degree courses, which within a few years disappeared from the Calendar.

Veterinary Science

In 1906 William Dick's Veterinary School was incorporated by Act of Parliament in the University of Edinburgh as the Royal (Dick) Veterinary College, administered by a Board of Management which included representatives of the Town Council, the University and other bodies.

Degrees of BSc and DSc in Veterinary Science were instituted in the Faculty of Science under University Court Ordinance No XXXVIII (Edinburgh No 13) of 24 July 1911. Of the eleven courses specified for the degree of BSc in Veterinary Science, three were taken at the Royal (Dick) Veterinary College and the remainder at the University, four in the Faculty of Science (Physics, Botany, Zoology and Genetics) and four in the Faculty of Medicine. The Department of Veterinary Science was created in the Faculty of Science at about the same time.

Zoology

[For antecedents *see* Natural History in previous chapters]

In 1893 **James Cossar Ewart**, Professor of Natural History since 1882, became a member of the newly-instituted Faculty of Science, but his Chair, together with those of Botany and Chemistry, was still based in the Faculty of Medicine. Although the Chair retained the title of Natural History, the Department, the courses and the Museum all seem to have become known as Zoology from about the time the Faculty of Science was founded.

As an extension of Ewart's notable research in animal genetics which finally disproved the theory of telegony, a University Lectureship in Genetics (Evolution and Heredity) was instituted in 1911 in the Department of Zoology. Arthur D Darbishire was appointed, but he died on war service in 1915 and in 1921 his successor was F A E Crew, who had been a student of both Ewart and Darbishire. The first chair of genetics in Britain was established at Cambridge in 1912, and it is believed that the Edinburgh lectureship was the first teaching post in the subject in a British university.

The University leased a farm at Fairslacks in 1913 where Ewart carried out experiments with sheep on fleece improvement. At this time, and for some years after the end of WWI, the Department occupied very inadequate accommodation on the west side of the Old College, but government support of research in animal genetics was being increased and the University was hopeful of a proposed national research institute being located in Edinburgh.

Some Notable Edinburgh University Scientists, 1893-1920

ANDERSON, Sir John, first Viscount Waverley PC, GCB, OM, FRS (1882-1958) Studied arts and science at Edinburgh (MA; BSc, 1903). Medal in chemistry under Crum Brown. Scottish Universities MP, 1938-50; Lord President of the Council, with overall responsibility for organising civilian and econmic resources, including atomic energy 1940-43. The Anderson air-raid shelter was named after him. [DNB, CBD, WWW]

BARBOUR, George FRSE, FRGS, FGS (1890-1977) Studied arts and sciences at Marburg, Edinburgh (MA, 1911), Cambridge and Columbia University, New York; achieved a distinguished career as a geologist in the field in China; held posts of Professor, Visiting Professor etc in Peking, Tientsin, Peiping, Columbia, Cincinnati and London Universities. Publ *Physiographic History of the Yangtze* (1935), *Ape or Man* (1949). [WWW]

BEWS, John FRSSA, FLS (1884-1938) Studied arts and science at Edinburgh (MA, 1906; BSc, 1907; DSc, 1912); lecturer in Plant Physiology at Edinburgh, 1908-10; first Prof of Botany, Natal University College, 1910-25 and 1927-30, then Principal, 1930-38. Publ *The Flora of Natal and Zululand* (1921), *The World's Grasses* (1929). [WWW]

HARRISON, Ernest (1886-1981) Studied agriculture at Edinburgh (BSc, 1909) and Ames, Iowa. Teacher of agriculture and administrator, South Africa, 1910-20, and in Kenya, 1921-30; Director of Agriculture in Tanganyika 1930-37; Prof of Agriculture in Imperial College of Tropical Agriculture, Trinidad, 1938-47. Agricultural consultant, Lima, Peru. [WWW]

HILL, James FRS (1873-1954) Studied science at the Royal College of Science, London and at Edinburgh (BSc, 1898; DSc, 1903). At Univ of Sydney, 1904-06, began life-long study of monotreme and marsupial embryology on which he became world expert. Jodrell Prof of Zoology, 1906-21, and of Embryology, 1921-38, at Univ of London. [CBES, WWW]

LEVY, Hyman FRSE (1889-1975) Studied at Edinburgh (MA-Maths & Nat Phil, 1911), and at Oxford and Göttingen (escaped in 1914). Asst Prof of Maths, Royal College of Science, 1920-23; Prof of Mathematics, Imperial College of Science and Technology, 1923-54, Dean, 1946-52. Publ many books on numerical analysis, statistics, science and society, etc. Active member of Communist Party, 1931-56; investigated and publicly denounced persecution of Jews in Russia, expelled from Party in 1958. [DNB, WWW]

McLINTOCK, William CB (1887-1960) Studied science at Edinburgh (BSc-with distinction in Botany, 1907; DSc, 1915). Curator of Geology, RSM, Edinburgh, 1911-21; planned the new Geological Musem in South Kensington 1930-5 and became its Director 1945-50. Reorganized the Geological Survey to advise on water and fuel resources. [DNB, WWW]

MATTHEWS, James CBE, FRSE, FLS (1889-1978) Studied at Edinburgh (MA, 1911); lecturer in Botany at Edinburgh, 1920-29; Prof of Botany at Reading, 1929-1934; Regius Prof of Botany and Keeper of the Cruickshank Botanic Garden at Aberdeen, 1934-59. Chairman of the Macaulay Institute for Soil Research, 1947-59. Helped to improve standards of land-use in Scotland. Publ *Origin and Distribution of the British Flora* (1955). [CSBD, WWW]

STAGG, James CB (1900-1975) Studied science at Edinburgh (BSc, 1920; MA, 1921); science master, Heriot's School, Edinburgh, 1921-23; joined Meteorological Office, 1924. Leader, British Polar Year Exped to Arctic Canada, 1932-33; Chief Meteorological Adviser to General Eisenhower (on Allied landings in Normandy, June 1944, etc) 1943-45; President, Royal Meteorological Society, 1950. Publ *Forecast for Overlord* (1971). [WWW]

WEDDERBURN, Joseph FRS (1882-1948) Studied mathematics at Edinburgh (MA, 1903; DSc, 1908); assistant in Natural Philosophy at Edinburgh, 1902-4, then lecturer in Mathematics, 1905-10; Assist/Assoc/Prof of Mathematics at Princeton University, 1910/21/28-1945. Did important work with Leonard Dickson on commutative and non-commutative algebras; proved in 1905 that every finite field is commutative. [CSBD, DSB, WWW]

CHAPTER   6

The King's Buildings and other developments, 1920 - 1939

The years between the wars were marked by a sense of unease in the universities, as in the rest of the country. People young and old gradually realised there was no such thing as a War to end all wars, no such place as a land fit for heroes. In 1921 Greece attacked Turkey; Mussolini, Stalin, Hitler and Franco seized power between 1922 and 1936; Britain suffered severely from the General Strike in 1926; Wall Street crashed in 1929; Japan invaded Manchuria; many of Britain's 2.8m unemployed marched on London. In the universities all shades of contemporary opinion could be found, from the notorious Oxford Union vote in 1933 for the motion 'That this house will refuse to fight for King and country', to the sacrifice of those who were killed in the Spanish Civil War. To their credit the British universities did not hesitate to offer asylum to the many academics who were forced to flee from Germany and other European countries in the 1930s.

Treasury grants to the universities, administered by the UGC from 1920, continued to increase fairly rapidly until the country's economic problems forced a change in government policy:–

	Recurrent grant	Non-recurrent grant
	£000	£000
1920-21	798	252
1924-25	1,238	79
1930-31	1,798	—
1935-36	1,828	—
1938-39	2,078	125

The inter-war years also brought substantial if unspectacular changes in industry. There was a rapid proliferation of research departments in some of the larger industrial firms in the early 1920s, spreading more slowly to smaller firms in the next decade so that by 1938 as many as 566 British firms were spending £5.4m annually on research and development. Naturally, however, most of their effort was on development rather than research. In fact, the Balfour Committee of 1929 said that 'nothing less than a revolution is needed .... imperfect receptivity towards scientific ideas on the part of British industry is, at the moment, the main obstacle to advance.'

The University of Edinburgh

In 1919 the area of ground known as West Mains Farm, bounded on the north and east by West Mains Road and Mayfield Road, and including part of the Craigmillar Park Golf Course (1906), was purchased by the University for the relocation and expansion of its science departments. Of its 115 acres (45 hectares) only about 90 acres (35 hectares) have been developed to date, the remainder being still leased to the Golf Club. Work on the first new building, for the Department of Chemistry, began in November 1919.

In 1921 the University launched an Appeal for £500,000 for the erection of laboratories and class-rooms on the Liberton site. King George himself endorsed the appeal in the following words:– 'I trust that in a Country and in a City where the value of education is thoroughly realised you will find generous donors able and willing to complete the plans which you have sketched with such a bold hand.' The object of the appeal was to provide accommodation adequate to the modern teaching of (a) Applied Chemistry, (b) Natural History (including Zoology in relation to Medicine, Diseases of Plants etc), and (c) Geology (the economic aspect of which must be further developed in connection with the proposed new Degree in Mining and Metallurgy).

The Faculty of Medicine

With the opening of the new Chemistry Building at the King's Buildings in 1922 that Department severed its more than two-hundred-year-old connection with the Faculty of Medicine. At about the same time the Departments of Botany and Natural History were transferred from the Faculty of Medicine to the Faculty of Science, although the Chairs of Botany and Natural History continued to be listed in the Calendars under the Faculty of Medicine until the 1960s. It is noticeable that this was not the case with Chemistry, presumably because a Chair of Chemistry in Relation to Medicine had been instituted in 1919 in the Faculty of Medicine.

In a history of the non-medical sciences at the University of Edinburgh we must beg leave of our medical colleagues to include the very distinguished scientist **Alexander Robertus Todd**, Baron Todd of Trumpington, OM, FRS, HonFRSE (1907-   ). He graduated DSc in organic chemistry at Glasgow and DPhil at both Frankfurt and Oxford before spending the years 1934-36 as Assistant in Medical Chemistry and Beit Memorial Research Fellow in the Faculty of Medicine at Edinburgh, where he began work on thiamine (vitamin B_1). From 1938 he was Professor of Chemistry at Manchester where he continued his studies of vitamins, and from 1944 to 1971 as Professor of Organic Chemistry at Cambridge he worked on the structure of DNA and RNA. He was awarded the **Nobel Prize for Chemistry** in 1957 for his work on the nucleotides and nucleotidic coenzymes which was a major contribution to our understanding of the biochemistry of growth.

The Faculty of Science

On 6 July 1920 the foundation stone of the new Chemistry Building on the West Mains Farm site was laid by His Majesty King George V, who was pleased to allow the name of The King's Buildings to be given to the University's future science departments. His Majesty said:– 'Looking round as we do upon a world devastated by the ravages of war, amazed at what it has accomplished, appalled at what it has lost, and concentrated in an

F*

endeavour to substitute for those old roads it may no longer travel, wider and better planned avenues of life, we pin our faith upon the possibilities emerging from the progressive application of science to the service of man.' In October 1922 the first classes were held in the new building, and it was officially opened by HRH the Prince of Wales on 3 December 1924. The total cost of the building, fittings and equipment was £182,000.

On the 14th and 15th of July 1921 the first eleven PhD degrees were awarded by the University of Edinburgh in the Faculties of Arts (4), Divinity (1), Science (5) and Medicine (1). Of the five science PhD graduates two were women, one of whom, Margaret White, MA, BSc, submitted a thesis entitled *Characteristic Frequencies in Elements of Low Atomic Weight (J Series)*. She was evidently one of the research students who had been persuaded by Prof Barkla to work on the J-phenomenon.

In October 1921 the Edinburgh University Court Ordinance No 35 came into force, instituting new regulations for the award of BSc and DSc degrees in Pure Science. The Bachelor of Science could be awarded as an Ordinary Degree, or with Honours in any one of 13 Schools in the Faculty of Science, after a period of study of not less than four years. Prior to that date, the degree of BSc could be awarded with 'Distinction' or 'Special Distinction' in one or more subjects. The Schools are listed below, demonstrating the wide range of the subjects that were considered to be encompassed by Pure Science in

King George V and Queen Mary at laying of foundation stone at the Chemistry Building, King's Buildings

both medical and non-medical sciences:–

(a)	Mathematics	(h)	Zoology
(b)	Applied Mathematics	(i)	Anatomy
(c)	Astronomy	(j)	Physiology
(d)	Physics	(k)	Bacteriology
(e)	Chemistry	(l)	Anthropology
(f)	Geology	(m)	Pathology
(g)	Botany		

Subsequent Court Ordinances introduced the degree of BSc with Honours into the Applied Sciences of Mining and Metallurgy (1921), Agriculture (1922), Technical Chemistry (1922), Engineering (1924) and Forestry (1924).

Since Charles Darwin and Robert Louis Stevenson studied science and engineering subjects respectively at Edinburgh without taking a degree, it seems to me very likely that our best-known science *graduate* must be **Eric Liddell** BSc (1902-1945). He matriculated in 1920 as just another first-year student, but when he graduated four years later he was 'capped' with an Olympic wreath of wild olive, chaired to the door of St Giles Cathedral for the Commemoration Service, and afterwards drawn through the streets of Edinburgh

Eric Liddell, chaired by fellow students after graduation

by a team of blues in an open carriage with the Principal, Sir Alfred Ewing. All that, because less than a week before he had won the 400 metres in the 1924 Olympic Games in Paris in a world record time of 47.6 seconds.

His firm Christian beliefs, his work as a missionary in China, and his tragic early death in a Japanese internment camp at Weifang in China in February 1945 are too well known to bear repetition here. Two recent ceremonies honouring his memory must be mentioned, however. In the first, in June 1991, the University, along with the Eric Liddell Foundation, arranged for a Mull granite memorial stone to be erected and dedicated at the site of his grave in Weifang; in the second, his daughter Mrs Patricia Russell handed over his three Olympic Medals into the safe keeping of the University of Edinburgh, where they are now on display in the Old College.

The year 1929 saw the completion of the new Zoology Building, now the Ashworth Building. The cost was met by a gift of £20,000 (originally anonymously) from Laurence Pullar of Bridge of Earn, a grant of £18,000 from the Carnegie Trustees, and a grant of £74,000 from the International Education Board which had been founded by John D Rockefeller, jun, in 1923. In March 1930 the new building for Animal Genetics, now the Crew Building, was ready for occupation. The International Education Board gave a grant of £30,000 which had to be, and was, matched by an equal sum from a variety of individuals and organisations. Outbuildings included houses for sheep, pigs, goats, poultry and the small animals which were the subjects of study.

By 1933 the membership of the Faculty of Science had increased from the original eleven to thirty-three, with both professorial and non-professorial additions. Five of the University's science departments had been transplanted to the King's Buildings site, and in session 1936-37 there were 569 matriculated students in the Faculty of Science out of a University total of 3763. The final pre-war development, long awaited by both students and staff, was the King's Buildings Union completed in 1938-39. It was formally opened on 11 January 1939 by Sir William Bragg, President of the Royal Society, replacing 'a Refectory and Women's and Men's Reading Rooms' which had been provided temporarily in the dilapidated wooden huts vacated by *Geology in 1931.

It deserves to be recorded, in the same spirit as the tale of the widow's mite, that the list of Recent Benefactions in a 1930s Calendar includes a gift of £2-2/- as 'a contribution to the funds of the University, with a view to founding a lectureship in Aeronautics.' The University still has no lectureship in aeronautics.

Agriculture

In 1922 **James Scott Watson**, an Edinburgh BSc of 1908, succeeded Robert Wallace as the fifth Professor of Agriculture and Rural Economy. Under his guidance the Agriculture Degree regulations were amended in 1922 to include BSc (Agric) with Honours in Economics, Chemistry, Botany, Zoology or Bacteriology. Scott Watson, with James A More, one of the Lecturers in the Department, wrote *Agriculture: the Science and Practice of British Farming* (1924; 9edn, 1949).

Ernest Shearer was appointed Principal of the College of Agriculture in 1924; he collaborated closely with Scott Watson until the latter resigned the following year, to take up an appointment as Sibthorpian Professor of Rural Economy in the University of Oxford. In 1926 **Ernest Shearer** was appointed the sixth Professor of Agriculture and Rural Economy, while retaining his post as Principal of the College of Agriculture. The increasing Government awareness of the importance of agriculture to the British nation was shown by the establishment in 1931 of the Agricultural Research Council.

By the mid-1930s it was apparent that the Faculty of Medicine was in need of room for expansion, as indeed were the Departments of Agriculture and Forestry in No 10 George Square, and the College of Agriculture in Nos 13, 14 and 15. Plans were accordingly drawn up for a new Medical Building on the north side of George Square, and a large new building in the north west corner of the King's Buildings site for the University Departments of Agriculture and Forestry, and the Edinburgh and East of Scotland College of Agriculture. Both schemes were abandoned in 1939 on the outbreak of WWII.

Astronomy

In 1921 Prof Sampson was one of the first astronomers to measure stellar spectra by the use of recording microphotometry – this work constituted a major and prestigious part of the ROE's research for the next 40 years or so. The Astronomy I course consisted of sixty lectures at the University and forty hours of practical work at the Observatory. Several successive Calendars also listed 'Courses II and III (to be announced later)', but it seems that in practice specialised courses for interested final honours year students were given only if there was sufficient demand.

A major re-equipment programme at the ROE was completed in 1932 with the installation of a Grubb Parsons 36-inch reflecting telescope and a new spectrograph with interchangeable long, medium and short focus cameras. The new equipment allowed him to extend his spectrophotometric work to fainter stars, and in 1934 he obtained an exceptionally good set of spectra of *Nova Herculis*.

William Greaves succeeded Sampson in 1938 as sixth Astronomer Royal for Scotland and seventh Regius Professor of Astronomy. Born in Barbados, he was the only son of Dr E Greaves, a medical graduate of Edinburgh University. Like Sampson before him he read mathematics at Cambridge and was awarded the Isaac Newton Studentship, then turned to astronomy first at Greenwich and later at the Cape of Good Hope. His main interest before coming to Edinburgh was the measurement of stellar temperatures.

Botany

William Wright Smith was appointed the eleventh Regius Professor of Botany in 1922, Balfour's own preference as his successor. He graduated MA at Edinburgh in 1896 and for a few years was a school teacher, but in 1902 accepted an invitation from Balfour to be his assistant. From 1907 he spent four years in India and Burma, then returned to Edinburgh as Deputy Keeper of the Royal Botanic Garden. He was a good lecturer who really enjoyed teaching, but he also continued his research on Sino-Himalayan plants, especially primulas and rhododendrons. At about the time of his appointment the Department of Botany was transferred from the Faculty of Medicine to the Faculty of Science. A few Calendar entries in the mid-1920s also put the Chair in the Faculty of Science, but (at a guess) Smith must have regarded this unfavourably, and the Chair was soon restored to the Faculty of Medicine where it remained until 1966.

Chemistry

Work on what is now known as the Joseph Black Building began in November 1919 at the King's Buildings site, and the first class was held there three years later. Walker was criticised at the time for providing so much space for research workers (more than 30 small rooms), and for planning the building so that it could be extended in height and in area. Both of these developments were subsequently found to be necessary.

One member of the first class was Neil Campbell, who retired as Professor of Chemistry in 1973 and recorded some of his recollections a few years later. The Chemistry Department was the only University building on the site until Zoology and Animal Genetics were completed about seven years later. West Mains Farm and its outbuildings still stood in the north west corner of the site, and cattle grazed on the fields not yet built upon. For amenities there were tennis courts, a hockey pitch and a soccer pitch.

A four-year Honours BSc Degree in Chemistry had been introduced in 1921, and in the following year a similar course in Technical Chemistry was instituted jointly with the Heriot-Watt College – 'to meet the needs of those students who desire definitely to prepare for the practice of chemistry in industry.' The teaching of Technical Chemistry in the final year of the University course was virtually a one-man speciality in the Department of Chemistry. Some topics could only be studied at the Heriot-Watt College, for example Metallurgy, Biochemistry, Oil Technology, and Foods and Drugs.

From its inception Technical Chemistry was nominally a Department, but in practical terms it was a small section within the Department of Chemistry until 1955, when it was renamed Chemical Technology and shared accommodation with the Heriot-Watt College, finally becoming the Department of Chemical Engineering in the University in 1960.

Neil Campbell judged Sir James Walker one of the best lecturers he had ever heard. His main drawback was that he made his points so clear and apparently so simple that it was not until afterwards that one realised how deeply into the subject he had gone and how much ground he had covered! He was also remarkable as being the last Professor of Chemistry who marked all four Honours papers single-handedly – he was an all-round master of physical, organic and inorganic chemistry, probably the last of the breed. Campbell also recalled that – 'Four of us took psychology as the optional third year subject, and in the intelligence tests one chap made a record score then six weeks later failed two of his other subjects, while the one who was a complete failure in psychology got a first class in chemistry – we all had a laugh about that.'

Prof Walker was in the first rank of physical chemists, and as Ostwald's first British student (1888-89) he was instrumental in making known in Britain the then new physico-chemical theories. Neil Campbell stayed on in the Department for four years to get his PhD, existing on a part-time demonstratorship at a salary of £100 per annum – which at the time he thought was a fortune. Probably the one feature of chemical research in the late 1920s which would cause most surprise to today's postgraduates would be the instrumentation, or rather the lack of it, plus the fact that in those days students had to do most of their own glass-blowing. Many of them went to Leiden, some every year, to attend a course on glass-blowing which enabled them to become quite expert in the art.

In 1928 Walker retired and **James Kendall** was appointed the tenth Professor of Chemistry. He had graduated at Edinburgh University (BSc, 1910; DSc, 1915) and in 1913 went to Columbia University, New York City where, apart from two years' service in the American Navy during WWI, he remained until 1926. He did most of his research at Columbia, publishing some fifty papers mainly on the physical chemistry of solutions. He also revised and enlarged Alexander Smith's famous series of textbooks on chemistry, and they remained in print until after WWII.

Neil Campbell became a Lecturer in the Department in 1932 and recalled that it was a very busy place in the 1930s both in teaching and research – '. . there was Percival on his carbohydrates, Butler on thermodynamics, Rule working on benzanthrones and naphthalene compounds, Ludlam on photochemistry, and Mowbray Ritchie on kinetics – altogether a very lively department, which might have flowered in the early 1940s had the war not come.' It is interesting that the holder of the Romanes Lectureship in Chemistry in session 1933-34 was **Heinrich Wieland** (1877-1957), a notable biochemist who in 1926 succeeded Willstätter at Munich. The following year he was awarded the **Nobel Prize for Chemistry** for his research on bile acids and analogous substances.

Engineering, and Mining
Under the Court Ordinance No 34 of October 1921, degrees of BSc and DSc were instituted in Mining and Metallurgy. In 1924 **Henry Briggs**, Professor of Mining at the Heriot-Watt College, was appointed conjointly to the newly-instituted James A Hood Chair of Mining in the University of Edinburgh. Degrees could be taken at the University or the (then) Heriot-Watt College, but there was never more than a handful of mining students at the University. Most of the first and second year courses were taken at the University, and most of the third and fourth years' at the Heriot-Watt College. In 1931 the designation of the degree was altered to simply 'Mining'. Prof Briggs was succeeded in 1936 by **William Macmillan**.

The Department of Engineering in 1920 was still in the old hospital buildings in High School Yards, which had rapidly become as inadequate in their turn as the awkwardly cramped spaces in the Old College had been two decades before. Admittedly the aftermath of WWI gave rise to a quite exceptional influx of ex-service students, but it is worth recording that in June 1922 just over a hundred degrees of BSc in Engineering were awarded, compared to seven in 1905 at the end of the Department's first year in High School Yards.

As with the other sciences, however, the University was quite unable to finance new buildings on the scale made necessary by increasing demands for laboratory facilities, and it was only in 1927 that a solution appeared for engineering. The Court was informed that under the will of the late James Sanderson of Galashiels a sum of about £50,000 would become available for the needs of the Departments of Chemistry and Engineering, and it was agreed that as Chemistry was by then well provided for, the greater part of the bequest should be used for the erection of a new engineering building. The official opening of the new Sanderson Engineering Laboratory by the Prime Minister, the Right Hon J Ramsay MacDonald, FRS, took place on 28 January 1932.

By 1939 the staff of the Engineering Department consisted of the Professor, a Reader, and five Lecturers. Electrical engineering was still taught by the Heriot-Watt College, but mechanical engineering was by that time studied at King's Buildings.

Forestry
In 1920 **Edward Stebbing** was elevated to the Chair, and the honorary degree of MA was conferred on him. For the next 20 years or more, the full-time teaching staff consisted of

the Professor and two lecturers, with an annual student intake of about twenty. There was nevertheless a strong emphasis on practical work throughout the course, including a First Year practical course by courtesy of the War Office on their estates at Dreghorn and Stobo, an Easter course on the Atholl or Murthly Estates based at Dunkeld, a Second Year tour of the Forest of Dean and surrounding areas, and the Final Year visit to France. The French tour occupied the whole of the summer term and included studies of broadleaf silviculture in Allier, the maritime pine in the Landes, and high level afforestation in the Auvergne, as well as the preparation by each student of a management plan in the Forest of Tronçais. Apart from the war years and other short interruptions these visits continued until 1967.

The Department's connection with the Atholl Estate and Professor Stebbing's acquaintance with the Duke, who was the King's Chamberlain at Holyrood Palace, had an unexpected outcome in 1923 when the Professor acquired as a gift some very large and ornate pieces of oak furniture from Holyrood Palace. A huge display cabinet 18 feet long and several throne-like chairs adorned Stebbing's room in No 10 George Square until the Department moved to the King's Buildings in 1966, when they were accepted by the Victoria and Albert Museum in London as fine examples of Austrian Gothic revival furniture.

Prof Stebbing was the author of more than twenty books on a wide range of subjects, including *Manual of Indian Forest Zoology* (1908), *Jungle By-ways in India* (1910), *British Forestry* (1916), *At the Serbian Front in Macedonia* (1917), *The Forests of India* (3 vols: 1921-26), *The Threat of the Sahara* (1937), *Forests and Erosion* (1941). When he was not writing, his recreations were fairly predictable:– '. . hunting, shooting, fishing and travelling in the wilds.'

In 1924 Ordinance No 43 superseded No 6, introducing one-year postgraduate BSc (Honours) degrees and the degree of DSc. The first to be awarded the DSc, in December 1924, was Mark L Anderson, who succeeded Stebbing in 1951. Also in 1924 the Edinburgh University Forestry Society was founded, with its annual publication *Sylva* which, unusually for a student periodical, survived for more than fifty years.

Genetics
The Board of Agriculture and Fisheries and the Development Commission appointed **F A E Crew** as Director of the Department of Research in Animal Breeding in 1920, and shortly afterwards the University Court appointed him University Lecturer in Genetics. This Lectureship had been instituted in 1911 and filled by A D Darbishire who died on war service in 1915. He is best remembered (by Crew at any rate in his 1971 paper) for his work on the genetics of the waltzing mouse – on which Crew unfortunately gives no further details. Crew himself became interested in animal breeding through a boyhood fascination with bantams, and on leaving school in 1906 came to Edinburgh to read medicine.

The Animal Breeding Research Department was the first of its kind in the UK, but was not fully integrated into the University until 1928. It began in very cramped accommodation in High School Yards, moved in 1924 into the Department of Chemistry at the King's Buildings, with the use of some seven acres of grassland for its animals, and by 1928 sufficient money had become available to start building the Institute of Animal Genetics, now the Crew Building, which was opened in 1930 by Sir Edward Sharpey-Schafer, the Professor of Physiology. Until 1945 a substantial contribution to the financing of the work was made by the Department of Agriculture for Scotland.

The research and the reputation of the Department grew rapidly in the 1920s, partly, as Crew himself admitted, because of the reluctance of his main rival, R C Punnett, Professor of Genetics at Cambridge, to allow postgraduate students to register for the PhD degree. Punnett was the outstanding poultry geneticist of his time, and many talented young scientists arrived in Cambridge hoping to work with him, only to be redirected to Edinburgh where many of them were welcomed by Crew.

Occasionally there was a move in the opposite direction. Among the first group of

Professor Crew with staff and visitors in 1924 (l to r): Arthur Walton, (Sir) D'Arcy Wentworth Thompson, Paul Kammerer, Lancelot Hogben, (Dame) Honor Fell, F A E Crew, M V Cytovich.

postgraduates in 1921 was Honor Fell, a budding histologist and cytologist. Crew thought it would be useful for her to learn the techniques of tissue culture at Cambridge under Strangeways, and in due course she went there. It did not take him long to recognise her potential, however, and she never returned to Edinburgh. **Dame Honor Bridget Fell**, DBE, FRS (1900-1986), BSc, PhD, DSc and Hon LLD of Edinburgh University, was Director of the Strangeways Research Laboratory in Cambridge from 1929 to 1970. She employed the organ culture method, largely developed at the Strangeways Laboratory, for her research in immuno-pathology.

In 1928 **Francis A E Crew** was appointed to the Buchanan Chair of Animal Genetics instituted in the Faculty of Science. The new subject of genetics was not welcomed by some of the more conservative academics in Britain, but it thrived in Edinburgh, even though under Crew there was a strong emphasis on physiology and livestock breeding. Poultry research was developed by **Alan Greenwood** who joined the Animal Breeding Research Department in 1923 and in 1947 became the first Director of the Poultry Research Centre until his retirement in 1962. Among research workers who spent shorter periods at the Institute was Lancelot Hogben, and his friends J B S Haldane and Julian Huxley were frequent visitors.

The distinguished geneticist **Hermann J Muller** (1890-1967) joined the Institute in 1937, having left the Soviet Union in disgust at the advent of Lysenkoism under Stalin. In Edinburgh he was mainly concerned with the study of chromosome variations and genetic differences between species. In 1927 he had first reported mutations in genes induced by exposure to X-rays, and his work in this field, continued in the USA after he left the Institute with a DSc in 1940, led to the award of a **Nobel Prize for Physiology or Medicine** in 1946. Among the young research workers who encountered Muller at the Institute were Charlotte Auerbach and Guido Pontecorvo, and Auerbach in particular was stimulated to take an abiding interest in mutagenesis which she developed over many years.

Guido Pontecorvo FRS FRSE FLS (1907-   ) graduated in agricultural science from the University of Pisa and joined the staff of the Institute in 1938, working with Muller on the genetic differences between species that produce sterile hybrids on crossing. He then studied the *Drosophila* species and gained his PhD in 1941, after which he turned his attention to fungal genetics. His work in this field, in association with that of Benzer, Roper and others, led to a much better understanding of the gene as a unit of function. In 1941 he moved to Glasgow University, where in 1956 he was appointed the first Professor of Genetics, a post he retained until 1968 when he moved to the research laboratories of the Imperial Cancer Research Fund in London. He was awarded the Darwin Medal of the Royal Society in 1978.

Some indication of the international reputation earned by the Institute in the 1930s was given by the decision to hold the Seventh International Congress of Genetics in Edinburgh in August 1939. Unfortunately the imminent outbreak of WWII disrupted the proceedings and many delegates had to return home in haste, or like Crew himself received their calling-up papers and had to report for military service.

Geology

The plight of Geology under Prof Jehu in its totally unsuitable accommodation in the Old College was made so much worse by the increase in student numbers after the end of WWI that urgent action had to be taken. The University Court purchased the wooden YMCA huts set up in St Andrew Square for the use of American troops during the war, and in the summer of 1923 they were removed and re-erected at the King's Buildings to house the Department of Geology. It was with great relief that the Principal Sir Alfred Ewing was able to announce in April 1929 that the University had received a gift of £50,000 from Sir Alexander Grant towards the cost of a new building for the Department of Geology. The official opening of the Grant Institute of Geology by the Prime Minister, the Right Hon J Ramsay MacDonald, FRS, took place on 28 January 1932.

The new building provided all the accommodation the Department of Geology would require for some time to come, though there were initially shortages of equipment which were gradually remedied as funds became available. It was fortunate that the new building was completed at a time when geology was becoming less of an observational science and more dependent on experimental work in the laboratory, and to some extent in the field. Full advantage was taken of the new facilities to expand teaching and research in mineralogy, petrology, paleontology and paleo-botany, using physical, chemical and microscopical methods of analysis.

Mathematics

Throughout the whole of the period covered by this chapter the Professor of Mathematics was Edmund Whittaker, an inspiring Head of Department who attracted some first-class members of staff and turned out a large number of distinguished graduates. Dr E M Horsburgh, for example, developed courses in Technical Mathematics for engineering students, and both William Edge and Ivor Etherington who were lecturers in the 1930s were appointed to Personal Chairs in the Department. Some of the more notable young lecturers who joined the department and then, sometimes after only a year or two, left to occupy chairs elsewhere, are noted at the end of this chapter – see Baker, McCrea, Oppenheim and Semple.

Possibly the most brilliant mathematics student of the 1920s and '30s was **Sir William Hodge** FRS FRSE (1903-1975), who graduated MA in mathematics at Edinburgh in 1923; at St John's College, Cambridge he was Smith's Prizeman, 1927; he taught at Bristol, Princeton and Cambridge before being appointed Lowndean Professor of Astronomy and Geometry at Cambridge in 1936. His work in algebraic geometry on the theory of harmonic integrals had an immense impact in both mathematical analysis and physics; he published *Methods of Algebraic Geometry* (3 vols, with D Pedoe, 1947, 1952, 1954). He was Royal medallist of the Royal Society in 1957, and Copley medallist in 1974, and he was given an Honorary LLD by Edinburgh University in 1958.

Natural Philosophy, and Mathematical Physics

With the introduction of Honours Degrees in Pure Science in 1921, Barkla proceeded to institute and develop the Honours School in the Department of Natural Philosophy. In 1922 the Tait Chair of Natural Philosophy was instituted in the Faculty of Arts, endowed largely by the Tait Memorial Fund launched almost 20 years earlier by Professor MacGregor. The intention was that the chair should be devoted especially to the teaching of Mathematical Physics. Charles G Darwin was appointed in 1923 the first Tait Professor of Natural Philosophy; he became in effect the Head of the Department of Applied Mathematics (Mathematical Physics). Grandson of the celebrated Charles Darwin, he later turned his attention to genetics and eugenics. He resigned in 1936 to become Master of Christ's College, Cambridge and two years later he became Director of the National Physical Laboratory.

In 1925 **Robin Schlapp** accepted the offer of the Lectureship in Applied Mathematics, thus beginning his more than forty years in the Department. He was an exceptionally respected mathematician, musician, mountaineer and man, but he was also modest and self-effacing, and his reward was to spend 21 years as a lecturer and 22 as a senior lecturer. When he retired in 1968 his friends and colleagues instituted an annual Robin Schlapp Lecture in his honour, and the Royal Society of Edinburgh, of which he had been a Fellow for 56 years, awarded him one of its Bicentenary Medals in 1983.

Max Born, who was appointed the second Tait Professor of Natural Philosophy in 1936, was one of the many talented refugees driven out of Nazi Germany in the 1930s. His research in quantum mechanics, and especially his invention of the statistical interpretation of the wave function, earned him the **Nobel Prize for Physics** in 1954. He published *Experiment and Theory in Physics*, 1943; *The Natural Philosophy of Cause and Chance*, 1949; *A General Kinetic Theory of Liquids* (with H S Green), 1949; *Dynamical Theory of Crystal Lattices* (with Kun Huang), 1953; *Principles of Optics* (with E Wolf), 1959. He had declined on moral grounds to take part in research during WWII aiming at the manufacture and use of an atomic bomb.

Ironically, one of Born's research students in Edinburgh in the late 1930s was the notorious **Klaus Fuchs** (1911-88), a brilliant mathematician who had become a member of the Communist Party while studying at Leipzig. During WWII he worked on atom bomb research in Britain and America. From

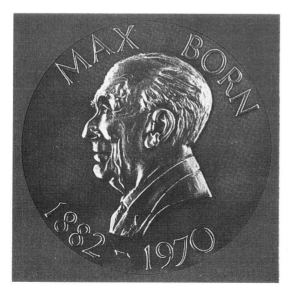

Max Born—Nobel Laureate

1943 (when he was granted British citizenship) he passed over much top secret information to the Russians, but in 1949, by which time he was head of theoretical physics at the Harwell Atomic Energy Establishment, he came under suspicion and eventually made a full confession. He was sentenced to 14 years imprisonment for treason, but was released in 1959 and became deputy Director of the Central Institute of Nuclear Research at Rossendorf near Dresden in East Germany.

Public Health

In 1925 **Col Percy Lelean** was appointed the second Professor of Public Health. He had served with distinction in the Royal Army Medical Corps, 1900-22, and soon after his arrival a number of major changes in the teaching of public health in the University took place. One of the most fundamental was that the BSc and DSc Degrees in Public Health, which since 1894 had been included in the programme of the Faculty of Science, with substantial teaching contributions from several science departments, were discontinued. Instead, the more popular one-year postgraduate Diploma in Public Health was offered by the Faculty of Medicine.

To close the story of the connection between Public Health and the Faculty of Science it only remains to add that in 1944 **Francis A E Crew**, who had been Professor of Animal *Genetics in the University from 1928 until war service took him to London in 1940, returned to Edinburgh and was invited to apply for the Chair of Public Health and Social Medicine, which he occupied until his retirement in 1955.

Statistics

In 1907 a Lecturer in Statistics and Mathematical Economics (Dr George A Carse) was appointed in the Faculty of Arts. The subject was part of the Honours course for the degree of MA in Economic Science, within the Department of Mental Philosophy. In 1919 two Lectureships in Actuarial Science were introduced into the subject of Mathematics within the Department of Science. Dr A C Aitken succeeded Dr Carse in 1925 as Lecturer in Statistics and Mathematical Economics, and was also one of three Lecturers in Actuarial Science. In 1937 Dr Aitken was appointed Reader in Statistics, and in 1946 he became the fifteenth Professor of *Mathematics. Courses in Statistics and Actuarial Science continued to be given within the Departments of Mental Philosophy and Science respectively in the Faculty of Arts.

Veterinary Science

In 1934 the College was affiliated to the University of Edinburgh and the degrees of BSc and DSc in Veterinary Science continued to be offered in the Faculty of Science. The subjects provided by the Faculty for the BSc degree were Physics, Mycology, Entomology and Parasitology, and Genetics in Relation to Animal Breeding.

Zoology

In Edinburgh's Place in Scientific Progress published on the occasion of the Edinburgh Meeting of the British Association in 1921, it was remarked that Edinburgh students had been occupying the four long-established Scottish Chairs of Natural History for some considerable time:– W C McIntosh and D'Arcy Thompson at St Andrews; Cossar Ewart at Edinburgh; J Arthur Thomson at Aberdeen; and J Graham Kerr at Glasgow. Among others farther afield were W A Herdman at Liverpool, J P Hill at London and W A Haswell at Sydney.

In 1927 **James Ashworth** succeeded James Cossar Ewart as the eighth Professor of Natural History. He had been appointed in 1901 to Ewart's staff as a lecturer in invertebrate zoology, and in 1919 to the newly-instituted Chair of Zoology in the Faculty of Science. When Ashworth was translated to the Chair of Natural History in 1927 the Chair of Zoology was left vacant, and it was not filled again until 1963.

Ashworth had a very positive and dynamic personality and he made a major contribution to the development of zoology at Edinburgh. He strengthened and reorganised the teaching of zoology in his department to students in medicine, veterinary medicine and agriculture. Between 1923 and 1927 money had been gradually accumulated to meet the cost of a new building, and in due course he presided over the re-housing of the Department at the King's Buildings in what is now known as the Ashworth Building, opened in May 1929 by HRH Prince George. The new building included a large museum space, and Ashworth set about the task of assembling the University's third natural history collection, with his usual energy and enthusiasm.

Zoology Building at King's Buildings

James Ritchie became in 1936 the ninth Professor of Natural History. He had been on the staff of the RSM for 24 years, latterly as Keeper of the Natural History Department, and left in 1930 to become Professor of Natural History in Aberdeen. It fell to him to run the Department during WWII, surmounting many difficulties.

Some Notable Edinburgh University Scientists and Engineers, 1920-1939

BAKER, Bevan B (later Bevan B BEVAN-BAKER) FRSE (1890-1963) Studied at London and Munich; lecturer in Mathematics at Edinburgh (DSc, 1923); Professor of Mathematics in London University, 1924-44. Publ *The Mathematical Theory of Huygens' Principle* (with E T Copson, 1939). [WWW]

GRAHAM, Alastair FRS (1906-   ) Studied arts and sciences at Edinburgh (MA, 1927; BSc, 1929) and at London (DSc); Prof of Zoology at the University of Reading to 1972, now Emeritus. Frink Medallist, Zoological Society, 1976. Publ *British Prosobranch Molluscs* (jtly, 1962), *Other Operculate Gastropod Molluscs* (1971). [WW]

GULLAND, John FRSE (1898-1947) Son of Edinburgh Prof of Medicine, G L Gulland. Studied chemistry at Edinburgh (BSc, 1921); research at St Andrews and Manchester on alkaloids, and at Lister Institute, 1931-36, on nucleic acids using new methods to study their structure; Prof of Chemistry at University College, Nottingham, 1936-47. [DSB, WWW]

HARVEY, Leslie (1903-1986) Studied science at Imperial College, London; lecturer in Zoology at Edinburgh, 1925-30; Prof, 1946-69 and Head of Department of Zoology at Exeter, 1930-69. Publ *Dartmoor* (with D StL Gordon, 1952). [WWW]

LICKLEY, Robert CBE, FRSE, FEng (1912-   ) Studied engineering at Edinburgh (BSc, 1932; Hon DSc, 1972); Prof of Aircraft Design at College of Aeronautics, Cranfield; Managing Director of Hawker Siddeley Aviation Ltd. 1960-76 then Head of Rolls Royce Support Staff, NEB, 1976-9. [WW]

LYON, Stanley (1917-1991) Studied engineering at Edinburgh (BSc, 1938); Major, RE, 1939-46; with ICI Ltd. from 1946, in the dyestuffs and agriculture divisions, rising to become Chairman of the Agriculture Division, 1966 and Deputy Chairman of ICI, 1972-77. [WWW]

McCREA, Sir William FRS, FRSE, FRAS (1904-   ) Studied at Cambridge and Göttingen; lecturer in Mathematics at Edinburgh, 1930-2, then lectured and held Professorships in Mathematics and Astronomy in universities and colleges world-wide. Research Prof of Theoretical Astronomy at Sussex, 1966-72, now Emeritus. Publ *Analytical Geometry of Three Dimensions* (1942); *Physics of the Sun and Stars* (1950); *Royal Greenwich Observatory* (1975); *History of the Royal Astronomical Society, 1920-80* (jtly, 1987). [WW]

MACDONALD, James FRSE (1908-   ) Studied agriculture at Edinburgh (BSc, PhD) and St.Andrews; lecturer in Botany, 1935, Prof of Botany, 1961-77 and Dean of the Faculty of Science, 1967-69 at St. Andrews. Publ *Introduction to Mycology* (1951). [WW]

MacLAREN, Sir Hamish KBE, CB, DFC (1898-1990) Studied engineering at Edinburgh (BSc, 1921); joined British Thomson Houston Co as a student apprentice, then on staff until 1926; joined Admiralty in 1926 and rose to become Director of Electrical Engineering, 1945-60. Pres, Instn of Electrical Engineers, 1960-61. [WWW]

MARTIN, Sir David CBE, FRSE, FRIC (1914-1976) Studied chemistry at Edinburgh (BSc, 1937; PhD, 1939; Hon DSc, 1968); his administrative abilities diverted him from chemistry to become general secretary of the Chemical Society 1945-7, and a very effective Executive Secretary of the Royal Society, 1947-76. [WWW]

MELVILLE, Sir Harry KCB, FRS (1908-   ) Studied chemistry at Edinburgh (BSc, 1930; PhD, 1932) and at Cambridge; Prof of Chemistry at Aberdeen 1940-8 and Birmingham 1948-56. Noted for his studies of the kinetics of polymerization chain reactions. Secretary to the DSIR, 1956-65; Principal of Queen Mary College, University of London 1967-76. Davy Medallist, Royal Society, 1955. Publ *Experimental Methods in Gas Reactions* (with A Farkas, 1938). [WW]

OPPENHEIM, Tan Sri Sir Alexander OBE FRSE (1903-   ) Studied at Oxford and lectured in Mathematics at Edinburgh, 1930-31; Professor of Mathematics, 1931-42, 1945-57 and Dep Principal, 1947, 1949 of Raffles College in Singapore; Vice-Chancellor of the University of Malaya, 1957-65. [WW]

RAEBURN, John CBE, FRSE (1912-) Studied agriculture at Edinburgh (BSc, 1932) and at Cornell, New York. Prof and Head of Department of Agriculture, Aberdeen, 1959-78. Vice-Pres, Intnl Assoc of Agricultural Economists, 1964-70. Publ *Problems in the Mechanisation of Native Agriculture in tropical African Territories* (jtly, 1950). [WW, WWIS]

ROBINSON, Harold FRS (1889-1955) Studied physics at Manchester and Cambridge; lecturer 1923-4 and Reader 1924-6 in Natural Philosophy at Edinburgh; Prof of Physics at Cardiff, 1926-30; Prof of Physics and Vice-Principal, Queen Mary College, London, 1930-55. Publ numerous papers on radio-activity and atomic structure. [WWW]

SEMPLE, John   MRIA   (1904-1985) Studied at Belfast and Cambridge; lecturer in Mathematics at Edinburgh, 1929-30, before being appointed to Chairs of Mathematics at Queen's University, Belfast, 1930-36 and King's College, London, 1936-69. He published several books and many papers, mainly on topics in algebraic geometry. [WWW]

SMITH, Robert CBE, FRS, PresRSE (1909-1980) Studied physics at Edinburgh (MA, 1930); worked at the Cavendish Lab, Cambridge then lectured at St Andrews and Reading until 1939 when he joined the TRE at Malvern; Prof of Physics at Sheffield, 1961-62 and at MIT, 1962-67. Principal of Heriot-Watt University, 1968-79. Publ *Radio Aids to Navigation* (1947), *The Physical Principles of Thermodynamics* (1952), *Semiconductors* (1959), *The Wave Mechanics of Crystalline Solids* (1961). [CSBD, WWW]

TAYLOR, Sir George FRS, FRSE, FLS (1904-1993) Studied botany at Edinburgh (BSc, 1926; DSc, 1934); member and leader of botanical expeditions in the Sino-Himalayan region and elsewhere; Director of the Royal Botanic Gardens at Kew, 1956-71. Publ

An Account of the Genus Meconopsis (1934). [CSBD, WWW]

WALKER, Arthur FRS, FRSE (1909-) Studied mathematics at Oxford and Edinburgh (PhD, 1933; DSc, 1945); Prof of Mathematics at Sheffield, 1947-52, and Prof of Pure Mathematics at Liverpool 1952-74. Publ *Harmonic Spaces* (with Ruse and Willmore, 1962). [WW]

WALLS, Henry (1907-   ) Studied chemistry at Edinburgh (BSc, 1930; PhD, 1933); research in physical chemistry at Munich, Edinburgh and Bristol; Director of Home Office Forensic Science Laboratory 1958-64, then Director of Metropolitan Police Laboratory 1964-68. Publ *Forensic Science* (1968 rev 1974); *Drink, Drugs and Driving* (with A Brownlie, 1969 rev 1985); *Expert Witness* (1972). [WW]

CHAPTER   7

War and austerity, 1939 - 1955

During 1938/39 many provisional arrangements affecting the universities 'in the event of hostilities' were discussed by the UGC and the CVCP with **Sir John Anderson** (MA, BSc, 1903), then Lord Privy Seal with special responsibility for anticipating such problems. Early in 1939 the CVCP sent a memorandum outlining the services that the universities might be able to offer in science, technology, medicine, agriculture and administration: the lessons of WWI had been learned and remembered.

The Ministry of Labour and National Service had already taken in hand the registration of the universities' academic staffs to ensure that the best use would be made of their expertise in the event of war. The Ministry of Works were making arrangements to coordinate demands by Service and other Departments for the requisition of university buildings. When war was declared on 3 September 1939 it had long been regarded by most people as inevitable; in April young men of 20-21 had already been called up; on 31 August women and children began to be evacuated from London; on 2 September the National Service Bill, making men aged 19-41 liable for military service, became law.

In December 1941 the age of conscription was lowered to 18½, and single women 20-30 became liable for military service. By 1943 the age of conscription had been further lowered to 18, but deferment was still granted under increasingly strict conditions to men and women undertaking courses in medicine and some of the sciences. After the success of the Allied landings in Normandy in June 1944 it was possible, indeed necessary, to plan realistically for peace and reconstruction, in education as in other spheres of life. The Education Acts of 1944 and 1945, for example, encouraged the notions of higher education for all, and university places for all who would benefit, aided by a much more widespread scheme of local authority and state grants. The school leaving age was raised to 15 in 1947 as a consequence of the 1944 Act – the intention was to raise it to 16 as soon as practicable, but that was only achieved in 1973.

The continuing disruption caused by the war and its aftermath was illustrated by the fact that the Ministry of Labour and National Service laid down that 90% of university places in 1946 were to be filled by ex-servicemen. The Barlow Committee (of which Sir Edward Appleton was a member) in its 1946 Report *Scientific Manpower*, recommended that the existing 55,000 total of undergraduate students in all faculties should be increased to 90,000 by 1955, and that in particular the universities' output of graduates in science and technology should be doubled. In fact this target was achieved within five years despite all the post-war shortages of building materials and laboratory equipment.

Also in 1946 extended terms of reference were laid down for the UGC, which had previously been limited to advising the Government on the financial needs of the universities and allocating the overall Treasury grant accordingly. In future it was to take

G

a broader and longer-term view of university education both at home and abroad, and assist in the preparation and execution of plans for the development of the universities in order to ensure that they were fully adequate to national needs. The UGC estimated a requirement of £40m for new buildings and £10m for sites and equipment during the quinquennium 1947-52 – in the event, in the very difficult post-war situation only £20m could be allocated, and only £13m was actually spent, because of restrictions on new building made worse by shortages of building materials. It might come as a surprise to readers under the age of fifty that several years after the end of the war food, sweets, clothing, petrol, paper, furniture and building materials were still rationed. That was what 'austerity' meant to the people of Britain.

Two significant changes in the pre-war and post-war funding of the universities should be mentioned: firstly, the proportion of their total income derived from the Treasury increased from 34.3 per cent in 1935-36 to 52.7 per cent in 1946-47, to 69.8 per cent in 1956-57 and to 75.4 per cent in 1966-67; and secondly, the provision of Treasury/UGC non-recurrent grants for buildings, sites and equipment was brought more into line with the universities' needs in a period of hectic expansion. Before the war it was very unusual for any substantial government grant to be given for a new university building; the pre-war King's Buildings, for example, were financed in most cases by generous individuals and charitable trusts, together with what the University itself could afford. It was recognised, however, that the planned expansion of the universities in the 1950s, involving an estimated expenditure in excess of £50m, could not be carried out on the same basis.

In 1947-48 the UGC introduced a scheme of grants to universities for the promotion of postgraduate studies, and in that year Edinburgh was given the sum of £7000 to be divided into studentships of £300 per annum, maintenance grants, and Fellowships of £650 or more per annum.

The University of Edinburgh

The effects of WWII on the University of Edinburgh, though considerable, were not as severe as on some other British universities. It was expected that the city of London would be subjected to heavy air attack and pre-arranged plans for the evacuation and dispersal of the whole University were put into operation in 1939. This proved to have been a wise precaution as damage was caused to many University buildings, some being completely destroyed. Edinburgh had been warned that it might have to accommodate some part of one of the London Colleges, but that did not happen.

The threat of air raids was taken very seriously everywhere, however, and to avoid black-out hazards time-tables were rearranged so that classes met only during daylight hours. The Christmas vacation was extended and the Easter vacation shortened. Air-raid shelters of various kinds were constructed by staff and students during the summer of 1939. From the outset of WWII most medical students and a good many in the Faculty of Science were deferred from liability to military service until they had completed their courses. On the other hand, about one in three of the medical and scientific members of staff, and others, were drafted into more essential war work, putting a heavy burden on those still engaged in teaching (including accelerated and special short courses), with increased administration and fire-watching or home guard duties.

Numbers of matriculated students did not show the dramatic fall that occurred in WWI, but the post-war increase, though less in percentage terms, was much larger numerically:–

	All Faculties: Total	Faculty of Science: Men	Women	Total
1938-39	3826	593	79	672
1939-40	3217	502	96	598
1940-41	3059	576	82	658
1941-42	3257	-	-	821
1942-43	3407	-	-	900
1943-44	3519	-	-	875
1944-45	3642	-	-	852
1945-46	4784	783	190	973
1946-47	5914	967	181	1148
1947-48	6457	1145	202	1347

By 1947/48 the Edinburgh University *Journal* was expressing anxiety about the growth in student numbers, and more than once stated its editorial view that a traditional Scottish University such as Edinburgh could not take more than about 4000 students 'without grave danger of losing its corporate identity and becoming a mere aggregate of technical departments.'

The University introduced in 1942 what it called 'War Degrees' in Arts and Pure Science, towards which twelve months' service in the Forces (after at least one year of study had been completed) would be reckoned as equivalent to one year of academic attendance. An Ordinary MA or BSc could thus be awarded after only two years, and an unclassed 'War Honours' Degree after three. At the same time the University acknowledged that special concessions would have to be made for those commencing their studies after war service, and for those who had completed a significant period of academic study as prisoners of war.

In the Edinburgh University *Journal* of Autumn, 1942, there was a reminder that even in the depths of WWII some thought was being given to a better future. Prof Ritchie, of the Chair of Natural History and at the time Dean of the Faculty of Science, was appointed to a Committee to investigate Nature Reserves, set up by the Standing Committee on Nature Preservation in Post-War Reconstruction.

In the autumn of 1946 a news item headed 'University Building Plans' appeared in the Edinburgh University *Journal*, referring guardedly to the anticipated large increases in student numbers and in government spending on university buildings, and to the University's building plans which had been submitted to the Town Council.

'The key to the whole plan is George Square, which might be said to be ready designed for an academic quadrangle . . . . it is proposed now to occupy all the four sides of the Square with buildings for teaching, for the Medical Library, and for the central administration; and some, at any rate, of the subjects now located at West Mains are to be transferred here, and so brought back into immediate contact with the rest. The King's Buildings will remain, but will be used mainly for advanced research work and other University purposes. . . Thus the three major Faculties of Arts, Medicine and Science will be adequately housed in one single continuous area.'

In the summer of 1951 the whole plan was still on the architect's drawing-board, with the exception of the extension to the Medical Buildings in the north west corner of George Square, which had been given planning permission by the Town Council as a particularly urgent requirement. It was to take another ten years of deliberation, debate and public argument before the redevelopment of the Square could begin with the construction of the David Hume Tower, and long before then all thoughts of moving any part of the King's Buildings back into the central area had vanished. In fact, although a planning statement as late as 1960 proposed that Mathematics should join Natural Philosophy at High School Yards, by the mid-sixties it had finally been decided that they should both, with a few other central area residents, pack their bags and head south to the King's Buildings.

The Faculty of Arts

The Faculty of Arts in 1949 consisted of the following Departments:-

Language and Literature	Science
Mental Philosophy	Education
History and Law	Commerce
Social Study.	

Under 'Department of Science' were listed courses in Mathematics, Mathematical Physics (Applied Mathematics), Natural Philosophy, Meteorology, Astronomy, Chemistry, Zoology, Botany, Geology and Geography.

The Faculty of Science

In 1940 **Prof James Ritchie** (Natural History) was elected Dean in succession to the late Prof Sir Thomas Hudson Beare, who had acted as Dean since 1914. Early in the war the universities instituted, at the request of the Service Departments, special six months' courses (later extended to one year) for cadets of the Royal Artillery, the Royal Engineers, the Royal Corps of Signals and the Royal Air Force. These courses, with a substantial content of science and technology, were attended by large numbers of enlisted men, and made considerable demands on university staff and resources already under pressure. In the summer of 1941 a scheme of state bursaries was introduced, meeting the full costs of tuition and residence, initially for students taking radio, engineering and chemistry courses. Two thousand bursaries were awarded in October 1941, and the range of qualifying subjects was later extended to other scientific and technical subjects.

In 1941 the University Court introduced a new Ordinance for Degrees in Pure Science, superseding No 35 of 1921, which rather illogically had required four years of study for both Ordinary and Honours Degrees. The principal effect of Ordinance No 68 was to reduce the period for an Ordinary Degree to three years, and the minimum number of courses to be attended from nine to seven.

Shortened war degree courses were introduced in 1943 to comply with revised regulations of the Ministry of Labour and National Service. To allow students in some branches of Applied Science, especially engineering, to obtain an Ordinary BSc in two years and three months a fourth term in the summer vacation was added in the first two years, and the course (of the full nine terms) was then completed by the end of the first term of the third year. In 1944 special arrangements were made by the Ministry of Supply for the universities and other research establishments to be allowed priority in obtaining useful items of equipment from the vast hoards of Government surplus stores that became available when the war ended.

In the 1950s there was a growing demand for science graduates in both old-established and new industries (electronics, chemicals, atomic power etc). At the same time came the realisation that there was a place in many industries for the pure scientists, such as mathematicians, for work in departments of economic analysis and statistics. There was one category of graduate, however, still not generally welcomed or even accepted by British industrial firms, and that was the woman scientist or technologist. Conversely it must be said that a career in industry was not the preferred choice of many women graduates in science or any other faculty.

The annual Summer Meeting of the British Association for the Advancement of Science was held in Edinburgh in August 1951, attracting more than 4000 members and guests. Most of the sections met in University premises and the plenary sessions were notable for the fact that the proceedings in the McEwan Hall were relayed by television to the Usher Hall, more than half a mile away. This was a remarkably successful experiment initiated by the Principal, Sir Edward Appleton, especially when it is remembered that it was the following year before the first BBC television reached central Scotland by microwave link to Kirk O'Shotts.

Agriculture

Towards the end of the war in 1944 **Stephen Watson** became the seventh Professor of Agriculture and Rural Economy and Principal of the Edinburgh and East of Scotland College of Agriculture. At that time the University teaching staff consisted of the Professor and two lecturers. Three years later a great step forward was taken with the purchase, by the University Court, of the Bush and Dryden Estates, extending to some 1300 acres of land on the southern outskirts of Edinburgh, and the establishment of the Edinburgh Centre for Rural Economy.

Prof Watson was an agricultural scientist of international stature through his work on the production and conservation of grass and forage crops, and on animal nutrition. His reputation was enhanced by the wide acceptance of the ten books he wrote, some in collaboration with his colleagues, including *Silage and Crop Preservation* (1938), *Feeding of Livestock* (1949) and *Silage* (with Dr A M Smith, 1951).

In 1949 the first year classes for the degree of BSc (Agric) were taught entirely by the departments of Pure Science ie Chemistry, Botany, Zoology and Physics. The second and third years each consisted of about 35 students, and in addition some 20 to 25 students took a special course in Agriculture of two terms' duration. About ten students annually took a postgraduate Diploma in Agricultural Science. There were also some 100 matriculated but non-graduating students attending classes in the University Department of Agriculture, 50 in each year of the course leading to the Scottish Diplomas in Agriculture, Horticulture or Dairying awarded by the College of Agriculture.

Astronomy

Professor William Greaves had occupied the Chair of Astronomy for only a year when WWII seriously interrupted the new spectrophotometric research he had initiated. The strict black-out regulations slowed up and finally halted all observational work 'for the duration', but the ROE maintained from the end of 1940 the vital national service of a back-up to the Greenwich time signals. Greaves had hardly completed the installation of the necessary equipment when in January 1941 Greenwich was put out of action by an enemy air raid and Edinburgh was able to take over without any interruption of the service.

In 1951 the first full-time University lecturer in Astronomy was appointed; prior to that time Prof Greaves had the assistance of a lecturer from the Department of Mathematical Physics. The Observatory's research in the 1950s was concentrated on star clusters, the mechanisms of star formation and the nature of the interstellar medium. Much intensive work was done on stellar spectrograms, but in the days before computers the calculations were extremely laborious and time-consuming. The results appeared in the new series of *Publications of the Royal Observatory Edinburgh*.

Botany

In 1949 under Prof Wright Smith the first year undergraduate class numbered about 100 students in Pure Science, Agriculture and Forestry. Medical students attending for the summer term numbered about 200. Students taking honours in botany attended for four years. There were also classes in Agricultural Botany and Agricultural Mycology, in Forest Botany, Forest Mycology, and in Indian and Colonial Forest Trees. The total number of students was little short of 500.

The research work being undertaken was very varied – problems in plant physiology, investigations into plant diseases, the analysis of timber, and the identification of plants from explorations abroad, entailing the description and publication of new species. The laboratories were extensively used by postgraduate students, and in addition there was a considerable amount of advisory work for Government departments, industrial firms and other organisations.

Chemistry

Throughout the whole of this period Prof Kendall occupied the Chair of Chemistry, but he was joined in 1947 by **Edmund Hirst** who was appointed to the new Forbes Chair of Organic Chemistry. A graduate of St Andrews University, where he worked with Norman Haworth, he had occupied chairs in Bristol and Manchester before coming to Edinburgh. He was an outstanding research chemist with an international reputation even before his arrival in Edinburgh, and he quickly revitalised the Department's research which had languished as Kendall became increasingly involved in administration and the many problems resulting from the war.

While at the University of Bristol during the war Prof Hirst was Head of the Armament Research Department and Chairman of the Chemical Explosives Committee. Hirst and Haworth collaborated over a long period in the field of carbohydrate chemistry, working on the structure and methods for the synthesis of various sugars. Their greatest achievement was the discovery of the structure of vitamin C, and its synthesis in the laboratory – the first vitamin to be made artificially.

In 1949 the first-year chemistry class was divided as follows:-

Pure Science, Tech Chem, Arts	110
Agriculture and Forestry	70
Engineering and Mining	60

The Industrial Liaison Committee brochure in 1949 noted that the staff of the Department of Chemistry were frequently called upon to advise Government Departments, industrial firms and private individuals on problems connected with all fields of chemistry – inorganic, physical, organic, analytical and technical.

The Department reassumed in 1952 responsibility for the teaching of chemistry to medical students, which it had given up in 1919 when the Department of Chemistry in Relation to Medicine (subsequently renamed Biochemistry) was founded in the Faculty of Medicine. This change brought four new lecturers and six assistants (who in turn became lecturers) – a substantial increase in the teaching staff.

Engineering, and Mining

In June 1940 Professor Sir Thomas Hudson Beare, in his thirty-ninth year in the Chair of Engineering, died at the age of 81. He had seen the Department grow from a handful of students in the basement of the Old College to more than a hundred occupying what the Edinburgh University *Journal* called 'one of the best planned and equipped engineering schools in the Empire.' He was Dean of the Faculty of Science for more than a quarter of a century, and held the record for the longest time, thirty-two years, as a member of the University Court.

The chair was left vacant during the war and **Major John B Todd**, Reader in Engineering, became the acting Head of Department. He graduated BSc with Distinction in Engineering in 1909 and commanded a siege battery in France in 1918, when he was mentioned in French Dispatches and received the *Croix de Guerre*. From 1943 to 1945 he carried a particularly heavy burden when the Department of Engineering had a four-term teaching session, as well as running special short courses for large numbers of prospective candidates for war service commissions.

In 1946 **Ronald Arnold** was appointed the fourth Regius Professor of Engineering. He graduated BSc in Mechanical Engineering at Glasgow in 1932, and later also took his DSc there. Although Edinburgh had only the one Department of Engineering, three-year ordinary and honours BSc degree courses were offered in civil, mechanical, and electrical engineering, and in mining. By 1949 there were about 70 students in each year, or just over 200 in all. The Department had never been particularly active in research, and Arnold lost no time in recruiting research staff to work in the field of applied dynamics.

The expansion and sub-division of the Department began in 1948 when W E J (Ewart) Farvis was appointed Lecturer in Applied Electricity. During the war he was a Senior Scientific Officer at the Telecommunications Research Establishment, Malvern. Some electrical teaching was taken over from the Heriot-Watt College and the first lines of research in gaseous electronics and radio engineering were established.

Sir Edward Appleton, Principal and Vice-Chancellor, 1949-65

Robert McAdam became in 1948 the James A Hood Professor of Mining, and Professor of Mining at the Heriot-Watt College. He graduated BSc and PhD at Edinburgh and thereafter gained practical experience in coal mines in Scotland and gold mines in India. His research covered mine surveying, production of oil from coal, geophysical prospecting and mine rescue work. He published *Colliery Surveying* (1953, 2edn, 1963), *Mine Rescue Work* (1955) and *Mining Explosives* (1958). The joint course, and the Chair, ceased to exist in the University of Edinburgh when the Heriot-Watt College became a University in 1966. Prof McAdam continued as Hood Professor of Mining Engineering at the Heriot-Watt University until his retirement.

In 1949 **Sir Edward Appleton** was appointed Principal and Vice-Chancellor of the University. Two years before his arrival in Edinburgh he had been awarded the 1947 **Nobel Prize for Physics** for his work on the physical properties of the upper atmosphere, and especially for his discovery of the eponymous Appleton layer. He looked to the Government for support in building up research in electronics at Edinburgh, and as a result in 1950 the UGC funded a one-year Post-Graduate Diploma course in Electronics and Radio. In addition to Electrical Engineering, the Department of Mathematical Physics, the Royal Observatory and the meteorology section of Natural Philosophy were also involved in this course.

Forestry

In March 1946 the Forestry Commission's Director of Research and Education wrote to the Principal saying that the Commission was in need of more graduate Forest Officers. The Department was already heavily loaded with about 30 students in the second year and 15 in the third, and the University had a commitment to the Indian Government to take up to 15 students per annum for the next ten years. The Forestry Commission therefore offered a grant of £7500, spread over five years, towards an increase in the teaching staff, on condition that some research would be undertaken. Some rather vague exchanges took place between Prof Stebbing and the Commission about research topics, but nothing was done until the arrival of Prof Anderson five years later.

In 1951 Prof Stebbing retired in his 81st year, after 41 years at the head of the Department of Forestry. He is best remembered in the world of tropical forestry for his letters to the press on the dangers of clearing large areas of savannah-woodland, when the East African Groundnuts Scheme was proposed soon after the end of WWII. His warnings, with those of W M Robertson, an Edinburgh Forestry graduate of 1922 who was then Chief Conservator of Forests in Tanganyika, went unheeded, and the grandiose groundnuts scheme ended in disaster.

Mark Anderson was appointed in 1951 the second Professor of Forestry. He graduated at Edinburgh with a BSc in 1919 and the first DSc in Forestry in 1924. He was in the forefront of British foresters because of his scientific approach, but for the same reason he was not universally popular with some of the older staff. From 1946 he had been in the Department of Forestry at Oxford University, and he had a clear idea of the changes needed to bring the Edinburgh course up to date.

Genetics

In August 1939 Prof Crew was recalled to the Royal Army Medical Corps and became involved with work in medical statistics for the War Office. In his absence **Alan Greenwood** became Acting Director of the Institute. Probably the most significant work done during the years of WWII was the research of Auerbach and Robson on chemical mutagenesis. A detailed historical review of their work with *Drosophila* on mustard gas mutagenesis was published in May 1993 by Geoffrey Beale in *Genetics*. Even the most casual reader of Beale's paper could not fail to be struck by the primitive nature of some of these experiments with mustard gas, carried out under conditions that would have made a health and safety officer blench.

On Crew's return from war service in 1944 he resigned from the Institute and took over the Chair of *Public Health and Social Medicine in the Faculty of Medicine. After the end of WWII the Agricultural Research Council decided to initiate a major effort in animal breeding research, centred in a location yet to be selected. **Robert White** was appointed in 1945 Director of the new centre, which was originally called the National Animal Breeding and Genetic Research Organisation; C H Waddington was appointed Chief Geneticist in charge of the genetics section. When shortly afterwards Waddington was offered the Chair of Animal Genetics in Edinburgh University, the decision was taken to locate the new organisation, the Animal Breeding and Genetics Research Organisation (ABGRO), in Edinburgh, with Waddington holding both posts.

C H Waddington was duly appointed to the Buchanan Chair of Animal Genetics in 1946. At Cambridge he graduated with Honours in Geology. During the war he served in the operational research section of Coastal Command, RAF, and for the last year of the war he was scientific adviser to the Commander-in-Chief. He always said that his experience of operational research during the war profoundly influenced his subsequent outlook on scientific research.

In 1947 the ABGRO moved to Edinburgh from its temporary quarters in London, the main part of it occupying at first a large house in the Grange district of Edinburgh. The Genetics Section was housed at the King's Buildings along with the University Department in what is now the Crew Building, at that time the Institute of Animal Genetics. A postgraduate Diploma in Genetics was introduced in 1949. In 1951 **Hugh Donald** succeeded White as Director of the ABGRO, and the opportunity was taken to divide the rather unwieldy organisation into two, the Genetics Section, and the Animal Breeding Research Organisation (ABRO), both (eventually) on the King's Buildings site.

Geology

In 1943 **Arthur Holmes** succeeded Prof Jehu as the fourth Regius Professor of Geology. His inaugural lecture on 28 October of that year was on the subject of 'The Age of the Earth', one in which, he said, he had been actively interested throughout his life as a geologist. A graduate of Imperial College, London in 1910, he was Professor of Geology at the University of Durham from 1925 to 1943. He was a shy, retiring man, not primarily a field geologist, but he was nevertheless a world authority on such major geological theories as the age of the earth and continental drift. He was the author of a large number of notable papers, an outstanding textbook *Principles of Physical Geology* (1944), and *The Age of the Earth* (1913) which passed through at least four editions.

Prof Holmes' wife, **Doris Reynolds**, was also a geologist, one of the first five women elected to membership of the Royal Society of Edinburgh in 1949, along with Charlotte Auerbach and Christina Miller. After lecturing in petrology at London and Durham she was an Honorary Research Fellow at Edinburgh, 1943-62. She published *Elements of Physical Geology* (1969) and undertook the revision of her husband's *Principles of Physical Geology* for the third edition in 1978.

In 1949 the numbers of students attending the various first-year undergraduate courses in geology were as follows:-

Arts	130
Pure Science	50
Mining	20
Agriculture, Engineering and Forestry	120

Advanced and Honours courses were attended by 10-15 and 4-12 students annually, and there were in the Department nine research workers aiming at higher degrees or pursuing their own researches. At that time research was largely concentrated on (a) the problem of the origin of granite and related rocks, and (b) palaeontology and its applications to historical geology. The advice of the staff was often sought on a great variety of geological problems, particularly in relation to water supply, and the identification of specimens.

Mathematics

In 1946 **Alexander Aitken** became the fifteenth Professor of Mathematics, in succession to Professor Sir Edmund Whittaker. Born in New Zealand, he entered Edinburgh University as a post-graduate student in 1923, becoming Reader in Statistics in 1937. He had a phenomenal faculty of rapid mental calculation and an equally impressive numerical memory; he could recite the value of π to a thousand places of decimals. He wrote an account of his WWI experiences, *Gallipoli to the Somme* (1963) which was awarded the Hawthornden Prize. In that book he recalled that when on active service in France the platoon roll-book had been lost, and he was able to provide from memory the full name and number of every man. He also acted as one of the General Editors, and wrote several volumes himself, of the University Mathematical Texts published by Oliver and Boyd from 1939 onwards.

The undergraduate classes in mathematics and the numbers attending in 1949 were as follows:–

First Ordinary Mathematics	90
Second Ordinary Mathematics	180
Intermediate Honours	70
Honours	40
Technical Mathematics (three years total)	180
Statistics (four years total)	100

Natural Philosophy, and Mathematical Physics

In 1945 **Norman Feather** succeeded Charles Barkla as twelfth Professor of Natural Philosophy. He undertook a radical overhaul of the undergraduate course, and instituted joint honours degrees with other science departments such as Astronomy, Chemistry and Electrical Engineering. His research was mainly on β-ray spectroscopy and nuclear ternary fission. His publications included *Life of Lord Rutherford* (1940); *Nuclear Stability Rules* (1952); *The Physics of Mass, Length and Time* (1959 repr 1968); *Vibrations and Waves* (1962); *Electricity and Matter* (1968); *Matter and Motion* (1970); and *Values in Education and Society* (1976). As well as being Dean of the Faculty of Science (1971-74), he also served, rather surprisingly, twice as Dean of the Faculty of Music.

In the Autumn Term of 1949 the ten Gifford Lectures were given by **Professor Niels Bohr**, of the University of Copenhagen, on *Causality and Complementarity: Epistemological Lessons of Studies in Atomic Physics*. On three days after the conclusion of his lectures Profesor Bohr participated in an informal conference on 'Elementary Particles' held in the Department of Natural Philosophy, attended by more than a hundred of Europe's most eminent physicists.

In 1949 the numbers of students taught in the natural philosophy classes were as follows:–

Arts and Science Ordinary	220
Agriculture and Forestry	60
Medical Physics	200
Veterinary Physics	40
Intermediate Honours	70
Final Honours (two years)	60

The main field of research was nuclear physics, and chiefly the development of new types of magnetic focusing instrument for fundamental studies of the radiations emitted by naturally and artificially β-radioactive substances.

The Chair of Mathematical Physics was occupied until 1953 by Max Born, who had the assistance of two lecturers in providing courses at all levels from first year to final honours. The syllabus of Course I concentrated on elementary mechanics and hydrostatics, while Course IV dealt mainly with statistical mechanics, thermodynamics and quantum theory. Research in the Department at that time included work on the dynamical theory of crystal lattices, the theory of quantised fields, the electronic theory of metals, and various topics in nuclear physics. The number of departmental research publications from 1935 to 1949 was about 125.

Veterinary Science

In 1951 the College became a constituent part of the University within the Faculty of Medicine and was designated the Royal (Dick) School of Veterinary Studies. The degree of BSc in Veterinary Science was replaced by the new degrees of BVMS and DVMS. The Professor of Veterinary Hygiene and Preventive Medicine was admitted to membership of the Faculty of Science. In 1964 the University created a Faculty of Veterinary Medicine.

Zoology

In 1949 the Department's undergraduate teaching was concerned with students of Medicine and Dental Surgery (250), Pure Science and Arts (100), Agriculture and Forestry (65), and Veterinary Science (20). Postgraduate classes were conducted in Entomology and Parasitology for the Diplomas in Public Health and in Tropical Medicine and Hygiene. There were ten research workers and associated technicians, some supported by grants from the ARC. Members of staff were frequently called upon to advise on problems connected with fresh-water fisheries, protection of wild birds, agricultural pests, parasites of domestic stock, insect damage in furniture and so on.

Michael Swann (Baron Swann, 1981) became in 1952 the tenth Professor of Natural History, in the Faculties of Science and Medicine. He was only 32 when appointed to the Chair from Cambridge, with a remit to switch the emphasis in the Department more strongly towards the cellular aspects of zoology. Not long after his arrival Murdoch Mitchison, who had worked with him in Cambridge, joined the staff and continued his research into aspects of cell division. Some time later they were joined by Peter Walker from King's College, London.

Within a short space of time Swann revitalised the Department and in the process managed to obtain funding to replace some of the more antiquated equipment, such as the microscopes for student use which had been presented by the Carnegie Trust in 1875! A small suite of research laboratories was built behind the Ashworth Building for staff and postgraduates, and in 1967 a large four-storey extension was added to the south end of the building.

Some Notable Edinburgh University Scientists and Engineers, 1939-1955

CALLAN, Harold (Mick) FRS, FRSE (1917-1993) Studied at St John's College, Oxford; TRE, Malvern, 1940-45; SSO in ARC Institute of Animal Genetics, Edinburgh, 1946-50; Prof of Natural History at St Andrews, 1950-82. Publ *Lampbrush Chromosomes* (1986), and many scientific papers, mostly on cytology and cell physiology. [WWW]

CASSELS, John FRS, FRSE (1922-   ) Studied mathematics at Edinburgh (MA, 1943) and at Cambridge (PhD, 1949). Lecturer and Reader at Manchester and Cambridge; Sadleirian Prof of Pure Mathematics at Cambridge 1967-84. Sylvester Medal, Royal Society, 1973; Hon ScD, Edinburgh, 1977. Publ *An Introduction to Diophantine Approximation* (1957); *An Introduction to the Geometry of Numbers* (1959); *Rational Quadratic Forms* (1978); *Economics for Mathematicians* (1981) and *Local Fields* (1986). [WW]

COWIE, John FRSE (1933-   ) Studied chemistry at Edinburgh (BSc, 1955; PhD, 1958); Assistant Lecturer at Edinburgh 1956-8. Research Officer, National Research Council of Canada, 1958-67; Lecturer and Senior Lecturer at Essex and Stirling, 1967-73. Prof of Chemistry at Stirling 1973-88; Prof of Chemistry of Materials at Heriot-Watt University, Edinburgh, since 1988. [WWIS, WWISIE]

CUNNINGHAM, Robert CMG (1923-   ) Studied zoology at Edinburgh (BSc, 1947) and

London (PhD). RAF, 1942-46. Research on soil chemistry and plant nutrition at Rothamsted and in various countries overseas. Prof of Chemistry and Soil Science in University of the West Indies, Trinidad, 1964-67. Adviser, then Chief Natural Resources Adviser, Overseas Development Administration, 1967-83. [WW]

GANE, Michael (1927-) Studied at Edinburgh (BSc Forestry, 1948), London (BSc Econ, 1963) and Oxford (DPhil, MA, 1967); Assistant Conservator of Forests, Tanganyika 1948-62; with Commonwealth Forestry Institute 1963-9; Director of Project Planning Centre for developing countries at Bradford University 1969-74 then Director, England, Nature Conservancy Council, 1974-81. [WW]

GLENNIE, Kenneth (1926-) Studied geology at Edinburgh, gaining the first MSc in a Scottish University; joined Shell Oil in 1954, eventually becoming a world figure in petroleum geology. Editor and a principal author of *Petroleum Geology of the North Sea* (3edn, 1990). Made a special study of ancient and modern deserts. [CSBD]

HENDERSON, James CVO (1923-) Studied at Glasgow (MA) and Edinburgh (DSc); from 1943 undertook extensive research in RAF and Air Ministry into air rockets and guns, becoming eventually Chief Scientist to the RAF (1969-73) and Scientific Advisor to British Aerospace 1978-82. President and Chief Executive of Mastiff Systems US Inc., since 1982. [WW]

LYON, Mary FRS (1925-   ) Studied genetics at Cambridge; member of the MRC Scientific Staff, Institute of Animal Genetics at Edinburgh, 1950-55. With the MRC Radiobiology Unit, Harwell from 1955; Head of the Genetics Division since 1962. Royal Medal of the Royal Society, 1984. [WW]

McCALLUM, Sir Donald CBE, FEng, FRSE (1922-) Studied engineering at Edinburgh (BSc, 1942). Admiralty Signal Establishment, 1942-46. Joined Ferranti, 1947; General Manager, Scottish Group, 1968-85. Chairman of Ferranti Defence Systems Ltd, and of Ferranti Industrial Electronics Ltd, since 1984. [WWIS, WW]

MANNERS, David FRSE (1928-   ) Studied chemistry at Cambridge; lecturer / reader in Chemistry at Edinburgh 1952-65; Meldola Medal, Royal Institute of Chemistry, 1957. Prof of Biochemistry at Heriot-Watt University, 1965, now Emeritus. [WWIS]

MONTEITH, John FRS, FRSE (1929-   ) Studied physics at Edinburgh (BSc, 1951) and London. Research at Rothamsted Experimental Station, 1954-67. Prof of Environmental Physics at Nottingham, 1967-86. Member of NERC, 1980-84. Hon Prof at Edinburgh University, 1989. Publ *Instruments for Micrometeorology* (ed, 1972); *Principles of Environmental Physics* (1973; with M H Unsworth, 2edn, 1988). [WW, WWISIE]

PRINGLE, Robert OBE, FRSE, FRS(Can) (1920-   ) Studied physics at Edinburgh (BSc, 1942; PhD, 1944) and lectured there from 1945-9; Prof of Physics at Manitoba University, 1949-56; founded in Edinburgh Nuclear Enterprises Ltd. in 1956, becoming President in 1976. Publ papers on nuclear spectroscopy and nuclear geophysics. [WW, CSBD]

RICHARDSON, Harold FRSE (1907-1982) Studied physics at London; research at Cavendish Laboratory, Cambridge, on the magnetic focusing of electrons and the design of magnets; lecturer in natural philosophy at Edinburgh, 1946-51 (DSc), Reader, 1951-52; Prof of Physics at Exeter, 1952-56, then London, 1956-73. [WWW]

TROTMAN-DICKENSON, Sir Aubrey (1926-   ) Studied chemistry at Oxford, Manchester and Edinburgh (DSc); lecturer in chemistry at Edinburgh 1954-60. Prof, Univ Coll of Wales, Aberystwyth, 1960-68; Principal, Univ of Wales College of Cardiff, since 1988 (Inst of Science and Technology, Cardiff, 1968-88); Vice-Chancellor, Univ of Wales, 1975-77 and 1983-85. Publ *Gas Kinetics* (1955); *Free Radicals* (1959); *Comprehensive Inorganic Chemistry* (ed, 1973) [WW]

WILSON, Sir Robert CBE, FRS (1927-   ) Studied at King's College, Newcastle upon Tyne and astro-physics at Edinburgh (PhD-Astrophysics, 1952); SSO, ROE, 1952-57. Director, SRC's Astrophysics Research Unit, Culham, 1968-72. Perren Prof of Astronomy and Director of the Observatories, University College, London, since 1972 and Head of Department of Physics and Astronomy, since 1987. Publ many papers on optical astronomy, plasma spectroscopy, solar physics and ultraviolet astronomy. [WW]

WOOD-GUSH, David FRSE (1922-1992) Studied at Witwatersrand, South Africa, and genetics at Edinburgh (PhD, 1945); SPSO, AFRC Poultry Research Centre, and Hon Prof at Edinburgh University (IERM), 1978-1992. A very distinguished animal behaviourist with a strong concern for animal welfare. Publ *Elements of Ethology*. [WWIS]

CHAPTER 8

Science galore – the expansive years, 1955 - 1970

It was about ten years after the end of the war before the British universities began to move forward from survival and recovery into a new era of expansion and progress. The period from 1955 to 1970 was one of steadily increasing student numbers, to an extent that had not been foreseen in the immediate post-war years. In the mid-fifties the demand for university places was expected to reach a total of 135,000 by the end of the sixties. In March 1962 the government stated that it aimed to provide about 170,000 places by 1973/74, but in the meantime it had appointed the Robbins Committee which reported in October 1963. As a result, the number of places to be provided was immediately increased to 197,000 (170,000 in the existing universities) by 1967/68 and 218,000 by 1973/74. In science and technology the universities and technical colleges were given the target of doubling their 1955 output of professional graduates by the late sixties, from about 10,000 to 20,000 a year.

The Reports of the UGC, on which Tables 8.1 and 8.2 are based, show the scale of the actual increase in Britain's university population from 1938 to 1968 – a four-fold increase in thirty years, with student numbers more than doubling in the last decade. The most striking change was in the number of post-graduate students, reflecting the increased willingness, even eagerness, of industry and commerce to employ their talents not only in research and development, but in management and production, accounts and sales, where higher degrees had previously been regarded as negative assets.

TABLE 8.1   Students in British Universities, 1938 - 1968.

	Under-graduates:	Post-graduates:	Total:
1938-39	46,908	3,094	50,002
1946-47	64,960	3,492	68,452
1949-50	78,064	7,357	85,421
1954-55	69,493	12,212	81,705
1960-61	89,863	17,836	107,699
1967-68	164,653	35,019	199,672

For a time after the war there was also a significant increase in the proportion of students in science and technology, a welcome trend for the new science-based industries that were finding it difficult to recruit well-qualified graduates in sufficient numbers. In many ways graduates in science and technology had never had it so good, but senior school pupils (and careers advisers) evidently were not convinced that science, let alone technology, could be a worth-while career for the brightest sixth-formers. The 'swing from science' which began in the sixties was a serious problem for which no long-term solution has been found, and it is now compounded by a lack of well-qualified teachers of mathematics and science in Britain's secondary schools.

In the second half of the sixties the availability of SRC grants encouraged many of the best science and technology graduates to stay on in the universities for their masters and doctors degrees, and a number of ways of countering this were suggested in the Swann Report, *The Flow into Employment of Scientists, Engineers and Technologists* (Cmnd 3760, HMSO, 1968). A measure of the government's concern about the escalating costs of higher education (Table 8.2) was the publication in 1969 of Shirley Williams' *13 Points* when she was Minister of State at the DES. It consisted of a review of possible economies in higher education, from student loans to shortening of courses, but they were almost all received unenthusiastically, not least by the CVCP in its response in 1970.

The costs involved in such a large-scale expansion of Britain's universities, and other areas of higher education, throughout a decade that was by no means free of economic problems and industrial strife, were further increased by inflation, as shown in Table 8.2.

TABLE 8.2   Totals of recurrent and non-recurrent grant from the UGC to all British universities, 1961-62 to 1981-82.

	Recurrent grant:		Non-recurrent grant:	
	£m	1962 prices	£m	1962 prices
1961-62	51.5	51.5	29.1	29.1
1966-67	139.5	109.5	59.1	46.4
1971-72	243.7	132.2	71.7	38.9
1976-77	607.0	163.8	79.1	21.3
1981-82	1016.2	136.6	103.4	13.9

In any discussion that touches on the growth of science it is refreshing to recall the much-quoted prophecy of Derek de Solla Price in his *Little Science, Big Science* (1963), emphasising the apparently relentless exponential growth of science:– 'By 2020, every man, woman, child and dog in the United States will be a scientist, and we will spend more on science than the whole GNP.' Certainly there was a growing awareness in America, Britain and other countries in the 1960s that some thought must be given to the *planning* of expenditure on science – should we plan for a levelling off, and if so when, and how. It underlined our lack of knowledge, and pointed to the fact that research was needed on science itself, as a social system. That was one of the *raisons d'être* of the *Science Studies Unit established at Edinburgh University in 1966.

In 1963 the Trend Committee, of which Prof C H Waddington was a member, was set up to review research provision. Two years later the Science and Technology Act was passed, dissolving the DSIR and setting up the SRC and the NERC, quickly followed by the SSRC. Proposals for research projects and applications for grants continued to come mainly from the academics, and those showing 'timeliness and promise' had a good

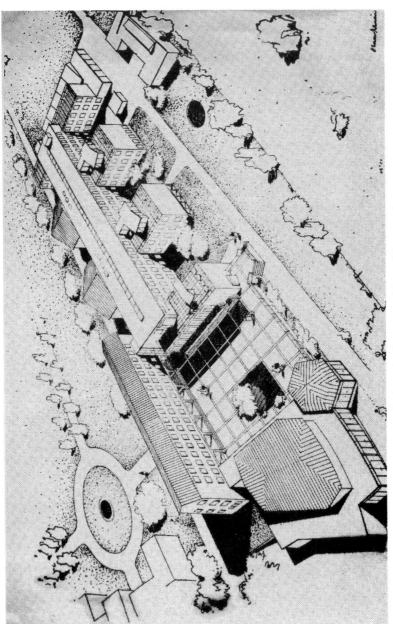

School of Agriculture—architects' impression

chance of getting support. By about 1972, however, a much more commercial attitude prevailed, questioning cost-effectiveness and relevance to the national interest. The universities began to be regarded as a national research resource which could be approached by government departments, private firms or even individuals, with contracts large or small for the research needed to solve specific problems.

Much of the expansion in university education in the late fifties and throughout the sixties was argued in terms of social justice for qualified school leavers more than on the need for technical manpower. It was a period of dramatic and extraordinary change throughout the higher education system, but it was also the period of considerable student unrest, from which Edinburgh was not immune. From our point of view it is perhaps best summed up by Stewart [1989], who saw the years 1960 to 1965 as a high point of public esteem and support for higher education, when optimism, new ideas, expansion and opportunity pervaded the UK universities. Towards the end of the sixties and in the early seventies restraint and control began to be increasingly felt by the universities from such bodies as the government, the UGC, the DES, the CVCP, the research councils, the academic trades unions, some student organisations – and last but by no means least, the economic recession of 1973-76.

The University of Edinburgh

The first of the post-war building projects at the King's Buildings was the ARC Poultry Research Centre begun in 1953, closely followed by the extensive group of buildings forming the Edinburgh School of Agriculture, erected between 1955 and 1960. The same period produced the first extension to the Ashworth Building (Zoology) and a new group of Engineering buildings, but it was the decade of the sixties that saw work in progress over the whole of the King's Buildings site, as the government responded to the pleas and pressures referred to in Chapter 7.

The principal beneficiaries among the Edinburgh science departments of this expansionist policy in the sixties were Botany (the Daniel Rutherford Building); Chemical, Civil and Electrical Engineering; Epigenetics; Forestry and Natural Resources with Molecular Biology (the Darwin Building); Geology; Mathematics, Meteorology, Physics and the Edinburgh Regional Computing Centre (the James Clerk Maxwell Building, Phase 1); the Royal Observatory (new laboratories for the Department of Astronomy); and last but not least, the King's Buildings Centre Refectory.

In the middle of the decade one other specially significant building was completed, an outpost of pure science among the arts and social sciences in and around George Square. This was the first-year science building, conceived by the Principal, Sir Edward Appleton, as an essential step towards the integration of a university divided not only by the gulf between C P Snow's two cultures but by a distance of two miles between the sciences and the non-sciences. The idea was good, enabling practically all science students to spend the greater part of their formative first year within easy reach of the whole range of interests and activities provided by a large cosmopolitan university.

Aerial view of the King's Buildings, looking north

In practice, however, there were problems for both staff and students, and it is doubtful if the benefits to the latter were as great as Sir Edward had hoped. He died almost exactly a year before the building was completed, and it was named after him the Appleton Tower. Today it is the venue for almost all the first-year lecture courses, and some of the laboratories, in applied mathematics, artificial intelligence, astronomy, biology, chemistry, computer science, engineering, geology, information systems, mathematics and physics. When completed in 1966 it was the largest and most expensive of the University's buildings, its 113,000 sq ft having cost rather more than £1.25m in total.

The recurrent grant to Edinburgh University increased from £1m in 1952 to £2.44m in 1962 and £12.47m in 1972. The University's income from research grants (including research contracts) was:-

1956-57	£53,000
1961-62	£185,000
1966-67	£984,000

Finally, at the risk of provoking a sharp attack of nostalgia in some of the older members of staff, it is worth mentioning that in 1965-66 the allocations to Faculties for purchase of Expensive Equipment were:-

Aerial view of George Square, looking north-west

Arts	£1,000
Social Sciences	5,000
Science	24,000
Medicine	16,500
Veterinary Medicine	2,500

The Faculty of Science

In 1953 Peter Schwarz came to Edinburgh as a post-doctoral Fellow in the Department of Chemistry. For more than twenty years until he retired in 1990 he served as Associate- or Vice-Dean, and some of the most interesting information on the Faculty of Science and the Department of Chemistry has been provided by him. Faculty Office in 1953 was situated in the Chemistry Building, with a full-time staff of not more than four or five, coping with about a thousand undergraduates. However, some work such as postgraduate administration was done in the Old College, and some things bore little or no resemblance to their present-day equivalents, such as the UFC breathing down everyone's neck all the time – but on the other hand UCCA didn't exist until 1964, so all applications had to be processed by the Faculty Office.

Professor Swann was the first Dean (in 1963) to appoint an Associate-Dean to assist with the ever-increasing volume of administrative paper-work; by 1967 two Associate-Deans were required. In 1965 Faculty Office moved into more spacious accommodation, a rather utilitarian building which had been originally a pig hut used by the Department of Animal Genetics. To celebrate the centenary of the Faculty in 1993, the Office moved into the refurbished Biophysics extension designed by the College of Art students in 1960. It is to their lasting credit that the Weir Building now has every appearance of having been designed for its present use.

Agriculture

In 1955 **Stephen Watson** had been Professor of the Department and Principal of the College of Agriculture for eleven years, and had seen his teaching staff increase from two to fourteen, enabling him to establish small groups of specialists in such areas as animal production, crop production, chemistry, agricultural economics, and management. He was able to continue this trend through the sixties until his retirement in 1968. He proved himself to be a man of vision and a good administrator as well as a notable scientist. Of his many publications *The Conservation of Grass and Forage Crops* (2nd edn, with M J Nash, 1960) has long been the standard reference on the subject, and has been translated into several other languages.

His greatest and certainly most lasting achievement was the planning and completion of the new Edinburgh School of Agriculture at the King's Buildings. Begun in 1955, it was opened by the Chancellor of the University, the Duke of Edinburgh, in October 1960. At a cost of £370k it provided accommodation for the University's Department of Agriculture and the Edinburgh and East of Scotland College of Agriculture, including the Advisory Service. From session 1964-65 the BSc (Hons) Degree in Agriculture could be taken in one of three Honours Schools:– General Agriculture, Agricultural Economics or Agricultural Science.

In 1966 a Sub-Department of General Microbiology was instituted within the Department of Agriculture. **John Wilkinson** transferred from the Department of Bacteriology in the Faculty of Medicine as Reader and Head of the Sub-Department. Three years later he was appointed to a Personal Chair in Microbiology, Head of the Department of General Microbiology, and first Head of the Microbiology Division of the School of Agriculture. With the assistance of Ian Sutherland who accompanied him from the Medical School, and members of the Agriculture microbiology staff, he established the Honours School in Microbiology. He was recognised as an authority on storage substances in bacteria and with the collaboration of Roger Whittenbury, he initiated work on the microbiology of hydrocarbons, particularly on bacteria capable of growing on methane. Initial support to the project and to the Department came from British Petroleum who then had an interest in the development of 'Single Cell Protein'. The Department was renamed Microbiology in 1971. The Staff of the Department later became involved in various aspects of biotechnology and were involved in the setting up of Bioscot Ltd, a joint venture with the Heriot-Watt University.

Stephen Watson was succeeded in 1968 by **Noel Robertson** as eighth Professor of

Agriculture and Rural Economy, and Principal of the Edinburgh and East of Scotland College of Agriculture. He was a graduate of Edinburgh in botany in 1944, then went as a Colonial Agricultural Service Probationer to Trinity College Cambridge, where he studied both botany and agriculture; for the rest of his life he found it difficult to choose between these two disciplines. He returned to Edinburgh from the Chair of Botany at Hull, and devoted himself with considerable success to building up the resources and the international reputation of the School of Agriculture and its two component parts. After he retired in 1983 he collaborated with Ian J Fleming in writing *Britain's First Chair of Agriculture at the University of Edinburgh, 1790-1990* (1990), from which much of the historical information in this account has been taken.

Artificial Intelligence and Machine Intelligence

The development at Edinburgh University of what were in the 1960s the peculiarly esoteric subjects of artificial intelligence, machine intelligence, cognitive science, metamathematics and epistemics, was due in large measure to a number of unusually perceptive individuals. They came from a remarkable variety of intellectual disciplines, which in itself was an important factor in the success of their collaborative efforts.

For example, **Donald Michie** was educated at Rugby, where he won an Open Major Scholarship in Classics to Oxford, and learnt to play chess. However, the state of the world being what it was in 1942, after setting what was believed to be a record for the shortest period of service as an infantry private, he was posted to Station X, the cypher school at Bletchley Park. There he worked as a member of Max Newman's group, which included Whitehead, Turing and other outstanding mathematicians, on the eventually successful unravelling of the Germans' *Enigma* encoding device. The machine they developed to do the job, which enabled Allied intelligence to decode messages the Germans confidently believed to be completely indecipherable, would today be called a computer.

In spite of this brilliant achievement, with the return of peace it was officially decided that such machines would be too complicated and unreliable to have applications in industry, commerce or scientific research, and the group at Bletchley was disbanded. Michie went up to Oxford, but switched from classics to medicine. In 1961 he was offered a non-teaching Senior Lectureship in Immunology in Edinburgh University's Faculty of Medicine, where he developed statistical tests for tissue matches in kidney transplants that are the standard technique today. From this period came his first book *An Introduction to Molecular Biology* (jointly, 1964).

His interest in computers, and his belief in the possibility of constructing thinking and learning machines, remained unshaken by official indifference, and in October 1962 there was published in the University of Edinburgh *Gazette* the substance of a talk given by him to the Edinburgh Philosophy of Science Group, entitled *The Effect of Computers on the Character of Science*. He began by saying:–

"I believe that computers are going to change the face of science in our lifetime. In

Plate 1.   James Hutton [Raeburn, c1785]
During a long weary tour including Birmingham, Bath, Wales and Anglesey Hutton
was saddlesore, weary and lonely long before he got home. He wrote to his friend
George Clerk Maxwell: – 'Lord pity the arse that's clagged to a head that will hunt
stones. I begin to be tired of speaking to stones and long for a fresh bit of mortality
to make sauce to them'.

Plate 2. Ornamental Table
Designed by D F Mackenzie of
Mortonhall and made by W R Swann of
Gilmerton, the table consists of nearly
1,000 pieces of 60 different home-grown
woods. It was awarded a Gold Medal by
the Royal Scottish Arboricultural
Society in 1883, and was presented by the
Mackenzie family to the Department of
Forestry and Natural Resources.

Plate 3. Waves breaking
Series of waves breaking in the
computer-controlled laboratory
wave tank in the Department of Physics.

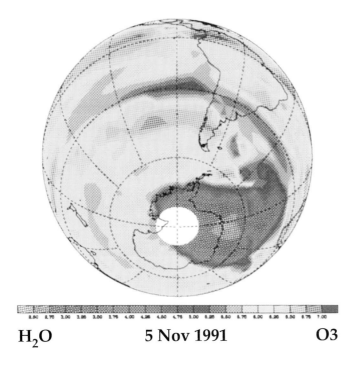

H$_2$O   **5 Nov 1991**   O3

Plates 4a, 4b. Upper atmosphere maps
The remnants of the ozone hole near the south pole in 1991 and unusually low ozone amounts over the northern hemisphere in 1993, as taken by the Microwave Limb Sounder instrument on NASA's Upper Atmosphere Research Satellite. The Department of Meteorology is part of the consortium which developed and operates this instrument.

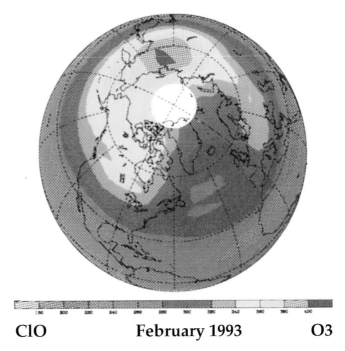

ClO   **February 1993**   O3

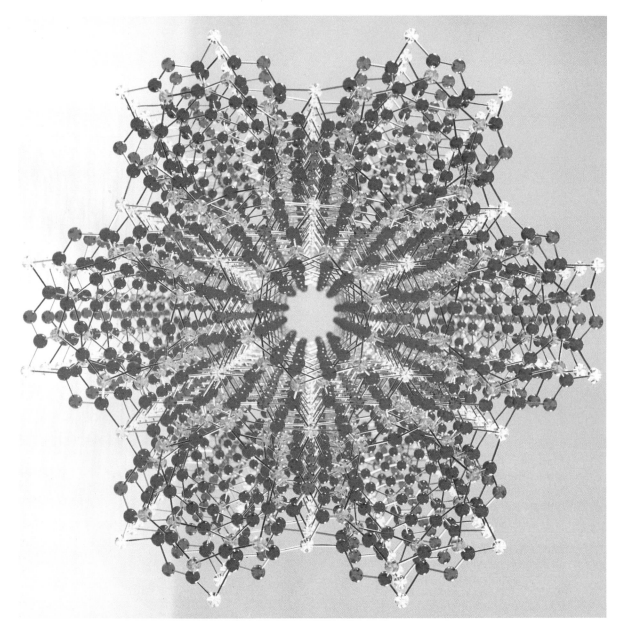

Plate 5.   Crystal of Beryl
Made from standard components produced by Beevers Molecular Models

Plate 6. X-ray Crystallography apparatus
Department of Chemistry

Plate 7. Fractal growth
A computer-simulated aggregation of particles.

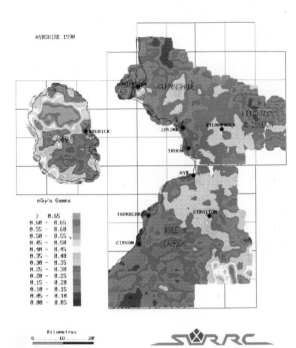

Plate 8.   Radiation maps
Maps produced by the Scottish
Universities Research and Reactor
Centre from data obtained by
airborne gamma-ray surveys.

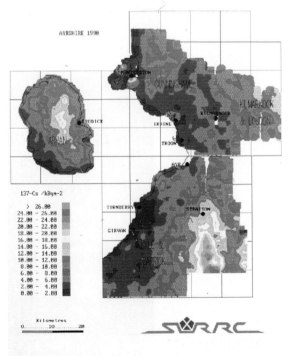

Plate 9. Micro-video camera
The image-sensing chip designed
by VLSI Vision Ltd.

Plate 10. High tech tartan
(l to r) Designer of the tartan; designer of
the chip on \which the tartan was based;
and the Rector of Edinburgh University,
Muriel Gray.

Plate 11.1 Hawaii View of the island showing shore-line and clouds below the summit ridge.

Plate 11.2 Hawaii Telescope domes on the summit of Mauna Kea.

Plate 11.3   Hawaii
An astronomer using the 1.2m
Schmidt Telescope on the
summitof Mauna Kea.

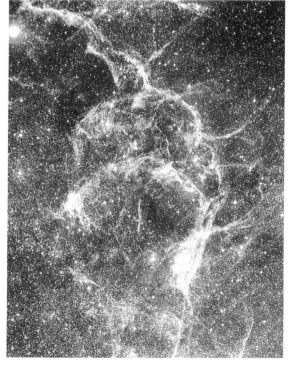

Plate 11.4   Hawaii
The Vela Supernova
remnant; a photograph
produced by combin-
ing three Schmidt Telescope
photographs using a
contrasting enhancement
technique.

Plate 12. Oil Rig
Scale model oil rig under test in wind tunnel.

Plate 13. Fire on Piper Alpha

Plate 14. Fire test on model of King's Cross Underground Station escalator.

Plate 15.   Riedel Shears
An NMR sandbox experiment showing the
complete 3D fault system extracted and
displayed.

Plate 16. The Edinburgh Turtle
A small computer-controlled robot
which could be programmed by school
children to draw regular shapes.

Plate 17.   CERN, Geneva
Human figures emphasize the scale of the machine with which physicists
hope to uncover the secrets of sub-nuclear particles such as the Higgs boson.

some cases I expect the changes to be so startling as to amount to a change in the *character* of science. The following are the main headings under which I expect these changes to occur:

1. Data retrieval
2. Multivariate systems
3. Simulation studies
4. Artificial intelligence."

That prediction was almost uncannily accurate, but five years later Michie wrote a short article *The Death of Paper* which, at least up to now, seems farther away from realisation than when it was written. The computers he described, with the capability of storing and accessing vast amounts of data and displaying any of it on demand, are on almost every desk – but so are the piles of paper he predicted would disappear! Perhaps it will become clear in due course that we have now reached roughly the half-way point, and it is only Michie's time-scale of '15 to 20 years in the future' (1982 to 1987) that was over-optimistic.

In 1963, with the backing of the Principal, Sir Edward Appleton, he established a small computer research group in a house at 4 Hope Park Square. Almost immediately it was supported by grants from the Science and Medical Research Councils, enabling it to acquire an Elliott 4100 Computer and set up the second multi-access time-sharing system in Britain. Users were able to 'converse' with the machine from any one of twelve remote terminals, by answering yes/no and multiple choice questions posed by the computer. In 1965 Michie's research group was formally incorporated in the University as the Experimental Programming Unit, and the first of a series of very successful annual Machine Intelligence Workshops was held in Edinburgh. In 1967 **Donald Michie** was appointed to a Personal Chair of Machine Intelligence.

One year later the Department of Machine Intelligence and Perception, and the Metamathematics Unit, were established by the University Court in the Faculty of Science. The former comprised three research groups - the Experimental Programming Unit (Dr Michie), the Bionics Research Laboratory (Richard Gregory), and the Theoretical Section (Prof H C Longuet-Higgins). The latter two groups transferred to Edinburgh from Cambridge University. The Department, believed to have been the first of its kind in any European university, had the long-term aim of clarifying the design principles of both artificial and biological learning, reasoning and perceiving systems.

The Metamathematics Unit was headed by **Bernard Meltzer** (Reader) who had been a member of the Department of Electrical Engineering since 1955. He spent the academic year 1964-65 at the Science Research Council's Atlas Computer Laboratory, exploring the possibility of programming computers in the logic of mathematical reasoning. As a result, the Unit quickly became a pioneer in the computer proof of mathematical theorems and established an international reputation as a centre for research in artificial intelligence.

An early photograph (c1968) showing Professor Michie sitting at a Teletype machine, surrounded by EPU staff members including Dr (now Professor) Rod Burstall, Ray Dunn and David Pullin

H

Professor Longuet-Higgins

Astronomy

In 1957 **Hermann Brück** was appointed seventh Astronomer Royal for Scotland and eighth Regius Professor of Astronomy. He took steps to introduce up-to-date electronic instrumentation for automatic measurement and data processing, while the spectro-photometric work was gradually wound down after publication of the results. The number of staff at the Royal Observatory Edinburgh (ROE) increased from single figures in 1957 to well over a hundred when he retired 18 years later.

The new instrumentation group began work in 1959 on the design of a measuring engine for the analysis of photographs to be taken with a Schmidt telescope; 'GALAXY' (*G*eneral *A*utomatic *L*uminosity *A*nd *XY* measuring machine) was installed at the ROE in 1967, along with the first main-frame computer, an Elliott 4130. A new 24-inch Schmidt telescope was completed at about the same time at the ROE outstation on Monte Porzio near Frascati in Italy. It was the first of a number of major new telescopes to be sited at optimum locations overseas, in order to give UK astronomers the benefit of observational conditions rarely if ever available at home. Several of these telescopes were designed solely or jointly by the staff of the ROE, and much of the instrumentation was developed and built in the workshops on Blackford Hill. Some of the astronomers from the ROE, including postgraduate research students, spend a good deal of their time at one or other of these outstations.

In 1965 governmental responsibility for the ROE was transferred from the Scottish Office to the newly created SRC. A new BSc Honours degree course in Astrophysics was introduced in collaboration with the Department of Physics, the first such course in a British university. By 1967 the lecturing staff had been increased from one to four, and a Department of Astronomy had been formally instituted in the Faculty of Science. In the same year an extension to the Royal Observatory was completed, providing additional staff accommodation and teaching laboratories.

During the sixties the ROE began work in the new field of infra-red astronomy, in which it was to develop facilities and expertise that brought it to the forefront of the world's research teams working in this difficult area. The UK Infra-red Telescope (UKIRT) was commissioned in 1979 on Mauna Kea in Hawaii. The Edinburgh Instrumentation Group was also involved in design work on the control of the new 150-

inch reflector, the Anglo-Australian Telescope. As a fitting acknowledgement of the ROE's reputation, in 1970 the International Astronomical Union held a formal Colloquium in Edinburgh on 'Automation in Optical Astrophysics'.

Biophysics

The Biophysics Unit was formed in 1952 in the Department of Natural Philosophy, on the initiative of Prof Feather, to teach (inter alia) a full first year physics course for all students taking MB ChB, BVMS or BDS degrees. It was headed by Jack Dainty, who had joined the Department's nuclear physics group in 1949; he was appointed Reader in Biophysics. In 1957 the Unit became the Department of Biophysics, and a small red-brick laboratory was built for it at the King's Buildings. Ben Malcolm joined the Department in January 1958, from Courtaulds Fundamental Research Laboratory at Maidenhead, making a total of six academic staff including Dainty.

In October 1957 there was a fairly serious leak of radioactive material at Windscale, and because there was a sudden realisation in official circles, following the Report of the Fleck Committee, that the nuclear industry lacked properly qualified health and safety staff, the accident led in a roundabout way to the setting up of a one-year Diploma course in Biophysics for physics graduates. The UGC funded an extension to the original building, and it was designed very competently as a student exercise by the Department of Architecture at the Edinburgh College of Art. The course was first offered in session 1960/61, but ran for only four years, although there was never any shortage of suitable applicants. It was very successful in turning out biophysicists of unusually high calibre, but none of them took a job as health and safety officer in the nuclear industry. At least four of them are now occupying chairs:– **Charles Randall House**, FRSE, Professor of Veterinary Cell Physiology in the University of Edinburgh; **Regis Kelly**, Professor of Biochemistry and Biophysics, University of California Medical Centre, San Francisco, USA; **Enid MacRobbie**, FRS, Professor of Plant Biophysics, University of Cambridge; and **Roger Spanswick**, Professor in the Division of Biological Science, Cornell University, Ithaca, USA.

By 1962 it was clear that Biophysics, still without a Professor to fight its battles in Faculty and Senate, and with few friends in other departments, was in a vulnerable position. Consequently when Dainty moved in 1963 to the Chair of Biology in the University of East Anglia he unwittingly sealed the Department's fate, for plans already made were then swiftly set in motion. Michael Swann, Dean of the Faculty of Science in 1963, and Acting Principal from April 1965, strongly supported by Waddington as Professor of Genetics, was master-minding a general reorientation of the biological sciences in Edinburgh. Dainty's departure allowed him to change a Department of rather traditional Biophysics into one of revolutionary *Molecular Biology almost overnight.

The Daniel Rutherford Building

Botany

On the death of Sir William Wright Smith in 1956 it was agreed that the burden involved in the two posts of Regius Keeper and Regius Professor being held by the one man was too great, and they were duly separated, but contact was maintained between the Botanic Garden and the University Department of Botany. The following year saw the end of the teaching of medical students in the Department of Botany after more than two hundred and fifty years.

In 1958 **Robert Brown** was appointed twelfth Regius Professor of Botany; he graduated first in agriculture, and taught for four years at an Agricultural College, before beginning his studies in botany at Imperial College, London. He was an outstanding plant physiologist who published many papers on the subject, and introduced that area of research as well as continuing the Department's long-established work in the field of plant taxonomy. Dr Peter H Davis was appointed head of a sub-department which offered a postgraduate diploma course in plant taxonomy, and he embarked on what turned out to be a life-long study of the flora of Turkey and the neighbouring Aegean islands, which together support five times the number of species found in the British Isles.

It is greatly to the credit of Robert Brown that the Department of Botany became one of the best in Britain. In 1958 it was small (five teaching staff), poorly equipped, with few technicians, and isolated at the Royal Botanic Garden from the rest of the University. Except in plant taxonomy it was relatively unknown outside Edinburgh. By 1965 the Department was housed in a fine new building on the King's Buildings campus, now known as the Daniel Rutherford Building. The teaching staff numbered thirteen, equipment and technical support were of a high standard, and some first-class research work had built up an international reputation for botany in Edinburgh. The Taxonomy Section continued, however, to occupy premises in the Botany building at the Botanic Garden. Shortly after the move to the King's Buildings the Chair of Botany was formally transferred from the Faculty of Medicine to the Faculty of Science.

Chemistry

In 1959 Professor Kendall, who had occupied the Chair of Chemistry since 1928, retired and Edmund Hirst, the Forbes Professor of Organic Chemistry, became Head of Department. The eleventh Professor of Chemistry was **Tom Cottrell**, who had graduated BSc at Edinburgh in 1943 and then worked, most of the time as a research chemist, in the Nobel Division of ICI at Ardeer. While with ICI he published some thirty papers, and in 1952 was awarded the Meldola Medal of the Royal Institute of Chemistry as 'the chemist under thirty years of age who, on the basis of published work, shows most promise'.

He quickly built up a flourishing research school in physical chemistry at Edinburgh, and himself published over twenty papers and several books, including *The Strengths of Chemical Bonds* (1954, 2nd edn 1958) jointly with J C McCoubrey; *Chemistry* (1963) and *Dynamic Aspects of Molecular Energy States* (1965). He was instrumental in setting up in Edinburgh the first group in Britain to work on molecular beams. In 1965 Professor Cottrell was appointed the first Principal and Vice-Chancellor of the new University of Stirling, and worked with all his energies and talents to build it up into a uniquely distinguished institution. Its first few years were unfortunately marred by outbreaks of student unrest, which may well have contributed to his sudden death at the age of fifty in 1973.

In 1966 **Charles Kemball** became the twelfth Professor of Chemistry. His research interests have covered many aspects of surface chemistry and catalysis, with particular emphasis on the study of exchange reactions with deuterium as a means of elucidating the mechanism of catalytic processes. This work is experimentally very difficult, and of great importance to the petrochemical industry. He won the Meldola Medal of the Royal Institute of Chemistry in 1951 and was President of the Institute in 1974-76. He was also President of the Royal Society of Edinburgh in 1988-91.

The first honours degree in Chemical Physics was awarded in 1966, and the following year **Evelyn Ebsworth** was appointed to the new Crum Brown Chair of Chemistry. Internationally honoured for his work in the fields of structural and synthetic chemistry, he has been a leading member of the Royal Society of Chemistry, the SERC and the Scottish Universities Council on Entrance. Prof Ebsworth resigned in 1990 on his appointment as Vice-Chancellor and Warden of the University of Durham.

Neil Campbell was appointed in 1967 to a Personal Chair of Chemistry. He was a member of the first class to begin their studies in the new Chemistry building at the King's Buildings in 1922. His main research interests have lain in the field of aromatic and heterocyclic compounds, on which he has published numerous papers. He was a member of the University Court from 1960 to 1968, and retired in 1973, after spending 51 years in the University of Edinburgh from student to Professor. His taped reminiscences are now part of the Departmental archive, a source of much valuable first-hand information on teaching, administration and research in days gone by, spiced with the occasional personal 'aside'. Neil Campbell was a good all-round athlete, and he recalls the more leisurely approach to studies which allowed him to play rugby for Watsonians and run for the University even in his final honours year. In training and in competition he was often in the same field of runners as Eric Liddell, the famous winner of the 400 metres race in the 1924 Olympics, and had many an opportunity of admiring his style from behind!

Computer Unit

The development of computing in the University of Edinburgh began on the first of April 1963 with the formation of the Computer Unit, the fore-runner of both the Department of Computer Science and the Edinburgh Regional Computing Centre. **Sidney Michaelson** from the Department of Mathematics at Imperial College, London, was appointed Director of the Computer Unit, which was initially housed in two rooms loaned by the Department of Chemistry at King's Buildings. Towards the end of 1963 the Unit moved into two flats at 7, Buccleuch Place; by that time Michaelson had three members of staff, but no computer, and little prospect of acquiring one in the immediate future. The University's computing service came into being, therefore, through the use of a Post Office line to transmit copies of programs prepared on punched paper tape to the Atlas computer at the University of Manchester, and in due course to get the answer back in the same way. In 1964 Edinburgh University's allocation of time on the Atlas was 15 minutes per day.

Those who remember Flexowriters and punched paper tape would no doubt agree that thirty years ago computing was in the stone age – and in practice it was even more primitive than the above procedure implies. To correct the inevitable minor errors in a program, unwanted holes in the paper tape were carefully covered with adhesive tape, and extra holes could be added, one at a time, with a small hand-held punch. Even with no errors on a tape, the readers which sent and received the telephone line signals were unreliable, and it was soon realised that it would be more efficient to send the tapes themselves to Manchester, using British Rail's Red Star parcel service! This was the system in use when the University instituted a post-graduate Diploma in Computer Science in 1964, and Edinburgh became known as the university with a commuter instead of a computer.

The government and its advisers were by this time gradually coming round to the idea that Britain might need more than the half-dozen large computers once reckoned to be sufficient for the universities, industry and commerce, and all other potential users. There was keen competition among the universities for funds to purchase computing equipment, and for a while in 1965-66 Edinburgh was allocated a share of time on Glasgow's newly-installed KDF9. This allowed the University to introduce the first undergraduate course, *Computer Science 1*, in 1965. Within the next few months the Computer Unit was able to purchase a Digital Equipment Corporation PDP8 computer, one of the first to be installed in Britain, for its immediate needs in teaching and research.

In the meantime the Flowers Committee had recommended that there should be regional computing centres at the Universities of London, Manchester and Edinburgh, with 'very large' computers, costing about £0.5m each, to which research workers from other universities and research institutions would have access. The Committee also recommended that Edinburgh should take a leading role in the development of conversational systems and advanced computing networks. As a result of the Flowers Report, in 1966 the Computer Unit was split into the Department of Computer Science under Michaelson, and the Edinburgh Regional Computing Centre (ERCC) under G E (Tommy) Thomas.

Computer Science

The Department of Computer Science was formed in 1966, with Michaelson as Head, to take over the teaching and research duties of the former Computer Unit. The following year, **Sidney Michaelson** was appointed the first Professor of Computer Science, and he occupied that Chair until his death in 1991.

He obtained funds to initiate a major joint research programme between the Computer Science department and English Electric-Leo-Marconi (later ICL). Known as the Edinburgh Multi-Access Project (EMAP), its objective was to design and implement software to run on a 'very large' main-frame computer in order to provide a multi-access and 'conversational' service for the whole university and neighbouring research institutions. Such a machine (an ICL 4-75) was due to be purchased by the ERCC at a later date. The project director was **Harry Whitfield** of the Computer Science Department and the resulting system was known as the Edinburgh Multi-Access System (EMAS). This was the first major research project in the UK to investigate the problems involved in such a system, and it introduced many original concepts. Development of EMAS progressed to the stage where a small number of users could be supported simultaneously, but when the ICL staff departed in 1970 on the scheduled completion of the project, there was still work to be done.

Dr John Oldfield and the Computer-Aided Design (CAD) Project, which had been initiated in 1966 with the support of the SRC, joined the Department of Computer Science, basing its graphical design and development work on a PDP7 machine linked to the Experimental Programming Unit's Elliott 4100. The computing facilities available on small machines by the end of 1967, and the promised installation of the 'very large' ICL 4-75 in the ERCC by 1968, allowed a *Computer Science 2* course to be introduced in 1968/69.

Edinburgh Regional Computing Centre (ERCC)

The ERCC came into formal existence in August, 1966, under its first Director, Dr G E **(Tommy) Thomas**, who was previously head of the Computer Group in the management services organisation of ICI Ltd. An ICL 4-75 main-frame computer was ordered and the Computer Science department were co-operating with ICL on writing an operating system (EMAS). In the meantime, a KDF9 was installed in January 1967 so that the University was no longer dependent on Glasgow's machine. Delivery of the ICL 4-75 took place in January 1969, by which time the staff of the ERCC already numbered over a hundred, and the registered users over two thousand.

Engineering

In 1955 **Kenneth Denbigh** was appointed to the new Chair of Chemical Technology and Chemical Engineering, again jointly with the Heriot-Watt College, housed along with their Department of Chemical Engineering in a new extension to their Chambers Street building. **Philip Calderbank** became the second Professor of Chemical Technology and Chemical Engineering in 1960, and in 1966 when the Department of Chemical Technology had its connection with the Heriot-Watt College severed on the latter's elevation to University status he had to arrange at very short notice for it to be moved into temporary accommodation at the King's Buildings. Shortly afterwards the Department and the Chair were renamed Chemical Engineering.

Ewart Farvis was appointed the first Professor of Electrical Engineering in 1961, and secured a start-up grant of £1080 to establish the new Department. He had joined the Department of Engineering as a lecturer in 1948. Over the next ten years research was directed mainly to the areas of solid state devices and materials science. The next separate engineering Chair to be established was in Civil Engineering, to which **Arnold Hendry** was appointed in 1964. Research was concentrated on the different forms of structural masonry, and large-scale load testing facilities were built up, including the Torphin Quarry test site.

Following the death of Professor Arnold in 1963 at the age of 55, **Leslie Jaeger** was appointed fifth Regius Professor of Engineering, from the Chair of Applied Mechanics at McGill University. By this time the Regius Chair was, in effect, the Chair of Mechanical

Full-scale testing of brick masonry structures at Torphin Quarry 1970

Engineering only, in spite of the fact that from 1868 to 1940 its first three occupants (Jenkin, Armstrong and Hudson Beare) had all been civil engineers. Jaeger saw all four engineering departments in a state of rapid expansion, and began to campaign for the creation of a Faculty of Engineering, but Principal Swann had decided otherwise – engineering must stay in the Faculty of Science, and furthermore must move towards engineering science, in the opposite direction to what he regarded as the regrettably vocational tendencies of the newly promoted Heriot-Watt University. The result was that Jaeger, after less than a year in Edinburgh, returned to McGill, and Hendry felt obliged to opt out and align the renamed Department of Civil Engineering and Building Science in another direction altogether.

Accordingly, in 1967 the School of the Built Environment was formed, consisting of the Departments of Architecture, Civil Engineering and Building Science, Geography, and Urban Design and Regional Planning. The joint first year course for students of architecture and civil engineering, instituted in 1968, was unpopular with most students and some staff, and after much effort had been expended by those who believed in its benefits, it was abandoned. At the same time the School of Engineering Science linked the Departments of Chemical, Electrical and Mechanical Engineering. The heads of the three departments worked closely together to evolve a new four year honours curriculum with a substantial number of common courses in the first two years. The flexibility this offered to students proved attractive at a time when numbers of engineering applicants were declining throughout the UK.

In 1967/68 an integrated circuit fabrication facility was established in the Department of Electrical Engineering, and the Wolfson Microelectronics Liaison Unit was formed with the aid of a grant from the Wolfson Foundation, as part of a Bosworth initiative in microelectronics. The Unit was subsequently renamed the Wolfson Microelectronics Institute. The first Director of the Unit was **James Murray**, and he was succeeded in 1972 by **David Milne**, OBE, who is now Managing Director of Wolfson Microelectronics Limited. These were the first steps in a process of expansion and specialisation that was to take the Department steadily nearer to its present pre-eminent position in microelectronics research and application.

James King became the sixth Regius Professor of Engineering in 1968. From 1961 he had been Chief Scientist in the Naval Construction Research Establishment at Dunfermline. He took over as head of the Department of Mechanical Engineering at a difficult time, and succeeded in imparting to it a new sense of direction and purpose within the School of Engineering Science. He continued and expanded the Department's research in vibrations, heat and mass transfer, and materials science.

Film Unit

Professor Waddington was approached by **Eric Lucey** in 1950 with the suggestion that a Research Film Unit be set up in the Department of Animal Genetics, to assist research workers (by the use of time-lapse techniques, for example) in the study of slow biological processes such as the development of embryos, and in other ways. Waddington was enthusiastic, and Lucey hoped that, as recommended in a number of reports published in the 1950s, the use of film in research and teaching would spread throughout the whole University.

Unfortunately, however, he met with more opposition than support, particularly from the first Director of the University's Audio-Visual Services Unit after he was appointed in 1970. So the one-man film unit remained in Genetics, making excellent films for a small number of enlightened research workers, and winning prizes at documentary film festivals in various parts of the world. In 1970, for example, the film *Shoreline Sediments* was awarded the first prize in the Geography/Geology Section at the Fifth International Festival of Scientific and Technical Films.

In 1989 Eric Lucey accepted an offer of early retirement, and the work of the Film Unit came to an end, though it should be added that both film and television are widely used today for teaching and research in many parts of the University.

Forestry and Natural Resources

Since 1951 Mark Anderson had been the Professor of Forestry. He improved the content of the undergraduate courses and made some long overdue changes to the postgraduate Honours course – in the past twenty years there had been only two honours graduates, both war-time Polish students. In 1959 the Department and College of Agriculture moved out of the upper part of 10 George Square to their new building at the King's Buildings, and Forestry was able to expand into the rooms they had vacated.

By 1961 it could be said that most of Prof Anderson's initial objectives had been achieved. In ten years three lecturers had been added to the staff, the Department now taught five subjects formerly taught by other departments, the whole curriculum had been revised, the postgraduate honours degree course revitalised, and some research projects initiated. The first internal PhD was awarded in 1955 and the first MSc in 1959.

He was a voracious but selective reader, self-taught in several languages, and he translated many works from French, German, Danish, Norwegian, Swedish, Finnish and Russian. Some of his major translations were Petrini's *Elements of Forest Economics* (1954), Kostler's *Silviculture* (1956), and Larsen's *Genetics in Silviculture* (1956). His own book *The Selection of Tree Species* (1950, 2edn 1961) was a valuable guide for the British forester, and his monumental *History of Scottish Forestry* (1967) was edited and published after his death by Dr C J Taylor.

In September 1961 Professor Anderson died suddenly, and **Charles Taylor** was appointed acting Head of Department. In November Senate set up a committee 'to consider the whole future of the Chair of Forestry'. For a time the very existence of the Department was in doubt, and it later emerged that only strong intervention by Professor Waddington, who wanted to see a department in the University with broad interests in the natural environment, had saved it from extinction. The University's long-term development plan for George Square allocated most of the north side (where Forestry had occupied No 10 since 1914) to the Faculty of Medicine, and a joint Forestry/Botany building had been contemplated at the King's Buildings. The uncertain future of Forestry in 1961-62, however, led to that building going ahead in 1962 as Botany alone.

In 1963 **John Black** was appointed the third Professor of Forestry and Natural Resources. He had graduated from Oxford in 1949 and since 1952 had been Reader in Ecology at the Waite Agricultural Research Institute in the University of Adelaide. He was appointed 'as from 1st January 1964' and was surprised to find the Department closed when he turned up for work that morning! He published *The Dominion of Man*, dealing with the ethics of man's utilization of natural resources, in 1970 and two books on his favourite 'recreational' subject of Italian opera in 1983/84.

Just over a year later work began on the multi-storey 'strong building forming a climax to the whole area' of the King's Buildings, as conceived by the University's architects. It was to accommodate the Departments of Forestry and Natural Resources and Molecular Biology. The gaunt steel framework invited much speculation when work was suspended for several months in the autumn of 1965 due to the UGC's freeze on building projects. However, when the unseasonal thaw came and work was resumed in January 1966, the Darwin Building took only another fifteen months to complete.

The academic year 1966/67 was the last in which BSc (Forestry) degrees were awarded. Over its sixty years of life there had been a total of 821 graduates, including one Director-General of the British Forestry Commission (Sir Arthur Gosling) and many other eminent foresters. It was replaced by the four-year BSc (Ecological Science) degree, with Honours in Ecology, Forestry, Resource Management or Wildlife and Fisheries Management.

Genetics

By 1955 **C H Waddington** had been in the Buchanan Chair of Animal Genetics for almost ten years, responsible as Professor for the University Department of Animal Genetics, and as Director for the Agricultural Research Council (ARC) Unit of Animal Genetics. The Institute of Animal Genetics (now the Crew Building) also housed the Medical Research Council (MRC) Mutagenesis Research Unit under Dr Charlotte Auerbach. In spite of (or perhaps because of) Waddington's attitude of supportive laissez-faire his staff accomplished a great deal of significant research, establishing Edinburgh as a primary centre for genetic research. In 1966 the Department was renamed Genetics.

Much of Waddington's own research centred on embryology and development, but, especially in his later writings, the overall impression is of the breadth of his interests, spreading into areas far removed from genetics itself. He was an immensely productive writer, publishing sixteen books as well as nearly 500 research papers and articles. His *Introduction to Modern Genetics* (1939) can still be read with profit today, as can *The Strategy of the Genes* (1957) and *The Nature of Life* (1962). For Pelican Books he wrote *The Scientific Attitude* (1941, 2nd edn, 1948), which though now very dated was a brave attempt to 'point out some of the contributions which the scientific attitude of mind can make to the creative tasks of social reorganisation with which the world is faced.' At the other end of the book scale, Edinburgh University Press published in 1969 a handsome volume *Behind Appearance: a study of the relations between painting and the natural sciences in this century*, which can be read with interest and pleasure by scientists and non-scientists alike.

Dr Henrik Kacser, FRSE, joined the Department in 1955 and pioneered the application of control analysis to metabolising systems, a development now widely recognised, for which the University of Bordeaux awarded him the degree of Docteur *honoris causa*.

In 1963 the MRC set up an Epigenetics Research Group, also under Waddington, and with funds from the Distillers Company, the Wellcome Trust, the MRC and the UGC, a new laboratory was built, equipped and occupied by the summer of 1966. The work of the Group was mainly concerned with the molecular basis of cellular differentiation. The underlying concept of epigenetics was consistent with Waddington's belief that non-DNA-determined 'epigenetic' phenomena were the key to understanding the complexities of multicellular development. It was perhaps this chink in his intellectual armour that led to his noticeable preoccupation with non-genetic topics towards the end of his life.

Geoffrey Beale, who joined the Department of Animal Genetics in 1948, was appointed a Royal Society Research Professor in 1963, and three years later he and his research team moved into a new laboratory for Protozoan Genetics adjacent to the Institute. He worked first on Paramecium, and later developed the new field of the genetics of the malarial parasite. He published *The Genetics of Paramecium aurelia* (1954) and *Extranuclear Genetics* (with J Knowles, 1978). His malaria research is being continued in the Centre for Parasite Biology under **David Walliker**, who joined the Department of Genetics in 1966 as an MRC Research Fellow. Since 1988 he has been on the MRC External Scientific Staff of the ICAPB, and an Honorary Professor in Edinburgh University.

In 1967 **Charlotte Auerbach** was appointed to a Personal Chair in Genetics. She was (during WWII) the first geneticist to demonstrate the mutagenic effect of chemical agents, and in the period covered by this chapter she developed in greater depth her studies of chemical mutagenesis, including the origin of the mutational effects of formaldehyde, alkylating agents and other compounds in the fruit-fly *Drosophila*. Her publications include *The Science of Genetics* (1961), *Heredity* (1965) and *Mutation Research* (1976).

In 1967 **Alan Robertson**, who had been a member of the ARC Unit, was made an Honorary Professor. He was a leading authority on quantitative genetics and animal breeding, and had a profound influence on animal breeding throughout the world. The following year **Douglas Falconer**, who joined the ARC Unit in 1947, was appointed to a Personal Chair in Genetics, and Director of the Unit in succession to Professor Waddington. He was Head of the Department from 1969 to 1977. His main interests lay in the genetics of continuously varying characters, and in particular with the efficacy of artificial selection as a means of changing these characters. He also established an international reputation for his work on the genetics of the mouse. His book, *Introduction to Quantitative Genetics* (1960, 3rd edn 1989) is widely used as a standard text in genetics and animal breeding courses.

Geology

The fifth Regius Professor of Geology, **Sir Frederick Stewart**, succeeded Arthur Holmes in 1956. Born in Aberdeen and educated there and at Cambridge, he like Holmes came to Edinburgh from the University of Durham. His main research interests in geology were in the fields of mineralogy and petrology, epecially evaporite deposits in Britain and the United States. His career might well have continued along such peaceful paths of science, had he not been persuaded to become Dean of the Faculty of Science in 1965. He rapidly became known throughout the University, belying his slightly unkempt look and friendly unassuming manner (which led to his nickname of 'Uncle Fred'), as a very considerable intellect and a formidable protagonist in committee debates.

Two years later his career as a statesman of science began when he became a member of the Council for Scientific Policy, followed by two years as Chairman of the Natural Environment Research Council, 1971-73. In 1972 he became a member, and from 1973 to 1979 Chairman, of the Advisory Board for Research Councils. He was knighted for his services to science in 1974. He was joint editor of *The British Caledonides*, and published *Marine Evaporites*, both in 1963, as well as numerous papers on igneous and metamorphic petrology and salt deposits. His wife Mary Stewart is also a prolific author, having written more than twenty novels, some of them adapted for television, as well as articles, poems and radio plays.

In 1955 the Department of Geology had six members of staff (in addition to the Regius Professor); by 1970 a second chair had been created in Geology with fifteen other members of staff, and the new Department of Geophysics had begun life with a chair and two members of staff. The rather futuristic extension for Experimental Petrology was opened in 1965 – the blast chimneys are designed to cope with unexpected explosions

*High Pressure and Temperature Study of
Materials*

from experimental 'bombs' which are subjected to prolonged periods of high temperature and pressure.

Gordon Craig was appointed to the James Hutton Chair of Geology in 1967, having joined the Department as Lecturer in Palaeontology in 1947. His main research interests have been in the field of palaeoecology – the study of fossils as living organisms in relation to their environment. He was a member and committee member of many scientific societies, with a special interest in the history of geology, and from 1984 to 1989 he was President of the International Commission on the History of the Geological Sciences. His publications include *This Restless Earth* (1962), *The Geology of Scotland* (editor: 1965; 3rd edn, 1991), and *James Hutton's Theory of the Earth: the Lost Drawings* (with D B McIntyre and C D Waterson, 1978).

Industrial Liaison (ILC)

The Industrial Liaison Committee (ILC) which was set up in 1947 on the initiative of the University Court is believed to have been the first such organisation in any British university. It consisted of representatives of local industry and the University, under the convenership of E P (later Sir Edmund) Hudson, the managing director of Scottish Agricultural Industries. It quickly became obvious that there was a good deal of ignorance on both sides about the other's needs and capabilities, and meetings and visits were arranged to remedy this.

In 1949 the ILC published a 57-page *Handbook of Departments in the University of Edinburgh related to Industry*. Twenty departments, almost all in the Faculty of Science, gave details of research projects and laboratory facilities likely to be of interest to industry, and brief biographies emphasising the 'industrial' research and expertise of members of staff. For the next two decades contacts with industry tended to be concentrated in a relatively small number of departments where there happened to be interested individuals, encouragement from the Head of Department (not by any means universal), and established contacts with industry often through graduates of the department.

Progress was steady if rather slow, though sufficient for the University to publish a revised and expanded edition of the *Handbook* in 1958. By the 1960s it was clear even at government level that British industry was not getting the graduates it needed, and that most university departments of science and technology were still too far removed from the industrial research laboratory let alone the factory floor. The reports by Dainton (1968), Jones (1967) and Swann (1968) led to the setting up by the UGC of a university/industry pump-priming reserve, and in 1969 Edinburgh took advantage of this to establish the Centre for Industrial Consultancy and Liaison (CICL) with **Dr John Midgley**, from the English Electric Company, as the first Director.

Mathematics

The atmosphere of the 1950s in the Department of Mathematics is recalled by Philip Heywood who joined the Department in 1954.

'Those were the days of coal fires in the Professors' retiring rooms, and Departmental teas in the so-called research room, where lectures (they would be called seminars today) were given by members of staff to colleagues and any students or visitors who cared to attend, while the kettle boiled on the open fire tended by the back row of the audience. Over tea stories would be told, such as Prof Aitken's tale of being taken, as a newcomer to the University in the 1920s, on a tour of Edinburgh in a car (a rarity then) owned by a colleague in the Faculty of Science – nearing the junction of Mayfield Road and West Mains Road, in the days before traffic lights, his colleague simply accelerated through it, explaining to the startled Aitken that he always drove according to the kinetic theory of gases, which he interpreted as 'the faster you travel, the fewer collisions you have'!'

'Another favourite motoring story was of the pre-war Professor who chose the wrong archway for driving out of the Old College quadrangle, and bounced his car down the steps before he could stop it!'

In 1958 Edinburgh University hosted the International Congress of Mathematics, the premier four-yearly conference in the subject. Robin Schlapp (Applied Mathematics) acted as secretary of the executive committee for the conference from 1955 to 1958.

A second Chair of Mathematics was instituted in 1963 by the University Court, influenced perhaps by the fact that Professor Aitken was in poor health by that time. **Arthur Erdélyi** was appointed to this Chair in 1964. Born in Hungary, he attended a technical institute in Czechoslovakia where his mathematical flair was soon apparent. The German occupation forced him to flee early in 1939 and he found a haven in Edinburgh University. He was invited in 1947/48 to inspect the Harry Bateman manuscripts at the California Institute of Technology and from 1949 he spent the next fifteen years there. For six years he was involved as coordinator of an international group of mathematicians who worked with him to transcribe, edit and publish Bateman's work in three volumes of *Higher Transcendental Functions* (1953-55) and two volumes of *Tables of Integral Transforms* (1954).

The Old College Quadrangle

By the time he returned to Edinburgh in 1964 his reputation was already international, and the following year on the retirement of Professor Aitken, Erdélyi became the sixteenth Professor of Mathematics. He was a man of great culture and had a very wide knowledge of mathematics. Special functions were his main expertise, but he also ensured by his appointments in the period of fast university expansion that the department could operate on a broad modern front.

After Erdélyi's 'promotion', **Frank Bonsall** was appointed to the Second Chair of Mathematics, known thereafter as the Colin McLaurin Chair. Coming to Edinburgh from King's College, Newcastle-upon-Tyne, he was internationally recognised as the leading authority on algebraic functional analysis in Britain. In 1973 he published with his former student Professor John Duncan *Complete Normed Algebras*, the definitive work on the subject. For the last few years in the Department he held an SRC Senior Fellowship.

In 1966 the Departments of Mathematics and Natural Philosophy were finally transferred from the Faculty of Arts to the Faculty of Science. Technical Mathematics continued until 1969 as a separate department under Dr L M Brown. **George Mackie** was appointed in 1968 to the newly-instituted Chair of Applied Mathematics in the Department of Mathematics. His research interests lay mainly in fluid dynamics and partial differential equations, and he was closely involved in developing a new curriculum in engineering mathematics. He published *Boundary Value Problems* (1965, 2nd edn, 1989), and a number of papers in mathematical journals.

Personal Chairs in Geometry and Algebra were bestowed in 1969 and 1972 respectively on **William Edge** and **Ivor Etherington**. Edge had joined the Department in 1932 and became Reader in 1948. At Cambridge in 1928 he won the Smith's Prize with a dissertation which grew into the book *Ruled Surfaces* (1931), still the authoritative work on the subject. He is an internationally recognized authority on classical algebraic geometry and at the age of 89 he is still publishing research papers today. Students found his lectures difficult, but those who made the effort also found them very rewarding. Edge and Schlapp were, like Aitken and Erdélyi, keen and accomplished musicians, and like Bonsall and Sinclair in the next generation, energetic hill-walkers.

Etherington joined the Department in 1933 and became Reader in 1963. He contributed to the abstract theory of non-associative algebra and as long ago as the 1930s became interested in the mathematics of population genetics, work that only recently has received renewed attention. A dedicated teacher, his efficient and energetic administration became legendary, and it was in no small degree due to him that the difficult period of Prof Aitken's illness was successfully weathered.

Prof Etherington's knowledge of departmental detail, past and present, was phenomenal – much of it he carried around in his pocket on small coloured cards. Naturally he had to use a kind of personal shorthand, in which 'E' represented Edge and 'e' Etherington, as befitted their physical stature. This meant that when Erdélyi returned to the Department in 1964 as a world-famous mathematician the only symbol left for him was ϵ, which in mathematics traditionally denotes a small positive quantity. Etherington is reputed to have arranged for the purchase of much-needed mathematical *tables* from the furniture grant when the library grant could not afford them.

Meteorology

James Paton, who was appointed Lecturer in Natural Philosophy in 1928 and had conducted research in upper atmosphere physics since 1934, was designated Lecturer in Meteorology in 1944. The following year he instituted an undergraduate course in Meteorology, the first in any British university, and later introduced a short Honours level course in Atmospheric Physics. He was promoted Senior Lecturer in 1950 and Reader in 1954, and when the Department of Meteorology was created in 1964 he was appointed Head of Department. In 1956 the Balfour Stewart Auroral Laboratory was established in Edinburgh with funding from the Royal Society of London, and Paton was appointed Director. A geophysical unit of the British Antarctic Survey was attached to the Auroral Laboratory in 1959 and remained there until the Laboratory was disbanded in 1975. The Department of Meteorology had a staff of three under Paton, who died in post just weeks before his intended retirement in 1973.

Molecular Biology

In 1962 Martin Pollock, then Head of the Division of Microbial Physiology at NIMR, and Bill Hayes, Director of the MRC Microbial Genetics Research Unit at Hammersmith, realized that the subjects of biochemistry and molecular genetics had converged to such an extent that combining them would result in a university department capable of making major advances in this important area of biological science. They shopped around newer and older universities, and Sussex and Edinburgh were the finalists. The scientific perception of Michael Swann ensured that 'Molecular Biology' came to Edinburgh. In 1964 **Martin Pollock** was appointed to a new Chair of Biology, and within a year he was joined by several others of his staff from NIMR, sharing space with the survivors of the renamed Department of *Biophysics (Molecular Biology).

The newcomers apparently found the King's Buildings campus distinctly dull and lacking in amenities. There was a fine lawn at the south end of the Biophysics Building, eminently suited in their view to the playing of croquet, so a splendid and rather expensive croquet set was ordered from Lillywhites – on the class grant. This was not viewed with favour by the university accountants, and a circular was sent to all academic departments defining very clearly what class grants could, and could not, be used for. It is interesting to note that one of the croquet players, many years later when Chairman of the SERC, issued a circular to all University Principals stressing the need to justify fully all overhead expenses included in grant applications.

The top three floors of the Darwin Building were occupied by the Department of Molecular Biology in 1968, and at that juncture **William Hayes** was appointed to a Personal Chair of Molecular Genetics. Most of the members of his Hammersmith Unit came with him to Edinburgh. The Department was formally opened by Nobel Prize

Winner Jacques Monod, someone who had had an immense philosophical influence on Pollock, in November 1968. The Pollock-Hayes plan envisaged a third main group in the Department, centred on nucleic acid research, and to lead this Ken Murray had joined them from Cambridge as a Senior Lecturer in 1967.

Even in its very first years the Department and Unit were productive in research. Highlights of these years were the recognition of bidirectional replication of DNA in *E. coli* by Masters and Broda, much progress in elucidation of the genetics, physiology and structure of various factors responsible for antibiotic resistance in bacteria (by Pollock, Richmond and Ambler), and the final edition of Hayes' classic book *The Genetics of Bacteria and their Viruses*. Julian Gross (at Edinburgh with the MRC Unit, 1968-74) initiated the genetic analysis of DNA replication, using *E. coli*, work that had considerable influence on those such as Arthur Kornberg in Stanford, who were defining the proteins required for chromosome replication using biochemical techniques. Elsewhere on the eighth floor of the Darwin Building, John Scaife was using genetic techniques to dissect the transcription machinery of *E. coli*, and Willie Donachie was laying the foundations of our understanding of cell division in bacteria.

Natural Philosophy (Physics) and Mathematical Physics

Max Born's successor in 1953 as Tait Professor of Natural Philosophy in the Department of Mathematical Physics was **Nicholas Kemmer**. His great-grandfather, Mikhail Petrovich Avenarius, was a Professor of Physics in Kiev, and had corresponded with Tait on the subject of thermo-electricity. While at Cambridge, Professor Kemmer had supervised a galaxy of future professors of theoretical physics (in part because P A M Dirac, the Lucasian Professor of Mathematics, wouldn't!). Previously, at Imperial College in 1938, he developed the first beautiful application of symmetry in elementary particle physics. The background to this was the understanding that the strong nuclear force appeared to be unchanged by the interchange of the proton and the recently-discovered neutron — the so-called isotopic spin symmetry. In the Yukawa theory, the force which held the nucleus together was associated with a particle, the π-meson, by analogy to the photon associated with the electromagnetic force binding electrons and nuclei into atoms.

Professor N Kemmer

At that time, it was believed that the charged particles π^+ and π^- had been observed experimentally. Kemmer showed that a necessary consequence of isotopic spin symmetry was the existence of a third particle, the electrically neutral π°, with roughly the same mass as the π^+ and π^-. In fact the charged particles which had been observed were later correctly identified as the μ^+ and μ^-, but the π^+, π° and π^- were all subsequently found and Kemmer's prediction was verified. In 1975 he was awarded the J Robert Oppenheimer Memorial Prize for his contributions to elementary particle physics. He published *The Theory of Space, Time and Gravitation*, 1959 (translated from the Russian of V Fock, 1955); *What is Relativity?*, 1960 (translated from the Russian of Landau and Rumer, 1959); and *Vector Analysis*, 1977.

It was during Kemmer's tenure that the title of the Chair was changed to the Tait Chair of Mathematical Physics, his Department became known as the Tait Institute of Mathematical Physics, and an Honours Degree in Mathematical Physics was instituted. In 1966 the Departments of Mathematics, Mathematical Physics and Natural Philosophy were at long last transferred from the Faculty of Arts to the Faculty of Science. A few years later the Faculty of Science decided that the title of the Department of Natural Philosophy should be changed to Physics – but in the Faculty of Arts, the courses in Physics are still referred to as Natural Philosophy. Finally in 1971 the Departments of Physics and Mathematical Physics were merged, and collaboration in both teaching and research is now well developed. The removal of all the mathematics and physics departments to the James Clerk Maxwell Building at the King's Buildings took place in stages from 1969 to 1975.

In 1955 **Norman Feather** had been Professor of Natural Philosophy and Head of the Department for ten years, and he continued in both capacities until his retirement in 1975 at the age of 70. By the mid-1950s the initial impetus of the nuclear research effort had been partially exhausted, and some research effort spread into other fields – fluid dynamics, solid state, electron and atomic physics, and quantum optics. The Fluid Dynamics Unit, for example, was created in 1969 within the Department, with **Dr Marion Ross** as Director. Nuclear physics conducted 'in house' continued to be the major concern. Feather was utterly convinced of the interdependence of undergraduate teaching, postgraduate training and research, and was loath to see two of these activities moved away to the large centralised research facilities which were then developing.

One of the more unusual careers followed by an ex-member of the Department's staff is that of the **Reverend Dr John Polkinghorne**, FRS, President of Queens' College, Cambridge since 1989, and member of the Church of England's General Synod. Dr Polkinghorne's first teaching appointment was as a lecturer in the Department of Mathematical Physics at Edinburgh, 1956-58, before returning to Cambridge where he became in 1968 the Professor of Mathematical Physics. He resigned his chair in 1979 to study for the Anglican priesthood and served in the parochial ministry for five years before again returning to Cambridge as a Fellow and Dean of Trinity Hall. He has since then been a member of the Science Research Council and Chairman of the Nuclear Physics Board. In 1993 he delivered the Gifford Lectures in Edinburgh University on the theme of 'Science and Christian Belief'. Among his publications are *The Analytic S-Matrix* (1966), *Models of High Energy Processes* (1980), *The Quantum World* (1984) and *One World* (1986).

The appointment of **William Cochran**, whose career in the Department began as an assistant lecturer in 1943, to a newly-established second Chair of Physics in 1964 was a great stimulus to work in solid state physics. His principal publications were in the same area – Vol III of *The Crystalline State* (with Prof H Lipson, 1954; 2nd edn, 1966) and *Dynamics of Atoms in Crystals* (1973). In 1967 **Peter Farago** was appointed to a Personal Chair of Physics. He joined the Department as a Senior Lecturer shortly after leaving Hungary in January 1957. His research interest was in the field of atomic and electron physics, especially problems related to the spin and magnetic moment of free electrons. Among his publications were *An Introduction to Linear Network Analysis* (1961) and *Free Electron Physics* (1971). The appointment of **Roger Cowley** in 1970 to the third Chair of Physics confirmed that the solid state was to be the Department's major research field for some time to come. He published *Structural Phase Transitions* (1981).

Science Libraries

The early development of class and departmental libraries at the King's Buildings is not well documented – probably in most cases they sprang from the professors' own collections, and in due course were added to with the aid of grants from the Library Committee. Two important large collections were donated to the University Library by Prof Crum Brown of Chemistry and the brothers Geikie of Geology; the volumes in these and other collections were added to the University Library catalogue, but the books remained in the departmental libraries, which by 1982 were eight in number. They all had to be staffed on a full-time basis, and were administered from the Main Library, but to a greater or a lesser extent they all suffered from shortage of staff, shortage of space for books and readers, and waste of money on duplications, especially of expensive journals.

In 1949 the first proposal was made for the establishment of a Central Science Library on the King's Buildings site, but nothing was done at the time. In 1962 a sub-committee of the Faculty of Science examined the situation and reported that the only satisfactory solution would be to build a unified Science Library at the King's Buildings. Again nothing was done, perhaps partly because the long-established departmental libraries had some very influential champions.

Science Studies Unit

The Science Studies Unit was founded in 1966 in the Faculty of Science (although it was never located at the King's Buildings) with the help of a generous grant from the Wolfson Foundation. The original proposal for the establishment of a unit of this kind had been made by Professor Waddington about two years previously. **David Edge** was the first Director, having been persuaded by Michael Swann to take on a task for which there were few precedents, and those that did exist were confusingly contradictory. The Dainton Report (1966) had just been published, and the Swann Report (1968) had been drafted; both called for the incorporation into science education of 'contextual studies', as a clear social need. Swann in particular looked forward to the day 'when all science, technology and engineering students gain some understanding of the society in which they will work.'

In 1967 a course of lectures called *Science Studies 1* was introduced into the Faculty of Science syllabus. A total of 224 students took this course in its first four years, all but 32 of them from the Faculty of Science. The Unit also arranged a large number of special lectures, and had working in it three Lecturers, three Research Associates and five Research Students. By this time the aim of the Unit was seen as 'to focus attention, by teaching and research, on those areas where scientific activities overlap with more general concerns of human societies.'

Statistics

Although the Department and Chair did not come into being until 1966, the subject had been taught since 1907, when a Lecturer in Statistics and Mathematical Economics (Dr George Carse) was appointed in the Faculty of Arts. The subject was then part of the Honours course for the degree of MA in Economic Science. In 1925 Dr A C Aitken, who twenty years later became Professor of Mathematics, was appointed Lecturer in Statistics and Mathematical Economics, and in Actuarial Science. By 1933 he was giving courses of lectures on Elementary and Advanced Statistics, and four years later he was made Reader in Statistics. In 1947 Dr D N Lawley succeeded Aitken as Lecturer in Statistics and Mathematical Economics in the Faculty of Arts.

In 1966 the Department and Chair of Statistics were instituted in the Faculty of Science. Dr Lawley transferred as Reader in Statistics, and **David Finney** was appointed the first Professor of Statistics.In 1954 he had founded the Department of Statistics and the ARC Unit of Statistics in the University of Aberdeen. When he moved to the new Chair in Edinburgh the ARC Unit (now the Scottish Agricultural Statistics Service) of which he was Director, 1954-84, moved with him. He was primarily interested in the application of statistical methods to biology, including agriculture and medicine. He was a member of the Adverse Reactions Committee of the Committee on Safety of Medicines, 1963-80, and President of the Royal Statistical Society, 1973-74. Among his publications are:- *An Introduction to Statistical Science in Agriculture* (1953, 4th edn 1972); *Experimental Design and its Statistical Basis* (1955); *Statistics for Mathematicians: an Introduction* (1968); *Statistics for Biologists* (1980). The courses in statistics were attended mainly by students from the Faculties of Science and Social Sciences.

Zoology

From Cambridge in 1955 **Peter Mitchell** came to the Department as Director of the Chemical Biology Unit, and with his life-long collaborator Jennifer Moyle worked in a small basement laboratory on the development of his chemiosmotic theory of cell metabolism. The key papers on which their subsequent research was based were published in 1960/61, but they were received with scepticism and even ridicule by some other biochemists. Mitchell and Moyle began to feel the pressures of working in a large institution hard to bear, and by 1963 they had decided to leave Edinburgh. Their work, which continued after 1964 in Mitchell's own Glynn Research Institute near Bodmin in Cornwall, led to his being awarded the **Nobel Prize for Chemistry** in 1978, for his contribution to the understanding of biological energy transfer through the formulation of the chemiosmotic theory. He published two books on chemiosmotic coupling in 1966/68.

By about 1960 the Chair of Natural History had become 'based' in the Faculty of Science, although the Professor of Natural History continued his membership of the Faculty of Medicine. In 1963 **Murdoch Mitchison** became the second Professor of Zoology; the Chair had been vacant since Ashworth was translated in 1927 to the Chair of Natural History. Swann and Mitchison together set the Department firmly on a new course more appropriate to the second half of the twentieth century. They participated with Waddington and others in discussions which, almost two decades later, were to lead to the integration of the biological sciences in Edinburgh University to a quite unprecedented extent, in the School of Biology which links all the departments with biological interests in the Faculties of Medicine, Science and Social Sciences. Mitchison published *The Biology of the Cell Cycle* (1971).

In 1966 Michael Swann was appointed Principal and Vice-Chancellor of the University, and **Peter Walker** became the eleventh Professor of Natural History in the Department of Zoology. He joined the Department as a Royal Society Research Fellow in cytochemistry in 1958, becoming Lecturer and Reader in Zoology in 1962/63. In his early research on genetic material in animal cells he had to make very precise measurements, and some of the special instruments he designed are now used in laboratories throughout the world. In this work he drew on his experience as a tool and instrument maker during WWII. He is the General Editor of *Chambers Science and Technology Dictionary*.

Michael M Swann, Baron Swann of Coln Denys

Expansion and Rationalisation

It was a distinct advantage to the science departments at Edinburgh that throughout the fifties and sixties the two Principals were themselves scientists, the physicist Sir Edward Appleton being succeeded in 1965 by the zoologist Michael (later Lord) Swann. He was one of the few recent Principals to be selected from the University's own professoriate, having been appointed to the Chair of Natural History in the Department of Zoology in 1952. He served as Dean of the Faculty of Science for the two years before he became Principal, so he was no doubt well aware of most of the Faculty's needs and aspirations.

Certainly in the two years after he became Principal an impressive programme of expansion and (equally necessary) rationalisation was carried out. A Sub-Department of Microbiology was created in the Department of Agriculture, and a Department of Astronomy was instituted in the Faculty of Science – the first full-time University Lecturer in Astronomy had been appointed only in 1950. The Department of Animal Genetics was renamed Genetics, the Chair of Botany was transferred from the Faculty of Medicine to the Faculty of Science, and the long-established BSc degree in Forestry was replaced by the BSc in Ecological Science.

The Departments of Mathematics and Natural Philosophy were transferred from the Faculty of Arts to the Faculty of Science, Meteorology became a separate department, and the Science Studies Unit was founded. The Computer Unit was separated into the Department of Computer Science and the Edinburgh Regional Computing Centre, and the Department of Machine Intelligence and Perception was established, along with the Metamathematics Unit. A Chair and Department of Statistics were instituted in the Faculty of Science, and Chemical Engineering had to be accommodated at the King's Buildings following the elevation of the Heriot-Watt College to University status. The Schools of Engineering Science and the Built Environment were established, membership of the latter extending into the Faculty of Social Sciences.

Some Notable Edinburgh University Scientists and Engineers, 1955 - 1970

BEVERIDGE, Gordon FRSE FEng (1933-   ) Studied chemical engineering at Glasgow, Strathclyde and Edinburgh (PhD, 1960). Lect at Edinburgh University and Heriot-Watt College, 1962-67. Prof of Chemical Enginering, Strathclyde, 1971. President and Vice-Chancellor, the Queen's University of Belfast, since 1986. [CSBD, WW, WWIS]

BOWMAN, John CBE (1933-   ) Studied genetics at Reading and Edinburgh (PhD, 1958). Prof of Animal Production, 1966-81 and Director of the University Farms, 1967-78, at Reading. Secretary, Natural Environment Research Council, since 1981. Publ *Animals for Man*, 1977; (jtly) *Hammond's Farm Animals*, 1983. [WW]

CATTANACH, Bruce FRS (1932-   ) Studied genetics at Durham and Edinburgh (PhD, 1962; DSc, 1966). MRC Induced Mutagenesis Unit, Edinburgh, 1959-62 and 1964-66. MRC Radiobiology Unit, Chilton, Oxford, 1969-86; Head of Genetics Division, since 1987. Publ papers on X-chromosome inactivation, sex determination and genetics generally. [WW]

CORMACK, Richard FRSE (1935-   ) Studied mathematics and statistics at Cambridge, London (external) and Aberdeen. Lect in statistics, Aberdeen, 1956-66; sen lect at Edinburgh, 1966-72; Prof of Statistics at St Andrews, since 1972. Publ *The Statistical Argument*; ed *Sampling Biological Populations, Spatial and Temporal Analysis in Ecology*. [WWIS]

HENDERSON, Richard FRS (1945-   ) Studied physics and molecular biology at Edinburgh (BSc) and Cambridge (PhD). Member of scientific staff at the MRC Laboratory of Molecular Biology in Cambridge, since 1973. Fellow of Darwin College, since 1981. Distinguished for his use of electron microscopy in the study of macromolecules. [CSBD, WW]

IRVINE, John FRAS (1939-   ) Studied physics at Edinburgh, Michigan and Manchester. Lect, sen lect, reader and in 1983 Prof of Theoretical Physics at Manchester. Head of Nuclear Theory Group, SERC Daresbury Laboratory, 1974-77. Principal and Vice-Chancellor at Aberdeen, since 1991. [WWIS]

KILGOUR, Alistair FBCS (1940-   ) Studied mathematics at Glasgow. Research Associate on the Computer-Aided Design Project at Edinburgh, 1966-74. Lect and sen lect in computing science at Glasgow, 1974-89. Prof in the Computer Science Department at the Heriot-Watt University, Edinburgh, since 1989. [WWIS]

McLAREN, Anne FRS (1927-   ) Studied genetics at Oxford (MA, DPhil) and London; ARC Unit of Animal Genetics, Edinburgh University, 1959-74. Director of MRC Mammalian Development Unit, since 1974. First woman officer (Foreign Secretary) of the Royal Society in its 332-year history; Member of Council, 1985. Hon DSc, Edinburgh, 1992. Publ *Mammalian Chimaeras* (1976); *Germ Cells and Soma* (1980). [WW]

MITCHISON, Avrion FRS (1928-   ) Studied zoology at Oxford (MA, 1949); Fellow, 1950-54; lect and reader at Edinburgh, 1954-62. Head of Division of Experimental Biology, National Institute for Medical Research, 1962-71; Jodrell Prof of Zoology and Comparative Anatomy, University College, London, since 1970. Hon MD, Edinburgh, 1977. [WW]

MOFFAT, Henry FRS (1935-   ) Studied maths at Edinburgh (BSc, 1957) and Cambridge (BA, PhD); lect in maths at Cambridge, 1961-76. Prof of Applied Mathematics at Bristol, 1977-80; Prof of Mathematical Physics at Cambridge, since 1980. Publ *Magnetic Field Generation in Electrically Conducting Fluids*, 1978 (Russian edn, 1980). [CSBD, WW]

MORRISON, Fraser (1948-   ) Studied civil engineering at Edinburgh (BSc, 1970); joined Morrison Construction Group in 1970, Managing Director, 1976-84; Chairman and Man Dir, since 1984. Chairman, Scottish Section, Federation of Civil Engineering Contractors; winner of the 1991 Scottish Business Achievement Award. [WWIS]

REES, David (Dai) FRS (1936-   ) Studied biochemistry at Univ College of North Wales, Bangor (BSc, PhD); lecturer in chemistry at Edinburgh, 1961-70 (DSc, 1970). Research with Unilever, 1970-82. Director, National Institute for Medical Research, 1982-87; Secretary, Medical Research Council, since 1987. Publ papers on carbohydrate

I

chemistry and biochemistry, and cell biology. [WW]

RICHMOND, Sir Mark FRS (1931-   ) Studied at Cambridge (BA, PhD, ScD); medical research, 1958-65; Reader in Molecular Biology at Edinburgh, 1965-68; Prof of Bacteriology at Bristol, 1968-81; Vice-Chancellor and Prof of Molecular Microbiology at Manchester, since 1981. Member and Chairman of SERC, 1981-1993; Chairman, CVCP, since 1987. [WW]

SLATER, Peter FRSE (1942-   ) Studied zoology at Edinburgh (BSc, 1964; PhD, 1968; DSc, 1983), dem in zoology, 1966-68. Lect in biology, Sussex, 1968-84. Kennedy Prof of Natural History, St Andrews, since 1984. Assoc Editor, *Advances in the Study of Behavior*, since 1982. Publ *Sex Hormones and Behaviour* (1978); *An Introduction to Ethology* (1985); *Collins Encyclopaedia of Animal Behaviour* (ed, 1986). [WW, WWIS]

THYNNE, John (1931-   ) Studied chemistry at Nottingham (BSc, PhD); lect in chemistry 1963-70 at Edinburgh (DSc). Principal, Department of Trade and Industry, 1970-73; Under Secretary, Electronics Applications Division, DTI, 1986-89; Under Secretary and Director, Information Engineering Directorate, DTI, since 1989. [WW]

CHAPTER 9

Science under pressure – the lean years, 1970 - 1991

The hectic expansion of higher education in the 1960s, characterised by the building of new universities, the raising of the CATs to university status, and large-scale building programmes at the existing universities, obviously could not go on for ever. A warning note was sounded by the government as early as 1965, when it announced that no more new universities were to be authorized for the next ten years. By the end of the sixties the percentage growth in Britain's GDP had decreased from 5.34 in 1964 to 1.52 in 1970; the Heath government in that year inherited an economic crisis which affected every aspect of Britain's economy.

The UGC's costing became increasingly difficult with rising inflation, which, boosted by the oil crisis in 1973, reached well over 25% in 1974, leading to the virtual abandonment of the university building programme along with the whole system of quinquennial planning and financing. For the next three years all UGC monies were arbitrarily reduced or deferred, and student intakes had to be reduced accordingly. In 1976 all the UK universities were told they faced a 4 per cent cut in real terms in their income the following year.

In the midst of this crisis, the worst faced by the universities in peace-time, a few statements of principle and changes in practice were made. In 1971 Lord Rothschild's proposals for the reorganisation of government-initiated R&D were published, clarifying the differences between basic and applied research. The Council for Scientific Policy was replaced in 1972 by the Advisory Board of Research Councils (ABRC), and in 1981 the Science Research Council (SRC) was renamed the Science and Engineering Research Council (SERC). In 1980 the CVCP produced a report *Research in Universities* which emphasised the strong and often unpredictable interrelationship between so-called basic, fundamental or pure research, and applied research, in science and technology.

The Labour government of James Callaghan gave place in 1979 to the Conservatives under Margaret Thatcher, and her views were echoed whole-heartedly first by Mark Carlisle, then from 1981 to 1986 by Sir Keith Joseph, at the Department of Education and Science. Monetarism ruled, and the universities were no longer to be funded on the Robbins principle of meeting the demand for places from candidates appropriately qualified, but on the new government attitude of 'make the best of what we decide we can afford to give you, and go out and get the rest of what you need from other sources.'

Towards the end of 1980 the UGC warned that greater intervention in the administration of individual universities was inevitable, and that in future resources were going to be taken away as well as added. Then in December 1980 the government reneged on their 'indication' to the UGC of level funding and imposed the first of the so-called 'volume cuts' in recurrent grant of £30m to take effect in the current academic year. This was coupled with the abolition of the subsidy for overseas students which led to significant losses in fee income over the next few years.

In 1981 Sir Keith Joseph announced in Parliament a further progressive reduction in the universities' recurrent grant between 1981/82 and 1983/84 of about 13 per cent, estimated by the UGC and the CVCP to represent a loss to the universities of about £130m to £150m. Considering the drastic consequences of these cuts the UGC contemplated resigning *en bloc*, but felt that that would be the coward's way out, and instead they stayed to try and make the best of the situation for the universities.

In an understandably defensive move the Scottish Vice-Chancellors and Principals formed their own standing committee in 1984 and proposed to the UGC a certain amount of devolution, perhaps even a Scottish UGC. This was firmly rejected at the time, but implemented in the form of the Scottish Higher Education Funding Council (SHEFC) in 1992. The percentage change in UGC funding to the Scottish universities from 1980/81 to 1986/87 ranged from a cut of 7.8% in Glasgow to 24.4% in Aberdeen, with Edinburgh third best at 11.6%. The average cut in all British universities was 17%.

In 1987 the ABRC produced *A Strategy for the Science Base*, at about the same time as Kenneth Baker's White Paper and Mrs Thatcher's new Advisory Council appeared. The strategy turned out to be for a three-tier university system:– R, funded for high-level research and teaching; T, without advanced research facilities, concentrating on undergraduate and master's degree teaching; and X, funded for advanced research in selected fields but not with the range of coverage to be found in R. It was not a new idea, and it was not welcomed any more warmly than before, but it happened to coincide more or less exactly with the recommendations of the UGC sub-committee on the earth sciences in 1988, and it may well be a pointer to the future of the universities in Britain.

The University Grants Committee (UGC) was renamed in 1989 the Universities Funding Council (UFC) and made answerable to Parliament as a non-departmental public body sponsored by the Department of Education and Science (now the Department for Education). The complementary Polytechnics and Colleges Funding Council (PCFC) was created at the same time.

THE UNIVERSITY OF EDINBURGH

In the Edinburgh University *Bulletin* of 25 November 1976 there appeared a 'Message from the Principal (Professor Sir Hugh Robson) to all Members of the University', which began starkly:– 'As you know, universities throughout Great Britain have been warned that they face in real terms a reduction in their income next year of around four per cent, and at Edinburgh—where this means saving a sum approaching £1m—as elsewhere, effecting these savings cannot be painless.' Almost hidden among the details of how the savings were to be achieved was the prescient warning that it was not impossible, in view of the national economic situation, that such reductions in income would endure or become even more acute after 1977-78.

In December 1980 the 'volume cut' of £30m in university funding, and withdrawal of the subsidy for overseas students, forced Edinburgh University to set a savings target of over £3m by the end of session 1980/81. This resulted in 294 staff posts being left vacant, including 91 academic staff; curtailment of library facilities; and deferment of building projects and planned maintenance. The sudden imposition of these severe cuts in government funding of the universities had very serious short-term consequences, but they rapidly achieved the government's aim of making the universities more accountable, more business-like, and more successful in raising money from other sources; in short, leaner and fitter.

Some of the most important 'other sources' of income were the industrial firms which supported research in their areas of interest. Edinburgh University was in 1947 one of the first to establish an industrial liaison committee and had been very successful in attracting income through research contracts, consultancies and patent licensing. In 1971-72 Edinburgh's research grants and contracts exceeded £2m for the first time (230 grants/contracts totalling £2,219,032).

In hard times, everyone tried even harder, and the increases in the University's total external research funding were impressive:–

1983-84	£10.8m	1991-92	£32.3m
1987-88	£19.2m	1992-93	£39.1m.

In June 1987 details of Edinburgh's Academic Plan for the three years 1987-1990 were published in the University *Bulletin*, **9**, xv. Full of unfamiliar terms such as 'academic strategy', 'rationalisation and repatterning', 'contractions and withdrawals', and 'cost centres', it conveyed a strong sense of the seriousness of the situation. A year later the Plan was updated and carried forward to 1991, showing how the University was coping with the loss of 12 per cent of its staff over the previous four years – with more staff losses still to come. The Faculty of Science had to defer plans to introduce an MEng in Chemical and Bioprocess Engineering and a BSc in Electronic Materials. The University itself had to defer the replacement, at an estimated cost of about £3m, of the obsolete and unreliable internal telephone network – assistance from the Department of Mechanical Engineering kept it operational in the meantime.

Overall, however, the University's financial position was worse in 1988 than it had been in 1987. Two of the principal reasons for this were stated to be, firstly, the UGC's planning decision in 1986 to reduce the number of students allowed to enter Edinburgh University in 1989/90 by 2.86% when the number entering the university system as a whole increased by 1.14%; and secondly, a substantial fall in investment income due to the reduction in interest rates during the year, and the much smaller sums available for short-term investment.

In the summer of 1989 another update, the University's *Academic Plan to the early 1990s*, was published. Strategies were outlined for finance, staff, students, and buildings and estates; prospects for each cost centre were summarised, but the advent of the UFC added yet another uncertainty to the already considerable difficulties faced by the University's Director of Finance. Nevertheless, he ventured to forecast that the deficit would be reduced from about £2.5m in 1989 to about £0.75m in 1989/90.

In October 1990, however, a statement by the Principal, Sir David Smith, on the University's financial position revealed that the new Director of Finance had discovered it to be some £2m worse than anticipated in his predecessor's 1989 forecast (ie about £3m instead of £1m) in terms of the recurrent deficit. Coming on top of the sacrifices already made, it was a crushing blow, and it says a great deal for the resilience of every member of staff that the University survived the most serious financial crisis in its four hundred year history. Its recovery was also due in no small measure to the determination of the Finance Committee which, among a number of other emergency measures, took the much-criticised decision to sell the University Library's copy of Audubon's *Birds of America* for the sum of $3.8m.

THE FACULTY OF SCIENCE

By 1983 the Faculty of Science comprised about 300 academic staff, 200 technical and 55 secretarial staff, 2500 undergraduates, 600 postgraduates and over 200 research staff. In session 1988-89 the Dean's corps of staff officers was increased to a Vice-Dean and three Associate-Deans. The present Dean, Prof John Mavor (Electrical Engineering), was elected in 1989. In February 1991 the Faculty of Science was renamed the Faculty of Science and Engineering, with Prof John Mavor remaining at the helm as Dean.

Agriculture

It had been recognised in Stephen Watson's time as Professor and Principal, that the burden of the two posts could not reasonably be carried by one man, but it was not until 1970 that **Francis Elsley** was appointed the first Professor of Animal Production and Head of the Animal Division. He gained an international reputation for his work on the relationship between nutrition and reproduction in sows, and with Colin Whittemore he wrote *Practical Pig Nutrition* (2nd rev edn, 1979) which has had a world-wide success. Two years later **Richard Macer** joined the School as the first Professor of Crop Production and Head of the Crop Division, having been Director of Scientific Development at Rothwell Plant Breeders for the previous six years. He resigned in 1976 to become Director of the Scottish Plant Breeding Station.

From 1973 to 1976 several new courses were introduced – the Postgraduate Diploma and MSc in Animal Breeding, in collaboration with the Department of Genetics and ABRO; BSc Honours options in Animal Production and Crop Production; the Postgraduate Diploma/MSc in Tropical Animal Production and Health in collaboration with the University Veterinary Faculty; and the Postgraduate Diploma/MSc in Seed Technology with the support of the Overseas Development Agency.

Two further professorial appointments were made in 1978. **Graham Milbourn** became the second Professor of Crop Production, continuing his research on the growth and yield of cereal and vegetable crops. He resigned in 1981 to become Director of the National Institute of Agricultural Botany at Cambridge. **John Prescott** was appointed the second Professor of Animal Production, with special interests in beef production and meat quality evaluation. He resigned in 1984 and is now Principal of Wye College, University of London.

In 1984 **Peter Wilson** was appointed ninth Professor of Agriculture and Rural Economy, Principal of the College and Head of the School. After graduating from Wye College, University of London, he studied for the Diploma in Animal Genetics at Edinburgh, 1950-51. He spent much of the next 13 years in the tropics, and in 1965 published *Agriculture in the Tropics* (2nd edn, 1980). He retired in 1990, to become Scientific Director of the Edinburgh Centre for Rural Research.

The third Professor of Animal Production, **Colin Whittemore**, joined the Department as a lecturer in 1970 and has won several awards for his research on the nutrition and growth of farm animals. **John Holmes** was the third Professor of Crop Production, his research covering many of the factors affecting crop productivity. From 1978 to 1988 he acted as consultant to the UN FAO in Africa and the Near East, advising on their training courses in agronomy and plant breeding.

In 1986 **Barry Dent** was appointed to the new Chair of Agricultural (later Rural) Resource Management and Head of the new Division of Rural Resource Management. The Chair has the financial backing of the Bank of Scotland and the Royal Bank of Scotland, and the support of the Department of Agriculture and the Department of Agriculture and Fisheries for Scotland. Professor Dent's research is concerned with regional resource planning and management in rural areas, aided by the creation of computer simulation models to integrate the biological, economic and behavioural aspects of farming. To reflect the broadening of the School's work in these areas, a joint Honours degree in Agriculture, Forestry and Rural Economy was introduced in 1982.

On the retirement of Prof Wilkinson in 1989, the Microbiology Division in the School of Agriculture was disbanded, but the University Department of *Microbiology continued in being with **Dr Ian Sutherland** as Head of Department from 1987 until 1990 when it was incorporated in the Institute of *Cell and Molecular Biology. At the same time the Department of Agriculture and Rural Economy was incorporated with the Department of Forestry and Natural Resources in the Institute of *Ecology and Resource Management, all within the Division of Biological Sciences in the Faculty of Science and Engineering.

Artificial Intelligence and Machine Intelligence

In 1971 the Metamathematics Unit became the Department of Computational Logic (Dr Meltzer) in the new School of Artificial Intelligence, along with the Bionics Research Laboratory (Dr Howe), the Department of Machine Intelligence (Prof Michie) and the Theoretical Psychology Unit (Prof Longuet-Higgins). Bernard Meltzer was appointed in 1972 to a Personal Chair of Artificial Intelligence, which was later renamed Computational Logic.

Prof Michie in 1972/73 wrote two interesting articles on machine intelligence describing what the Department's computer-controlled robots could, and could not, do. They could assemble a heap of parts into an object such as a toy car, but an inordinate length of time was involved in 'teaching' them to do this. Nevertheless, 'Freddy' the robot was hardly surpassed anywhere else in the world at that time, and his accomplishments were described in American and Japanese, as well as British, scientific journals. As long ago as 1974 Prof Michie was suggesting that undersea inspection, assembly and repair of North Sea oil installations would one day be performed more safely and economically by robots than by divers.

The FREDDY robot, mark 2 (c1973)
The XY platform moved objects around, enabling them to be lifted by the manipulator. It was used for pioneering work on automatic assembly of objects from parts. From left to right, Dr (now Professor) Harry Barrow, Mr (now Professor) Steve Salter, Mr Gregan Crawford and Mr (now Professor) Robin Poppleston

In order to understand the downs and ups in the history of Artificial Intelligence at Edinburgh it is necessary to refer to the Lighthill Report. Early in 1972 the SRC's Computing Science committee expressed concern about the different and apparently incompatible opinions being expressed about the nature and aims of research in artificial intelligence. Some, like Michie, viewed it as a kind of engineering; while others, like Longuet-Higgins, saw it as a new kind of theoretical psychology (which in course of time became cognitive science). Accordingly, the SRC invited Sir James Lighthill, Lucasian Professor of Applied Mathematics at Cambridge, to undertake a personal review of the subject.

Briefly, Lighthill saw the building of robots as the main case for the existence of AI as a separate field of research, and on the strength of his personal view of successes and failures in current AI research, his report concluded that the sense of discouragement about the research in category B (the Building of robots) "seems altogether more widespread and profound, and this raised doubts about whether the whole concept of AI as an integrated field of research is a valid one".

The effects of the report were widespread and very damaging. While the Department's research programme included work on mathematical logic, theory of computation, computational modelling of psychological phenomena, and the design and testing of computer-based learning environments, the robotics work formed its solid core. It provided the *raison d'être* for the Department's infrastructure, including workshops, laboratories, programming development team, and so on. Almost overnight, SRC funding for work in robotics ceased, resulting in the loss of a number of extremely talented research workers.

The School of Computer Science and Artificial Intelligence was created in 1974 to strengthen and promote communication between the two Departments, which otherwise remained quite independent. An article by Prof Meltzer in the Edinburgh University *Bulletin* (16 Apr 1975, 1-2) described the work of the Artificial Intelligence Department in perception, cognitive development, mathematical reasoning, theory of computation, operational research, and the development of high-level programming languages. At this stage the first undergraduate course, *Artificial Intelligence 2*, was started, followed four years later by *Artificial Intelligence 1*.

At about the same time Prof Michie detached himself and re-established Machine Intelligence as an independent Research Unit, and Prof Longuet-Higgins moved to the Centre for Research in Perception and Cognition at the University of Sussex. Stephen Salter, a lecturer in the Bionics Research Laboratory where he had already built the first prototype of the Salter Duck, moved to the Department of Mechanical *Engineering.

In 1978 **Rod Burstall** was appointed to a Personal Chair of Artificial Intelligence, having come to Edinburgh University in 1964 as a Senior Research Fellow, with an industrial background in the field of operational research. Prof Burstall transferred in 1979 to the Theory Group in the Department of *Computer Science.

What helped to keep the Department together in the 1970s despite continuing losses of senior staff was Jim Howe's SSRC funded research into the design and development of computer-based learning environments, undertaken in collaboration with a number of local primary, secondary and special schools. The practical fruits of the research included the development of the Edinburgh Turtle (a small robot), over one thousand of which were used in the classrooms of Britain during the 1980s, and an implementation of the children's programming language *LOGO*.

The downward spiral in the Department's fortunes continued, despite some notable achievements, until it was saved by the launch in 1983 of the government's R & D programme in Information Technology, the Alvey Programme, together with associated funding schemes such as the IT Lectureship scheme and the Engineering and Technology Programme.

Since 1982 the Department of Artificial Intelligence has been able to introduce joint Honours Degrees in Linguistics and Artificial Intelligence (1982); Artificial Intelligence and Computer Science (1987), with support from the Engineering and Technology Programme; and Artificial Intelligence and Mathematics (1992). In 1983 the MSc/Diploma course in Information Technology: Knowledge Based Systems was launched, with SERC pump-priming support, and it has now become the largest MSc course in the Faculty of Science and Engineering, with an annual intake of about 50 students. The topics covered include natural language, visual processing, intelligent assembly, intelligent sensing and control, expert systems, inference techniques, speech processing and database design.

In 1983 the School of Computer Science and Artificial Intelligence was dissolved and replaced by the School of *Information Technology, bringing the Department of Electrical Engineering into a tripartite collaboration. By 1985, the Department's annual research income had grown to £4m, compared to £400,000 in 1982; academic staff numbers had increased from four to eleven.

Jim Howe, who joined the Department as a Research Fellow in 1967 and became its Head in 1978, was appointed Professor of Artificial Intelligence in 1985. Recently Prof Howe has been concerned with the problems of transferring high-technology skills from

Exploring mathematics by computer

university to industry, and he was instrumental in the creation of the Artificial Intelligence Applications Institute (AIAI) in 1984 to assist in that process. Another of his research projects (the most challenging?) is CARoM, the Computer Aided Recognition of Misconceptions, which aims to develop a system that will support the diagnosis of a wide range of students' mistaken beliefs about physical systems. In 1989 Artificial Intelligence and *Cognitive Science combined with a number of other departments in Glasgow, Durham and Edinburgh Universities to form the Human Communication Research Centre.

Also in 1989 the School of Information Technology was combined with the School of Engineering to form the School of Engineering and Informatics, which has a co-ordinating rather than an executive role. At the same time Artificial Intelligence combined with the Departments of Electrical Engineering and Linguistics to form the Centre for Speech Technology Research (CSTR), which took on the role of coordinator in a joint university/industry project funded by the Alvey Directorate. The budget for Edinburgh University's research over the following five years was £3m, the aim being to develop the innovative software and hardware necessary to create a word-processing system responsive to spoken instructions.

Artificial Intelligence Applications Institute
The Institute was formally established in 1984 by the University Court, with most of its initial income being derived from ongoing contracts. Subsequent development of the Institute was assisted by additional funding from Lothian Region Development Authority and the Scottish Development Agency (now Scottish Enterprise). Its Advisory Board is chaired by the head of the Department of Artificial Intelligence, and for the first year Prof Jim Howe of the Department of Artificial Intelligence was the Acting Director. In 1985 **Dr Austin Tate**, who gained his PhD in the Machine Intelligence Research Unit in 1975, was appointed Director; currently he is Technical Director. The Institute is mainly concerned in the application by industry and commerce of the basic research undertaken by the Department of Artificial Intelligence, which with Cognitive Science and Computer Science gives Edinburgh University the largest concentration of such expertise outside the USA.

On 16 June 1986 the formal inauguration took place of the £2.25m national facility for technology development and transfer in knowledge representation systems and parallel computer architectures, funded by industrial sponsors under the Alvey Programme, and by the DTI and SERC. The two new laboratories forming part of the Artificial Intelligence Applications Institute are designed to introduce potential industrial and academic users to some of the most advanced computer hardware and software in the world, with expert assistance being provided by AIAI staff. Additional funding to allow a 50 per cent increase in the number of potential 'customers' visiting AIAI was received in 1987 from the City of Edinburgh District Council.

In 1989 **Austin Tate,** Technical Director of AIAI, was appointed to a Professorial

Fellowship. The Institute won an award in 1990 of £30,000 from the Department of Trade and Industry, for successful long-term collaboration with an industrial firm – in this instance, ICL.

Astronomy
The last five years of Professor Brück's term as Regius Professor and Astronomer Royal were marked by intensive work on three major new telescopes. Location surveys were carried out for the Northern Hemisphere Telescope, and a site was eventually selected on La Palma in the Canary Islands. At the Siding Springs site in Australia, Dr V C Reddish was given charge of the erection of the UK 48-inch Schmidt telescope (UKST), designed for similar photographic work in the southern hemisphere to that undertaken by the comparable Schmidt Camera on Mount Palomar in California. The Royal Observatory Edinburgh (ROE) also carried out site surveys for the UK Infrared Telescope (UKIRT) on Mauna Kea (4,200m) in Hawaii, and since its commissioning in 1979 it has been operated by the ROE as a shared facility with the University of Hawaii.

In 1975 Prof Brück retired, and in 1983 he published *The Story of Astronomy in Edinburgh from its beginnings until 1975*, on which much of the account of astronomy at the University of Edinburgh in this volume is based. He was succeeded by **Vincent Reddish** as the eighth Astronomer Royal for Scotland and ninth Regius Professor of Astronomy. Under his guidance 'GALAXY' was redesigned and rebuilt, both faster and able to measure faint (elliptical) galaxies as readily as (circular) stars. It was renamed 'COSMOS' from its ability to measure '*C*oordinates, *S*izes, *M*agnitudes, *O*rientations and *S*hapes' of images on Schmidt photographs. In 1976 COSMOS became a national facility operated like UKIRT and UKST by ROE staff for the benefit of all British astronomers.

Prof Reddish published *Evolution of the Galaxies* (1967), *The Physics of Stellar Interiors* (1974), and *Stellar Formation* (1978). He retired in 1980 to Rannoch Station in Perthshire (a move that might be termed 'the Reddish shift'), and was succeeded by **Malcolm Longair**, the ninth Astronomer Royal for Scotland and tenth Regius Professor of Astronomy. Among his many publications were *The Large-Scale Structure of the Universe* (ed jtly, 1978), *High Energy Astrophysics: an informal introduction* (1980), *Astrophysical Cosmology* (ed with H A Brück and G Coyne, 1982), and *Theoretical Concepts in Physics* (1984).

Two major ROE projects made impressive progress in the 1980s. The joint ROE/Durham University southern galaxy catalogue project received further SERC funding, reflecting the very successful collaboration of the UKST in Australia and COSMOS in Edinburgh. In 1987 the James Clerk Maxwell Telescope (JCMT) with a 15m diameter paraboloidal reflector was commissioned on Mauna Kea. It was the largest of a new generation of radio telescopes designed to work at sub-millimetre wavelengths, and is operated by the ROE in association with the University of Hawaii, the National Research Council of Canada and the Netherlands Foundation for Pure Research.

Prof Longair resigned in 1991 on his appointment to the Jacksonian Chair of Natural Philosophy in the University of Cambridge, leaving Edinburgh as an internationally recognised centre for cosmological research. It was decided as an economy measure not to refill the Regius Chair at that time, and **Peter Brand**, Reader in Astronomy, was elected Head of Department.

BIOLOGICAL SCIENCES, DIVISION OF

In 1987 the then Dean of the Faculty of Science, Prof Ebsworth, set up a Planning Group covering all the biological sciences in the University of Edinburgh. One of its first proposals was the setting up of a new biology teaching organisation to integrate all courses in biological subjects up to third-year level. The other radical proposal was that existing departmental structures should be completely reorganised, in the interests of more efficient use of dwindling resources and staff numbers, and more effective work in research. Two years later the *Biology Teaching Organisation came into being, and on 1st August 1990 the Division of Biological Sciences in the Faculty of Science and Engineering was created, consisting of:-

> The Biology Teaching Organisation (BTO)
> The Institute of *Cell, Animal and Population Biology (ICAPB)
> The Institute of *Cell and Molecular Biology (ICMB)
> The Institute of *Ecology and Resource Management (IERM).

The three new Institutes comprised the most appropriate groupings of staff from the former Departments of Agriculture, Botany, Forestry and Natural Resources, Genetics, Microbiology, Molecular Biology and Zoology. The Division is technically a single department, by far the largest in the University, with more than 80 full-time lecturing and academic-related staff. **John Dale**, Professor of Plant Physiology (ICMB), was designated Head of Division with overall responsibility for integration of the biological sciences.

Biology, School of

The School of Biology was established in May 1973 as a loose federation of all the departments involved in the teaching of biological subjects in the Faculty of Science and Engineering and the Faculty of Medicine, together with the Department of Psychology in the Faculty of Social Sciences.

To take just one of the Medical Departments as an example, the Chair of Chemistry in Relation to Medicine was established in the Faculties of Medicine and Science in 1919, and renamed Biochemistry in 1960. Since 1984 **Andrew Miller** FRSE (1936-   ) has been Professor of Biochemistry. An Edinburgh graduate, he was Assistant Lecturer in Chemistry at Edinburgh University, 1960-62; Lecturer in Molecular Biophysics, Oxford University and (from 1967) Fellow of Wolfson College, 1966-83. In 1987 a joint research project on collagen was initiated in the Departments of Biochemistry and Chemistry with an SERC Grant of £118,840 over three years. The Professor of Biochemistry is currently a member of the Faculty of Science and Engineering.

Biology Teaching Organisation

This is an inter-faculty organisation which coordinates undergraduate teaching of the biological sciences under the Science, Forestry and Agriculture Ordinances, and represents the teaching executive of the School. It had its origins in the Biology Teaching Unit which was set up in 1966 by **Dr Ron Kille** (Zoology), who was succeeded as Director in 1985 by **Dr D E S Truman** (Genetics). The Unit had both administrative and technical staff, and was responsible for a major teaching facility in the Appleton Tower. It was transformed into the Biology Teaching Organisation in 1988 and directed initially by Dr **John Phillips**, on a five-year secondment from the Department of Biochemistry. He was appointed to a Personal Chair in Biology Teaching in 1992.

Botany

After twenty years in the Chair Robert Brown was succeeded in 1978 by **Michael Yeoman** as the thirteenth Regius Professor of Botany. He joined the Department in 1959 and first developed an interest in the regulation of cell division. After 1975 his research moved towards studies of secondary metabolic pathways in immobilised cells, a topic of considerable commercial interest which attracted extensive funding from industry. He edited *Cell Division in Higher Plants* (1976) and *Plant Cell Technology* (1986), and

Volumes comprising field study "Flora of Turkey"

The Turkish Poppy, adopted as the study logo

published a *Laboratory Manual of Plant Cell and Tissue Culture* (jtly, 1982).

In 1979 **Peter Davis** was appointed to a Personal Chair in Taxonomic Botany; his definitive *Flora of Turkey and the East Aegean Islands*, the product of a life-time's interest in the region, was completed in 1988 in ten volumes, published by the Edinburgh University Press.

Two Personal Chairs were created in 1985/86; the first in Plant Physiology, for **John Dale**, Lecturer and Reader in Botany since 1961, and the second in Plant Molecular Biology, for **Christopher Leaver**, Lecturer and Reader in Botany since 1969. Prof Dale has a particular interest in the cerrado vegetation of central Brazil, and maintains links with botanists in Brazil and elsewhere with a similar interest. Prof Leaver resigned in 1990 to become Sibthorpian Professor of Botany at Oxford.

A major development in the late 1980s benefitting the whole University was the establishment of the Science Faculty Electron Microscope Facility within the Department of Botany. It consists of one transmission and two scanning electron microscopes, with facilities for cryo-preparation of biological specimens, a back-scattered electron detector, and an image analyser. The last of these can of course be equally useful in the analysis of non-microscopic images, for example in estimating the forest canopy gap fraction from aerial photographs.

A research project which even the purists would have to label 'Scotch' rather than Scottish was funded in 1987 by the North British Distillery Company, with the aim of getting a better understanding of the reactions involved in the traditional methods of converting starch to sugar in the malting process. Since the export earnings of the Scotch Whisky industry are around £1,000m per annum, even a small increase in productivity would be of benefit to the industry and the country as a whole.

In 1990 the Department of Botany, after more than three hundred years of independent existence, was incorporated in the Institute of *Cell and Molecular Biology within the Division of Biological Sciences in the Faculty of Science and Engineering.

Chemistry

In 1969 **John Cadogan** was appointed to the Forbes Chair of Organic Chemistry, from the Purdie Chair of Chemistry at St Andrews. One of his innovations was to introduce the study of Environmental Chemistry, first as a second year half-course in 1973/74, then as a four-year Honours Degree course, the first of its kind in Britain, two years later. Students were encouraged to take support courses in such subjects as biology, geology, meteorology and business studies, while the Department's own input included chemistry in relation to man's activities, and monitoring the environment. The Honours course in

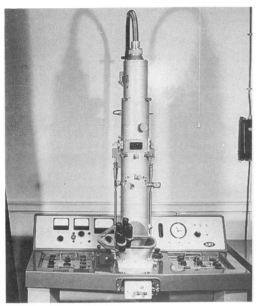

Early Electron Microscope

Environmental Chemistry has proved very popular, and the Department now offers a one-year postgraduate Diploma course in the same subject.

Prof Cadogan resigned in 1979 to become Chief Scientist and, in 1981, Director of Research, British Petroleum. He was knighted in 1991, at about the time of his retirement from BP. In addition to more than 200 scientific papers, he published *Principles of Free Radical Chemistry* (1971) and *Organophosphorus Reagents in Organic Synthesis* (1979).

The Department was awarded a grant of £92,500 by the Wolfson Foundation in 1972 to set up a Unit for High Speed Liquid Chromatography as part of the Foundation's scheme for linking scientific research with industry. Two years later **John Knox** was appointed to a Personal Chair in Physical Chemistry, and Director of the Wolfson Liquid Chromatography Unit. Himself an Edinburgh graduate, he returned to the Department of Chemistry in 1953 as a lecturer, and developed a special interest in liquid chromatography. His theoretical and practical expertise led to many fruitful links with industrial firms, and after his retirement in 1984 he was given the Martin Award of the Chromatographic Society at their 16th International Symposium in 1987.

In 1979 **Robert Donovan** was appointed to a Personal Chair in Physical Chemistry, and in 1986 he became the thirteenth Professor of Chemistry. He joined the Department as Lecturer in Physical Chemistry in 1970, and has earned an international reputation for his spectroscopic and photochemical studies, using laser and synchrotron radiation, in the experimentally difficult ultraviolet region of the spectrum. He was awarded the Corday-Morgan Medal and Prize of the Royal Society of Chemistry in 1975. The research group led by Prof Donovan was awarded £326,000 in 1985 under the UGC Additional Equipment Grant scheme, to enable them to bring their laser research equipment up to the highest international standard.

The Department was fortunate in being allocated the necessary funding (of the order of £300,000) in 1979 to acquire a very high field strength Nuclear Magnetic Resonance (NMR) spectrometer, the first of its kind in a British university. **Ian Scott** was appointed to the Forbes Chair of Organic Chemistry in 1980. A graduate of Glasgow University, he had previously held chairs in British Columbia, Sussex, Yale and Texas A & M Universities. Soon after his arrival in the Department he was awarded a grant of £365,000 over four years by the SRC to pursue research into metabolic processes in living cells, using the NMR technique. An expanded NMR Unit was opened in May 1981, but unfortunately Prof Scott could not resist an invitation to return to Texas A & M as Davidson Professor of Chemistry and Biochemistry later that year.

There was however no shortage of research workers keen to use the facilities of the NMR Unit, which in any case was funded on the basis that up to 80% of its time would be at the disposal of other UK universities. Early in 1985 the SERC announced a further grant of £200,000 in support of the NMR Unit over the next five years. Both grants included an allowance for the regular maintenance and up-grading of the machine and its ancillary equipment to the latest specification.

In 1984 **Robert Ramage** was appointed to the Forbes Chair of Organic Chemistry, having occupied a similar Chair in Manchester (UMIST) since 1977. His principal research interests are concerned with the synthesis of polypeptides and antibiotics. In the late 1980s the Department began work in three new areas which underlined its growing interest in the biological sciences. A joint research project on collagen telopeptides was initiated with an SERC grant of £119,000 over three years. The telopeptides were synthesised in the Department of Chemistry using new methodology developed by Prof Ramage, then studied in the Department of Biochemistry.

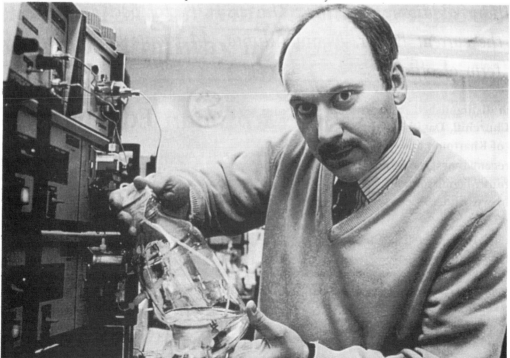

OSWEL DNA facility

An important service for research workers investigating the structure of DNA was set up in the Department of Chemistry with the support of the Wellcome Trust. The OSWEL DNA manufacturing facility can make up to 30 fragments of high quality DNA per week on an automatic synthesizer, operating more or less continuously with computer monitoring and control. OSWEL is one of a number of central facilities in chemistry and biology expected to be set up at Edinburgh University over the next few years.

Vitamin research group (l to r): Robert Baxter, Keith Milne, Helen Baxter, Dominic Murphy and Andrew Ramsay

The Vitamins Research Group, made up of chemists and biochemists, was awarded a grant of £90,000 over three years by the SERC, to investigate the enzymes involved in the biological formation of a number of key vitamins. Because of the commercial importance of this work, additional funding has been received from the Food Research Institute and a number of industrial sponsors.

In 1989 **David Rankin** was appointed to a Personal Chair of Structural Chemistry, having joined the Department as a Research Fellow in 1969. He has been using electron diffraction to investigate the structure of chemical compounds for the past twenty years, progressing from relatively simple to more and more complicated structures. Recently he has combined electron diffraction with NMR analysis to increase the accuracy of his results, and now provides a service to research workers in all the other British universities.

Having over the past ten years attracted much praise for its management of the original NMR Unit, the Department in 1989 was given a grant of a further £1m from the SERC to support a new ultra-high-field NMR facility, the only one of its kind in Scotland and one of only two in the UK. It is being used by chemical and biological research workers from all parts of the UK, allowing them to probe molecular behaviour and environment at levels not previously possible.

Cognitive Science

The School of Epistemics was created in the Faculty of Science in 1969, with the objective of bringing together all those having 'a common concern with the nature of knowledge and understanding and the means whereby knowledge and understanding may be achieved.' The Chairman of the School was Royal Society Research Professor **Christopher Longuet-Higgins** of the Department of Machine Intelligence and Perception. At Cambridge he was one of the leading figures in post-war theoretical chemistry, but turned his attention to information processing in biological systems, and problems of the mind. He was co-author of *The Nature of Mind – The Gifford Lectures*, 1972.

On the meaning of *epistemics* (a word coined by Christopher himself), he wrote in the University *Bulletin* (10 June 1969):–

"By tradition the philosophical theory of knowledge is known as *epistemology*. The word *epistemics* implies an intention to reformulate some of the key questions about knowledge and to construct formal models of the processes – perceptual, inferential and linguistic – by which knowledge and understanding are achieved."

The other members of the School, about twenty in number, worked in the Departments of Computer Science, Molecular Biology, English Language, Linguistics, Philosophy and Psychology, and in the research units of Computer-Aided Architectural Design, Metamathematics, Science Studies, and Speech and Communication. The computational modelling of language in relation to the cognitive processes employed in its use became the hallmark of Cognitive Science at Edinburgh.

Following the departure of Christopher Longuet-Higgins in 1974 to the Centre for Research in Perception and Cognition at the University of Sussex, **Barry Richards**, Lecturer, later Reader, in the Department of Philosophy, was appointed Director. His work in logic and formal semantics played a leading part in establishing the School's computational orientation. He was appointed in 1985 to a Personal Chair of Cognitive Science, from which he resigned in 1989 to become Professor of Computer Science at Imperial College, London.

In 1978 the Postgraduate Programme in Epistemics was introduced, which led to the degrees of MPhil and PhD. An MSc degree was added in 1981. During this time the Academic Secretary was **Keith Brown**, a Senior Lecturer in Linguistics. He moved to Essex University in 1983 where he subsequently became Research Professor of Linguistics.

During the formalization of the structure of the School in 1982, the name of the Programme was changed from Epistemics to Cognitive Science and its Director, designated Academic Secretary for the Programme, was elected by the membership of the School. **Terry Myers**, Lecturer in Psychology and subsequently Senior Lecturer in Cognitive Science and Psychology, directed the Programme from 1982 to 1987. He is now a University Fellow in the CCS, and editor of the *Encyclopedia of Cognitive Science*.

The School of Epistemics became in 1985 the Centre for Cognitive Science (CCS), a 'department' within the Faculty of Science. It continued to be devoted exclusively to research and postgraduate teaching in Cognitive Science, involving the Departments of Artificial Intelligence, Computer Science, English Language, Linguistics, and Psychology. **Ewan Klein**, Reader in Cognitive Science, was appointed Head of Department in 1986. Principally through his success in securing ESPRIT funding, the Centre has achieved a prominent position within a network of research and training collaborations that are both interdisciplinary and international.

In session 1988/89 the **Human Communication Research Centre** (HCRC), proposed as a joint venture by Edinburgh and Glasgow Universities, was founded as the first Inter-disciplinary Research Centre (IRC) of the Economic and Social Research Council (ESRC). With additional funding from the UGC and the two Universities, and a small staff input by the University of Durham, the aim of the Centre was to pursue research in the areas of real spoken language and memory and inference, and to contribute to technology transfer in those areas. Its senior staff were seconded from the Departments of *Artificial Intelligence, Cognitive Science, Linguistics and Psychology in Edinburgh, Glasgow and Durham Universities. The first Director of HCRC is **Keith Stenning**, appointed as a 'new blood' lecturer in 1983, and in 1989, Senior Lecturer in Cognitive Science and Psychology, later Professorial Fellow.

The CCS was incorporated in 1989 in what is now the School of Engineering and Informatics. Students who enrolled for the modular MSc in Information Technology were able to take some components of the course in Cognitive Science, which encompassed computational linguistics, cognitive psychology, logic and formal methods, and theoretical linguistics, to which was added in 1991 neural networks. In 1991, **Elisabet Engdahl**, Reader in Artificial Intelligence and Cognitive Science, was appointed Head of Department. Under her leadership the course began diversification, allowing students to specialise on a broad base.

Computer being hoisted out of building

Computer Science

The decade of the 1970s began with the introduction of the *Computer Science 3* and *4* courses, leading to joint Honours Degrees in Computer Science and Mathematics, and single Honours in Computer Science. In later years joint Honours Degrees with Artificial Intelligence, Electronics, Management Science, Physics and Statistics were also introduced.

In 1971 the Department moved to King's Buildings, to the newly-completed Phase 1b of the James Clerk Maxwell Building, adjacent to Phase 1a which already housed the ERCC. Thanks to the foresight of Sidney Michaelson, Computer

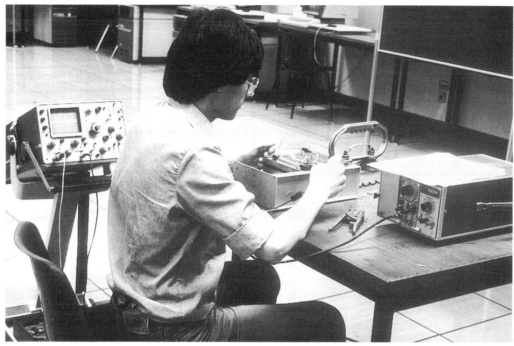

Micro-computer Kits

Science had its own machine halls, large enough for the Computer-Aided Design project under **John Oldfield** to move into the same accommodation as the rest of the department, which had never been possible in Buccleuch Place.

However, the first year Computer Science class (CS1) remained in the centre of town, with access via card readers at Alison House to the ERCC's IBM 360/50. In 1973, CS1 students moved at last on to the Edinburgh Multi-Access System (EMAS) and a room full of Olivetti terminals was provided in the Appleton Tower. Although the main-frame computers running the system changed several times over the following years and the Olivetti (hard-copy) terminals were replaced by visual display units, the class continued using EMAS until 1987.

By 1975 Sidney Michaelson had been Head of Department in the Computer Unit and then in Computer Science for a total of twelve years, and he indicated a desire for a change. **Peter Schofield**, a Senior Lecturer in the Department, was elected for three years although eventually he also served for twelve. After early years in the Royal Navy and then Imperial College London, he had joined the original Computer Unit in 1963.

An MSc course in Computer Systems Engineering was started in 1978. Two years later, following the Report of the Roberts Committee, the SERC selected Edinburgh as one of three universities for additional funding to run MSc courses in Integrated Circuit

Design. The Departments of Computer Science and Electrical Engineering participated jointly in this development, which was built on a modular basis on top of their existing MSc courses, so that students could take some modules from each department. Other departments (Artificial Intelligence, Cognitive Science, and Linguistics) joined in this modular structure later.

In 1978 John Gray took leave of absence to direct the Silicon Structures Project at the California Institute of Technology. On his return the department became very much involved in the Mead and Conway approach to VLSI chip design. In 1980 John Gray and two other members of staff, Irene Buchanan and Peter Robertson, left the department to form a start-up company *LATTICE LOGIC*, which developed one of the world's first silicon compiler products, *Chipsmith*, still in use today. Sidney Michaelson, John Gray, David Rees and others from the department co-operated with Electrical Engineering to set up a series of international conferences on VLSI, which took place annually from 1981 to 1991, the first and last being held in Edinburgh.

By the end of the 1970s, the department urgently needed additional computing power – the subject was developing rapidly and overall student numbers had doubled in three years. Fortunately, prices were dropping and in 1979 the department was able to buy a Digital Equipment Corporation (DEC) VAX 11/780 computer; DEC's multi-access operating system, known as VMS, provided a service to staff and students in second year onwards. In 1980 a new first-year course entitled *Information Systems 1* was introduced, aimed specially at non-scientists. A separate laboratory was set up in the Appleton Tower, funded jointly by Computer Science and ERCC.

In 1981 a small experimental project was started to design and build a modular computer system that would enable students and staff to experiment with a variety of architectures and processors. The project soon became diverted, however, towards a small number of architectures needed to meet the demands of teaching, which were once again overtaking supply. Thus the 'Advanced Personal Machine', otherwise known as the 'Fred Machine', after Fred King the hardware designer, was born. Forty of these personal workstations had been assembled in the department by 1984, the total increasing to 60, mostly with colour graphics, by the end of 1985. They were in use for second and third year teaching until the spring of 1993.

The next round of (overlapping) changes in computing equipment began in 1987. The use of EMAS for *Computer Science 1* teaching came to an end, and *Sun* workstations running under the UNIX operating system were provided instead in the Appleton Tower laboratory and in a small number of other locations. As funds have become available, this change has spread throughout the department, and there are now about 280 *Sun* workstations or similar equipment in use.

From the beginning, the success of the department's work relied on strong support from the technical staff. In that connection it is interesting to note that in 1971 one member of the technical staff read a paper at an international DEC conference; later, another left the department to take up a Lectureship in Electrical Engineering at the Heriot-Watt University, returning after five years to a Lectureship in Computer Science at Edinburgh University.

The department is unique among the *academic* departments in having a significant number (about one-third) of its academic-related staff appointed as Computing Officers. This situation developed from the massive increase in scale and complexity of departmental computing facilities in the 1980s. The department had to create a single coherent internal computing service, and it did so by employing graduate academic-related staff to handle systems management and development. The department thus enjoys an efficient and state-of-the-art computing service, while the academic staff have more time for teaching and research.

Another start-up company, which now employs seven people, sprang from the department in 1984. *CLAN SYSTEMS* was set up by Hamish Dewar and Igor Hansen as a system house engaged in combined hardware and software design. The main area of activity is laser printer controllers, and Clan-designed controllers are to be found in the products of such major manufacturers as Fujitsu and Ricoh.

Professor Rod Burstall and **Dr Gordon Plotkin** transferred from the Department of Artificial Intelligence to Computer Science in 1979. In conjunction with Robin Milner and his colleagues already in Computer Science, they formed a group with a considerable international reputation. The title of Rod Burstall's personal chair was changed to Computer Science. Since making the move, Rod Burstall has been best known for his research contributions to computer-aided proof, program specification, functional programming and applications of category theory to computing. He was awarded a 5-year SERC Information Technology Senior Fellowship.

Robin Milner, who had joined the Department as a lecturer in 1973, was appointed to a Personal Chair of Computation Theory in 1984. He has a number of important advances in computer science to his credit, especially CCS, a Calculus for Communicating Systems, and a large part of the development of ML, originally a language for expressing and manipulating logical proofs, and now widely used as a functional programming language. The research group led by Professors Milner and Burstall was awarded the British Computer Society 1987 Technical Award for Standard ML. Robin Milner is a Distinguished Fellow of the British Computer Society.

Gordon Plotkin was appointed to a Personal Chair of Computation Theory in 1986, having joined the University in 1971 as a Research Associate in Artificial Intelligence. His work concerns the application of logic to computer science. He is particularly known for his contributions to the semantics and logic of programming languages, and he has also worked on automated theorem proving.

In 1986, the three Professors mentioned above (Burstall, Milner and Plotkin) set up the **Laboratory for Foundations of Computer Science** (LFCS) within the Department of Computer Science. The twin aims were to intensify the already strong programme of theoretical research, and to deepen the formal links with industry to ensure the application of this basic research in practical environments. Significant funding to set up the Laboratory was obtained from the SERC, national and international informatics programmes and industry. The three founders of the Laboratory are serving three years each as Director. After the first few years of operation, the LFCS has stabilised at a little above its originally planned size of some sixty members, including research students; it is generally accepted as a leading world centre for theoretical computer science.

The work of the LFCS has strongly influenced the development of computation theory particularly in the fields of semantics, specification, concurrency, complexity, machine assisted proof and implementations (of both languages and proof systems). It is naturally the software products that have been most visible, in particular the functional programming language *Standard ML*, which is now in use in many places around the world both in education and in research and development. Methodologies have also been exported, for example the Specification Language *CLEAR* and the algebraic Calculus of Communicating Systems.

Despite the promotion of three members of Computer Science to personal chairs, until 1985 there was only one established chair, held by **Sidney Michaelson**. From the new funds then becoming available, two more established chairs were created.

In 1985, **Roland Ibbett** was appointed to the Second Chair of Computer Science, from the University of Manchester, where he was best known for his work as designer of the MU5 computer. His research interests lie in the area of computer hardware, and in particular the design and simulation of parallel and high performance architectures. In 1987, he took over as Head of Department from Peter Schofield.

In 1988, **Michael Fourman** was appointed Professor of Computer Systems (Software), from Brunel University. His early work was on connections between category theory and logic; more recently he has also been developing applications of formal methods to chip design. This work has led to the formation of a company, *ABSTRACT HARDWARE LTD*, which is now successfully marketing formally based design tools.

In 1987, the year of its twenty-first 'birthday', the Department of Computer Science expanded into an extension of the JCMB built with funds from the UGC Engineering and Technology Programme. In that time the Department had grown from six to eighty staff and research workers, and from a handful of students to over 350 undergraduates and postgraduates. Two years later the Department was incorporated in what is now the School of *Engineering and Informatics. In February 1991 the death occurred of Prof Michaelson after almost 28 years of sterling service to the science of computing in the University and beyond.

A resounding success was scored by a team of six second-year students from the Department of Computer Science, who won the final of the 1989 British Computer Society programming competition. With an upper age limit of 30 most of the teams contained considerably more experienced programmers, and Prof Ibbett as Head of Department was delighted at this demonstration of the effectiveness of its teaching.

In the modern world we depend increasingly on complex systems controlled by computers, and we depend in many cases on that control being safety-critical. Computer programs being notoriously capricious, how can we guarantee the safety of such systems? A research team in the LFCS, working on Mathematically Proven Safety Systems (MPSS), has had notable success in the design and analysis of safety-critical systems. David May, Head of Transputer Architecture at Inmos, and a member of the Advisory Board of LFCS, has expressed the opinion that 'with microprocessor chips now containing over a million transistors we can no longer verify designs by simulation alone. New mathematical techniques which allow us to ensure correct design *by construction* are essential to the semiconductor industry of the 1990s.'

In his PhD research in 1988, Tom Kean had invented a configurable logic architecture for VLSI. He showed how this could be used to achieve a dramatic speeding up of some types of computation. In order to exploit this work, he was joined by John Gray and Irene Buchanan, and they created *ALGOTRONIX*, the third company to spin-off from the department. In 1993, Algotronix needed capital to expand and it was voluntarily acquired by Xilinx, the world leader in this technology.

Computing Services and Edinburgh Parallel Computing Centre

The scheduled (and re-scheduled) completion date for the Edinburgh Multi-Access Project (EMAP) finally arrived in September 1970 – ICL staff were withdrawn, but the system based on the ICL 4-75 was at that time not capable of meeting the specification. The Computer Science staff who had been working on the project were joined by members of ERCC in a team which had to complete (and in the process largely rewrite) what became in 1971 the Edinburgh Multi-Access System (EMAS).

By 1974 a second ICL 4-75 was in service, ERCC had taken over responsibility for development work on EMAS, and a reliable service was available throughout the University and beyond. The number of registered users had grown to over 4000, and a Regional Computing Organisation (RCO) had been set up linking Edinburgh with Glasgow and Strathclyde Universities. Interactive computing was transformed by the gradual introduction of monitors (visual display units or VDUs in those days) instead of punched paper tape or cards for input, and hard copy output on concertinas of continuous computer paper.

The largest and most powerful computing resource in Scotland was opened in October 1976 on Edinburgh University's Bush Estate, about five miles south of the King's Buildings. The ICL 2980 computer in the new ERCC building was the largest built by International Computers up to that time, and was valued at about £2m. It was funded by the National Computer Board to serve the needs of the RCO and government research institutes in central Scotland. Further improvements to the University's computing facilities have been made more or less continuously since then, in an effort to keep pace with developments in hardware (*smaller* and better, fortunately), software (constantly expanding to fill just a few Mb *more* than the space available for it), and user demand (what do they *do* with all that data?).

A new approach to high-performance computing began in 1980 when members of the Department of Physics began to use parallel computing processes, at first on the ICL Distributed Array Processor (DAP) at Queen Mary College in London, to run molecular dynamics and high energy physics simulations. Two years later Edinburgh University acquired one ICL DAP for its own use, part of the cost being met by SERC and part off-set by ICL against software to be supplied to them by ERCC for a collaborative project both parties were involved in at the time. The Department of Physics continued to generate widespread recognition of its advanced work in the field of parallel computing, and in 1983, as a 400th Anniversary gift to the University, ICL donated a second DAP, based on an upgraded dual processor ICL 2976.

In 1986 **Dr Brian Sutton** was appointed to succeed Dr Thomas as Director of the newly-renamed Edinburgh University Computing Service (EUCS), which consisted of the Edinburgh Regional Computing Centre and the Centre for Applications Software and Technology (CAST). He had previously been IT Systems Manager with Britoil plc. Under his guidance the decision was taken in 1989 to plan for the closure of EMAS after its twenty years of sterling service, and move all the multi-access facilities on to the recently-installed UNIX system based on three Amdahl 470 series computers.

Largely due to the very successful results achieved by research staff using the ICL DAP, the Edinburgh Concurrent Supercomputer Project was initiated in 1987, based on the Meiko Computing Surface installed the year before. This very powerful machine uses a modular array of transputers, the 'computer on a chip', manufactured by the British company Inmos. An even more powerful Meiko was purchased in 1987 with the aid of a £350,000 SERC grant. By September 1990 the Edinburgh Concurrent Supercomputer Project had developed to such an extent that the Edinburgh Parallel Computing Centre (EPCC) was established by the University as a separate group within the Faculty of Science and Engineering. Its mission is to promote the use of these very high power systems by universities and industry. **Prof David Wallace** of the Department of Physics was appointed Director of the EPCC.

It is appropriate to close this chapter in the story of multi-access computing at Edinburgh University by recording that the last machine running EMAS was switched off in July 1992.

ENGINEERING (SCIENCE), SCHOOL OF

Since 1967 the Engineering Departments had been in two distinctly different Schools:– Civil Engineering and Building Science had joined the Departments of Architecture, Geography, and Urban Design and Regional Planning in the School of the Built Environment; Chemical, Electrical and Mechanical Engineering had combined in the School of Engineering Science. In 1973 the Department of Fire Safety Engineering was instituted, and joined the School of the Built Environment. Soon afterwards, however, it became increasingly obvious that there was not as much common ground among the members of that School as had been hoped, and it was dissolved in 1975.

Another factor in the demise of the School of the Built Environment was the realisation that any fragmentation of the Engineering Departments, in times of increasingly severe competition for limited resources, would be liable to affect any or all of them adversely. It made good sense, therefore, when in January 1979 the School of Engineering

Science was re-constituted as the School of Engineering, adding the Departments of Civil Engineering and Building Science, and Fire Safety Engineering. After a good deal of effort it proved to be possible to devise a joint first year course acceptable to all four main departments, and this has continued to allow a few students each year to change to another branch of engineering after completing a 'taster' first year.

The existence of the School undoubtedly helped the engineering departments through these difficult times, though not without losses of staff in all departments; the general moratorium on the filling of vacant posts imposed in July 1981 had a particularly severe impact on Chemical, Civil and Mechanical Engineering which were already depleted in staff numbers at that time. In 1989 the four Departments in the School of Engineering combined with the Departments of Artificial Intelligence and Computer Science, and the Centre for Cognitive Science, to form the School of Engineering and Information Technology, which in 1992 was renamed the School of Engineering and Informatics.

Chemical Engineering

After the separation from the Heriot-Watt University the Edinburgh University staff moved at very short notice in 1967 into make-shift accommodation at the King's Buildings, where the present two-storey brick and concrete building was completed in 1971. This provides office space, research laboratories and workshops; the teaching laboratories and classrooms are shared with the other Engineering departments. When Prof Calderbank retired in 1980 the University did not immediately move to appoint a successor, and in July 1981 this hesitation took a much more serious turn when the general moratorium on the filling of vacant posts supervened.

It was then proposed by the UGC, as part of its economy drive, that consideration should be given to 'integration of activities' between the Departments of Chemical Engineering in Edinburgh and Heriot-Watt Universities, and it was only after more than a year of protracted discussions that this idea was dropped.

By about 1985, with the Chair of Chemical Engineering still unfilled, the Department had clearly survived the crisis. Under the guidance of senior members of staff acting in turn as Head of Department, an atmosphere of strong mutual loyalty was generated which turned the department into a highly effective though still rather small unit. First year student numbers were increasing and research activity was gathering momentum; for example, the Department launched in 1986 a joint project with specialists in Respiratory Medicine and the City Hospital, to develop improved biopsy procedures for the early diagnosis of lung cancer.

The Department's large and heterogeneous group of research students and research workers contains, in addition to Chemical Engineers from Edinburgh and elsewhere, graduates in areas as diverse as physics, mathematics, computer science, chemistry and microbiology. The areas in which they work are correspondingly diverse.

The large group engaged in a rolling programme of research in process simulation, integration and control has attracted continuing and very substantial SERC funding totalling over £2m. The programme also involves the Glasgow Department of Control Engineering and the Dundee and Edinburgh Departments of Mathematics. The stated aim is 'Better processes through better design', and the means are related to the provision of improved computational aids to the design engineer. The four main areas of activity are:– integrated process design; process synthesis and optimisation; process simulation; and process control.

The new and powerful Particle Image Velocimetry (PIV) technique has been applied to fluid-particle flows as diverse as the 'roping' in gas-particle transport ducts that causes control problems in power-station pulverised fuel combustion; the rapidly reversing and chaotic flows around prosthetic heart valves in pulsatile flow; and particle carry-over in the freeboard region of fluidised bed combustors and chemical reactors. This work is being carried out in collaboration with the Departments of Mechanical Engineering and Physics. Useful links have been forged with the power generation companies and equipment manufacturers.

Image processing projects have included the motion of particles in a rotating drum and the development of a computer aided tomography system to help surgeons take biopsies of specific regions of lung tissue ('shadows') for diagnostic purposes. A project now in progress with industrial funding is developing a system for aiding the discharge of industrial filter presses. A vision system has been developed that can recognise and remove undischarged deposits automatically, with great potential savings in labour costs and (since a major application is sewage sludge filtration) improvements in job satisfaction!

In 1990 **Jack Ponton**, who had joined the Department as an assistant lecturer in 1967, was appointed ICI Professor of Chemical Engineering, and **Dr Colin Pritchard** was elected Head of Department. In 1991 a new Lectureship in Safety Engineering was funded by Elf UK, to which Dr Jennifer Black, a graduate of the Department, was appointed.

Quantitative risk assessments (QRAs) are being increasingly used to analyse the risks presented by large scale industrial installations. Most major incidents have involved significant human factors in their causation and without proper consideration of human error any QRA is incomplete. Methodologies currently used for incorporating human reliability in QRA in a range of industries and the use of 'near-miss' reporting systems as a source of human reliability data are being studied. Hazard identification in the process industries is often carried out using a structured technique known as 'Hazard and Operability Study' (HAZOP). The Department's work aims to modify this technique to allow inherent safety to be built into the design at an early stage.

Civil Engineering and Building Science

In Civil Engineering research continued in structural masonry, the results contributing to the revision of national and European codes of practice. The carefully monitored testing

Load testing of masonry bridge

to destruction of a small number of redundant masonry road bridges furnished valuable new information on the strength of such structures under the much heavier traffic loads common today. Other topics of growing importance included numerical modelling, non-destructive testing, the performance of earthmoving equipment and hydraulic model testing.

In 1989 **Michael Rotter** became the second Professor of Civil Engineering and injected a new sense of purpose into the Department. From the University of Sydney he brought with him some of the group with whom he had been conducting research into structures for the bulk storage of solids, which has since become a major departmental activity. Environmental engineering (water supply, treatment and disposal of liquid and solid wastes, control of pollution, irrigation and flood control, and coastal protection) is of great and growing importance today, and the Department is expanding its work in that area. **Mike Forde** was appointed Tarmac Professor of Civil Engineering Construction in 1990.

Financial stringency in 1985 led to the Department of *Fire Safety Engineering becoming the Fire Safety Engineering Unit within the Department of Civil Engineering and Building Science. It has preserved an international reputation for its fire safety research, and provides courses of lectures to undergraduates in several departments (three at Edinburgh, one each at the Heriot-Watt and Glasgow Universities), at all levels from first year to honours options. In 1990 **Dr Dougal Drysdale**, an Edinburgh chemistry graduate, was appointed Reader, and Director of the Fire Safety Engineering Unit. His book *An Introduction to Fire Dynamics* was published in 1985. He is also CIGNA Visiting Professor in Fire Protection Engineering at Worcester Polytechnic Institute, Massachusetts, USA.

Fire Safety Engineering

David Rasbash was the first Professor of Fire Engineering; he joined the staff of the Fire Research Station in 1949, becoming Head of the Fire Protection Division before his move to Edinburgh in 1973. He introduced a one-year postgraduate course in Fire Engineering, the first anywhere in the world, leading to either a Diploma or a Masters Degree. The name of the Department was changed from Fire Engineering to Fire Safety Engineering in 1977, after a wittily apposite remark by the Chancellor, HRH the Duke of Edinburgh, at a fund-raising function. One of the original aims of the Department was to develop an undergraduate course, but this was not achieved. The postgraduate course ceased in 1983, but the University's venture into this new field has made a major contribution to the recognition and development of Fire Safety Engineering as an academic and professional discipline. Courses at both undergraduate and postgraduate level are now evolving at various centres around the world.

Fire Safety Engineering at Edinburgh was incorporated in 1985 into the Department of *Civil Engineering and Building Science.

Electrical Engineering

In 1970 **Jeffrey Collins** was appointed SRC Research Professor in the Department of Electrical Engineering. The post was converted into a Personal Chair of Industrial Electronics in 1973. The results of his research were published as *Computer-Aided Design of Surface Acoustic Wave Devices* (1976). Shortly after the appointment of Prof Collins the University was fortunate to receive from 'a distinguished Edinburgh financier' a sum of money sufficient for a new building for the Department of Electrical Engineering. After the building had been completed in 1974 it became known that the money had been donated by the Alrick Trust, through the generosity of Mr James Gammell, the Chairman of Ivory and Sime, investment managers. The Alrick Building gave the Department more space for its teaching and research in the rapidly-expanding area of microelectronics.

Jeffrey Collins succeeded Ewart Farvis in 1977 as Professor of Electrical Engineering, and under his energetic leadership the Department's research proliferated in the areas of microelectronics and microfabrication. He also continued the process of strengthening the Department's links with the growing number of electronics firms in and around Edinburgh, realising that many of them would need the high-level research and development facilities and expertise that a university could provide. Prof Collins resigned his chair in 1984, and became Director of the Automation and Robotics Institute and Professor of Electrical Engineering at the University of Texas at Arlington, USA.

In 1978 the Wolfson Microelectronics Liaison Unit was renamed the Wolfson Microelectronics Institute, which in 1985 became the spin-off company WOLFSON MICROELECTRONICS LTD. Also in 1978 the Edinburgh Microfabrication Facility (EMF) was set up in the Electrical Engineering Department as one of five central facilities throughout the UK funded by the SRC. They were intended to act as focal points for research and to provide support for other SRC teaching and research programmes in Information Technology, in the case of the EMF by the design and fabrication of customised integrated circuits. **Dr John Robertson** of Electrical Engineering was the first Director of the EMF, which over the next few years attracted a large measure of support in recognition of its success in bridging the gap between university research and its application in industry.

Research in the Department of Electrical Engineering in the 1980s was concentrated in microelectronics, but at the same time diversified as new projects were started, emphasizing the remarkably astute choice of this general area of research by Prof Farvis twenty years before. Towards the end of 1980 a new LSI microcircuit design facility was opened, complementing the Edinburgh Microfabrication Facility established the year before. The sophisticated instrumentation of these facilities was intended to be used for undergraduate and postgraduate teaching, for research and to some extent for the benefit of local electronics firms without such resources of their own.

In 1983 Hewlett-Packard donated one of their 'state-of-the-art' desk-top computers, the HP9000, to the Department of Electrical Engineering. In handing over the gift, the General Manager of their South Queensferry factory emphasized how important it was that students should *not* have to be trained on out-of-date equipment because of the universities' current financial cutbacks. He went on to admit that Hewlett-Packard had a vested interest in giving an HP9000 to the Department, since about ten per cent of their graduates at South Queensferry had come from Edinburgh University.

Edinburgh University's largest-ever award for research, in two linked grants from the SERC totalling just over £2·5m, was received in 1982 by the Edinburgh Microfabrication Facility. Some £0·75m was in support of the Facility's service to research units in other British universities, the remainder for the acquisition of specialist equipment which enabled it to move forward into the realm of VLSI microcircuit technology. In 1987 the largest single research grant ever made to Edinburgh University, £1·79m from the SERC, was made to the EMF. In the previous six years over 450 different integrated microcircuits had been designed and fabricated, and the next stage required the Facility to grapple with the problems of automation and control in a batch manufacturing process.

Later that year the Edinburgh Microfabrication Facility was the recipient of a 'package' of funding amounting to £1·5m from the SERC and six key firms in the electronics industry, for research into computer-aided manufacturing (CAM) techniques. It was already clear that they would be essential for precise control in the manufacture of the next generation of integrated circuits, which would have more than a million transistors per chip. In 1988 **Dr R J Holwill** succeeded Prof John Robertson as Director of the Edinburgh Microfabrication Facility.

In Electrical Engineering by 1980 there were 18 academic members of staff, including two professors, one of whom was **John Mavor** who was appointed in 1980 to the Lothian Chair of Microelectronics, the first such chair in the UK, funded to the extent of £35,000 per annum by Lothian Regional Council. The next ten years saw an increase in staff numbers to 30, including six professors:– **Alan Owen** was appointed in 1981 to a Personal Chair in Physical Electronics; **John Mavor** became in 1986 the third Professor of Electrical Engineering, and **John Robertson** succeeded him in the Lothian Chair of Microelectronics; **Peter Denyer** was appointed in 1986 to the Advent Chair of Integrated Electronics, which was converted four years later into a Personal Chair; and **Peter Grant** was appointed in 1987 to a Personal Chair of Electronic Signal Processing.

Mervyn Jack was appointed in 1988 to a Personal Chair of Electronic Systems, and Director of the Centre for Speech Technology Research (CSTR), founded in 1984 as an inter-departmental research institute and granted independent departmental status in the Faculty of Arts in 1991. Since 1988 the CSTR has generated over £5m in grants from UK and EC research councils, and in R&D contracts from industrial firms in Britain, the United States and Japan.

A substantial £1.2m extension to the Electrical Engineering Department's Alrick Building was opened in 1988 by the Chancellor, HRH the Duke of Edinburgh. The extension provided more teaching and research space (funded by the UGC) and two floors for the Technology Transfer Centre Ltd (funded by Edinburgh District Council). Funding from the DTI through the National Electronics Research Initiative (NERI) of about £1m, plus a similar level of support (in the form of staff secondments) from six companies, was received for the Silicon Architectures Research Initiative (SARI) directed by Professors Denyer and Grant.

At the end of 1988 details of the new five-year undergraduate MEng Degree in Electronics were published. A key feature of the new degree was that each student would be sponsored by a company through the last two years of the course, including an industrial project based on the work of their sponsoring company. A good example of the benefits of collaboration between the university and industry was the Queen's Award for Technological Achievement won by Racal-MESL in 1989 for the development of a new type of radar, using a technique called Surface Acoustic Wave Pulse Compression. The resulting dramatic improvement in performance of radar equipment for surveillance of ships and aircraft, increasing safety at sea and in the air, was the result of work carried out jointly by Racal-MESL, the Royal Signals and Radar Establishment, and the Department of Electrical Engineering.

As a small postscript to this account of large-scale engineering research costing huge sums of money, it is refreshing to record that in 1988 Teresa Anderson, a postgraduate student from the Energy Systems Group in the Department of Electrical Engineering, visited Nepal. She took with her a set of demo disks of a *CRYSTAL* expert system created to help engineers design economically viable microhydro schemes in remote mountainous areas. Further progress with this project was assisted by an Overseas Development Agency Research Award for 1989-91, and a substantial number of microhydro schemes are now in operation in Nepal and elsewhere.

Mechanical Engineering
In the Department of Mechanical Engineering research began in 1974 under Stephen Salter (who had arrived there from the rather distant world of the Bionics Research Laboratory) into wave power, leading to the development of the 'Salter duck' and the construction of one of the most sophisticated wave testing tanks in the world. In 1983 the Department of Mechanical Engineering gained **Joe McGeough** as the new occupant of the Regius Chair of Engineering, and three years later **Stephen Salter** was appointed to a Personal Chair in Engineering Design.

Prof McGeough brought with him a research group working on the development of unconventional manufacturing processes such as electrochemical machining and spark erosion. These researches were supported initially by the SERC, then in 1987 further

The wave tank at King's Buildings

funding from the Wolfson Foundation allowed the Centre for Advanced Machining Technology to be established, with equipment for laser cutting and ultrasonic machining of brittle materials. The Centre has attracted many overseas visitors, especially from China, Japan, Egypt and Israel. In 1992 Prof McGeough was made an Honorary Professor in the Nanjing University of Aeronautics and Astronautics. He has also initiated research in the field of bio-engineering materials, with particular emphasis on the effects of ageing on the mechanical properties of bone and cartilege.

Forestry and Natural Resources

Prof Black resigned in 1971 to become Principal of Bedford College in the University of London, and in 1972 Frederick Last became the fourth Professor of Forestry and Natural Resources, while continuing in his post as Head of the Institute of Tree Biology (later absorbed into the Institute of Terrestrial Ecology), situated on the Bush Estate. Prof Last soon found that he could not do justice to the two jobs, and he resigned as Professor of Forestry and Natural Resources in 1974, since when he has held an Honorary Professorship. One of the Department's major research projects at that time was concerned with the management of red deer in the Scottish highlands, and a report on this by Dr Bill Mutch appeared in the Edinburgh University *Bulletin*, 8, 10.

Paul Jarvis was appointed the fifth Professor of Forestry and Natural Resources in 1974. After graduating from Oxford in 1957 he had spent four years in Sweden and 15 months in Australia before returning in 1966 to the Botany Department of Aberdeen University. Under him research flourished, and innovations in TLA (teaching, learning and assessment) were progressively put into practice. **Dr Charles Taylor** was appointed to a Personal Chair of Forestry in 1976; three years later he retired, and wrote an interesting history of *Forestry and Natural Resources in the University of Edinburgh* which was published in 1985.

In 1977 a one-year course in Resource Management was introduced, leading to an MSc degree. By 1989 there were 55 postgraduate students in the department, of whom 28 were taking the MSc course in Resource Management.

In 1981 Prof Jarvis was granted leave of absence to pursue research in Australia and New Zealand. **Dr W E Scott Mutch** took over as Head of Department for three years, and this was renewed in 1984. He retired in 1988 from the Department he entered as a student in 1944, subsequently serving four years as Chairman of the South East Region of the Nature Conservancy Council for Scotland.

Two grants from the Scottish Forestry Trust and the Dulverton Trust totalling £32,000 were awarded to the Department in 1986 for research into agro-forestry, the integration of farming and forestry, in collaboration with the Hill Farming Research Organisation and the Northern Research Station of the Forestry Commission. In 1987 an SERC grant of £72,000 over three years was awarded to members of the Departments of Artificial Intelligence and Forestry and Natural Resources for joint research into the computer modelling of ecological systems. Much interest has been shown in this work by FERN, the Forest Ecosystem Research Network, sponsored by the European Science

Foundation, and an international research workshop on forest growth modelling was held in Edinburgh in 1988.

It is worthy of note that three members of the Department's staff have successively been President of the Institute of Chartered Foresters, the UK professional body – Dr C J Taylor, 1977-78; Dr W E S Mutch, 1983-84; and Dr D C Malcolm, 1988-90. **Dr Douglas Malcolm**, OBE also acted as Head of Department from 1987 to 1990, when the Department of Forestry and Natural Resources was incorporated with the Department of Agriculture and Rural Economy in the Institute of *Ecology and Resource Management within the Division of Biological Sciences.

Genetics

In 1971 **Max Birnstiel** was appointed to a Personal Chair in Epigenetics. He joined the MRC Epigenetics Research Group at Edinburgh in 1963, and quickly achieved recognition as a leader in studies of the fine structure of DNA; he was credited with the first chemical isolation of a single gene in pure form, a major advance in our understanding of chromosome structure. He resigned in 1972 to become Professor in the Institute of Molecular Biology in the University of Zürich.

The joint degree of MSc in Animal Breeding was introduced in 1973 in collaboration with the Department of Agriculture. It was the only course of its kind in the UK and attracted students from all over the world, many of whom went on to take PhDs and then returned home to found centres of research in quantitative genetics or animal breeding in their own countries.

A notable discovery was made in 1975 by **Ed Southern** of the Mammalian Genome Unit, when he invented the technique of the 'Southern blot', which can reveal rare DNA fragments in a complex mixture of DNA. The term *Southern blot* is now included in the Oxford English Dictionary, as well as most scientific dictionaries. Analogous procedures were developed for RNA and proteins. Dr Southern received an honorary DSc from the University of Edinburgh in 1991, and is now Professor of Biochemistry in the University of Oxford.

The death in office of Prof Waddington in September 1975 presaged an era of contraction in some areas of genetics at Edinburgh, although the prime cause lay in the economies forced on the universities by the government's financial problems. In 1976 **John Fincham** was appointed as Waddington's successor to the Buchanan Chair of Genetics, from the same post in the University of Leeds. His research work was concentrated mainly on the effects of mutations on enzyme structure and function. He was the editor of *Heredity*, 1971-78, and he published *Fungal Genetics* (with P R Day, 1963; 4th edn 1979), *Microbial and Molecular Genetics* (1965), *Genetic Complementation* (1966) and *Genetics* (1983). He resigned in 1984, moving to the Arthur Balfour Chair of Genetics in the University of Cambridge.

On the retiral of Prof Falconer in 1980 the ARC terminated the Unit of Animal Genetics, as they are in the habit of doing when a Director retires. The Poultry Research Centre (PRC) subsequently moved to new premises at Roslin, while ABRO, under its

Director **Roger Land**, remained at the King's Buildings. During this period ABRO scientists Richard Lathe (now of the AFRC Centre for Genome Research) and John Clark (now of the Roslin Institute) pioneered the technology of pharmaceutical production in transgenic sheep milk. This discovery led to the establishment of a company, PHARMACEUTICAL PROTEINS LTD, to exploit the commercial applications of the technology. In 1981 **Dr Grahame Bulfield** was appointed Head of the newly formed Genetics Group at the AFRC Poultry Research Centre.

In 1983 **William Hill**, who had joined the Department as an assistant lecturer in 1965, was appointed to a Personal Chair of Animal Genetics. His research interests are in theoretical, population and quantitative genetics, and their application to livestock improvements. This involves him in close collaboration with the School of Agriculture and ABRO, a partnership which is characteristic of the interlinking of research at Edinburgh University today. Following the resignation of Prof Fincham in 1984, the Buchanan Chair was left vacant until 1990. In the intervening period **Dr D E S Truman** was Head of Department, 1984-89.

In 1989 **John Bishop** was appointed to a Personal Chair in Molecular Cell Biology. A native of Edinburgh, he studied under Profs Waddington and Beale, from whom he says he learned scientific scepticism. After three years in the United States he returned to Edinburgh and joined the Department of Genetics in 1962. For almost twenty years he has been involved in recombinant DNA technology and its application to problems of cell biology, and this interest led him to take up work with transgenic animals. He initiated in 1987-88 the bid which resulted in the location of the AFRC Centre for Genome Research at Edinburgh University, and he is currently Associate Director of the Centre.

Adrian Bird was appointed in 1990 to the Buchanan Chair of Genetics. He graduated in 1968 from the University of Sussex, then studied for his PhD at Edinburgh under Max Birnstiel. From 1975 to 1986 he was a member of the MRC Mammalian Genome Unit, for the last two years as Acting Director. His principal research interests are in genome organisation and evolution, and CpG islands as gene markers in the vertebrate nucleus. He is currently a member of the Editorial Boards of *Chromosoma* and *Nucleic Acids Research*.

In 1990 the members of the Department of Genetics were incorporated in the Institutes of *Cell and Molecular Biology, and *Cell, Animal and Population Biology within the Division of Biological Sciences.

Genome Research, AFRC Centre for

In 1989 the AFRC Centre for Genome Research (CGR), an Interdisciplinary Research Centre, was established at the King's Buildings in the former ABRO building, under an agreement between the University and the AFRC, which provides a substantial proportion of the funding. **Richard Lathe**, a graduate of Edinburgh in Molecular Biology, was appointed Director and Professorial Fellow. The Centre, a non-teaching Department of the University, comprises a modern transgenic unit with full laboratory facilities for molecular biology, stem cell manipulation (gene targeting), cell culture and mammalian genetics. It is closely associated with the Division of Biological Sciences, several of whose staff are also members of the Centre.

Geology and Geophysics

The first Professor of Geophysics, **Alan Cook**, was appointed in 1969, from the National Physical Laboratory. Educated at Corpus Christi College, Cambridge, he resigned in 1972 to return there as Jacksonian Professor of Natural Philosophy. Among his many publications were Gravity and the Earth (1969) and Global Geophysics (1970). In 1973 **Ken Creer** was appointed the second Professor of Geophysics, from the Department of Geophysics and Planetary Physics at Newcastle. He was best known for his work in South America where he made outstanding contributions to the understanding of the rock magnetism of that part of the world. He also made important comparisons of the South African basalts with those in Brazil in relation to the ancient geological history of Africa and South America.

Michael O'Hara was appointed to a Personal Chair of Petrology in 1971 in the Department of Geology, which he had joined as an assistant lecturer in 1958. He resigned in 1978 to become Professor of Geology in the University College of Wales, Aberystwyth.

The 1971 centenary celebrations of the Department of Geology, marked by one of the largest gatherings of geologists ever seen in Britain, were held in Edinburgh in mid-September. Nearly five hundred attended, and due homage was paid to Edinburgh's early pioneers, Hutton, Jameson, Hall, Playfair and the brothers Geikie. During the celebrations a turf-cutting ceremony took place on the site (leased from Edinburgh University) of what is now Murchison House, Scottish Headquarters of the British Geological Survey.

In 1982 **Brian Upton**, who joined the Department in 1962, was appointed to a Personal Chair in Petrology. His research into the generation, ascent and evolution of magmas has been carried out in Greenland and the western United States, as well as in the Scottish highlands and islands. The Edinburgh University Bulletin, **20**, 1 in October 1983 carried a review of modern developments in ocean floor research, by Dr Roger Scrutton, joint editor of The Ocean Floor published in 1982. The same journal in October/November 1986 featured an article by Dr Godfrey Fitton giving his explanation of the gas eruption from Lake Nyos in Cameroon which killed over 1500 people.

The Department acquired a new Head in 1986 when **Geoffrey Boulton** was appointed the sixth Regius Professor of Geology, from the School of Environmental Sciences at the University of East Anglia. The Chair had been vacant since the retirement of Sir Frederick Stewart in 1982. Prof Boulton's primary interests have been in the field of quaternary geology, and he is internationally recognised for his work on glacial erosion and sedimentation processes.

In 1987 a committee of the UGC began a major review of all the UK universities' Earth Sciences Departments, and in due course their report made it clear that they envisaged a small number of large departments with 'well-found' laboratories for postgraduate research, complemented by a larger number of more modest departments, many of which would concentrate on undergraduate teaching. Edinburgh's submission proposed a merger of the Departments of Geology and Geophysics, which was accepted by the committee and implemented in 1989, giving Edinburgh University the second largest (after Cambridge) Earth Sciences Department in Britain.

Outdoors in Dorset

The new Department of Geology and Geophysics grew in terms of staff numbers from 22 to 33, including the transfer of **Prof Ian Parsons** from Aberdeen to the Chair of Mineralogy, and **Prof Barry Dawson** from Sheffield as a Professorial Fellow. The number of postgraduate students increased from about 30 to 85, and a major extension to the Grant Institute of Geology was constructed.

The NERC's largest-ever grant of £827,000 was awarded to the Department of Geology in 1989 for the purchase of an ion microprobe, which can quantitatively analyse trace amounts of elements or isotopes in minute samples of crystals or minerals. With its aid it is possible to decipher the growth history of individual mineral grains in rocks whose ages may be tens or hundreds of millions of years. As well as the Department's own research it will also be used for selected collaborative projects with earth scientists from other UK universities. In the same year the **Petroleum Science and Technology**

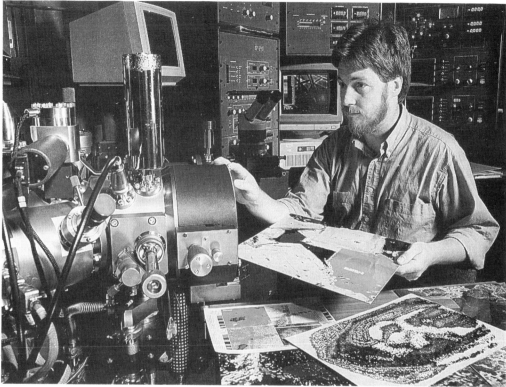

Ion Microprobe

Institute (PSTI) was established jointly with the Heriot-Watt University, funded by a consortium of oil and gas companies and the then Department of Energy, for an initial period of five years with an income of about £1·5m per annum.

History of Science

In 1965 **Eric Forbes** was appointed Lecturer in the History of Science in the Department of History in the Faculty of Arts. He graduated with Honours in Astronomy at the University of St Andrews in 1954, and pursued a career in astronomy, physics and mathematics before specialising in the history of medicine and science. His lectures were popular with students in all Faculties, and he also built up, with the support of the Manpower Services Commission, a group of young people who undertook research and produced a series of publications on *Scotland's Cultural Heritage*. In 1978 he was promoted to a Personal Professorship in the History of Science. Among his publications were the first volume of the history of *Greenwich Observatory* (1975), and *The Birth of Navigational Science* (1974); he also edited *The Gresham Lectures of John Flamsteed* (1975). Prof Forbes' early death in 1984 at the age of 51 was a sad loss to his chosen subject and to the University of Edinburgh.

Industrial Liaison (CICL, UnivEd)

The Centre for Industrial Consultancy and Liaison (CICL) was created in 1969, with the objective of building up all forms of mutually profitable University/industry collaboration. In 1971 the Centre promoted an 'Open Day for Industry' at the King's Buildings; twenty-five departments presented projects and facilities of interest to the 500 industrialists who attended. A revised and enlarged third edition of the Handbook for Industry was published. New developments in microelectronics, computers, materials science and medical engineering were on display, along with materials testing and other services. At the Open Day press conference the Principal contrasted Edinburgh University's average non-UGC research budget of about £50,000 per annum in the 1950s with the total of almost £2m in 1971.

As a measure of the increasing amount of industrial collaboration, Dr Midgley was able to report that during session 1977-78 CICL:-

   (i) assisted 25 Department and Units;
   (ii) negotiated 60 contracts, including 23 consultancies;
   (iii) increased patent royalties by 50% to £27,264; and
   (iv) arranged three international conferences.

Throughout most of the 1960s and '70s it was not too difficult to obtain funds from one source or another for university research, and one of the few real problems was to persuade members of staff to include a realistic percentage for overheads. By the early 1980s, however, the climate had begun to change, and it was clear that a more businesslike approach, with more accurate costings and stricter accountability, would have to be adopted for the funding of research projects.

In 1983 Dr Midgley retired and **Mike Weber**, a lecturer in the Department of Business Studies with experience of marketing in the pharmaceutical industry, was appointed Director. Shortly afterwards CICL was replaced by a company, wholly controlled by the University, known as UnivEd Technologies Limited, with the broad remit to market in a more positive way the University's R&D resources to industry and commerce. One of the anticipated advantages was purely psychological, but none the less important – it had become evident that many people in industry felt more at ease dealing with another company than with a university.

The Quantum Fund was set up in May 1985, managed by UnivEd Technologies, to provide a fund of venture capital, initially £100,000, backed by the University of Edinburgh, the British Linen Bank, 3i and the Scottish American Investment Company. On similar lines, the British Technology Group (BTG) and the University of Edinburgh concluded an agreement in 1986 making available nearly £400,000 of BTG research funding for the University over the next three years.

In June 1988 the Edinburgh Technology Transfer Centre (ETTC), located on the top two floors of the new Electrical Engineering Building at the King's Buildings, was formally opened by HRH the Duke of Edinburgh. The Centre has office accommodation for UnivEd staff, and a number of small laboratories in which individual scientists can develop ideas with commercial potential. The cost of the ETTC was met by a grant from Edinburgh District Council, and by the end of 1989 several projects were approaching the pre-production development stage.

In the first full year after it was established in 1984, the total value of the contracts negotiated by UnivEd was £2.2m. During the next few years its role expanded into training, consultancy, company formation and other commercial activities. In 1988/89 UnivEd handled around £10m of industrial and government contracts on behalf of the University, negotiated 89 consultancy contracts worth £278,000 for staff in 21 different departments, and generated £318,000 of income from 66 training courses.

The influence of the European Community on the universities in member countries began to be felt more strongly after the Single European Act came into force on 1 July 1987. The Act set out the objectives for implementation of research and technological development within the Community, and introduced or promoted a whole range of programmes with catchy acronyms and attractive offers of support for university research. UnivEd urged members of staff not to neglect these potentially important sources of funding, which included DELTA (Developing European Learning through Technological Advance), ESPRIT (European Strategic Programme for Research and development in Information Technology) and JOULE (Research and Technological Development Programme in the Field of Energy).

In the autumn of 1990 UnivEd emerged from a restructuring exercise carried out on the initiative of the University Court, one outcome of which was that Mike Weber became Director of UnivEd Technologies Ltd and Director of Industrial Liaison for the University of Edinburgh.

Five of the 19 Scottish SMART (Small firms Merit Award for Research and Technology) Awards for 1991 were given to projects on the King's Buildings site, three of them based in the ETTC.

Information Technology
The School of Information Technology was established in 1983, as a relatively loose federation of the Departments of *Artificial Intelligence, *Computer Science and *Electrical Engineering, and the Centre for *Cognitive Science. Diploma and MSc courses in Information Technology were offered, using the combined resources of the School together with the Departments of Physics, Geophysics, Meteorology and Linguistics. In 1989 the School combined with the School of Engineering to form the School of Engineering and Information Technology, which in 1992 was renamed the School of *Engineering and Informatics.

In 1984 SERC thought it necessary to encourage research in the field of Information Technology and to this end offered a limited number of IT Fellowships. Of the twelve awarded up to 1990 four came to Edinburgh University members of staff:– Prof Alan Bundy (Artificial Intelligence), Prof Mervyn Jack (Electrical Engineering), Prof Jim Jordan (Electrical Engineering) and Dr H S Thompson (Artificial Intelligence).

Mathematics

In the early 1970s the Mathematics Department was situated mainly in Chambers Street with an Applied Mathematics outpost at the King's Buildings. The academic staff of about 30 covered a wide range of mathematical expertise, with the group in mathematical analysis being particularly well known internationally.

The Department acquired an EAL 380 Analogue Computer in 1972, and began to include instruction in this technique in their undergraduate courses. The computer was also utilised for teaching and research by the School of Engineering Science. In 1976 the Department of Mathematics moved from the Mathematical Institute in Chambers Street to the James Clerk Maxwell Building at the King's Buildings. At that time, under the auspices of CICL, a group was formed with the aim of bringing the range of mathematical expertise available in the Department to the attention of R&D staff in local industrial firms.

In 1979 **Elmer Rees** was appointed the seventeenth Professor of Mathematics. He studied at Cambridge and Warwick Universities, and lectured in mathematics at Oxford, 1971-79. Prof Rees is a modern geometer who works in algebraic topology and algebraic geometry, and is also interested in the interface of geometry with theoretical physics. His presence has stimulated much activity and he has recently been instrumental in the establishment of an International Centre for the Mathematical Sciences in Edinburgh, in collaboration with John Ball of the Heriot-Watt University.

Terence Lyons was appointed in 1985 to the Colin McLaurin Chair of Mathematics, from Imperial College, University of London. His research field is probability theory and he interacted usefully with the Department's interests in analysis and geometry. In 1993 Imperial College tempted him to return with an offer he could not refuse, but over the next few years arrangements have been made to enable him to maintain his research links with the Department of Mathematics in Edinburgh. In 1989 **David Parker** was appointed to the Chair of Applied Mathematics, from the Department of Theoretical Mechanics in the University of Nottingham. His research interests centred on nonlinear waves in gas dynamics and elasticity, more recently concentrating on surface acoustic waves and fibre optics. He has participated in nine Mathematical Study Groups with Industry, becoming involved in the investigation of such topics as synthetic fibre manufacture, an industrial gas separation process and electro-discharge machining.

Allan Sinclair was appointed in 1991 to a Personal Chair of Operator Algebras and Mathematical Analysis. Born in Johannesburg, he had been Reader in the Department since 1977. His main research interests are the relationships between the algebraic and geometrical properties of operator algebras, and structures related to them, within the broad area of mathematical analysis. Also in 1991 the Departments of Mathematics and Statistics were merged into a combined Department of Mathematics and Statistics – proving that two into one *will* go.

Three examples of mathematicians applying mathematics to unusual problems end this section on a lighter note. Frank Bonsall invented a rule that helps to decide whether or not two neighbouring mountain tops should be regarded as separate mountains. Applied to Scottish mountains over 3,000 feet high it reproduced Munro's list almost exactly, a gratifying result for Bonsall, who had himself climbed all the Munros by 1977.

George Mackie applied mathematics and statistics to the games of snooker and billiards, writing a computer program which would calculate the difficulty factor for any given potting position, and then work out the probability of a player of known ability being successful. This was featured in a BBC TV programme in the *QED* series in 1985.

The principal field of research of Dr Douglas Heggie, a Reader in the Department, is theoretical astronomy, but for many years he has taken a keen interest in stone circles, of which there are almost a thousand in the British Isles alone. He has undertaken a thorough reappraisal of the work of Alexander Thom and others who have made what seem to be somewhat exaggerated claims for the knowledge and mathematical abilities of the megalithic astronomers. He published his conclusions in *Megalithic Science: Ancient Mathematics and Astronomy in Northwest Europe* (1981).

Meteorology

After James Paton's retirement **Dr Douglas McIntosh** became Head of Department in 1973. He joined the Meteorological Office on graduating from St Andrews, and during the war rose to become Deputy Chief Meteorological Officer for South-East Asia. He entered the Department of Physics to teach meteorology in 1955, and with Alasdair Thom wrote a teaching text Essentials of Meteorology. His research was principally concerned with the physics and dynamics of the upper atmosphere. Douglas McIntosh retired in 1982, and since then the position of Head of Department has been held in rotation by several members of the staff.

In 1976 the Department moved with Mathematics and Physics to the James Clerk Maxwell Building at the King's Buildings, and the following year introduced a new one-session course leading to an MSc or Diploma in Meteorology, the only one of its kind in Scotland. A joint research project with physicists from the Heriot-Watt University was initiated in 1986 to measure the amount of ozone and water vapour in the upper atmosphere using satellite-borne equipment. Edinburgh University is one of six institutions cooperating in the UK Universities Global Atmospheric Modelling Project (U-GAMP) using the Cray Y-MP computer at the Rutherford-Appleton Laboratory. The overall aim of the project is to develop a state-of-the-art climate model for both the troposphere (where the weather is) and the stratosphere (where the ozone layer is), capable of displaying the results of interactions between them.

Microbiology

Prof Wilkinson had been head of the Department of General Microbiology for two years when in 1971 it was renamed Microbiology. This period saw the development of interests in microbial exopolysaccharides (Ian Sutherland), radiation resistance (Bev Moseley) and yeast genetics (Ian Dawes) following the departure of Roger Whittenbury to one of the Foundation Chairs in biological sciences at the new University of Warwick. There was close co-operation and support from the Department of Energy in their Enhanced Oil Recovery programme. The Department was also greatly strengthened by the appointment of a Visiting Industrial Professor, Graeme Gould, from the Unilever Colworth Laboratory. The appointment of a mycologist, Jim Deacon, further widened the interests of the Department to include biological control and 'green' pesticides. For much of this period, until 1990, the University Department of Microbiology worked in close collaboration with the staff of the Edinburgh School of Agriculture (which at that time comprised the Scottish Agricultural College and the University Department of Agriculture) as the School's Division of Microbiology. However, with the reduction in interest and staffing on the part of the School of Agriculture, the University Department had to become totally self-sufficient until its incorporation into the Division of Biological Sciences on its formation in October 1991. By that time Ian Dawes had left to accept a Chair in Biochemistry at the University of New South Wales, and Bev Moseley had been appointed head of the AFRC Food Research Institute and titular professor at Reading.

Molecular Biology

Prof Hayes resigned in 1973 at the age of 60, to spend the remainder of his active years in a warmer climate at the Australian National University, Canberra. It has always been MRC policy to encourage the dispersal of talent from Units on the retirement of the Director, so about a third of the MRC staff moved on, while the other six stayed in the Department. Five of them have since obtained chairs, and three are still at Edinburgh.

Martin Pollock retired in 1976, having created the Department of Molecular Biology by his personal inspiration and his skill in attracting the right sort of staff. He was too outspoken to be a success in university politics, but he was one of the earliest advocates of the reorganization of biology, and was trying to erode departmental boundaries at least as early as 1970. It was largely due to his initiative that the School of Biology had been established by 1973.

He was succeeded in the Chair of Molecular Biology by **Ken Murray**, who in 1984 became Biogen Research Professor. Four years later his wife **Noreen Murray** was appointed to a Personal Chair of Molecular Genetics. They were married in 1958 when both were working for a PhD at the University of Birmingham, and their careers have run in parallel ever since; their mutual interest in protein-DNA interactions led to the development of the first bacteriophage vectors for recombinant DNA technology and their application in the cloning and manipulation of genes from any organism.

The Murrays' work clearly had commercial potential, and in 1978 Ken Murray was one of an international group of molecular biologists who founded BIOGEN, one of the original independent biotechnology companies. One of the company's first projects was initiated at Edinburgh, and directed by Ken Murray, whose group succeeded in producing hepatitis B virus antigens in microbial cells. This led to the production of an important subunit vaccine against the virus which is now in widespread use throughout the world, and together with related diagnostic reagents constitutes a major commercial development. Prof Murray devoted a very large part of his share to found the Darwin Trust, which since 1983 has made multi-million-pound contributions to much-needed developments in the natural sciences at Edinburgh University.

From 1970 the Department's teaching consisted of a final year Molecular Biology Honours course, which could also usefully be attended by any postgraduates who had not previously studied the subject in depth. The cuts in direct UGC funding inflicted on the universities in the 1970s and '80s affected Molecular Biology as seriously as most other departments in the University, and disastrous results for both teaching and research were only avoided by the transfer of staff to non-UGC funded positions, largely with the aid of the Darwin Trust.

In 1982 **Neil Willetts** was appointed to a Personal Chair of Molecular Genetics, having joined the MRC Molecular Genetics Unit in 1968. He achieved a high reputation for his research into the bacterial plasmids, but resigned in 1985 to move to the University of New South Wales. In 1984 **John Scaife** was appointed Professor of Molecular Parasitology, having joined the Department in 1975. From 1980 he was head of a research team funded by the MRC working on the development of a malaria vaccine, and significant progress was being made, only to be cut short by his tragic death in 1991. However, work has since continued both in Edinburgh and elsewhere.

Two members of the Department's staff, John Collins and Andrew Coulson, realized in 1981 that the rapid growth in knowledge of amino acid and nucleotide sequences would soon overload the existing computer methods of handling such data. They believed that the very powerful Distributed Array Processor (DAP) used by the Department of *Physics would be particularly suitable for this purpose, and when this had been established the Biocomputing Research Unit was set up in 1988, with funding from the Darwin Trust.

Richard Ambler was appointed to a Personal Chair of Protein Chemistry in 1987, having joined the Department in 1965. He is an international authority on the determination of primary protein structure, with an enviable reputation for extremely high standards of accuracy in his experimental work. In 1983 his interest was aroused by an article in the journal *Science* in which the writer claimed to have identified the species to which blood residues on prehistoric stone tools and weapons belonged. With a grant from the Nuffield Trust in 1988 he began a series of tests using first the technique described in the original article, and later some other methods which he believes might be more effective. In 1990 Prof Ambler became Head of the Institute of *Cell and Molecular Biology when it was set up within the Division of Biological Sciences.

Physics

The Department of Physics finally completed its move to the James Clerk Maxwell Building in 1975, and following the retirement of Prof Feather in that year, **William Cochran** vacated the second Chair of Physics to become the thirteenth Professor of Natural Philosophy. One of his main research interests was the use of neutrons to investigate interatomic forces in crystals, and solid-state phase transitions.

After Prof Kemmer retired in 1979, **David Wallace**, an Edinburgh graduate of 1967 in mathematical physics, returned from the University of Southampton to became the fourth Tait Professor of Mathematical Physics. He continued the tradition of the mathematical physics group in elementary particle and statistical physics. In recent years a major activity in the Department has been high performance computing, and this resulted in 1990 in the establishment of the Edinburgh Parallel Computing Centre, with Prof Wallace as Director; it has currently more than 40 professional staff funded on external grants and contracts.

Among those present at the opening of the Tait Institute in 1955, as an assistant lecturer, was **Peter Higgs**, who was appointed to a Personal Chair in Theoretical Physics in 1980. He is renowned for his discovery of the mechanism which led to the theory of the unified weak and electromagnetic interaction between elementary particles, for which Glashow, Salam and Weinberg were awarded the Nobel prize for Physics in 1979.

Professor Peter Higgs

It is amusing to note that Higgs' theory predicts the existence of particles in incomplete multiplets of the underlying symmetry group, a concept that was so unacceptable to Kemmer that he was led to predict the π°!

The nuclear physics research group in the Department occupied some of their time over several years preparing for the completion in 1982 of the new 30 million volt Van de Graaff accelerator at the SERC Daresbury Laboratory. The accelerator is used by nuclear physicists in many other universities and research institutions, and Edinburgh is fortunate in having been provided with a data analysis workstation on-line to Daresbury, to aid efficient transfer and processing of the huge amounts of data now being generated.

Right at the other end of the scale of research in physics, a grant of £2,383 from SERC was given to Murray Campbell and Clive Greated in 1982 to enable them to examine the fluid mechanics of the flute, using the Department's anechoic chamber and a variety of acoustic instrumentation. In 1987 they published jointly *The Musician's Guide to Acoustics*.

In 1985 **Stuart Pawley**, who joined the Department in 1964, was appointed to a Personal Chair in Computational Physics. He is an authority on molecular lattice dynamics, and in the use of computer modelling in this complex field of study. For the massive computations required he initially, in the early 1980s, used the two ICL DAP computers, which for a short time constituted probably the most powerful facility in the world for dealing with these exceptional problems. However, he and many others were later able to take advantage of the even more powerful computing facilities in the Edinburgh Parallel Computing Centre.

Alan Shotter joined the Department in 1970 and was appointed to a Personal Chair in Experimental Physics in 1989. While he was at the Berkeley Laboratory of the University of California on sabbatical in 1978-79 he discovered a new type of nuclear reaction process – a kind of tidal mechanism analogous to that responsible for the formation of planetary rings. More recently he has pioneered the development of silicon nuclear detectors and their associated microelectronics.

Two of the smaller but none the less very active research groups in the Department of Physics work in the areas of fluid dynamics and applied optics. **Dr Marion Ross** retired in 1973 as Director of the Fluid Dynamics Unit and was succeeded by **Dr Clive Greated**. The Unit's large wind tunnel has recently been used for such diverse investigations as the effect of wind gusts on offshore structures, and the evaporation characteristics of tree canopies. In 1989 the Unit launched a new initiative on wind energy, concentrating on the design of the turbine blade tip in an attempt to improve the speed and accuracy of its response to wind gusts. This research will include wind tunnel tests as well as computer simulations, and will make use of experimental data from the full-scale wind turbines in Orkney and Shetland.

The Applied Optics Group was formed in 1983, initially to look into new ways of enhancing optical images and recognising patterns, using combinations of techniques in computing, microelectronic optical devices and liquid crystal technology. The Group's field of interest has since widened to include neural networks, optical switching systems and digital optics, though the main activity remains the development and application of spatial light modulators. One of its founder members, R M Sillitto, wrote *Non-Relativistic Quantum Mechanics* (1960, 2nd edn 1967).

In 1990 **Peter Pusey** was appointed Professor of Physics, from the Royal Signals and Radar Establishment at Malvern where he was a Senior Principal Scientific Officer. His main research interests are in the structure and dynamics of colloidal and polymeric systems, which he studies by means of laser light scattering.

Three other notable books written by members of the Department of Physics between 1970 and 1990 were Clive Greated (with T S Durrani) *Laser Systems in Flow Measurement* (1977); P J Kennedy (with A P French) *Niels Bohr – A Centenary Volume* (1985); and W D McComb *The Physics of Fluid Turbulence* (1990).

Science Libraries

In the late 1960s architects' plans were drawn up for Phase I of a Central Science Library (Biology) which was to be built on to the south end of the King's Buildings Centre, along with a new Science Faculty Office. Unfortunately, before the contract could be put out to tender it was axed in the first round of the UGC non-recurrent grant cuts.

By 1971 the numerous problems affecting the library services at the King's Buildings could no longer be ignored, and a Faculty Library Committee was set up. The Central Science Library was no nearer realisation, but the Committee put in hand a number of relatively inexpensive changes which resulted in a significant overall improvement. In 1972 the King's Buildings Library was opened in temporary accommodation in the James Clerk Maxwell Building, providing some basic indexing and abstracting publications, encyclopedias and other works of general reference which individual libraries could not be expected to purchase.

In 1980 the KB Library Centre was set up, and two years later **David Ferro** was appointed as the first Science Librarian. The Centre gradually took over much of the administrative and cataloguing work formerly done in the Main Library, and in 1988 it was renamed the Science Libraries Centre. At the same time the King's Buildings Library was closed and the stock relocated to the various departmental science libraries. In October 1990 the new Darwin Library was completed, allowing much of the biological sciences material from five separate collections to be housed in the one library.

In January 1991 **Richard Battersby** was appointed the second Science Librarian.

Science Studies Unit

In 1986 the SERC awarded a three-year research grant of £50,000 to Dr David Edge, Director of the Science Studies Unit, and Mr James Fleck of the Heriot-Watt University's Business Organisation Department, to examine how best use may be made of resources in Artificial Intelligence.

In 1989 the Science Studies Unit was transferred to the Faculty of Social Sciences.

Statistics

Research continued on spatial processes, partly supported by an SERC Research Fellowship, and on modelling, multivariate analysis and Bayesian inference, with applications in forensic science, medicine and genetics.

Courses given by the Department of Statistics included those for students taking Joint Honours Degrees in Statistics with Computer Science or Mathematics, as well as service courses for other students in the Faculties of Science, Social Sciences and Veterinary Medicine. The Department also offered a one-year course leading to an MSc or a Diploma in Statistics.

After Prof Finney retired in 1984 the James Gregory Chair was left vacant, and in 1991 the Department of Statistics was amalgamated with the Department of Mathematics.

Zoology

In the early 1970s the Department took on the unaccustomed role of retirement home, when within a few months of each other two very eminent newly-retired professors chose to continue their work at Edinburgh University. **Sir Maurice Yonge** FRS PresRSE (1899-1986) gained his PhD at Edinburgh in 1924, went up to Cambridge, and led the expedition to the Great Barrier Reef in 1928-29 which largely determined its origin and structure. He retired from the Regius Chair of Zoology at Glasgow in 1964 and came back to his old Department as an Honorary Fellow in 1971 to continue his research and writing. He published *A Year on the Great Barrier Reef* (1930) and *The Sea Shore* (1949) in Collins' New Naturalist series as well as more than 140 scientific papers.

Sir John Randall FRS FRSE (1905-1984) graduated MSc in physics at Manchester in 1926 and began his remarkably varied career with the General Electric Company at Wembley, 1928-37. With H A H Boot he invented the cavity magnetron, a high-power microwave transmitter vital to Britain's radar defences, in 1940; he held the Wheatstone Chair of Physics at King's College, London, 1946-61 and at the same time was Hon Director, MRC Biophysics Research Unit, 1947-70. After his retirement he joined the Department of Zoology as an Honorary Professor and set up a research group to continue his biophysical structural studies.

In 1973 Prof Walker left the Department to become Director of the MRC Mammalian Genome Unit, and **Aubrey Manning** was appointed twelfth Professor of Natural History. He joined the Department as a lecturer in 1956, being promoted to Reader in Zoology in 1968. His main personal research interest has been in behaviour genetics, through studies of mice and fruit flies. He is also active in the field of conservation and population control, and is particularly concerned with promoting conservation as a subject of study in schools. He was Secretary-General of the International Ethological Committee, 1971-79, and published *An Introduction to Animal Behaviour* (1992).

Another example of the ever-increasing fuzziness in the always somewhat artificial distinction between the 'medical' and 'non-medical' biological sciences can be found in the career of **Michael Gaze**. He became the Head of the MRC Neural Development and

Regeneration Group in 1984, and an Honorary Professor in 1985, in the Department of Zoology, having qualified in medicine at the Medical School of the Royal Colleges of Edinburgh in 1949 and thereafter engaged in medical teaching and research. He had been working since 1970 in the National Institute for Medical Research in London with a substantial MRC grant, on a study of the formation of nerve connections during development and regeneration, and his move to Edinburgh was part of a major redistribution of research projects by the MRC.

A Manpower Services Commission Community Programme project was initiated in 1988 to create a Centre for Resources in Animal Biology (CRAB) based on the University's extensive Natural History museum collections. These were largely amassed between 1860 and 1970 as teaching material in animal biology, and needed to be brought up-to-date and made more accessible to students, visiting school-children and the general public.

In 1988 **Spedding Micklem** was appointed Professor of Immunobiology, having been Reader in Zoology in the Department since 1973. **David Saunders** was appointed Professor of Insect Physiology in 1990, having been Reader in Zoology in the Department since 1974. He joined the Department in 1958 and has been working in the field of parasitology, researching the tsetse fly, insect time clocks and insect endocrinology. He has published *Insect Clocks* (1972; 2edn 1982) and *Introduction to Biological Rhythms* (1977).

In 1990 the majority of the staff of the Department of Zoology were integrated into the Institute of *Cell, Animal and Population Biology within the Division of Biological Sciences, along with staff of similar research interests from Agriculture, Forestry and Natural Resources, and Genetics.

A Leaner and Fitter University

The twenty years covered by this chapter certainly saw the most fundamental and far-reaching changes in the whole of the University's history. Compared to the abolition of the regenting system in 1708, or the foundation of the Faculty of Science in 1893, both of which would have registered no more than 4.5 to 4.8 on the Richter scale ('wakes sleeping persons'), the worst of the many shocks in the 1980s must have reached at least 6.2 – 'strong enough to cause some structural damage' to ivory towers!

Edinburgh University survived better than most, perhaps partly because of its four centuries of tradition, and partly in spite of its many academic and administrative traditionalists. Between 1980 and 1991 the University was obliged to leave unfilled for varying periods of time a substantial number of UGC/UFC-funded staff posts; most of these vacancies were subsequently filled by the appointment of externally-funded staff. The level of UGC/UFC recurrent grant decreased by well over ten per cent in real terms, but the total of external research income increased from just over £2m in 1971-72 to more than £32m in 1991-92. By 1991 the ivory tower was being rebuilt, on the same solid foundations, as the headquarters of a very large organisation engaged in the *business* of teaching, research and marketing its skills to the world at large.

Edinburgh University Scientists and Engineers, 1970 - 1991

The problems involved in compiling a select list of notable Edinburgh University scientists and engineers have been increasing with each succeeding chapter, and I now have to admit that with the graduates of 1970 to 1991 the attempt would be not merely very difficult but positively foolhardy! Sources of biographical information such as *Who's Who* don't even try to predict who's *going* to be who in another ten or twenty years' time, and the University's alumni database, though impressively comprehensive nowadays, naturally suffers from the same limitation. So, regretfully but sensibly, since I am unable to make a sufficiently informed choice, I have made no choice at all from the graduates of 1970 - 1991, any of whom may yet become as notable as those who appear in earlier chapters.

Surprisingly, however, you will find at the end of chapter 10 that I have not been similarly inhibited in making a selection from the graduates of 1994 - 1997!

CHAPTER 10

The Faculty of Science and Engineering today and tomorrow

Looking back from this final chapter it is clear that over the past four hundred years radical changes have often been imposed on the universities of Britain as a result of changing economic conditions, religious affirmations, public attitudes and political policies. In common with most other non-commercial institutions, those in positions of authority in the universities could always produce good reasons for maintaining the *status quo*, and fundamental changes had to be imposed from without, rather than initiated from within. The last ten years in particular have been extremely difficult, but perhaps the worst of the latest upheaval is over, at least for the present. What then can be said about the situation the universities find themselves in today?

The University of Edinburgh Magazine *Edit*, Issue 3, Winter 1992/93, featured an article entitled *KNOWLEDGE plc* by Douglas Fraser, the Education Correspondent of *The Scotsman*. He noted that 'today's universities are full of the jargon . . of the market –. . customer satisfaction, planning units, cost centres, the client learning environment and, inevitably, the mission statement.' This is certainly true of Edinburgh today, and doubtless also of Glasgow, whose Rector, Pat Kane, coined the term *KNOWLEDGE plc* to express his disapproval of the changes taking place in the Scottish universities. 'Their work', he complained, 'has lost its breadth, its pace, its ability to question and its identity.'

He went on to say that the move from students to 'customers' may appear to enhance their status, but in fact those same clients have become widgets, being processed in dramatically increasing numbers through a degree machine. The analogy of a 'degree machine' is not new, and it tends to be used by critics whenever there is a change in the system. The short-term consequences of radical change in a complex system almost inevitably take the form of an initial over-reaction, followed by more gradual adjustments until a new state of equilibrium is reached.

My own recollections of Edinburgh University as an engineering student nearly fifty years ago constitute a generally unfavourable comparison with today – large classes, distant professors, feverish note-taking, exams testing memory rather than understanding (nothing but a slide rule, log tables, pen and pencil and a bottle of ink in the exam room in those days!). As members of staff in the sixties, my colleagues and I had to come to terms with stencil-duplicated hand-outs, open-book exams, staff-student committees, continuous assessment, audio-visual aids, honours projects, calculators and computers. They were all criticised by some, and rejected by a few, but who now would denigrate them as mere cogs in a degree machine?

Until very recently the situation in the universities was that their teaching and research had moved with the times, but their administration had not – by and large, it had not needed to, relying on spoon-feeding by the UGC and the research councils.

However, the largest institutions such as Edinburgh University found as inflation ran riot in the seventies and eighties that their annual budget was no longer £x million but tens of millions and eventually more than £100 million, and miscalculations of only a few per cent could become headline news. A more businesslike attitude was long overdue at all levels down to the smallest 'cost centre', and I am still enough of an optimist to believe that, as so often in the past, when the dust has settled the changes will be seen to have benefitted students as well as staff, teaching as well as research.

The Principal of the University, Sir David Smith, speaking at the November 1993 Graduation Ceremony, surveyed some of the changes in his six-year term of office. The number of students had grown by 36 per cent, but the number of teaching staff had decreased by 7 per cent. At the same time the amount of money in real terms available to teach a student had declined by no less than 19 per cent. Sir David emphasised that this situation was not unique to Edinburgh, and that in fact many universities were in a worse position.

An important change in the administration of higher education in Britain, rejected by the government in 1984, was announced in 1992 – the functions of the UFC in relation to the Scottish Universities were to be transferred to the Scottish Higher Education Funding Council (SHEFC) as from April 1993. Then on 27 May 1993, as if to challenge my belief that the worst might be over, the White Paper *Realising our Potential. A Strategy for Science, Engineering and Technology* (Cmnd 2250, HMSO, 1993) was published.

It proposed widespread changes throughout the various interfaces between government, industry and the universities – a new Council for Science and Technology, reorganised Research Councils with explicit commitments to 'wealth creation and the quality of life', and a new post of Director-General of Research Councils in the Office of Science and Technology. The dual-funding mechanism would be rationalised and retained while the Rothschild customer-contractor principle would be maintained and strengthened, but there is a prospect of the privatisation of some of the government research establishments.

The White Paper goes on to propose that training of postgraduate scientists and engineers will be developed so that the MSc can become the normal initial postgraduate degree, and PhD training can be properly underpinned. Those postgraduates who go on to a career in academic research should be better managed, and there will be a new campaign to spread the understanding of science and technology in schools and among the public. *Plus ça change, plus c'est la même chose.*

The writer of a recent note in the Newsletter of the Faculty of Science and Engineering was referring to his own Department of Geology and Geophysics, but surely speaks for university staff everywhere:–

"It would be very pleasant if we could feel that after several years of intense effort to adjust to new national research and teaching policies, we were able to exploit our success in a stable environment in which goals and processes were explicit. Sadly, like all our colleagues, we recognise that the only certainty is uncertainty. As we adjust ourselves to the demands of the White Paper on Science and Technology, which we are well placed to do, and anticipate further, unknown changes beyond, we must depend upon our enthusiasm and commitment to carry us through, in the hope that the ultimate performance indicator is not a heart attack!"

THE UNIVERSITY OF EDINBURGH

The changing public image of the University of Edinburgh can be measured in various ways, but one in particular has impressed itself upon me when delving into the University archives in the course of writing this history. The publications of an academic institution are a good guide to how it sees itself, and to how it wants the world to see it – or, indeed, whether or not it cares how the world sees it. A century ago when the Faculty of Science was founded the University Calendar was already 34 years old, and on the whole neither more nor less interesting than its counterpart today. A century ago, however, the Calendar was the University's *only* publication, its only contact with potential students, their parents and advisers. Today the University's public image as projected by its publications is very different.

The Undergraduate and Postgraduate Prospectuses are attractive, informative and readable; departmental brochures are well-produced and widely available; our graduates . . . sorry, Alumni, almost 90,000 of them, have their own magazine, and the University of Edinburgh Development Trust reports annually on the success of its fund-raising efforts; the University's Magazine *Edit* won four awards in the 1993 competition run by the British Association of Industrial Editors in Scotland; and the Annual Report is a thoroughly professional full-colour document, more interesting than most of its commercial equivalents.

The University of Edinburgh today consists of eight Faculties, listed here with dates of foundation – approximate in those cases where Faculties were not created by statute, but came into being by use and wont:-

Arts	1583
Divinity	c1620
Law	c1722
Medicine	1726
Science	1893
[Science and Engineering, from 1991]	
Music	1894
Veterinary Medicine	1953
Social Sciences	1963

The size of the Faculties, as may be imagined, covers a very large range indeed, and the University has established four Faculty Groups which provide a better balance in terms of student numbers, budgets and resources:-

Arts, Divinity and Music
Law and Social Sciences
Medicine and Veterinary Medicine
Science and Engineering.

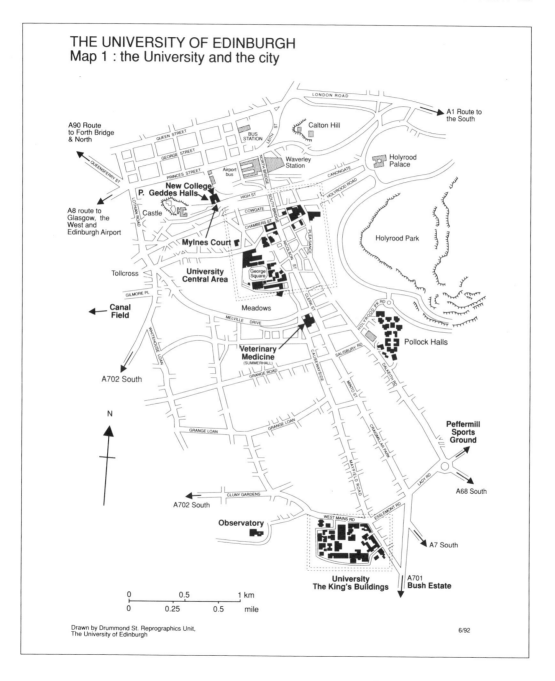

THE UNIVERSITY OF EDINBURGH
Map 1 : the University and the city

A90 Route
to Forth Bridge
& North

LONDON ROAD

A1 Route to
the South

Calton Hill

BUS
STATION

Waverley
Station

Holyrood
Palace

QUEEN STREET

GEORGE STREET

PRINCES STREET

Airport
bus

CANONGATE

QUEENSFERRY ST

New College
P. Geddes Halls

HIGH ST

A8 route to
Glasgow, the
West and
Edinburgh Airport

Castle

LOTHIAN ROAD

COWGATE

CHAMBERS ST

Mylnes Court

Holyrood Park

University
Central Area

George
Square

NICOLSON ST

PLEASANCE

Tollcross

GILMORE PL

Meadows

CLERK ST

HOLYROOD PK RD

Pollock Halls

Canal
Field

MELVILLE   DRIVE

WHITEHOUSE LOAN

Veterinary
Medicine
(SUMMERHALL)

SALISBURY RD

CAUSEWAYSIDE

DALKEITH RD

A702 South

GRANGE ROAD

N

MINTO ST

CRAIGMILLAR PARK

Peffermill
Sports
Ground

GRANGE LOAN

GRANGE LOAN

MAYFIELD ROAD

LADY RD

A68 South

CLUNY GARDENS

A702 South

ESSLEMONT RD

Observatory

WEST MAINS RD

A7 South

University
The King's Buildings

A701
Bush Estate

0   0.5   1 km
0   0.25   0.5   mile

Drawn by Drummond St. Reprographics Unit,
The University of Edinburgh

6/92

In the Principal's address to the summer meeting of the General Council in June 1992, Sir David Smith was able to report the welcome news that the operating deficit for 1991/92, which could have been as much as £3.75m, was likely to be reduced to break-even point. In fact, when the final figures were available they showed a net surplus of just over £2m, justifying his optimistic forecast that despite threats of declining funding per student, Edinburgh's distinctive pattern of teaching in a research-led environment would be sustained. At the time of going to press, the results for 1992/93 were announced, showing a net surplus for the financial year of just over £5m, on a total income of £191m. The Principal was able to say, three months before his retirement at the end of March 1994, that the University was firmly back in the black, and beginning to build up its reserves against uncertain times ahead.

THE FACULTY OF SCIENCE AND ENGINEERING

The Faculty of Science and Engineering now constitutes one of Edinburgh University's four Faculty Groups. The Dean of the Faculty, Prof John Mavor of Electrical Engineering, became Provost of the Faculty Group, and he will be succeeded as Provost and Dean in October 1994 by Prof Geoffrey Boulton of Geology and Geophysics. Nine Planning Units have been created in Science and Engineering, each with its own Head of Planning Unit (HoPU). At the same time preparations were put in hand for the Teaching Quality Assessment exercises which are expected to be introduced throughout the UK higher education system in the near future.

In 1992 the Government announced new arrangements for Research Council Grants, modifying the 'dual support' system of research funding which had become almost traditional in British universities. From the beginning of the 1992/93 academic year the Research Councils became responsible for meeting all the costs of the research they support, apart from academic salaries and premises costs, through money previously distributed to universities as part of the UFC block grant. To assist staff in the Faculty of Science and Engineering in the preparation of fully costed grant applications UnivEd appointed Dr Jane Polglase to the post of Research Council Officer.

At the end of 1992 Edinburgh University was awarded a block of twelve European Commission research contracts, totalling £1.2m, as part of the *ESPRIT* programme in the field of Information Technology. The recipients included the Departments of Artificial Intelligence and Computer Science, the Human Communication Research Centre, the Laboratory for Foundations of Computer Science, the Centre for Cognitive Science, and the Centre for Speech Technology Research.

As a measure of the level of research activity throughout the Faculty of Science and Engineering, it should be put on record that in the financial year 1991/92, the Faculty attracted a total of over £20m in research grants and contracts.

Two engineering alumni of the Faculty were in the news as this chapter was being written. **Sir Francis McWilliams** graduated BSc (Eng) in 1945 as a civil engineer, and after a few years in Edinburgh went out to Malaysia. He became Town Engineer for

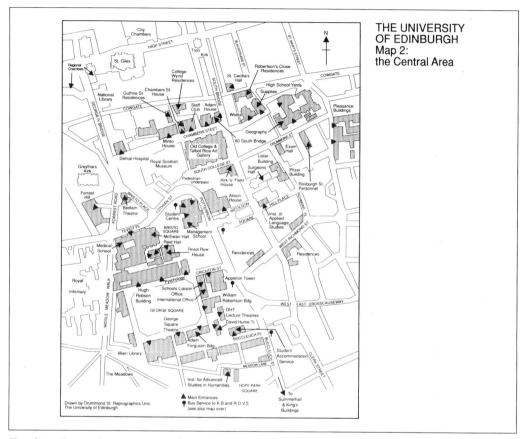

Petaling Jaya, the country's first industrial new town, which he helped to build from scratch over the next decade. For his services to the State of Selangor the Sultan appointed him a *Dato*, the equivalent of a Knight. He also became involved in arbitration work, and on his return to London qualified as a Barrister in 1978. His membership and chairmanship of the residents' association in the Barbican, and his election as Alderman for the Ward, eventually brought him in November 1992 the signal honour of being installed as the 665th Lord Mayor of London.

The University of Edinburgh / Royal Bank of Scotland Alumnus of the Year 1993 was **Dr Roualeyn Fenton-May**, who graduated BSc in Chemical Engineering in 1967. He won a Fulbright Scholarship to the University of Wisconsin at Madison, where he completed a PhD thesis on food processing. He then joined the Coca-Cola Company and by 1976 was responsible for the development and implementation of worldwide quality assurance programmes. In 1980 he moved to Hong Kong, and six years later was made

Sir Francis McWilliams, Lord Mayor of London, 1992-93

Dr Roualeyn Fenton-May, Alumnus of the Year, 1993

President, Coca-Cola China Limited, in which capacity he greatly expanded the company's business in that area. Last year he returned to company headquarters in Atlanta, Georgia, to take up the post of Director of Operations Development worldwide.

BIOLOGICAL SCIENCES, DIVISION OF

For the earlier history of the Biological Sciences see entries in previous chapters for the Departments which are now incorporated in the Division:-

Agriculture	Botany	Genetics
Forestry and Natural Resources		Microbiology
Molecular Biology		Zoology

The spectrum of teaching and research activity covers the whole range of biology, from molecular and cell biology on the one hand to ecology and resource management on the other. No other UK university spans this range so effectively and in such depth, within a single 'mega-department'. The Division aims to use the quality and diversity of its research activity to maintain its undergraduate and postgraduate teaching at a very high standard. When taken together with the other University departments and research

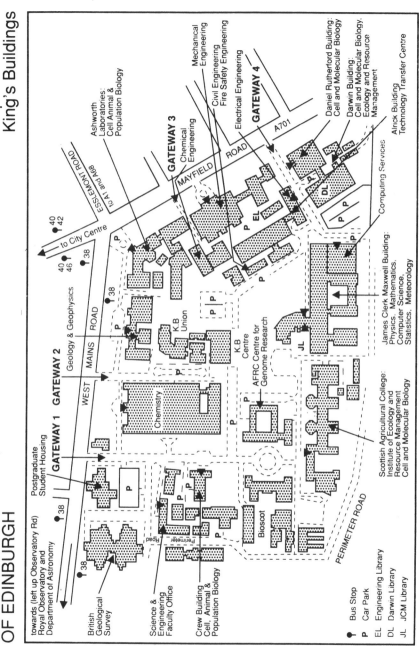

THE UNIVERSITY
OF EDINBURGH

Map 3:
King's Buildings

towards (left up Observatory Rd)
Royal Observatory and
Department of Astronomy

British
Geological
Survey

Science &
Engineering
Faculty Office

Crew Building
Cell, Animal &
Population Biology

GATEWAY 1

GATEWAY 2

Postgraduate
Student Housing

WEST   MAINS   ROAD

Geology & Geophysics

ESSLEMONT ROAD
to A1 and A68

to City Centre

Ashworth
Laboratories:
Cell Animal &
Population Biology

GATEWAY 3

Chemical
Engineering

Mechanical
Engineering

Civil Engineering
Fire Safety Engineering

Electrical Engineering

GATEWAY 4

MAYFIELD   ROAD

A701

Daniel Rutherford Building:
Cell and Molecular Biology

Darwin Building:
Cell and Molecular Biology,
Ecology and Resource
Management

Alrick Building
Technology Transfer Centre

Computing Services

James Clerk Maxwell Building:
Physics, Mathematics,
Computer Science,
Statistics, Meteorology

Scottish Agricultural College:
Institute of Ecology and
Resource Management
Cell and Molecular Biology

K.B
Union

K.B
Centre

AFRC Centre for
Genome Research

Chemistry

Bioscot

PERIMETER ROAD

Perimeter Road

Bus Stop
P   Car Park
EL   Engineering Library
DL   Darwin Library
JL   JCM Library

institutes involved in collaborative research programmes, the Division is part of a very large, active and well funded research community which gives Edinburgh University a major international presence in biology.

The latest Annual Report of the Division of Biological Sciences summarises its current research under eleven broad headings, which convey quite effectively its variety:- the structure and function of macromolecules, molecular genetics, gene expression and development, population genetics, immunology, parasite biology and genetics, plant development, fungal biology, animal ecology and behaviour, ecology and environmental physiology, animal agriculture, management of agriculture and forest resources. One example of research which builds on the Division's strengths in molecular and population genetics is the highly interactive programme investigating the molecular genetics of quantitative traits in laboratory, natural and farm animal populations and the mechanisms by which variation is maintained in them. This research spans Institutes in the Division and also involves the AFRC Roslin Institute.

A new Centre for HIV Research funded by the MRC was established in 1993 at the King's Buildings, the first of its kind in the UK. Its specialist research facilities will be used by staff from the Departments of Medicine, Medical Microbiology, Haematology and Infectious Diseases in the Faculty of Medicine, and from the Division of Biological Sciences and the Department of Chemistry in the Faculty of Science and Engineering. One research group led by Dr Andrew Leigh Brown (ICAPB) has identified four different strains of the North American AIDS virus, and work is continuing with the aim of finding an effective AIDS vaccine.

Construction of a major new Biological Sciences centre has been started, financed by £1m from the University and a further £14m from the Wellcome Trust, the Wolfson Foundation and the Darwin Trust. The Michael Swann Building will provide first class facilities for up to 170 research workers in genetics and molecular biology, with library, computing and other support functions, and a 400-seat lecture theatre. Interest has already been expressed by a number of eminent biological scientists in joining the expanded research teams which will occupy the new building on its completion in 1995.

The Division has recently acquired two major items of equipment on research grants, a laser scanning confocal microscope and a *FACSTAR* cell sorter, the latter being the only one of its kind in Scotland. Other facilities essential to biological research include the Biocomputing Research Unit, originally set up in 1988 in the Department of *Molecular Biology, and the Faculty electron microscope facility which is managed by the ICMB.

In October 1993 **Bill Hill**, Professor of Animal Genetics in the ICAPB, succeeded Prof Dale as Head of Division and Head of the Planning Unit. The three Institutes within the Division of Biological Sciences welcomed more than 400 first year students in October 1993. Fifteen honours courses are offered, and there are 140 students currently in the fourth year. On the research front there are over 150 research staff backed by more than 120 technical staff, plus about 180 research postgraduates. A recent development is the formation of a Graduate School, with Prof Ian Sutherland (ICMB) as Convener, to coordinate and advise on such matters as research topics, choice of supervisor, graduate training courses, seminars, supervision and assessment.

Institute of Cell, Animal and Population Biology

The Institute was formed in 1990 as a constituent part of the Division of Biological Sciences within the Faculty of Science and Engineering. It is at present accommodated mainly in the Ashworth Laboratories and the Crew Building, but a major relocation of staff will take place on completion of the new Biological Sciences building.

The Institute initially included the following professorial staff (previous department in brackets):-

John Bishop (Genetics) Professor of Molecular Cell Biology.

William Hill (Genetics) Professor of Animal Genetics and Head of the Institute, 1990-93.

Aubrey Manning (Zoology) Professor of Natural History.

Spedding Micklem (Zoology) Professor of Immunobiology. Retired in 1992.

David Saunders (Zoology) Professor of Insect Physiology, and Head of the Institute from October 1993.

The Faculty Group of Science and Engineering plans to fill the Chair of Zoology in session 1993/94.

Linda Partridge, who joined the Department of Zoology in 1977 and became Reader in 1987, was appointed in 1992 to a Personal Chair in Evolutionary Biology. She left Edinburgh in January 1994 to take up an appointment at University College, London.

Dr Nick Barton, Darwin Trust Senior Fellow in ICAPB, has been listed in *Science* as one of 49 rising young European biologists expected to make names for themselves in future. He is a member of the team working on various aspects of population biology, helping to foster new interactions between population geneticists and colleagues working in animal behaviour and ecology.

The MSc/Diploma course in Animal Breeding, instituted twenty years ago and still the only one of its kind in the UK, is now offered jointly by the ICAPB and the IERM. It continues to attract new sponsorship, both from industry and from such organizations as the UK Meat and Livestock Commission. Students are accepted for the course with honours degrees in agriculture, veterinary medicine, genetics, statistics or related subjects.

Institute of Cell and Molecular Biology

The Institute was formed in 1990 as a constituent part of the Division of Biological Sciences within the Faculty of Science and Engineering. It is accommodated in the Darwin and Daniel Rutherford Buildings.

The Institute initially included the following professorial staff (previous department in brackets):-

Richard Ambler (Molecular Biology) Professor of Protein Chemistry and Head of the Institute, 1990-93.

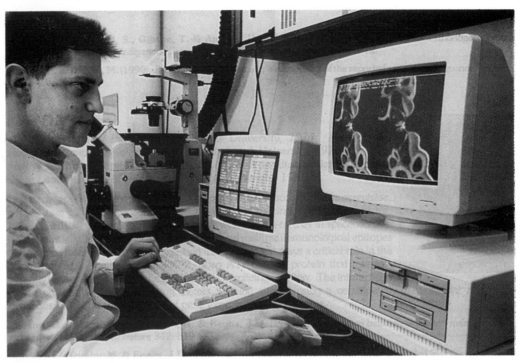

The Faculty Electron Microscope facility

Adrian Bird (Genetics) Buchanan Professor of Genetics. One of the four most-cited Scottish scientists, according to a survey commissioned by the Edinburgh International Science Festival. In December 1992, on the occasion of the European Summit in Edinburgh, Prof Bird gave a public lecture entitled *Understanding the Human Genome – Scottish Science in Europe*, in which he pointed out that the contribution of scientists working in Scotland to the study of genetics has been out of all proportion to the size of the country. Prof Bird received one of the 22 Howard Hughes Medical Institute awards to UK medical scientists for 1993.

John Dale (Botany) Professor of Plant Physiology, and Head of the Division of Biological Sciences from 1990 until he retired in 1993.

Sir Kenneth Murray (Molecular Biology) Biogen Research Professor of Molecular Biology. Prof Murray was awarded a knighthood in 1993 for 'services to science', and in particular for his work in genetic engineering, in the development of the world's first artificial vaccine against hepatitis B. The numerous contributions to the funds of the

Professor Sir Kenneth Murray at the Institute of Cell and Molecular Biology at King's Buildings

University from Prof Murray's Darwin Trust have up to the end of 1993 amounted to a total of some £7m, the largest sum from any individual benefactor.

Noreen Murray (Molecular Biology) Professor of Molecular Genetics.

John Scaife (Molecular Biology) Professor of Molecular Parasitology. Died in June 1991.

Michael Yeoman (Botany) Regius Professor of Botany. Retired in 1993.

Since the foundation of the Institute a number of additional professorial appointments have been made. In 1991 **Ian Sutherland**, Reader in the Department of Microbiology, was appointed to a Personal Chair of Microbial Physiology, and **Tony Trewavas**, Reader in the Department of Botany, was appointed to a Personal Chair of Plant Biochemistry.

In 1993 **William Donachie**, Reader in the Department of Molecular Biology, was appointed to a Personal Chair of Bacterial Genetics, and **Dr D J Finnegan** succeeded Prof Ambler as Head of the Institute.

At the time of writing applications have been invited for the vacant Regius Chair of Botany, which is jointly funded by the University and the Royal Botanic Garden, Edinburgh.

Institute of Ecology and Resource Management

The Institute was formed in 1990 as a constituent part of the Division of Biological Sciences within the Faculty of Science and Engineering. It is accommodated principally in the School of Agriculture and Darwin Buildings, the latter also housing the Edinburgh Centre for Tropical Forests (ECTF). The Institute now offers ten different MSc courses, which in 1992-93 attracted a total of 72 students.

It initially included the following professorial staff (previous department in brackets):-

Colin Whittemore (Agriculture) Professor of Agriculture and Rural Economy and Head of the Institute (1990 to date).

Barry Dent (Agriculture) Professor of Agricultural Resource Management.

Paul Jarvis FRSE (Forestry) Professor of Forestry and Natural Resources.

The ECTF is an association comprising the University's Schools of Forestry and Ecological Sciences, the Royal Botanic Garden, the NERC Institute of Terrestrial Ecology,

Edinburgh Centre for Tropical Forests—Chinese visitors in Scotland

Land and Timber Services International, and the Forestry Commission. It reflects the city's unique concentration of expertise, accumulated over more than two centuries, in the area of tropical forestry. In September 1993 it was announced that the ECTF is to undertake a consultancy contract worth more than £0.5m for the Chinese Government on behalf of the Overseas Development Administration. The contract is to provide training, travel and equipment over a three year period to assist in the development of a programme for the conservation and sustainable management of temperate and sub-tropical forests in China.

In 1992 **John Grace**, Lecturer and Reader in Ecology, 1970-92, in the Department of Forestry and Natural Resources and the IERM, was appointed to a Personal Chair of Environmental Biology.

In April 1993 HRH the Prince of Wales formally launched Sustainable Farming Systems (SFS), a joint initiative between the University of Edinburgh and the Scottish Agricultural College. The project is the largest single EC-funded investigation of the sustainability concept and aims to develop food production methods that depend on biological processes rather than chemicals. Funding for the initiative is also being provided by the Scottish Office, Scottish Natural Heritage, and the Horticulture Development Council. Prof Barry Dent is joint Chairman of the SFS steering committee.

A major research commitment of the Institute is the Edinburgh University Biosphere-Atmosphere Programme (EUBAP), which also involves the Scottish Agricultural College, the Institute of Terrestrial Ecology at the Bush, the Macaulay Land

Use Research Institute and the Northern Forestry Research Institute. EUBAP aims to improve understanding of the impact of *global change*, particularly rising levels of atmospheric carbon dioxide and temperature, on vegetation, and the role of vegetation in influencing the composition of the atmosphere, especially carbon dioxide, methane and water vapour. EUBAP includes studies of man-made and natural forests, heathlands and crops, extending from the tropics to the boreal region. This and other international cooperative research programmes have brought about £1.8m in grants from the EC and a number of other sources within the past eighteen months.

AFRC Centre for Genome Research

In 1992 the building now occupied by the CGR, and originally by ABRO, was named the Roger Land Building. **Prof Richard Lathe** is Director of the CGR, which undertakes a core research programme utilising transgenic technology to address questions of relevance to agriculture, medicine and fundamental biology. It also provides a centralised resource of expertise and technology for collaborative research with academic and industrial research workers in Britain and abroad. There are currently over 100 permanent and visiting scientists working in the Centre. In 1993 Dr Rosa Beddington, Senior Research Fellow in the CGR, received one of the 22 Howard Hughes Medical Institute awards to UK medical scientists.

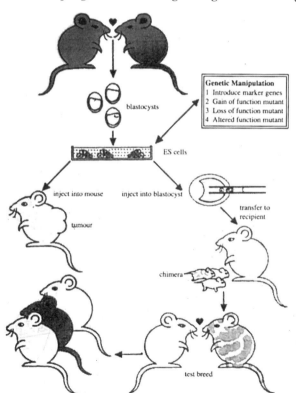

Mouse genetic manipulation

Biology Teaching Organisation

On 1 October 1993 **Dr Simon van Heyningen** (Biochemistry) succeeded Prof John Phillips as Head of the Biology Teaching Organisation.

Chemistry

The Chemistry Department in the University of Edinburgh is one of the largest in the UK, with an international reputation for research in all three of its divisions, organic, physical and inorganic chemistry.

There are in the Department at present more than 120 PhD students and postdoctoral research workers. Undergraduate teaching leads to the BSc degrees in Chemistry, Chemical Physics or Environmental Chemistry. Two new honours courses with a forward-looking slant have been introduced in the current session, *Chemistry with a year in Europe* and *Environmental Chemistry* with a year in Europe; students will spend their third year on an approved course of study in a designated European university.

A major achievement in biological organic chemistry has been the synthesis of the important protein, ubiquitin, in crystalline form allowing a study to be made of the protein folding. Using polymer-assisted peptide synthesis, advances have been made in the design of inhibitors of the enzymes involved in inflammatory response and heart disease. The Biological Chemistry Group has a key role in the SERC-supported Edinburgh Centre for Molecular Recognition due to its particular strengths in peptide/protein synthesis, recombinant and synthetic DNA methodology and biological NMR spectroscopy.

Chemical physics and physical chemistry at Edinburgh is concerned with understanding the properties of isolated molecules, especially in excited electronic states, and in the results of molecular collisions, either as isolated events or as parts of more complex sequences occurring at phase interfaces. In this area of research lasers and molecular beams are particularly useful, especially the latter which allow unstable and exotic species to be 'frozen' far from thermodynamic equilibrium.

Spectroscopic measurements can be used as a powerful probe in the study of surface processes that can bring about catalytic reactions. It is possible to extend the technique, from processes occurring on clean single crystal surfaces at ultra high vacuum, to practical industrial plant conditions involving mega-ton production at many times atmospheric pressure. Expertise in the synthesis of new zeolites and molecular sieves plays an important part in this area and in the interface with industry. Electrochemistry has many uses in analytical, environmental and synthetic chemistry. Work on the use of electrochemical sensors to monitor specific medical conditions has grown enormously in recent years, and work in this area has grown from fundamental studies to the formation of a commercial enterprise.

The Department of Chemistry is now especially strong in the area of structural chemistry, with leading authorities on the staff in X-ray and electron diffraction studies, using some of the most up-to-date equipment in any British university. These facilities complement the extensive programme of synthetic work and also permit studies of the dynamic nature of materials in the solid state. The use of electron diffraction in the study of compounds in the gas phase, where the molecules are relatively free of induced distortions, has centred almost exclusively on neutral molecules at or above room temperature, but is now being extended by the construction of special apparatus to allow structural studies of molecules cooled to temperatures near absolute zero in the gas phase.

Brian Johnson was appointed Crum Brown Professor of Chemistry in 1991, from Fitzwilliam College in Cambridge. He was awarded the Corday-Morgan Medal and Prize of the Royal Society of Chemistry in 1976. In 1993 **Tom Brown** was appointed to a Personal Chair of Nucleic Acid Chemistry. He and his research colleagues are noted for their chemical studies of the nucleic acids, from a physical rather than a biological standpoint. The interfaces group was strengthened in 1993 by the arrival of **Prof Lovat Rees**, who retired recently from Imperial College, London. His specialism is the absorption of sorbates and their binary mixtures in natural zeolites and their ion-exchanged forms.

The Department's teaching continues to reflect the needs of a changing world, and in 1993 a one-year Master of Science degree in Environmental Chemistry was introduced.

Computing Services

Dr Richard Field was appointed Director of Computing and Information Technology Services in the University from October 1990. Since 1981 he had been Director of the University of London Computer Centre, and shortly after his arrival in Edinburgh the EUCS was renamed Computing Services.

Edinburgh now has the most extensive computing facilities in any British university, with a high-speed fibre optic network known as EdLAN linking the King's Buildings, George Square and Old College areas. Departments' ethernets are connected to the FDDI backbone cable through electronic networking switches (routers). The main operating configurations are now Unix based on two large Sequent Symmetry systems with a VMS service supported on a DEC VAX system. Microcomputer laboratories have been established in most parts of the University campus, and they are used both for class instruction and for individual work. They have a variety of computing equipment, mainly IBM compatible and Apple Macintosh, all linked to the network.

The very latest development (February 1994) is that the University of Edinburgh has been selected by the Science and Engineering Research Council to host Europe's fastest supercomputer, representing an investment of about £8m. When the 40 Gflops (40 billion arithmetic operations per second) 256-processor Cray T3D is commissioned later this year by the University's Computing Services it will be among the ten fastest computers in the world. The University itself has committed additional funding in order to increase significantly the size and speed of the new machine. This funding from EPCC, the Departments of Geology and Geophysics, Physics, ICMB and EUCS will enable the University to utilise the supercomputer most effectively for its own academic research and in collaborative projects with leading industrial companies.

The EPCC will support scientists using the Cray T3D for research into some of today's most complex scientific problems such as mapping the human genome, modelling climatic changes, simulating airflow around complicated geometries, understanding how new drugs work, designing new materials and uncovering the secrets of sub-nuclear particles – the so-called *Grand Challenges* of science.

Edinburgh Parallel Computing Centre

In 1991 a CM-200 Connection Machine was placed in the EPCC by Thinking Machines Corporation of Cambridge, Massachusetts, whose Vice President on handing it over declared that the University of Edinburgh was one of the foremost centres of parallel processing systems in the world. It was at the time the most powerful supercomputer in the UK, with a peak speed of 8 Gflops (8×10^9 FLOating Point operations per Second), roughly the equivalent power of 10,000 personal computers. By 1992 the CM-200 was being used to simulate traffic flows in and around Edinburgh, analysing the movements of up to 250,000 vehicles on 1,500 roads with 6,000 junctions. The EPCC has another twelve major research contracts to be carried out for UK commercial and industrial firms in the next two years, including Rolls Royce (computational fluid dynamics), the Meteorological Office (weather forecasting), and British Telecom (network management software).

The EPCC has expanded rapidly and now has a staff of more than 50, the majority working on collaborative projects with industry. It has been selected as a European large-scale facility under the EC's Human Capital and Mobility Programme, in recognition of the fact that it has one of the most significant concentrations of high performance computing resources and experience in any European university. Over the next three years Edinburgh University research workers will be able to apply for EC funding to support short-term visits by European university scientists on collaborative research projects.

Prof David Wallace resigned at the end of 1993 to take up the appointment of Vice-Chancellor of Loughborough University of Technology, and was succeeded as Director of the Edinburgh Parallel Computing Centre by **Dr Richard Kenway**, Reader in the Department of Physics.

ENGINEERING AND INFORMATICS, SCHOOL OF

The School was formed in 1989 as the School of Engineering and Information Technology, to coordinate the interests and activities of the Departments of Artificial Intelligence, Chemical Engineering, Civil Engineering and Building Science, Computer Science, Electrical Engineering and Mechanical Engineering, and the Centre for Cognitive Science. The title of the School was changed in 1992 to Engineering and Informatics.

Artificial Intelligence

Alan Bundy was appointed Professor of Automated Reasoning in 1990. He joined Edinburgh University's Metamathematics Unit in 1971, and from 1987 to 1992 held an SERC Senior Fellowship. His research involves the building of problem solving programs for different branches of mathematics, such as number theory, algebra, mechanics, ecological modelling and logic/functional programming. He is also working in conjunction with the Department of Sociology on the sociology of proof; in other words, the sociological factors which may influence approaches to mathematical proof. As part of an international working group from twenty universities in Europe and the USA, Prof Bundy has begun a collaborative research programme on the automation of mathematical proofs requiring induction.

Current research in the Department of Artificial Intelligence is concentrated in four areas:– intelligent robotics, knowledge based systems, mathematical reasoning, and natural language. In robotics, an innovative hybrid architecture has been developed for the hierarchical control of reactive robotic devices. Using vision and force sensing, this architecture has been successfully applied to industrial assembly tasks using a low cost manipulator. Research will now be undertaken into the problems of the recognition and location of complex industrial parts, and the grasping and manipulation of unknown objects for applications such as radioactive waste disposal.

FREDDY Twenty years on. Demonstrating the assembly of shapes made from SOMA parts

A major research project has been awarded to the University in the form of a DTI/SERC grant of £600,000 under the Safety-Critical Systems Programme. The work will involve the Departments of Artificial Intelligence, Computer Science and Sociology (Faculty of Social Sciences), and the Human Communication Research Centre, as well as the participation of a number of industrial firms.

Another example of the cross-faculty collaboration that is becoming the rule rather than the exception in Edinburgh University is the new joint Honours Degree in Artificial

Intelligence and Psychology which is to be launched in October 1994. The Department of Artificial Intelligence began in 1971 as a small research department with 3.5 academic staff and about 40 FTE students, and over the past twenty years or so it has now reached 13.6 academic staff and about 200 FTE students, divided roughly equally between undergraduates and postgraduates.

Artificial Intelligence Applications Institute

David Parry, the former Managing Director of Ferranti Infographics Ltd, was appointed Managing Director of AIAI in 1992. Prof Austin Tate, Technical Director of AIAI, was made a Fellow of the American Association of Artificial Intelligence in 1993 – one of only eight Europeans to be given that honour for research and services in the field of AI. The Institute is now one of the top centres world-wide for Artificial Intelligence applications in planning and scheduling.

Work began in 1993 on a multi-million pound project, supported by the Department of Trade and Industry, in enterprise modelling. The Artificial Intelligence Applications

First Year Teaching Session

Institute is leading a consortium including Unilever, IBM, Logica and Lloyd's Register of Shipping.

Chemical Engineering

In response to rapidly rising student numbers, three new lecturers have recently been appointed in Chemical Engineering. The undergraduate body at present totals 125, a figure expected to rise further in the next few years, reflecting strenuous staff activity devoted to recruitment in response to the University's recent policies. Recently-developed recruitment activities include the organisation of a two-day residential 'Chemistry to Chemical Engineering' course for schoolteachers, generously funded by BP Chemicals Ltd. The Department runs a single four-year Honours degree course leading to the degree of BEng in Chemical Engineering.

The Department now holds one of the best research ratings for the subject in the UK. More than £1m in new research grants and contracts was received in the twelve months up to November 1992. The complement of almost thirty research workers and postgraduate students includes graduates in physics, mathematics, computer science, chemistry and microbiology as well as chemical engineering. They form a coherently active group with much mutually beneficial cross-fertilisation of ideas. One of the largest areas of research is process simulation, integration and control, which has attracted substantial SERC funding, in association with the Glasgow Department of Control Engineering and the Dundee and Edinburgh Departments of Mathematics. Other current research topics include fluid and fluid-particle mechanics, biochemical and medical engineering, energy recovery, and gas-solid non-catalytic reactions.

The student Chemical Engineering Society promotes a social programme which results in a lively and cohesive student body. A one-week industrial tour is undertaken in the Easter vacation to centres of the chemical industry beyond the range of the term-time works visits.

Laboratory teaching is an important component of all the years of the course, taking the form of a one-week full-time laboratory project in Third Year and an Honours research project lasting the whole of the Final Year. The Final Year also contains a group Design Project intended to be a realistic introduction to industrial design practice, and this is supervised jointly by academic staff and part-time industrial lecturers. Two recent developments are the provision of a pilot French language intermediate course for undergraduate students and the institution of a new-venture MEng degree in Chemical Engineering with European Studies. The introduction of an MEng and an MSc in Process Systems Engineering is planned.

Civil Engineering and Building Science

The BEng degree with Honours in Environmental Engineering was introduced in 1992, and is expected to lead to a significant increase in student numbers as it becomes better known. Already over the past four years since the arrival of Prof Michael Rotter all the main indicators of activity have more than doubled – external research income and numbers of undergraduates, postgraduates and publications. The bulk solids storage group led by Prof Rotter is now one of the largest in the world, with research projects including full scale experiments on industrial silos, model studies of flowing solids, investigation of the properties of granular materials, model tests to explore structural failure modes, and numerical (ie computer) modelling of all these aspects.

Cognitive Science

The Centre for Cognitive Science (CCS) currently has a population of around 60 postgraduate students, about half-and-half MSc and PhD, distributed roughly one-third each from the UK, the EC and other countries. In 1993-94 a new half course *Introduction to Cognitive Science* became available to Honours undergraduates.

The collaborative research initiated by the Centre has built up an excellent network of links with European research groups, and has played a prominent role in obtaining EC funding for Cognitive Science. The Centre was awarded the first ESPRIT grant to come to Edinburgh University, and since then has been concerned in many other successful EC grant applications. The newly formed European Network of Excellence in Language and Speech (ELSNET) makes CCS and HCRC the joint organisational node for coordinating EC academic and industrial research in speech and language.

Human Communication Research Centre

The HCRC was founded in April 1989 as the first Interdisciplinary Research Centre of the ESRC, with its staff drawn from the Universities of Edinburgh, Glasgow and Durham. In Edinburgh it is closely associated with the Centre for Cognitive Science and other departments in the School of Engineering and Informatics. Its first four years' work achieved a substantial integration of the computational, linguistic and psychological aspects of human and machine (ie computer) communication. It is now extending the application of formal techniques for analysing natural language to multi-modal comm-unication, especially that involving combinations of diagrams and language. The wide range of interest in its work is shown by the fact that external support for its research comes from three Research Councils (ESRC, SERC and MRC) and three EC research funding programmes, as well as a number of British and European companies.

Computer Science

In the early days of computer science at Edinburgh, all of thirty years ago, the scope of the subject could fairly be described as 'the design and use of computers', but it has now developed into a proper science involving an investigation of the 'structure and behaviour of discrete dynamic systems'. There is a mutual interplay between scientific theory and engineering practice. The major practical concern is to ensure that computation is reliable, efficient and secure, and that computer-based systems achieve what is required of them.

The Department of Computer Science is now one of the best known in the UK, with an international reputation for its teaching and research. It has three established Chairs (including one vacancy), three Personal Chairs, 20 other teaching staff, 23 research workers and 27 support staff. In terms of FTEs there are nearly fifty research students and 275 taught students, of whom 243 are undergraduates. The undergraduate degrees offer a route to Chartered Engineer status. General computing facilities consist of about 280 *Sun* workstations in the JCMB and the Appleton Tower, plus other computers and a rich variety of software, much of it developed within the department.

The **Laboratory for Foundations of Computer Science** (LFCS) continues to be a key component of the department, and its research is currently supported by grants totalling almost £5m. In 1993, the LFCS became the co-ordinating node for the EC-funded Network of Excellence in the Logical Foundations of Computer Science - EuroFOCS.

Foundational research is pursued in the LFCS on a broad front on complexity and algorithms, concurrency theory and tools, formal development of programs and systems, languages and applied semantics, and logic and proof.

Systems research centres around the development of high-performance architectures and parallel computation. This work has well- developed connections with the Edinburgh Parallel Computing Centre and its strong industrial liaison programme. Other areas of research include human-computer interaction, performance modelling, database systems, computer graphics and computer-aided design for VLSI.

It is satisfying to note that Steven Beard, who graduated recently with a joint degree in Artificial Intelligence and Computer Science, was the Scottish Young Software Engineer of the Year in 1993. His winning project involved a computer vision system capable of identifying and classifying nematodes, worms which cause parasitic diseases in sheep. The award was made by the Scottish Software Federation.

Staff members continue to earn high honours. In 1991, **Robin Milner** received the A M Turing award, the highest award of the Association for Computing Machinery – the 'Nobel Prize' in computing. The following year **Gordon Plotkin** was awarded a 5-year SERC Senior Research Fellowship, and also became the department's second Fellow of the Royal Society.

Electrical Engineering

The seventh professorial appointment in the Department of Electrical Engineering was the elevation of **Jim Jordan** in 1991 to a Personal Chair of Electronic Instrumentation. He first joined the Department as a lecturer in 1970, and since 1989 has held an SERC Senior Information Technology Fellowship. His early industrial experience of control and electronic instrumentation has developed into current research interests in fieldbus instrumentation/systems and fast product prototyping using electronic system emulators.

In July 1992 ten students completed the five-year Master of Engineering degree course and graduated MEng in Electronics, the first example of an extended first degree in the Faculty of Science and Engineering. The Department aims to have about fifteen MEng students each year from now on, compared to about 85 taking the BEng. The majority of graduates are awarded a BEng with Honours in Electronics and Electrical Engineering, the alternatives being Microelectronics, Electrical and Mechanical Engineering, Computer Science and Electronics, or Electronics and Physics. In 1993 the first students embarked on the BEng joint degree in Electronics with Business Studies, and in October 1994 a new degree course in Communications Engineering will be available.

Electrical Engineering is by far the largest of the engineering departments, with (approximately, at the last count!) 34 academic staff, 20 clerical and technical staff, 25 research staff, 75 postgraduate students and 280 undergraduates. In April 1993 Edinburgh University hosted the Third International Conference on Microelectronics for Neural Networks, reflecting the fact that there are currently groups active in developing and applying synthetic neural networks in the Departments of Electrical Engineering, Physics, Artificial Intelligence, Cognitive Science and Pharmacology, and in the Centre for Speech Technology Research.

The Department has the largest annual research income from external sources of any department in the University, currently in excess of £3 million. Much of the research comes under the heading of microelectronics, in which the Department has been a pioneer for several decades, but there are also active research groups in instrumentation, control and computing, signal processing, and energy systems. Professor Alan Owen, Head of the Department, was one of five Scottish engineers given an award by the Edinburgh International Science Festival on the basis of citations of his research papers from 1981 to 1992.

Mechanical Engineering

Current research is concentrated in five main areas; fluid dynamics, manufacturing planning, advanced machining, wave energy and dynamic systems. A particularly notable success was registered by the design team led by Dr Bill Easson (Mechanical Engineering) and Prof Clive Greated (Physics) which developed an award-winning device for measuring the flow in non-opaque fluids – the automated particle image velocimetry (PIV) analysis system. Using pulsed laser illumination, the device produces photographs of air flows in aeroengines and turbomachinery, which when analysed by computer with specially designed software, yield detailed information about velocities, turbulence and flow patterns.

In wave kinematics a move is being made towards the study of coastal engineering problems, as these are perceived to be of major importance in Europe over the coming

*Automated Particle Image Velocimetry
Analysis System*

decade, and the techniques developed at Edinburgh can provide valuable insights into coastal erosion and the transport mechanism of waves. The Department's energy group are preparing the Solo Duck for prototype testing in the near future with DTI funding, and they are also collaborating with the Department of Physics on aspects of wind turbine design. Research on waves and wave energy has led to advances in computer controlled hydraulics, and this work is continuing with support from the Department of Trade and Industry and from the EC under the JOULE programme.

The Department awards degrees of BEng with Honours in Mechanical Engineering or in Electrical and Mechanical Engineering, both accredited by the Institution of Mechanical Engineers. For the future, maintaining the recent growth in student numbers will be a principal objective. One area to develop will be mixed-discipline degrees, linking mechanical engineering with such subject areas as languages or management, perhaps involving the exchange of students with other European countries.

Geology and Geophysics

Since the amalgamation of the Departments of Geology and Geophysics in 1989 research has been undertaken generally within one of four main groups:– igneous, metamorphic and experimental petrology; tectonics and earth history; geophysics; and quaternary environmental change. Support is also given to work carried out by individual scientists, such as the internationally recognised palaeontologist Euan Clarkson, who collaborates with a world-wide circle of experts in his subject area. Close contact and active collaboration is maintained with other Edinburgh University Departments such as Biological Sciences, Physics, Electrical and Civil Engineering, Mathematics, Chemistry and Biochemistry. There is a particularly strong link with the centre of excellence in isotope geology funded by several of the Scottish universities at the Scottish Universities Research and Reactor Centre. In addition to supporting the consortium, the department has located some of its own equipment and technical staff at the SURRC in the interests of efficient collaboration.

In 1992 the Petroleum Science and Technology Institute endowed the PSTI Chair of

The University of Edinburgh Grant Institute of Geology and Geophysics extension. Opened by HRH The Prince Philip, Duke of Edinburgh, KG, KT, Wednesday, 20 May 1992
Back row, left to right: Professor Jim Briden, Professor Ian Parsons, Professor Barry Dawson, Dr Martin Lowe, Professor Geoffrey Boulton, Professor Ron Oxburgh, Professor Tony Harris, Professor Ken Creer, Professor Gordon Craig, Professor Brian Upton, Professor Ben Harte
Front row, left to right: Professor Anton Ziolkowski, Professor John Mavor, Sir David Smith, HRH Prince Philip, Sir Gerald Elliot, Professor Alan Cook, Robert Johnston (PSTI)

Petroleum Geoscience, to which **Professor Anton Ziolkowski** from Delft University of Technology was appointed; he also became Head of the Predictive Geoscience Research Unit. The Unit will address fundamental problems associated with the exploitation of ores and hydrocarbons, through the combined resources of five research groups in predictive geoscience, geophysical computing, seismic and sequence stratigraphy, fluid-rock interactions, and shear waves and anisotropy. A key member of the Unit from the time of his appointment in April 1992 was **Stuart Crampin**, who joined the department from the British Geological Survey as Professor of Seismic Anisotropy.

The new wing of the Grant Institute of Geology and Geophysics, which had been completed at the end of 1991, was officially opened by the Chancellor, HRH the Duke of Edinburgh, on 20 May 1992. It allowed the physical integration of the two departments now combined as Geology and Geophysics, and provided greatly improved facilities for the 60 research staff and 90 postgraduate students in the recently designated Graduate School of Geology and Geophysics. The School has been set up to provide a focus for the large number of research students and staff working in the Department, and to facilitate collaborative projects with industry.

Ben Harte, Reader in the Department since 1981, was appointed Professor of Metamorphism; he acted as Editor of the *Journal of Petrology* from 1978 to 1985. His research interests include the nature and metasomatism of upper mantle rocks, using the ion microprobe.

In April 1992 a ship docked at Leith with an unusual cargo – more than 70 Russian geophysicists attending the XVII General Assembly of the European Geophysical Society, which brought 2,400 delegates to the University of Edinburgh. The ship belonged to the Moscow Institute of Oceanology, and was hired by the EGS for the benefit of the Russian scientists, who could not otherwise have afforded to come to Scotland on their salaries of the equivalent of £10 per month. At the Assembly, Prof Ken Creer of the Department of Geology and Geophysics was installed as President of the Society for 1992-94, and one of its sessions was named the *Hutton Symposium* to honour the career of Dr Rosemary Hutton in the Department of Geophysics at the University of Edinburgh.

In October 1992 a new undergraduate course in Environmental Archaeology was launched, the participating departments being Archaeology, Geography, and Geology and Geophysics. Combining laboratory work with extensive fieldwork, the course is designed to introduce students to new techniques making use of evidence from the soils, plant and animal remains found on archaeological sites to piece together a detailed picture of the environments and economies of people in the past.

Colin Graham, who joined the Department of Geology in 1979, was appointed to a Personal Chair of Experimental Geochemistry in 1993.

The funding of the PSTI from 31 oil and gas companies, plus the DTI (OSO), was extended beyond the end of 1993 on a three year 'rolling subscription' basis. The new funding, totalling £4.5m for the period 1994-96, enables PSTI to continue its investment in research designed specifically to meet the needs of the oil industry in Scotland, working from its bases in Edinburgh and Aberdeen. Selected by the EC as an Organisation for Promotion of Energy Technology, the Institute functions as a research intelligence centre at the interface between the oil industry and the research community as a whole.

In the summer of 1993 the Department of Geology and Geophysics acted as host to a NATO Advanced Study Institute on 'Feldspars and their reactions'. These Institutes are held in particular subject areas only once every ten years in different European locations, funded by NATO's science division, bringing together a small group of acknowledged experts and a larger number of younger scientists working in the same field. It has been found that such exchanges of information and opinion can move a whole community of research workers forward by the equivalent of one or two years' work almost overnight.

The Faculty Group of Science and Engineering plans to fill the vacant Chair of Geophysics in session 1993/94. It is worth recording, as a measure of the success enjoyed recently by Geology and Geophysics, one of the Faculty's most enterprising departments, that between 1988 and 1991 grants from Research Councils increased by a factor of four, funding from industry by a factor of sixteen, and grants from the EC by a factor of five.

In response to the latest swing in government policy towards a sharp increase in undergraduate student numbers, the Department has introduced a joint degree in Geology and Physical Geography, and a new single honours degree in Environmental Geoscience. The latter is designed to explore the applications of the Earth Sciences to environmental problems such as pollution, waste disposal, water supply, coastal protection, seismic and other natural hazards, climate and environmental changes. The first students embarked on this course in October 1993.

Industrial Liaison (UnivEd)

In October 1992 UnivEd made a number of new appointments to strengthen its marketing of the University's R&D, consultancy and training facilities. Dr Keith Winton, Contracts Manager for the Faculty of Science and Engineering, was appointed (in addition) Deputy Director of UnivEd. A Technology Audit was carried out in the Faculty of Science and Engineering to identify marketable expertise whose full potential had not yet been realised. This exercise was funded by the DTI under its 'Innovation: Support for Technology Audits' scheme.

The latest annual report of UnivEd Technologies Ltd presents a very satisfactory picture of the University's achievements in making the most of its marketable assets. The number of training courses organised by UnivEd rose to 151 with over 4,000 participants, generating more than £1m in gross income, an increase of 64% from the previous year. The number of R&D contracts rose by 55% to 192, giving an income of £17.9m, of which the largest slice, £7.29m, went to the Faculty of Science and Engineering. The number of consultancies undertaken increased by no less than 87%, spread over 115 members of staff in 53 departments, bringing in a total gross income of £1.16m.

The Technology Transfer Centre (TTC) at the King's Buildings is almost fully occupied by potential spin-off businesses at various stages of development. It is to be hoped that some at least of them will have a measure of the success of VLSI Vision Ltd, the company set up to manufacture Prof Peter Denyer's revolutionary image-sensing chip. Having found its feet in the helpful environment of the TTC it moved out into its own premises and now employs a staff of about forty.

Mathematics and Statistics

Terry Lyons, the Colin McLaurin Professor of Mathematics, resigned in 1993 and moved to a chair at Imperial College, London with an SERC Senior Fellowship. He intends to maintain his research links with some members of the Mathematics Department over the next few years, and he is now an Honorary Professor in Edinburgh University. During session 1993/94 the Faculty Group of Science and Engineering plans to fill the Colin McLaurin Chair of Mathematics, and the Chair of Statistics which has been vacant since the retirement of Professor David Finney in 1984.

The combined Department of Mathematics and Statistics which was formed in 1991 now has 36 full-time teaching staff including three professors; there are about a dozen research fellows, several visiting fellows, and about 30 postgraduate students. Degree courses offered include BSc Honours in Mathematics, Mathematics and Statistics, and Mathematics or Statistics with various other subjects – 54 such degrees were awarded in 1993. However, the department's major teaching commitment is to around 1,600 students (600 undergraduate FTEs) who are taking degrees in other subjects, and much of this 'service' teaching takes place two miles away from the department, at the Appleton Tower in George Square. Few things in the whole University can have changed more dramatically since 1893, when Professor Chrystal taught mathematics with only one assistant.

The Department is involved in two MSc mathematics courses, one in nonlinear mathematics with the Heriot-Watt University and one in mathematical education with the Department of Education. A further collaboration with the Heriot-Watt made feasible the establishment in 1991 of the International Centre for Mathematical Sciences (ICMS) which has organised several conferences and workshops encouraging interaction with industry and commerce. The ICMS programme 'Harmonic Analysis and Partial Differential Equations' in April-July 1994 is expected to bring eminent analysts to the Department from many countries.

Up to now the ICMS has been based at the King's Buildings, but it will move in April 1994 to a singularly appropriate new home, the classically elegant house in India Street in the New Town of Edinburgh where James Clerk Maxwell was born in 1831. It will continue to develop as a centre of excellence in areas of mathematics relevant to science, industry and commerce. In October 1993 **Professor Angus Macintyre** FRS, the distinguished Oxford mathematician, was appointed Scientific Director of the Centre. Its high standing after only two years was shown by its selection as the host for the fourth International Conference on Industrial and Applied Mathematics in 1999.

Different kinds of mathematics are the concern of the Edinburgh Centre for

Mathematical Education (ECME), ranging from Mathematical Challenge, the Mathematics Masterclasses, the Number Shop (an open-access advice centre for the public), and Access programmes. The ECME, which is externally funded, is the department's focus for mathematics in schools; it pursues curriculum training and educational research in collaboration with SOED and SEB. New teaching materials have been produced and new courses developed, and in-service training courses are held regularly.

Most of the staff in the department are engaged in research with one or more of the well-established research groups:– analysis, dynamical systems, geometry and topology, algebra and number theory, stochastic processes, statistics, operational research and optimisation, waves, fluid flow and modelling, and mathematical astronomy. The department places great stress on regular seminars to stimulate and monitor the research of both staff and students, and to promote the free interchange of information and comment. A notable feature is the number of collaborations with other universities in the UK and overseas, including Göttingen, Halle, Moscow, Copenhagen, Texas, Illinois, and Stanford.

The applied mathematicians naturally have more contact with other departments – agriculture, astronomy, biology, business studies, engineering, geophysics and physics – and with industry, though it is not unknown for a very awkward practical problem to require a perfectly pure mathematician to solve it. The statisticians most of all, perhaps, are in demand by research workers in other departments for advice in the planning of experiments and analysis of the results. They also have externally funded work in forensic statistics for the Home Office and in

James Clerk Maxwell's home—exterior and interior

medical statistics for the Department of Psychiatry. There is a close relationship with the Scottish Agricultural Statistics Service, strengthened by the recent appointment to the SASS of two Edinburgh mathematics graduates.

Meteorology

In October 1988 an agreement was signed on collaboration and exchanges between the department in Edinburgh and the Institute of Meteorology in Nanjing, which has about 360 academic staff and well over 1200 students. The agreement provides funding for an association which has existed since 1984, jointly by the British Council and the State Meteorological Administration in the People's Republic of China. Exchanges of staff and students continue to take place on a regular basis.

For some time now, two major areas have dominated the department's research effort, both concerned with large-scale atmospheric composition and dynamics:–

observational studies, principally based on remote sensing from space, and complementary theoretical studies with a significant component of numerical simulation. These areas involve a substantial amount of UK and international collaboration and support, the space studies for example being dependent on data from the microwave limb sounder on NASA's upper atmosphere research satellite (UARS), launched in September 1991. It makes daily global measurements of stratospheric ozone, water vapour and active chlorine, the data being transmitted almost instantaneously to Edinburgh over a dedicated link. Analysis of the data is making a significant contribution to our understanding of the ozone 'holes' in the earth's atmosphere, and this phase of the research is expected to continue for another five years.

The UARS project is a collaboration with a group at NASA's Jet Propulsion Laboratory in California, SERC's Rutherford-Appleton Laboratory at Oxford, and the Physics Department at the Heriot-Watt University, Edinburgh. The department is also engaged in the design of enhanced instrumentation for the future launch of NASA's earth observing system, which is intended to be the principal series of environmental satellites for the first two decades of the twenty-first century. This part of the project, funded by SERC, will require increased effort from the department as the time of launch approaches.

Physics and Astronomy

Housed for the first time (after almost four hundred years!) in accommodation designed and built for its present purpose, the Physics Department has experienced a period of striking development and change, exemplified by its recent amalgamation with the Department of Astronomy. The new Department of Physics and Astronomy now has six Professors, of whom two are Fellows of the Royal Society, five Readers, and about 25 lecturing staff. Three chairs are vacant at the time of writing:– Astronomy, Natural Philosophy and the Tait Chair of Mathematical Physics. There are also 34 research staff, 96 research students, 28 technical and 6 clerical staff - though these figures necessarily fluctuate from year to year.

In 1992 **Richard Nelmes** was appointed to a Personal Chair in Physical Crystallography. An Edinburgh PhD (1969), in 1989 he was awarded a five-year SERC Senior Fellowship, one of only four throughout all UK universities that year, and at the same time became a Professorial Fellow of Edinburgh University. Much of his work is done at Daresbury and Rutherford-Appleton Laboratories (RAL), where his research team has established what is believed to be a world-leading position in high-pressure powder diffraction, both with (synchrotron) x-rays at Daresbury and neutrons at RAL.

Clive Greated, Director of the Fluid Dynamics Unit since 1973, was appointed to a Personal Chair in Fluid Dynamics in 1993. The current research interests of the Unit extend over a wide range, but much of the experimental work makes use of particle-image velocimetry (PIV) as the measuring technique. With PIV the whole velocity field at a single instant is measured and this technique, which has undergone considerable development in the Unit, is extremely powerful in the investigation of a wide variety of flows.

For more than 150 years the Regius Chair of Astronomy was combined with the post of Astronomer Royal for Scotland, and there was almost the same degree of integration between the teaching of astronomy and the work of the Royal Observatory in Edinburgh. It is expected that the University will be able to fill the Regius Chair of Astronomy, funded jointly with the SERC, in 1994. The ROE has a staff of 110 of whom 17 work in Hawaii at the telescopes. The joint research effort of the University and the Royal Observatory astronomers has two main themes – cosmology, concentrating on the initial creation process and the origins of our own galaxy, and star formation.

In addition to providing courses for students taking general degrees and degrees in subjects other than Physics – some from other Faculties, such as Arts and Music – the Department teaches for Honours Degrees in Physics, Astrophysics, Mathematical Physics and Computational Physics, as well as for joint Honours Degrees in Chemical Physics, Computer Science and Physics, Electronics and Physics, Geophysics, and Mathematics and Physics.

Experimental, theoretical and computational research is conducted in-house and at research centres elsewhere in Britain and Europe. Current fields of research include theoretical and experimental studies of fundamental particles, nuclear structures, statistical mechanics, condensed matter physics, molecular dynamics, atomic physics, fluid mechanics, the acoustics of musical instruments, optoelectronic devices, light scattering, and archaeological dating. The Department is a major user of the immensely powerful computers in the Edinburgh Parallel Computing Centre, which grew from the department's initiatives, in 1980 and subsequently, on the use of powerful parallel computing techniques to solve complex problems in physics.

Research activity is organised into five main groups - astronomy, nuclear and particle physics, condensed matter physics, computational physics, and applied physics. Each of these groups has established collaborations with academic and/or industrial researchers in the UK, Europe, and the USA, and attracts very substantial financial support from appropriate outside sources, such as central government, the research councils, industry, and the European Community. Long-term planning is necessary – for instance, the high-energy experimenters are involved with their collaborators at the European Centre for Nuclear Research (CERN) in the planning of experiments that will not come on stream until 1999.

But planning, however careful and long-term, can be completely negated by other organisations' expedients – the work of the nuclear structures group at the SERC Nuclear Structures Facility at Daresbury, which had resulted in the discovery of a new and rare mode of proton radioactivity, was abruptly halted by the SERC's decision to close down this internationally important facility as an economy measure. However, thanks to the group's widespread international contacts, this will hopefully be a delay rather than a disaster.

In the same vein, the search for the *Higgs boson* (the W-boson), which could turn out to be the missing 'dark matter' of the universe, was to have been a focus of the multi-billion dollar accelerator facilities planned for the Superconducting SuperCollider in Texas. Having already cost £1.35bn over the past ten years, the project was 'finally cancelled' by the US House of Representatives' refusal in October 1993 to vote any more funds for it. So the physicists using the CERN LEP (Large Electron Positron collider), among whom are some members of the Edinburgh particle physics group, may be the first to discover the exact nature and properties of the elusive W-boson predicted on purely theoretical grounds by Peter Higgs 25 years ago.

Science Libraries

Alterations were in progress to the KB Centre during the summer vacation of 1993 to provide a larger Engineering & Science Library (to be known as the Robertson Library) in the old refectory, and a Central Science and Engineering Library has been adopted as the major Appeal objective in the Faculty's Centenary year.

Today . . . . . and tomorrow?

The 'research plan – future developments' submitted by the Department of Geology and Geophysics for the UFC's Research Assessment Exercise in 1992/93 was presented in each major research area as a series of questions, such as:– how do magma chambers fill, evolve and evacuate?; what are the implications of the diameter and transience of the Jurassic doming of the North Sea?; what factors influenced the origin and character of hydrocarbon reservoirs?; did ice sheets have a major impact on continental geohydrology? That such fundamental geological questions, and innumerable others in every branch of science, remain unanswered as we approach the end of the twentieth century prompts even more searching questions:– is there any chance that we will ever know everything?; is there in fact a finite body of knowledge to be discovered, a finite number of questions to be answered?

In the past four hundred years science has advanced at first gradually from ignorance and uncertainty to the apparently ever-increasing knowledge and certainty of pre-quantum physics, then quite suddenly in the 1920s to the certainty of *un*certainty, following the revelations of Einstein, Heisenberg and other theoretical physicists.

So now, in some senses at least, the wheel has turned full circle. The eighteenth century scientific professor, dependent for his livelihood on the class fees of his students, had to be a teacher, a showman, a clerk, a businessman, a writer of textbooks – no profess-orial entourage in those days! For a few golden decades of the present century ivory towers were there to be occupied by academics who wanted to escape from the world about them, but like other structurally unsound high-rise buildings they had to be demolished. More than ever today the scientific professor has to be a teacher, a business manager and fund-raiser, a research team-leader, a consultant, a committee-member and conference-attender, a writer of papers for prestigious journals – differences of emphasis rather than differences of character, between him and his eighteenth century predecessor.

One thing is certain – the future of science and engineering is beyond even the mind's eye of today's scientists and engineers. The writing of this book has taught me how the task of the historian becomes progressively more difficult as the scene changes from the distant past to the recent past, until he is faced with a near-insoluble problem in writing about the present day. Not for me, then, to speculate about the future. Since the world of tomorrow will be shaped by the students of today, it seems only fair that some of them should have the last word in this last chapter.

Some of Edinburgh University's 'Scientists and Engineers of Tomorrow'

NOTE: I am very grateful to the Edinburgh University students who provided the material for most (but not all) of these biographical fantasies in response to my request for 'the CV you could imagine yourself writing for a job application in the year 2020'.

BARBOUR, Paul (1971-) Studied agricultural economics at Edinburgh (BSc, 1994), and development economics at Oxford (MSc, 1995); economic advisor to Min of Agric, Malawi, 1995-7, and the World Bank, 1997-2000; Prize Fellow, Harvard Inst for Intnl Devel, 2000-05; economist, Overseas Development Administration, 2005-11. Reader and consultant in the agricultural policy research unit at Sussex, since 2011. Publ *Redefining the Role of British Overseas Aid*, 2008; *Technological Change and Agricultural Production*, 2015.

BARKER, Sir David (1969-) Studied medical sciences and mathematics at Edinburgh (BSc, 1991; BSc, 1994); actuarial trainee with Guardian Royal Exchange, 1994-8; joined Standard Life as actuary, 1998; MBA, 2003; Director, 2007-18; planned financial rescue of Lloyds of London, 2018; Director of Lloyds, since 2018. Kt, 2020. Wife became first female Chief Whip, 2019. Publ *The Politics of Risk*, 2015 and *The Risk of Politics*, 2019.

BATES, Stephen FRS, FEng, FIEE (1972-) Studied electrical engineering at Edinburgh (BEng, 1994), and analytical science at DIAS, UMIST (PhD, 1997); after working with Defence Science Group on first fusion generator was head-hunted by U.S. Government to work on fusion drives for space program, 2002-10; headed Viking 2 project to found a colony on Mars with first manned fusion drive space vehicle, 2010-20. Bill Clinton Award for management in Government Agencies, 2018. President of Fusion Consultants Inc, since 2020. Publ *Nuclear Fusion and its Impact on the Electricity Generating Market*, 2002; *Fusion Driven Interplanetary Vehicles*, 2005; *Fusion Driven Interstellar Vehicles – Will Man Colonise the Galaxy?*, 2020.

BRAITHWAITE, Emma CEng, EurIng (1972-) Studied electronic and electrical engineering at Edinburgh (BEng, 1994), and at Cranfield (PhD, 1997). Post-doctoral research on interactive television at MIT, 1998-2002; worked with Sony in Japan on new generation low power TV, 2002-10, then with Thomson Interactive HDTV in Paris. Consultant on low radiation emitting TVs and monitors for use in business and the home, since 2015; consultant to A2 (French TV) on integration of new technology.

BROWN, Ruth (1969-) Studied chemistry, environmental chemistry and psychology at Durham and Edinburgh (BSc, 1990; PhD, 1995; MSc, 2007). Joined Greenpeace, 1995, and took part in unsuccessful attempt to reach North Pole, 1996. Re-trained with Polymers Intnl, patented polymeric rope using super-conducting elastomer for sub-zero temperatures, and made successful solo conquest of Mount Everest in 2002. Lost Green Party seat in West Cumbria local elections, 2010; won Women's Liberation Front seat, 2011; MP for West Cumbria, since 2015. Director of the Emily

Pankhurst Equality Society, since 2006. Publ *To Everest by Rope Bridge and Tackle*, 2003; *Women as the Male Alter-Ego: A Treatise*, 2005; *Can Too Many Degrees Confuse The Mind?*, 2019.

HERRERO, Mario (1967-) Studied tropical animal production and health, and mathematical modelling of biological systems at Edinburgh (MSc, 1992; PhD, 1995). Post-doctoral Fellowship at Massey Univ, New Zealand, 1996-8; FAO Animal Production Consultant, 1999-2005. Director, Division of Tropical Crops and Pastures, CSIRO, Australia, 2006-14; Professor and Head of Animal Science Department, Cornell Univ USA, since 2015. Publ *Modelling of Tropical Grazing Systems*, 1998; *Simulation of Atomic Interactions in Ruminants*, 2009; *Advanced Artificial Intelligence for Biologists*, 2017.

KINGSHOTT, Ruth FRS, FRSE (1972-) Studied biological sciences, specialising in sleep disorders, at Edinburgh (BSc, 1994; PhD, 1997). Worked on cystic fibrosis in Sick Children's Hospital, London, 1997-2000; as a Research Assistant at Univ of Sydney, discovered a salivary beetle enzyme with mucus breakdown properties which was patented and sold (2003) to ICI for cystic fibrosis research. World tour, 2003-4. Set up own company "Night School" for research into subliminal learning during sleep for people with special needs; developed a machine which stimulates cortical areas involved in learning; won the Innovative Design of the Year Award, 2005. Fellow of the American Inst of Child Health. Publ *Nocturnal Mucus Levels in Cystic Fibrosis*,1998; *Analysis of Dreams – Study of an Australian Sub-population*, 2002; *Human Hibernation*, 2011.

McDONALD, Lynne (1972-) Studied animal sciences at Edinburgh (BSc, 1994) then specialised in pig nutrition and behaviour at Guelph Univ, Canada (PhD, 1997). After a period in commerce pursuing research into pig nutrition and breeding, became major shareholder in "McDonalds" and Director, since 2010. Publ *CREEP* (Clinically Re-cycled Experimental Effluent Protein) *Feeding of Piglets*, 1994; *Good Fast Food Guide*, 2011.

MURDOCH, Zoe FIBiol FCIB (1969-) Studied biology at Edinburgh (BSc, 1992; PhD, 1996); research scientist, Greenland Research Assoc, 1996-2002; qualified as accountant by part-time study, 1998-2002; joined Bank of Europe, 2003. Director, Westminster Investment Management Ltd, London, since 2010. Publ *A heuristic study of peat bog ecology*, 1998; *Investing for Profit*, 2008; *Top People's Guide to the Bahamas*, 2015.

PIRIE, Sir Angus (1970-) Studied physics, specialising in condensed matter, at Edinburgh (BSc, 1992; PhD, 1995). Research physicist, 1995-2015. Volunteered for first test of experimental Virtual Reality Drive, 2015, with fatal results; met God; was successfully reanimated, 2016. International 'talk show' host, since 2016; interviewed the DNA-reconstructed Genghis Khan, 2020. Chief consultant to the BBC on religious philosophy, since 2018. Kt, 2020. Publ *One foot out of the Grave*, 2017; *There and Back Again – The Not So Grim Reaper*; 2018; *How Dying Can Seriously Improve your Career Prospects*, 2020.

WINCHESTER, Andrew FSGT FIBS (1972-) Studied chemistry at Edinburgh (BSc, 1994); postgraduate studies in brewing and distilling at Cork (DSc, 2004). Joined Guineas plc as head of research, 2007; patented method of producing Guineas by adding chemical tablet to glass of water, 2010; unemployed, 2010-12. General Manager of Irish Railairbus International, since 2012. Publ *Winchester's Almanac*, 2011 to date.

APPENDIX A

CHRONOLOGICAL SUMMARIES

AGRICULTURE

1790	Chair of Agriculture instituted in the Faculty of Arts.
	Andrew Coventry FRSE (1764-1830) first Professor.
1831	**David Low** FRSE (1786-1859) second Professor.
1854	**John Wilson** FRSE (1812-1888) third Professor.
1885	**Robert Wallace** (1853-1939) fourth Professor.
1922	**Sir James A Scott Watson** CBE MC (1889-1966) fifth Professor of Agriculture and Rural Economy. Resigned 1925.
1924	**Ernest Shearer** appointed Principal of the College of Agriculture.
1926	**Ernest Shearer** (1879-1945) sixth Professor, and Principal of the College.
1944	**Sir Stephen J Watson** CBE FRSE (1898-1976) seventh Professor, and Principal of the Edinburgh and East of Scotland College of Agriculture.
1968	**Noel F Robertson** CBE FRSE (1923-) eighth Professor, and Principal of the School of Agriculture. Retired 1983.
1969	**John F Wilkinson** (1925-) appointed to a Personal Chair in Microbiology, and first Head of the Microbiology Division in the School of Agriculture. Retired 1989.
1970	**Francis W H Elsley** FRSE (1934-1977) first Professor of Animal Production and Head of the Animal Division.
1972	**Richard C F Macer** (1928-) first Professor of Crop Production and Head of the Crop Division. Resigned 1976.
1978	**Graham M Milbourn** (1930-) second Professor of Crop Production. Resigned 1983.
	John H D Prescott (1937-) second Professor of Animal Production. Resigned 1984.
1981	**David G M Wood-Gush** FRSE (1922-1992) appointed Honorary Professor in the Division of Animal Production.
1984	**Peter N Wilson** CBE FRSE (1928-) ninth Professor of Agriculture and Rural Economy, Principal of the College and Head of the School. Retired 1990.
	Colin T Whittemore (1942-) third Professor of Animal Production.
	John C Holmes (1925-) third Professor of Crop Production. Retired 1990.
1986	**J Barry Dent** (1937-) first Professor of Agricultural (later Rural) Resource Management and Head of the new Division of Rural Resource Management.
1990	The Department of Agriculture and Rural Economy was incorporated in the Institute of *Ecology and Resource Management.

ARTIFICIAL INTELLIGENCE

1970	Metamathematics Unit established in the Faculty of Science.
	Staff consisted of B Meltzer (Reader) and Prof J A Robinson (Hon Fellow).
1972	Metamathematics Unit became the Department of Computational Logic in the new School of Artificial Intelligence.

Bernard Meltzer FRSE (1913-   ) appointed to a Personal Chair of Artificial Intelligence, renamed Computational Logic in 1978. Resigned 1979.

1974   School of Artificial Intelligence renamed Computer Science and Artificial Intelligence.

1979   Rodney M Burstall (1934-   ) appointed to a Personal Chair of Artificial Intelligence in the Department of Computer Science.

1983   School of Computer Science and Artificial Intelligence dissolved.

1984   Artificial Intelligence Applications Institute (AIAI) established.

1985   James A M Howe (1937-   ) Professor of Artificial Intelligence.

1989   Department incorporated in what is now the School of Engineering and Informatics.
Austin Tate (1951-   ) Director of AIAI since 1985, appointed Professorial Fellow.

1990   Alan R Bundy FRSA (1947-   ) Professor of Automated Reasoning.

1992   David Parry Managing Director of AIAI, with Prof Tate as Technical Director.

ASTRONOMY

From 1583   Astronomy was studied as part of Mathematics and Natural Philosophy in the four-year courses given by the Regents.

1785   Regius Chair of Practical Astronomy instituted in the Faculty of Arts.
Robert Blair FRSE (1748-1828) first Professor, but gave no lectures.

1834   Thomas Henderson FRS FRSE (1798-1844) appointed to the joint post of Astronomer Royal for Scotland and Regius Professor of Astronomy.

1846   Charles Piazzi Smyth FRSE (1819-1900) second Astronomer Royal for Scotland and third Professor of Astronomy. Retired 1888.

1889   Ralph Copeland FRSE (1837-1905) third Astronomer Royal for Scotland and fourth Professor of Astronomy.

1893   The Professor of Astronomy became a member of the newly-instituted Faculty of Science.

1894   Completion of the new Royal Observatory, Edinburgh on the Blackford Hill.

1905   Sir Frank W Dyson KBE FRS (1868-1939) fourth Astronomer Royal for Scotland and fifth Professor of Astronomy.

1910   Ralph A Sampson FRS FRSE (1866-1939) fifth Astronomer Royal for Scotland and sixth Professor of Astronomy. PresRAS, 1915-17.

1938   William M H Greaves FRS FRSE (1897-1955) sixth Astronomer Royal for Scotland and seventh Professor of Astronomy.

1950   First full-time University Lecturer in Astronomy appointed.

1957   Hermann A Brück CBE FRSE (1905-   ) seventh Astronomer Royal for Scotland and eighth Professor of Astronomy.

1967   Department of Astronomy instituted in the Faculty of Science.

1975   Vincent C Reddish OBE FRSE (1926-   ) eighth Astronomer Royal for Scotland and ninth Professor of Astronomy. Retired 1980.

1980   Malcolm S Longair FRSE (1941-   ) ninth Astronomer Royal for Scotland and tenth Professor of Astronomy. Resigned 1991.

1991   Peter W J L Brand (1941-   ) Reader, appointed Head of Department.

1993   Departments of Astronomy and Physics combined.

BOTANY

1676 **James Sutherland** (1638-1719), intendant of the 'Edinburgh Physick Garden', appointed by the Town Council to teach in the Town's College.

1695 The Town Council created for Sutherland a Chair of Botany in the College (ie the University of Edinburgh). He resigned from this post in 1706.

1705-6 **Charles Preston** (1660-1711) second College Professor of Botany, Keeper of the College Garden and the Botanic Garden at Trinity Hospital.

1712 **George Preston** (c1665-1749) (brother of Charles) third College Professor of Botany, intendant of the College Garden and the Botanic Garden. Resigned 1738.

1716 **Charles Alston** received a commission from George I appointing him King's Botanist, third Regius Professor of Botany and Materia Medica, and Overseer of the Royal Garden.

1738 **Charles Alston** (1685-1760) appointed by the Town Council fourth Professor of Botany and Materia Medica, in the Faculty of Medicine, in succession to George Preston, combining the posts of King's Botanist in Scotland with the Chair of Botany in the University of Edinburgh.

1760 **John Hope** FRS FRSE (1725-1786) fifth Professor of Botany and Materia Medica in the University of Edinburgh. In 1761 he was appointed also King's Botanist in Scotland and Superintendent of the Royal Garden.

1763 New Botanic Garden established on a five-acre site in Leith Walk.

1786 **Daniel Rutherford** FLS (1749-1819) sixth Professor of Medicine and Botany.

1820 **Robert Graham** FRSE (1786-1845) seventh Professor of Medicine and Botany. He moved the Botanic Garden to its present site at Inverleith.

1845 **John Hutton Balfour** FRS FRSE (1808-1884) eighth Professor of Medicine and Botany.

1879 Title of the Chair reverted to Botany.

1880 **Alexander Dickson** FRSE (1836-1887) ninth Professor of Botany.

1888 **Sir Isaac Bayley Balfour** KBE FRS FRSE (1853-1922) (son of John Hutton Balfour) tenth Professor of Botany.

1893 The Professor of Botany became a member also of the Faculty of Science.

1896 Patronage of University Chair transferred to the Crown.

1922 **Sir William Wright Smith** FRS PRSE (1875-1956) eleventh Regius Professor of Botany.

1956 On Smith's death the posts of Regius Keeper and Regius Professor were separated.

1958 **Robert Brown** FRS (1908-   ) twelfth Regius Professor of Botany.

1965 Official opening of the new building for the Department of Botany at the King's Buildings, now known as the Daniel Rutherford Building.

1966 Chair of Botany transferred from the Faculty of Medicine to the Faculty of Science.

1978 **Michael M Yeoman** FRSE (1931-   ) thirteenth Regius Professor of Botany Retired 1993.

1979 **Peter H Davis** FRSE (1918-1992) appointed to a Personal Chair in Plant Taxonomy.

1983 **Douglas M Henderson** CBE FRSE (1927-   ) Regius Keeper of the Royal Botanic Garden since 1970, appointed to an Honorary Professorship.

1985   **John E Dale** FRSE (1932-   ) appointed to a Personal Chair in Plant Physiology.

1986   **Christopher J Leaver** FRS FRSE (1942-   ) appointed to a Personal Chair in Plant Molecular Biology. Resigned 1990.

1990   The Department of Botany was incorporated in the Institute of *Cell and Molecular Biology within the Division of Biological Sciences.

CELL AND MOLECULAR BIOLOGY, Institute of (ICMB)

[For antecedents see Botany, Genetics, Microbiology and Molecular Biology]

1990   The Institute was formed as a constituent part of the Division of Biological Sciences within the Faculty of Science and Engineering.

Head of the Institute – **Prof Richard P Ambler.**

1991   **Ian W Sutherland** (1935-   ) appointed to a Personal Chair of Microbial Physiology.

Anthony Trewavas (1939-   ) appointed to a Personal Chair of Plant Biochemistry.

1993   **William Donachie** (1935-   ) appointed to a Personal Chair of Bacterial Genetics.

Dr David J Finnegan succeeded Prof Ambler as Head of the Institute.

Professor Sir Kenneth Murray knighted for services to science.

Douglas M Henderson CBE FRSE (1927-   ) Regius Keeper, Royal Botanic Garden, Edinburgh 1970-87; Honorary Professor.

David Ingram FRSE (1941-   ) Regius Keeper, Royal Botanic Garden, Edinburgh, since 1990; Honorary Professor.

CELL, ANIMAL AND POPULATION BIOLOGY, Institute of (ICAPB)

[For antecedents see Genetics, Natural History and Zoology]

1990   The Institute was formed as a constituent part of the Division of Biological Sciences within the Faculty of Science and Engineering.

Head of the Institute – **Prof William G Hill.**

1992   **Linda Partridge** FRSE (1950-   ) appointed to a Personal Chair of Evolutionary Biology. Resigned at the end of 1993.

1993   **Prof David S Saunders** succeeded Prof Hill as Head of the Institute.

Grahame Bulfield FRSE (1941-   ) Head of the AFRC Roslin Institute (Edinburgh), since 1988; Honorary Professor.

Peter M B Walker CBE FRSE (1922-   ) Honorary Professor.

David Walliker (1940-   ) MRC External Scientific Staff; Honorary Professor.

CHEMICAL ENGINEERING

1922   BSc in Technical Chemistry instituted jointly with the Heriot-Watt College.

1955   **Kenneth G Denbigh** FRS (1911-   ) appointed to the new Chair of Chemical Technology, jointly with the Heriot-Watt College, Edinburgh.

1960   **Philip H Calderbank** (1919-   ) first Professor of Chemical Engineering. Retired 1980.

1966   The Department's connection with the Heriot-Watt College was severed on the latter's elevation to University status.

1967   School of Engineering Science instituted, consisting of the Departments of Chemical, Electrical and Mechanical Engineering.

1971   Completion of new building for Chemical Engineering at the King's Buildings.

1979, Jan 1	School of Engineering Science re-constituted as the School of Engineering, adding the Departments of Civil Engineering and Building Science, and Fire Safety Engineering.
1982	UGC proposed 'integration of activities' with the Heriot-Watt University, but after much discussion no action was taken.
1989	The Department joined what is now the School of Engineering and Informatics.
1990	**Jack Ponton** (1943-) appointed ICI Professor of Chemical Engineering.
1991	**Dr Colin Pritchard** (1943-) elected Head of Department.

CHEMISTRY

1713	Chair of Chemistry and Medicine instituted by the Town Council. **James Crawford** (1682-1731) appointed, with no salary.
1726	Faculty of Medicine established by Act of the Town Council – Crawford gave up the Chair of Medicine and Chemistry. **Andrew Plummer** (1697-1756) and **John Innes** (d.1733) were both involved in the teaching of chemistry.
1755	**William Cullen** FRS FRSE (1710-1790) appointed joint Professor of Chemistry with Plummer until the latter's death.
1756	Cullen succeeded Plummer as third Professor of Chemistry.
1766	**Joseph Black** FRSE (1728-1799) fourth Professor of Chemistry.
1795	**Thomas C Hope** FRSE (1766-1844) appointed Professor of Chemistry and Chemical Pharmacy conjointly with Joseph Black. From October 1797 Hope was effectively the sole (fifth) Professor of Chemistry in the University.
1844	**William Gregory** FRSE (1803-1858) sixth Professor of Chemistry.
1858	**Sir Lyon Playfair** GCB FRS FRSE (1818-1898) seventh Professor of Chemistry.
1869	**Alexander Crum Brown** FRSE (1838-1922) eighth Professor of Chemistry.
1893	The Professor of Chemistry became a member also of the newly-instituted Faculty of Science.
1908	**Sir James Walker** FRS FRSE (1863-1935) ninth Professor of Chemistry.
1920, July 6	Foundation stone of the new building for the Department of Chemistry at the King's Buildings laid by His Majesty King George V.
1928	**James P Kendall** FRS PRSE (1889-1978) tenth Professor of Chemistry.
1947	**Sir Edmund L Hirst** CBE FRS PRSE (1898-1975) appointed to the new Forbes Chair of Organic Chemistry.
1959	**Tom L Cottrell** (1923-73) eleventh Professor of Chemistry.
1966	**Charles Kemball** CBE FRS FRSE (1923-) twelfth Professor of Chemistry. Retired 1983.
1967	**Evelyn A V Ebsworth** (1933-) appointed to the new Crum Brown Chair of Chemistry. Retired 1990. **Neil Campbell** OBE FRSE (1903-) appointed to a Personal Chair in Chemistry. Member of the University Court, 1960-68. Retired 1973.
1968	**John I G Cadogan** CBE FRSE (1930-) appointed to the Forbes Chair of Organic Chemistry. Resigned 1979.
1975	**John H Knox** FRS FRSE (1927-) appointed to a Personal Chair in Physical Chemistry. Retired 1984.

1979   **Robert J Donovan** FRSE (1941-   ) appointed to a Personal Chair in Physical Chemistry.

1980   **Alastair I Scott** (1928-   ) appointed to the Forbes Chair of Organic Chemistry. Resigned 1982.

1984   **Robert Ramage** FRS FRSE (1935-   ) appointed to the Forbes Chair of Organic Chemistry.

1986   **Prof Donovan** appointed thirteenth Professor of Chemistry.

1989   **David W H Rankin** FRSE (1945-   ) appointed Professor of Structural Chemistry.

1991   **Brian F G Johnson** FRS FRSE (1938-   ) appointed Crum Brown Professor of Chemistry.

1993   **Tom Brown** FRSE (1952-   ) appointed to a Personal Chair of Nucleic Acid Chemistry.

CIVIL ENGINEERING AND BUILDING SCIENCE

[For antecedents see Engineering]

1964   **Arnold W Hendry** FRSE (1921-   ) first Professor of Civil Engineering.

1967   School of the Built Environment instituted, consisting of the Departments of Architecture, Civil Engineering and Building Science, Geography, and Urban Design and Regional Planning. Dissolved 1975.

1979, Jan 1   School of Engineering Science re-constituted as the School of Engineering, adding the Departments of Civil Engineering and Building Science, and Fire Safety Engineering.

1989   **J Michael Rotter** (1948-   ) second Professor of Civil Engineering.
The Department joined what is now the School of Engineering and Informatics.

1990   **Michael C Forde** (1945-   ) appointed Tarmac Professor of Civil Engineering Construction.
Dougal Drysdale (1939-   ) appointed Reader in Fire Safety Engineering, and Director of the Unit of Fire Safety Engineering..

COGNITIVE SCIENCE, Centre for

1969   Creation of the School of Epistemics in the Faculty of Science.
Chairman – **Prof H C Longuet-Higgins** FRS FRSE (1923-   ) of the Department of Machine Intelligence and Perception. Resigned 1974.

1974   **Dr E Barry Richards**, Lecturer in the Department of Philosophy, appointed Director of the School of Epistemics.

1985   **Barry Richards** (1942-   ) appointed Professor of Cognitive Science. Resigned 1989.

1986   The School of Epistemics became the Centre for Cognitive Science.
Dr Ewan H Klein, Reader in Cognitive Science, appointed Director.

1989   The Centre joined what is now the School of Engineering and Informatics.

1992   **Dr Elisabet B Engdahl,** Reader in Artificial Intelligence since 1991, appointed Director of the Centre.

COMPUTER SCIENCE

1963, April 1   Formation of the Computer Unit, the fore-runner of both the Department of Computer Science and the Edinburgh Regional Computing Centre (ERCC). **Sidney Michaelson** appointed Director.

1966   The Unit was split into (a) the Department of Computer Science under Michaelson, and (b) the ERCC [*Computing Services].

1967   **Sidney Michaelson** FRSE (1925-1991) first Professor of Computer Science. Dr John Oldfield and the Computer-Aided Design (CAD) Project joined the Department of Computer Science.

1971   The Department and the CAD Project moved into the James Clerk Maxwell Building.

1974   School of Computer Science and Artificial Intelligence created.

1979   **Professor Rodney Burstall** (1934-   ) and Dr Gordon Plotkin transferred themselves from Artificial Intelligence to Computer Science.

1984   **Robin G Milner** FRS (1934-   ) appointed to a Personal Chair of Computation Theory.

1985   **Roland N Ibbett** FRSA (1941-   ) appointed to the Third Chair of Computer Science.

1986   **Gordon D Plotkin** FRS (1946-   ) appointed to a Personal Chair of Computation Theory.

1988   **Michael P Fourman** (1950-   ) appointed Professor of Computer Systems Software.

1989   Department joined what is now the School of Engineering and Informatics.

COMPUTING SERVICES   [For antecedents see Computer Science]

1966   The Edinburgh Regional Computing Centre (ERCC) came into formal existence in August. Director: **Dr G E (Tommy) Thomas**.

1971   EMAS (Edinburgh Multi-Access System) service began.

1980   Department of Physics staff began to use parallel computing processes. [*Edinburgh Parallel Computing Centre]

1982   JANET (Joint Academic NETwork) inaugurated.

1986   **Dr Brian R Sutton** appointed Director of ERCC. Resigned 1990.

1987   Formation of the Edinburgh University Computing Service (EUCS).

1990   **Dr Richard Field** appointed Director of Computing and Information Technology Services in the University of Edinburgh.

1992   EUCS renamed Computing Services.

ECOLOGY AND RESOURCE MANAGEMENT, Institute of

[For antecedents see Agriculture, and Forestry and Natural Resources]

1990   The Institute was formed as a constituent part of the Division of Biological Sciences within the Faculty of Science and Engineering. Head of the Institute – **Prof Colin T Whittemore**.

1992   **John Grace** (1945-   ) appointed to a Personal Chair of Environmental Biology.

1993   **Grahame Bulfield** FRSE (1941-   ) Head of the AFRC Roslin Institute (Edinburgh), since 1988; Honorary Professor. **William Heal** (1934-   ) Northern Director of the Institute of Terrestrial Ecology, the Bush Estate; Honorary Professor.

John Hillman FRSE (1944-) Director of the Scottish Crop Research Institute; Honorary Professor.

John W B King FRSE (1927-) Head of AFRC Animal Breeding Liaison Group; Honorary Professor.

Frederick T Last FRSE (1928-) NERC Institute of Terrestrial Ecology; Honorary Professor.

Thomas J Maxwell (1940-) Director of the Macaulay Land Use Research Institute since 1987; Honorary Professor.

John L Monteith FRS FRSE (1929-) NERC Institute of Terrestrial Ecology; Honorary Professor.

Norman W Simmonds FRSE (1922-) Director of the Scottish Plant Breeding Station 1965-76; Honorary Professor.

Phil Thomas (1942-) Principal and Chief Executive of the Scottish Agricultural College since its foundation in 1990; Honorary Professor.

Brian D Witney (1938-) Head of the Division of Agricultural Engineering and Director of the Scottish Centre of Agricultural Engineering at the Bush Estate; Honorary Professor.

EDINBURGH PARALLEL COMPUTING CENTRE

1990   David J Wallace FRS FRSE (1945-) second Tait Professor of Mathematical Physics, appointed Director of the Edinburgh Parallel Computing Centre. Resigned Dec 1993.

1994   Dr Richard Kenway, Reader in the Department of Physics, appointed to succeed Prof Wallace as Director.

ELECTRICAL ENGINEERING   [For antecedents *see* Engineering]

1961   W E J (Ewart) Farvis CBE FRSE (1911-) first Professor of Electrical Engineering.

1967   School of Engineering Science formed, consisting of the Departments of Chemical, Electrical and Mechanical Engineering.

1970   Jeffrey H Collins FRSE (1930-) appointed SRC Research Professor. The post was converted into a Personal Chair of Industrial Electronics in 1973.

1977   Jeffrey Collins succeeded Ewart Farvis as second Professor of Electrical Engineering. Resigned 1984.

1979, Jan 1   School of Engineering Science re-constituted as the School of Engineering, adding the Departments of Civil Engineering and Building Science, and Fire Safety Engineering.

1980   John Mavor FRSE (1942-) appointed to the Lothian Chair of Microelectronics.

1981   Alan Owen FRSE (1928-) appointed to a Personal Chair in Physical Electronics.

1986   John Mavor third Professor of Electrical Engineering.

Peter B Denyer (1953-) appointed to the Advent Chair of Integrated Electronics.

John Robertson (1943-) Director of the Edinburgh Microfabrication Facility since 1981, appointed to the Chair of Microelectronics.

1987   **Peter Grant** (1944-   ) appointed to the Chair of Electronic Signal Processing.
Mervyn Jack (1949-   ) appointed to the Chair of Electronic Systems, and Director of the Centre for Speech Technology Research.

1989   **James R Jordan** (1938-   ) appointed Professorial Fellow.
Electrical Engineering joined what is now the School of Engineering and Informatics.

1990   **Peter Denyer** appointed to a Personal Chair in Integrated Electronics. Currently seconded as Managing Director to VLSI Vision Ltd.

1991   **Jim Jordan** appointed to the Chair of Electronic Instrumentation.
John Mavor appointed Dean and Provost of the Faculty Group of Science and Engineering.

ENGINEERING

1855   Regius Chair of Technology instituted in the Faculty of Arts; the holder also to be Director of the proposed Industrial Museum of Scotland in Edinburgh.
George Wilson FRSE (1818-1859) appointed to the combined post.

1859   When Wilson died at the age of 41 the Government, supported by Senate, promptly abolished the chair.

1868   Regius Chair of Engineering instituted in the Faculty of Arts.
Henry Charles Fleeming Jenkin FRS FRSE (1833-85) first Regius Professor of Engineering.

1885   **George F Armstrong** (1842-1900) second Regius Professor of Engineering.

1893   The Regius Professor of Engineering became a member of the newly-instituted Faculty of Science.

1901   **Sir Thomas Hudson Beare** FRSE (1859-1940) third Regius Professor of Engineering.

1932   The Department of Engineering moved into the new Sanderson Building at the King's Buildings.

1940   Prof Hudson Beare died at the age of 81. **Major John B Todd** (1883-1954), Reader in Engineering, became Head of Department.

1946   **Ronald N Arnold** FRSE (1908-63) fourth Regius Professor of Engineering. [*Mechanical Engineering]

1955   **Kenneth G Denbigh** FRS (1911-   ) Professor of Chemical Technology. [*Chemical Engineering]

1961   **W E J (Ewart) Farvis** CBE FRSE (1911-   ) first Professor of *Electrical Engineering.

1964   **Arnold W Hendry** FRSE (1921-   ) first Professor of *Civil Engineering.

1967, Oct 1   School of Engineering Science instituted, consisting of the Departments of Chemical, Electrical and Mechanical Engineering.
School of the Built Environment instituted, consisting of the Departments of Architecture, Civil Engineering and Building Science, Geography, and Urban Design and Regional Planning. Dissolved 1975.

1973   **David J Rasbash** (1921-   ) first Professor of Fire Engineering, 1973-77; Professor of *Fire Safety Engineering, 1977-82.

1979, Jan 1   School of Engineering Science re-constituted as the School of Engineering, adding the Departments of Civil Engineering and Building Science, and Fire Safety Engineering.

ENGINEERING AND INFORMATICS, School of

1989   School of Engineering combined with the Departments of Artificial Intelligence and
              Computer Science, and the Centre for Cognitive Science, to form the School of
              Engineering and Information Technology.
1992   School renamed Engineering and Informatics.

FIRE SAFETY ENGINEERING

1973   **David J Rasbash** (1921-   ) first Professor of Fire Engineering. Retired 1983.
1977   Department renamed Fire Safety Engineering.
1985   Financial stringency led to the Department of Fire Safety Engineering becoming the
              Fire Safety Engineering Unit within the Department of *Civil Engineering and
              Building Science.

FORESTRY AND NATURAL RESOURCES

1889   **Sir William Somerville** KBE (1860-1932) appointed to the new University
              Lectureship in Forestry.
1891   **Lt Col Fred Bailey** RE (d. 1912) appointed to succeed Somerville as Lecturer.
1910   **Edward P Stebbing** FLS FRSE (1870-1960) appointed Lecturer in Forestry.
1919   Chair of Forestry endowed by public and private subscription.
1920   **Edward Stebbing** was elevated to the Chair as the first Professor of Forestry, and
              the honorary degree of MA was conferred on him. Retired 1951.
1951   **Mark L Anderson** (1895-1961) second Professor of Forestry.
1961   **Dr Charles J Taylor** appointed acting Head of Department.
1963   **John N Black** FRSE (1922-   ) third Professor of Forestry and Natural Resources.
1967   The newly-completed Darwin Building was occupied by the Departments of
              Forestry and Natural Resources, and Molecular Biology.
1971   **Frederick T Last** FRSE (1928-   ) fourth Professor of Forestry and Natural
              Resources. Resigned 1974.
1975   **Paul G Jarvis** FRSE (1935-   ) fifth Professor of Forestry and Natural Resources.
1976   **Charles J Taylor** MBE CBE FRSE (1912-   ) appointed to a Personal Chair of
              Forestry. Retired 1979.
1990   Department of Forestry and Natural Resources incorporated in the Institute of
              *Ecology and Resource Management.

GENETICS   [For antecedents see Natural History, 1882]

1911   University Lectureship in Genetics (Evolution and Heredity) instituted in the
              Faculty of Science; **Arthur D Darbishire** (d. 1915) appointed.
1920   **F A E Crew** appointed Director of the Department of Research in Animal Breeding,
              and also University Lecturer in Genetics.
1928   **Francis A E Crew** FRS FRSE (1886-1973) appointed to the Buchanan Chair of
              Animal Genetics instituted in the Faculty of Science. Resigned 1944.
1930   Department moved into the new Institute of Animal Genetics (now the Crew
              Building) at the King's Buildings.

1945   The Agricultural Research Council (ARC) decided to establish a major new centre for animal breeding research, and **Robert G White CBE** (1885-1976) was appointed Director, with **C H Waddingto**n as Chief Geneticist. When shortly afterwards Waddington was offered the Buchanan Chair of Animal Genetics in Edinburgh University, the decision was taken to locate the new organisation in Edinburgh, with Waddington holding both posts.

1946   **Conrad H Waddington** CBE FRS FRSE (1905-1975) second Buchanan Professor of Animal Genetics.

1951   **Hugh P Donald** CBE (d. 1989) succeeded White as Director, and the organisation was divided into two, the Genetics Section and the Animal Breeding Research Organisation (ABRO).

1957   The Genetics Section was designated the Unit of Animal Genetics.

1966   **William Hayes** FRS FRSE (1913-1994) appointed to a Personal Chair of Molecular Genetics. Resigned 1973.
          Department renamed Genetics.

1967   **Charlotte Auerbach** FRS FRSE (1899-   ) appointed to a Personal Chair of Genetics. Retired 1969.

1968   **Douglas S Falconer** FRS FRSE (1913-   ) appointed to a Personal Chair of Genetics, and Director of the ARC Unit. Retired 1980.
          Geoffrey H Beale MBE FRS FRSE (1913-   ) Royal Society Research Professor. Retired 1978.

1971   **Max L Birnstiel** (1933-   ) appointed to a Personal Chair of Epigenetics. Resigned 1972.

1976   **John R S Fincham** FRS FRSE (1926-   ) third Buchanan Professor of Genetics. Resigned 1984.

1980   Following the retiral of Prof Falconer, the ARC Unit of Animal Genetics was wound up.

1983   **William G Hill** FRS FRSE (1940-   ) appointed to a Personal Chair of Animal Genetics.

1989   **John O Bishop** FRSE (1935-   ) Professor of Molecular Cell Biology.

1990   **Adrian P Bird** FRS (1947-   ) fourth Buchanan Professor of Genetics.
          The Department of Genetics was incorporated in the Institutes of *Cell and Molecular Biology, and *Cell, Animal and Population Biology.

GENOME RESEARCH, AFRC Centre for

1973-80   Prof Peter Walker was Director of the MRC Mammalian Genome Unit.

1989   The Genome Interdisciplinary Research Centre (IRC) was established jointly by the University and the Agricultural and Food Research Council (AFRC).

1993   The AFRC Centre for Genome Research is closely associated with the Division of Biological Sciences, many of whose staff are also members of the Centre.
          Director: **Professor Richard Lathe.**

GEOLOGY   [For antecedents see Natural History]

1871   Regius Chair of Geology instituted in the Faculty of Arts.

Sir Archibald Geikie KCB FRS FRSE (1835-1924) first Regius Professor of Geology. Succeeded by his younger brother.

1882   **James Geikie** FRS PRSE (1839-1915) second Regius Professor of Geology.

1893   Regius Chair of Geology incorporated in the newly-instituted Faculty of Science.

1914   **Thomas J Jehu** FRSE (1871-1943) third Regius Professor of Geology.

1932   Official opening of the Grant Institute of Geology at the King's Buildings.

1943   **Arthur Holmes** FRS FRSE (1890-1965) fourth Regius Professor of Geology.

1956   **Sir Frederick H Stewart** FRS FRSE (1916-   ) fifth Regius Professor of Geology. Retired 1982.

1967   **Gordon Y Craig** FRSE (1925-   ) appointed to the James Hutton Chair of Geology. Retired 1984.

1971   **Michael J O'Hara** (1933-   ) appointed Professor of Petrology. Resigned 1978.

1982   **Brian G J Upton** FRSE (1933-   ) appointed to a Personal Chair of Petrology.

1986   **Geoffrey S Boulton** FRS FRSE (1940-   ) sixth Regius Professor of Geology.

GEOLOGY AND GEOPHYSICS

1989   The Departments of Geology and Geophysics were combined.

       Ian Parsons FRSE (1939-   ) appointed Professor of Mineralogy.

1992   Opening of the new wing of the Grant Institute of Geology and Geophysics. Graduate School of Geology and Geophysics instituted.

       Stuart Crampin FRSE FRAS (1935-   ) appointed Professor of Seismic Anisotropy in the Predictive Geoscience Research Unit.

       Ben Harte FRSE (1941-   ) appointed Professor of Metamorphism.

       Anton Ziolkowski (1946-   ) appointed to the PSTI Chair of Petroleum Geoscience, and Head of the Predictive Geoscience Research Unit.

1993   **Colin M Graham** FRSE (1946-   ) appointed to a Personal Chair of Experimental Geochemistry.

GEOPHYSICS

1969   **Alan H Cook** FRS (1922-   ) first Professor of Geophysics.

1973   **Kenneth M Creer** FRAS FRSE (1926-1993) second Professor of Geophysics.

INDUSTRIAL LIAISON (UNIVED TECHNOLOGIES LTD)

1947   Industrial Liaison Committee formed.

1969   Creation of the Centre for Industrial Consultancy and Liaison (CICL).

       Dr John W Midgley first Director.

1983   **Mike Weber**, from the Department of Business Studies, second Director of CICL, and from 1984 Director of UnivEd Technologies Ltd.

1984   CICL superseded by UnivEd Technologies Limited.

1990   Mike Weber appointed also Director of Industrial Liaison.

INFORMATICS

1983 Established as the School of Information Technology, comprising the Departments of *Artificial Intelligence, *Computer Science and *Electrical Engineering, and the Centre for *Cognitive Science.

1989 Combined with the School of Engineering to form the School of Engineering and Information Technology.

1992 School renamed *Engineering and Informatics.

MACHINE INTELLIGENCE

1967 **Donald Michie** FRSE (1923-   ) appointed to a Personal Chair of Machine Intelligence. He joined Edinburgh University in 1958 in the Faculty of Medicine, and in 1965 was appointed Director of the Experimental Programming Unit. In 1966-67 he was Reader in the Department of Brain and Automata Studies.

1968 Department of Machine Intelligence and Perception created.
 Richard L Gregory FRSE (1923-   ) appointed to a Personal Chair of Bionics. Resigned 1970.

1969 **H Christopher Longuet-Higgins** FRS (1923-   ) joined the Department as Royal Society Research Professor. Resigned 1974.

1972 Department renamed Machine Intelligence, and incorporated in the newly-instituted School of *Artificial Intelligence.

1974 Prof Michie detached himself from the newly-renamed School of Computer Science and Artificial Intelligence, and re-established Machine Intelligence as an independent Department.

1984 On Prof Michie's resignation the Department was disbanded.

MATHEMATICAL PHYSICS

1922 The Tait Chair of Natural Philosophy was instituted, the intention being that the chair should be devoted to the teaching of Mathematical Physics.

1923 **Sir Charles G Darwin** KBE FRS FRSE (1887-1962) first Tait Professor of Natural Philosophy. Grandson of Charles Robert Darwin.

1936 **Max Born** FRS FRSE (1882-1970) second Tait Professor of Natural Philosophy; he was awarded the Nobel Prize for Physics in 1954.

1953 **Nicholas Kemmer** FRS FRSE (1911-   ) third Tait Professor of Natural Philosophy. During his tenure of the Chair its title was changed to the Tait Chair of Mathematical Physics. Retired 1979.

1971 Mathematical Physics combined with *Physics when both Departments moved to the James Clerk Maxwell Building at the King's Buildings.

MATHEMATICS

1583 Chair of Mathematics considered to have been instituted at the time of the foundation of the Tounis College.

1620 **Andrew Young**, the senior Regent, given the title of 'public Professor of Mathematics', in addition to his duties as regent.

1640 **Thomas Craufurd** (d. 1662) succeeded Andrew Young.

1674 **James Gregory** FRS (1638-1675) first separate Professor of Mathematics.

1683	**David Gregory** FRS (1659-1708) nephew of the preceding, and fourth Professor of Mathematics, appointed at the age of 24.
1692	**James Gregory** (1666-1742) brother of the preceding, and fifth Professor of Mathematics.
1725	**Colin McLaurin** FRS (1698-1746) sixth Professor of Mathematics (jointly with James Gregory until the latter's death in 1742).
1747	**Matthew Stewart** FRS FRSE (1717-1785) seventh Professor of Mathematics.
1775	**Dugald Stewart** FRSE (1753-1828) eighth Professor of Mathematics.
1785	**Adam Ferguson** FRSE (1723-1816) who had already held the chairs of Natural Philosophy and Moral Philosophy, was appointed ninth Professor of Mathematics with John Playfair FRSE (1748-1819) as his assistant. Playfair became Professor of Natural Philosophy in 1805.
1805	**Sir John Leslie** FRSE (1766-1832) tenth Professor of Mathematics. He also moved from Mathematics to Natural Philosophy, succeeding Playfair in 1819.
1819	**William Wallace** FRSE (1768-1843) eleventh Professor of Mathematics.
1838	**Rev Philip Kelland** FRS PRSE (1808-1879) twelfth Professor of Mathematics.
1879	**George Chrystal** FRSE (1851-1911) thirteenth Professor of Mathematics.
1893	The Professor of Mathematics in the Faculty of Arts became also a member of the newly-instituted Faculty of Science.
1912	**Sir Edmund Whittaker** FRS PRSE (1873-1956) fourteenth Professor of Mathematics.
1946	**Alexander C Aitken** FRS FRSE (1895-1967) fifteenth Professor of Mathematics.
1964	**Arthur Erdélyi** FRS FRSE (1908-1977) sixteenth Professor of Mathematics.
1965	**Frank F Bonsall** FRS (1920-) appointed to the McLaurin Chair of Mathematics. Retired 1984.
1966	Departments of Mathematics and Natural Philosophy finally transferred from the Faculty of Arts to the Faculty of Science.
1968	**Andrew G Mackie** FRSE (1927-) appointed Professor of Applied Mathematics. Retired 1988.
1970	**William L Edge** FRSE (1904-) appointed Professor of Mathematics – Geometry. Retired 1975.
1972	**Ivor M H Etherington** FRSE (1908-1994) appointed Professor of Mathematics – Algebra. Retired 1974.
1976	Department of Mathematics moved from Chambers Street to the James Clerk Maxwell Building at the King's Buildings.
1979	**Elmer G Rees** FRSE (1941-) seventeenth Professor of Mathematics.
1985	**Terence J Lyons** FRSE FRSA (1953-) appointed to the Colin McLaurin Chair of Mathematics. Resigned 1993, now an Honorary Professor.
1990	**David F Parker** (1940-) appointed to the Chair of Applied Mathematics.
1991	**Allan M Sinclair** FRSE (1941-) appointed to a Personal Chair of Operator Algebras and Mathematical Analysis. The Departments of Mathematics and Statistics were combined.

MATHEMATICS AND STATISTICS

| 1991 | The Departments of Mathematics and Statistics were combined. |

1993   **Terence J Lyons** FRSE FRSA (1953-   ) Honorary Professor.
              Henry D Patterson FRSE (1924-) Honorary Professor.

MECHANICAL ENGINEERING   [For antecedents see Engineering]

1965   **Leslie G Jaeger** FRSE (1926-   ) fifth Regius Professor of Engineering. The Regius Chair was then, in effect, the Chair of Mechanical Engineering only.
1967   School of Engineering Science instituted, consisting of the Departments of Chemical, Electrical and Mechanical Engineering.
1968   **James L King** (1922-   ) sixth Regius Professor of Engineering.
1979, Jan 1   School of Engineering Science re-constituted as the School of Engineering, adding the Departments of Civil Engineering and Building Science, and Fire Safety Engineering.
1983   **Joseph A McGeough** FRSE (1940-   ) seventh Regius Professor of Engineering.
1986   **Stephen H Salter** FRSE (1938-   ) appointed to a Personal Chair of Engineering Design.

METEOROLOGY

1944   Specialist lecturer (James Paton) appointed in the Department of Physics for the teaching of Meteorology.
1956   Balfour Stewart Auroral Laboratory (funded by the Royal Society of London) instituted, with **James Paton** as Director.
1967   Meteorology became a separate Department under James Paton, Reader, who retired in 1973.
1973   **Douglas H McIntosh** OBE FRSE (1917-1993) Head of Department until he retired in 1982.
1976   Department of Meteorology moved to the King's Buildings.
1992   Head of Department - **Dr R S Harwood.**

MICROBIOLOGY

1913   Robert Irvine Chair of Bacteriology instituted in the Faculties of Medicine and Science. Bacteriology is now known as Medical Microbiology in the Faculty of Medicine.
1969   Department of General Microbiology instituted in the Faculty of Science.
1970   **John F Wilkinson** (1925-   ) appointed to a Personal Chair of Microbiology, and Head of the Division of Microbiology in the Edinburgh and East of Scotland College of Agriculture.
1971   Department renamed Microbiology.
1989   On the retirement of Prof Wilkinson the Division of Microbiology in the Edinburgh and East of Scotland College of Agriculture was disbanded.
1990   The Department of Microbiology was incorporated in the Institute of *Cell and Molecular Biology in the Division of Biological Sciences.

MINING

1924	**Henry Briggs** OBE (1883-1935) Professor of Mining at the Heriot-Watt College, Edinburgh, appointed conjointly to the James A Hood Chair of Mining in the University of Edinburgh.
1936	**William H Macmillan** (d.1947) second James A Hood Professor of Mining, and Professor of Mining at the Heriot-Watt College.
1948	**Robert McAdam** FRSE (1906-1978) third James A Hood Professor of Mining, and Professor of Mining at the Heriot-Watt College.
1966	The joint course, and the Chair, ceased to exist in the University when the Heriot-Watt College became a University.

MOLECULAR BIOLOGY

1952	Biophysics Unit formed in the Department of Natural Philosophy, headed by **Jack Dainty**, who resigned in 1962.
1957	Unit became the Department of Biophysics.
1964	**Martin Pollock** FRS (1914-) appointed to a new Chair of Biology in the Department of Biophysics. Retired 1976.
1965	Department renamed Molecular Biology.
1966	**William Hayes** FRS FRSE (1913-1994) appointed to a Personal Chair of Molecular Genetics. Resigned 1973.
1968	Department moved into part of the new Darwin Building at the King's Buildings.
1976	**Kenneth Murray** FRS FRSE (1930-) appointed Professor of Molecular Biology.
1982	**Neil S Willetts** (1939-) appointed to a Personal Chair of Molecular Genetics. Resigned 1985.
1984	**Kenneth Murray** appointed Biogen Research Professor of Molecular Biology. **John G Scaife** FRSE (1934-1991) Professor of Molecular Parasitology.
1987	**Richard P Ambler** (1933-) appointed to a Personal Chair of Protein Chemistry.
1988	**Noreen Murray** FRS FRSE (1935-) appointed to a Personal Chair of Molecular Genetics. Biocomputing Research Unit set up, with funding from the Darwin Trust.
1990	Department of Molecular Biology incorporated in the Institute of *Cell and Molecular Biology within the Division of Biological Sciences.

NATURAL HISTORY

1767	Chair of Natural History instituted in the Faculty of Medicine.
1770	**Robert Ramsay** (d. 1779) first Professor of Natural History. There is no record of any lectures having been given by him.
1779	**John Walker** FRSE (1731-1803) second Professor of Natural History.
1804	**Robert Jameson** FRSE (1774-1854) third Professor of Natural History.
1854	**Edward Forbes** FRS FRSE (1815-1854) fourth Professor of Natural History, but died six months after taking up the appointment.
1855	**George J Allman** FRS FRSE (1812-1898) fifth Professor of Natural History.
1870	**Sir Charles Wyville Thomson** FRS FRSE (1830-1882) sixth Professor of Natural History.
1871	Regius Chair of *Geology endowed by Sir Roderick I Murchison.

1872	Wyville Thomson set off on the Challenger expedition, which in four years circumnavigated the globe and brought back a great variety of specimens.
1882	**James Cossar Ewart** FRS FRSE (1851-1933) seventh Professor of Natural History. Retired 1927.
1893	The Professor of Natural History became a member of the newly-instituted Faculty of Science.
1919	**James H Ashworth** FRSE (1874-1936) appointed to the newly-instituted Chair of Zoology.
1927	The Department of Natural History was renamed *Zoology. Ashworth was translated to the Chair of Natural History as the eighth Professor, and the Chair of Zoology remained vacant until 1963.

NATURAL PHILOSOPHY

1583	Chair of Natural Philosophy considered to have been instituted at the time of the foundation of the Tounis College.
1708	**Sir Robert Stewart** (1675-1747), a Regent of Philosophy since 1703, was appointed the first Professor of Natural Philosophy, in the Faculty of Arts.
1742	**John Stewart** was associated with his father, then became the second Professor of Natural Philosophy in 1747.
1759	**Adam Ferguson** FRSE (1723-1816) third Professor of Natural Philosophy. In 1764 he resigned to take up the Chair of Moral Philosophy.
1764	**James Russell** fourth Professor of Natural Philosophy, another incumbent of whose life and teachings little is known.
1774	**John Robison** FRSE (1739-1805) fifth Professor of Natural Philosophy, the first to raise the Edinburgh chair to a position of eminence.
1805	**John Playfair** FRSE (1748-1819) sixth Professor of Natural Philosophy, having been Professor of Mathematics for the previous twenty years.
1819	**Sir John Leslie** FRSE (1766-1832) seventh Professor of Natural Philosophy, had been Professor of Mathematics from 1805 to 1819.
1833	**James D Forbes** FRS FRSE (1809-1868) eighth Professor of Natural Philosophy.
1860	**Peter G Tait** FRSE (1831-1901) ninth Professor of Natural Philosophy.
1893	The Professor of Natural Philosophy became a member also of the newly-instituted Facultyof Science.
1901	**James G MacGregor** FRS (1852-1913) tenth Professor of Natural Philosophy.
1913	**Charles G Barkla** FRS (1877-1944) eleventh Professor of Natural Philosophy. He was awarded the Nobel Prize for Physics in 1917.
1945	**Norman Feather** FRS PRSE (1904-1978) twelfth Professor of Natural Philosophy.
1964	**William Cochran** FRS FRSE (1922-) appointed to the second Chair of Physics in the Department of Natural Philosophy.
1966	The Departments of Mathematics and Natural Philosophy were finally transferred from the Faculty of Arts to the Faculty of Science.
1967	**Peter S Farago** FRSE (1918-) appointed to a Personal Chair in Physics. Retired 1982.
1969	The Fluid Dynamics Unit was created within the Department of Natural Philosophy, with **Dr Marion A S Ross** as Director.

1970	In the Faculty of Science, the title of the Department of Natural Philosophy was changed to *Physics – but in the Faculty of Arts, the courses in Physics are still referred to as Natural Philosophy.

PHYSICS   [For antecedents *see* Natural Philosophy]

1970	**Roger A Cowley** FRS FRSE (1939-) appointed to a Personal Chair in Physics. Resigned 1988.
1971	The Department of Mathematical Physics (Prof Kemmer) was amalgamated with the Department of Physics (Prof Feather).
1973	Dr Ross retired and was succeeded as Director of the Fluid Dynamics Unit by **Dr Clive Greated**.
1975	Following the retirement of Prof Feather, **William Cochran** became the thirteenth Professor of Natural Philosophy.
1979	**David J Wallace** FRS FRSE (1945-) fourth Tait Professor of Mathematical Physics, and Director of the *Edinburgh Parallel Computing Centre.
1980	**Peter W Higgs** FRS FRSE (1929-) appointed to a Personal Chair in Theoretical Physics.
1985	**G Stuart Pawley** FRS FRSE (1937-) appointed to a Personal Chair in Computational Physics.
1989	**Alan C Shotter** FRSE (1942-) appointed to a Personal Chair in Experimental Physics.
1990	**Peter N Pusey** (1942-) appointed to a Personal Chair in Physics.
1992	**Richard J Nelmes** (1943-) appointed to a Personal Chair in Physical Crystallography.
1993	**Clive A Greated FRSE** (1940-) Director of the Fluid Dynamics Unit since 1973, appointed to a Personal Chair in Fluid Dynamics. Departments of Physics and Astronomy combined.

PUBLIC HEALTH

1875	Degrees of BSc and DSc in Public Health instituted in the Faculty of Science; candidates had to be graduates in Medicine.
1898	Chair of Public Health endowed by Bruce and John Usher in the Faculties of Medicine and Science. **Charles Hunter Stewart** (1854-1924) first Professor of Public Health.
1902	Formal opening of the John Usher Institute of Public Health. A Department of Public Health was created in the Faculty of Science at about the same time.
1925	**Col Percy S Lelean** (1871-1956) second Professor of Public Health. Soon afterwards Public Health was removed from the Faculty of Science, continuing as a Department in the Faculty of Medicine.
1944	**Francis A E Crew** FRS FRSE (1886-1973) third Professor of Public Health and Social Medicine. An Edinburgh medical graduate (MB, ChB 1912), he was Professor of Animal *Genetics, 1928-44, in the Faculty of Science.

SCIENCE DEGREES COMMITTEE

1864 Degrees of Bachelor of Science and Doctor of Science were first offered in session 1864-65, administered by the Science Degrees Committee of the Senate.

1866 The first degrees in science were three in number, one of DSc and two of BSc, out of a total of 153 degrees conferred.

1892 The total numbers of Science Degrees conferred by Edinburgh University before the Faculty of Science was instituted in 1893 were:
DSc - 65, and BSc - 224.

SCIENCE, Faculty of

1893 Faculties of Science were instituted in the Universities of Aberdeen, Edinburgh and Glasgow under the terms of Ordinance No 31 of the Commissioners appointed under the Universities (Scotland) Act, 1889.
Prof James Geikie (Geology) first Dean of the Faculty of Science.

1914 **Prof Sir Thomas Hudson Beare** (Engineering) Dean, until his death in 1940.

1922 New regulations provided for the award of BSc with Honours in any one of 13 schools in the Faculty of Science, including Botany.

1940 **Prof James Ritchie** (Natural History) Dean.

1948 **Prof Ronald N Arnold** (Engineering) Dean.

1954 **Prof James P Kendall** (Chemistry) Dean.

1955 **Prof Ronald N Arnold** (Engineering) Dean.

1957 **Prof James P Kendall** (Chemistry) Dean.

1959 **Prof Sir Edmund L Hirst** (Chemistry) Dean.

1963 **Prof Sir Michael M Swann** (Zoology) Dean.

1965 Appleton Tower completed and brought into use for first year science teaching.

1966 **Prof Frederick H Stewart** (Geology) Dean.

1967 Faculty meetings ceased to be held in the Old College.

1968 **Prof Hermann A Brück** (Astronomy) Dean.

1971 **Prof John N Black** (Forestry) Dean. (January-June only)

1971 **Prof Norman Feather** (Physics) Dean. (from October)

1974 **Prof Noel F Robertson** (Agriculture) Dean.

1975 **Prof Charles Kemball** (Chemistry) Dean.

1978 **Prof William Cochran** (Physics) Dean.

1981 **Prof Michael Yeoman** (Botany) Dean.

1984 **Prof John M Mitchison** (Zoology) Dean.

1985 **Prof Evelyn A V Ebsworth** (Chemistry) Dean.

1989 **Prof John Mavor** (Electrical Engineering) Dean.

1990 The Faculty of Science was renamed the Faculty of *Science and Engineering.

SCIENCE AND ENGINEERING, Faculty of

1990 The Faculty of Science was renamed the Faculty of Science and Engineering.
Prof John Mavor (Electrical Engineering) Dean.

STATISTICS

| 1966 | **David J Finney** CBE FRSE (1917-   ) first Professor of Statistics. Retired 1984. |
| 1991 | The Departments of Mathematics and Statistics were combined. |

UNIVERSITY OF EDINBURGH

1583	'Tounis College' of Edinburgh founded under a Charter of King James VI.
1685	Creation (in effect) of a Faculty of Medicine by two Acts of the Town Council, in March and September, instituting four Professorships in the practice of medicine. The Act of 24 March also for the first time referred to the Town's College as a University.
1708	Abolition of the regent system of teaching.
1826	Royal Commission on the Universities of Scotland. It reported to Parliament in 1830, but for the next quarter of a century nothing was done.
1863, Feb	Lyon Playfair, the Professor of Chemistry, proposed in the Senate 'That a committee be appointed to consider the best means by which a Degree in Science may be initiated in this University.'
1864, Feb	The committee's proposals were generally accepted.
1864, Oct	Degrees of BSc and DSc were instituted in the academic year 1864-65, administered by the *Science Degrees Committee of the Senate.
1876	Royal Commission on the Universities of Scotland. One of its remits was the regulations for the granting of Degrees in Science.
1889	The Universities (Scotland) Act, 1889, 'An Act for the Better Administration and Endowment of the Universities of Scotland', was passed on 30 August 1889 and came into operation on 1 January 1890.
1893, June 5	In Ordinance No 31 – Glasgow, Aberdeen, and Edinburgh, No 1, under the said Act, the Commissioners specified the Composition of the Faculties and the Institution of Faculties of Science in the three Universities.
1893, Nov 23	Ordinance No 31 was approved by Order in Council.

VETERINARY SCIENCE

| 1911 | BSc and DSc degrees in Veterinary Science instituted in the Faculty of Science. The Department of Veterinary Science was created in the Faculty of Science at about the same time. |
| 1964 | The University created a Faculty of Veterinary Medicine. |

ZOOLOGY   [For antecedents see Natural History]

1927	**James H Ashworth** FRSE (1874-1936) eighth Professor of Natural History. He presided over the re-housing of the Department at the King's Buildings in what is now known as the Ashworth Building, opened in May 1929.
1936	**James Ritchie** CBE FRSE (1882-1958) ninth Professor of Natural History.
1952	**Michael M Swann** (Baron Swann, 1981) FRS FRSE (1920-1990) tenth Professor of Natural History. Principal and Vice-Chancellor 1965-73.

1963   **J Murdoch Mitchison** FRS FRSE (1922-   ) second Professor of Zoology. Retired 1988.

1966   **Peter M B Walker** CBE FRSE (1922-   ) eleventh Professor of Natural History. In 1973 he left the Department to become Director of the MRC Mammalian *Genome Unit, from which he retired in 1980.

1973   **Aubrey W G Manning** FRSE (1930-   ) twelfth Professor of Natural History.

1988   **H Spedding Micklem** (1933-) appointed Professor of Immunobiology.

1990   **David S Saunders** (1935-) appointed Professor of Insect Physiology.
The majority of the staff of the Department of Zoology were integrated into the Institute of *Cell, Animal and Population Biology, along with staff of similar research interests from Agriculture, Forestry and Natural Resources, and Genetics.

APPENDIX B
ASSOCIATED INSTITUTIONS

There are in all 27 research units and scientific institutes formally associated with the University of Edinburgh by virtue of their contribution to its academic activities. The following are directly associated with the Faculty of Science and Engineering.

AFRC ROSLIN INSTITUTE, EDINBURGH
Started life as part of the Animal Breeding Research Department of the University [*Genetics] during the First World War. In recent years the Institute has usually had some 30 to 40 PhD students at any one time, and its members of staff are heavily involved in university teaching at undergraduate and MSc levels, in close collaboration with the Division of *Biological Sciences. The Acting Director of the Institute is **Prof Grahame Bulfield** FRSE.

BRITISH GEOLOGICAL SURVEY, EDINBURGH

FORESTRY COMMISSION NORTHERN RESEARCH STATION

MACAULAY LAND USE RESEARCH INSTITUTE, CRAIGIEBUCKLER, ABERDEEN

NERC INSTITUTE OF TERRESTRIAL ECOLOGY

ROYAL BOTANIC GARDEN, EDINBURGH

ROYAL MUSEUM OF SCOTLAND, EDINBURGH

ROYAL OBSERVATORY, EDINBURGH

SCOTTISH AGRICULTURAL COLLEGE, EDINBURGH

SCOTTISH AGRICULTURAL SCIENCE AGENCY

SCOTTISH AGRICULTURAL STATISTICS SERVICE

In 1984 when Prof Finney retired from the Chair of *Statistics **Dr H D Patterson** FRSE was appointed Acting Director and Honorary Professor. He retired in 1985 and the following year **Mr R A Kempton** was appointed Director, with a remit to establish a unified statistics service for all. the Scottish Agricultural Research Organisations.

The Scottish Agricultural Statistics Service was established in 1987 with core funding from the Scottish Office Agricultural and Fisheries Department. There are currently about 25 research staff, half of them based at the King's Buildings.

SCOTTISH CROP RESEARCH INSTITUTE, INVERGOWRIE, DUNDEE

SCOTTISH UNIVERSITIES RESEARCH & REACTOR CENTRE, EAST KILBRIDE

The Centre was established in 1963 by a consortium of universities to provide a research facility – a 100kW research reactor – that would have strained the resources of any one institution. It is located at East Kilbride near Glasgow, and is now a joint facility receiving its core funding from the Universities of Glasgow, Edinburgh and Strathclyde.

The establishment of the Isotope Geology Unit in 1967 marked the beginning of an expansion of the Centre to provide radiometric dating for geology departments, and at the same time the reactor was upgraded to a power of 300kW, with a concomitant increase in the neutron flux.

After the Chernobyl nuclear reactor disaster the Centre undertook an extensive programme of measurements of radioactivity in the Scottish population, and contributed to the development of a new system of aerial g-ray spectrometry. The Director of the Centre is **Dr Roger D Scott.**

WOLFSON MICROELECTRONICS LIMITED, EDINBURGH

The Wolfson Microelectronics Liaison Unit was established in 1969 within the School of Engineering Science, with a start-up grant of £130,700 from the Wolfson Foundation.

Dr James Murray was appointed the first Director, and the Unit quickly developed an international reputation as a centre of microelectronics expertise.

Dr A David Milne succeeded Jim Murray as Director in 1973 at about the same time as the Unit first became self-supporting, and since then it has been an increasingly profitable commercial organisation, engaged in the design and development of custom integrated circuits and many other microelectronics applications. In 1976 it was renamed the Wolfson Microelectronics Institute and in 1985 it became an independent company, Wolfson Microelectronics Limited, in which the University is a major shareholder.

APPENDIX C

SPIN-OFF COMPANIES

Some examples of companies that originated within the Faculty of Science and Engineering.

ALGOTRONIX LTD

Department of *Computer Science.

BEEVERS MOLECULAR MODELS
Department of *Chemistry.

BIOSCOT LTD now COGENT DIAGNOSTICS
A joint venture by Edinburgh and Heriot-Watt to exploit the potential of both Universities in the field of biotechnology. The name was changed following a substantial injection of capital by the venture fund Cogent, and the company has since successfully developed and marketed a range of diagnostic kits.

CLAN SYSTEMS LTD
Department of *Computer Science.

EDINBURGH TECHNOLOGY TRANSFER CENTRE LTD
A joint venture by the University and the Edinburgh District Council providing fully managed and serviced accommodation on the King's Buildings campus in which promising commercial projects can be developed until they become self-sustaining and move out into their own premises.

EUMOS LTD
A company originally established by the Department of Electrical Engineering to provide training courses in MOS design – hence the name. Rapidly diversified to provide a wide range of short post-experience courses in electrical and electronic engineering, and was able to achieve charitable status because of its primarily educational objectives.

INMAP LTD
Originally set up as a joint venture with the Heriot-Watt University to combine Edinburgh University's skills in VLSI microcircuit design, much of which at the time resided in the Department of Electrical Engineering, with the expertise of the Heriot-Watt's Computer Applications Centre. Subsequently wound up.

LATTICE LOGIC LTD
Department of *Computer Science.

PETROLEUM SCIENCE AND TECHNOLOGY INSTITUTE LTD
Joint venture between the Department of *Geology and Geophysics and the Heriot-Watt University. The Institute acts as a catalyst and facilitator of industry-led, university-based hydrocarbon research and development. It has attracted more than fifty sponsors for its activities in both research and teaching, aimed primarily at increasing exploration efficiency and lowering production costs in the industry.

THE QUANTUM FUND LTD
This development support fund was established with relatively small sums of money from the University and a number of local financial institutions. Its main objective is to assist promising new developments to reach the stage where they can bridge the 'credibility gap' by demonstrating the commercial feasibility of a prototype to prospective industrial backers. The Quantum Fund's

responsibility extends to the whole of the University, but its major successes to date have been in the Faculty of Science and Engineering.

TROPAG CONSULTANTS LTD
A company established to provide training and consultancy services in all aspects of tropical agriculture, essentially taking over the business built up through CICL by staff in the Departments of Agriculture and Forestry, and the Centre for Tropical Veterinary Medicine. It attracted support from some of the world's top funding agencies such as the British Council, the UN FAO and the World Bank, but changing circumstances made its existence anomalous and it was wound up. The steadily increasing number of tropical agriculture courses and consultancies is now managed by UnivEd.

VLSI VISION LTD
The most successful outcome to date of the Quantum Fund's sponsorships, the basic imaging technologies were developed from the requirements of an earlier fingerprint recognition project, also supported by Quantum. The advantages of the new technique are the low cost of production and the ability to directly interface the image sensing with digital processing. After a two-year development programme, based in the Technology Transfer Centre, the company launched the world's smallest video camera, and after successfully arranging its second-round refinancing moved to its own premises in Edinburgh early in 1993.

WOLFSON MICROELECTRONICS LTD
Established as the Wolfson Microelectronics Liaison Unit in the Department of *Electrical Engineering, by the late 1970s it had achieved an international reputation. In 1985 it was incorporated as a limited company and moved off campus to its own premises, with the University remaining a major shareholder, to further develop its business of designing and supplying integrated circuits.

REFERENCES

[ ] Abbreviation used in text.

BALFOUR REPORT 1929 *Factors in Industrial and Commercial Efficiency* London, HMSO.

BARLOW REPORT 1946 *Scientific Manpower* Cmnd.6824 London, HMSO.

BIRSE, R M 1983 *Engineering at Edinburgh University: a short history 1673-1983* Edinburgh University, the School of Engineering.

BIRSE, R M 1989 Scotland's Contribution to the Scientific and Industrial Advance of Europe, 1750-1914. Unpublished paper read at Symposium on *The History of Technology, Science and Society 1750-1914*, University of Ulster, September 1989.

BRITISH ASSOCIATION 1921 *Edinburgh's Place in Scientific Progress* [BA] Edinburgh, W & R Chambers.

BRÜCK, H A 1983 *The Story of Astronomy in Edinburgh from its beginnings until 1975* Edinburgh University Press.

BURNETT, J 1969 *A History of the Cost of Living* London, Penguin Books.

CALDER, J and ANDREWS, S M 1986 A Source of Inspiration: Robert Jameson. In: CALDER, J (ed) *The Enterprising Scot* Edinburgh, the Royal Museum of Scotland.

CAMPBELL, N and SMELLIE, R M S 1983 *The Royal Society of Edinburgh 1783-1983* [RSE] The Royal Society of Edinburgh.

CARDWELL, D S L 1971 *From Watt to Clausius: the rise of thermodynamics in the early industrial age* London, Heinemann.

CHAMBERS, R (ed) 1875 *A Biographical Dictionary of Eminent Scotsmen* (6 vols, rev by Rev Thos Thomson) [BDES] Glasgow, Blackie.

CHAMBERS 1992 *Scottish Biographical Dictionary* [CSBD] Edinburgh, Chambers.

CLEMENT, A G and ROBERTSON, R H S 1961 *Scotland's Scientific Heritage* Edinburgh, Oliver & Boyd.

COLVIN, S and EWING, J A (eds) 1887 *Papers Literary, Scientific, etc, by the late Fleeming Jenkin, with a Memoir by Robert Louis Stevenson* (2 vols) London, Longmans, Green.

DAICHES, D and JONES, P & J (eds) 1986 *A Hotbed of Genius: the Scottish Enlightenment 1730-1790* Edinburgh University Press.

DAINTON REPORT 1968 *Enquiry into the Flow of Candidates in Science and Technology into Higher Education* Interim Report (1966) and Final Report (1968) London, HMSO.

DALZEL, A 1862 *History of the University of Edinburgh from its foundation* (ed Laing) Edinburgh.

DARWIN, Charles 1859 *The Origin of Species* London, John Murray.

DAVIE, G E 1964 *The Democratic Intellect: Scotland and her Universities in the Nineteenth Century* 2ed Edinburgh University Press.

DAVIES, M 1982 A Survey of British Scientists *Sci. Prog., Oxf.* (1982) 68, 1-18.

DICTIONARY OF AMERICAN BIOGRAPHY [DAB] 1928-36 (20 vols) New York, Charles Scribner's Sons.

DICTIONARY OF NATIONAL BIOGRAPHY [DNB] 1885-1993 (22 + 9 vols, & supplement) Oxford University Press.

DICTIONARY OF SCIENTIFIC BIOGRAPHY [DSB] Ed C C Gillispie 1970-80 (16 vols) New York, Charles Scribner's Sons.

EDINBURGH EVIDENCE 1837 *Evidence, Oral and Documentary, taken and received by the Commissioners for Visiting the Universities of Scotland: Volume 1, University of Edinburgh* London, HMSO.

EMMERSON, G S 1973 *Engineering Education: a Social History* Newton Abbot, David & Charles.

FLEMING, I J and ROBERTSON, N F 1990 *Britain's First Chair of Agriculture at the University of Edinburgh 1790-1990* Edinburgh, the East of Scotland College of Agriculture.

FORBES, E 1983 Philosophy and Science Teaching in the Seventeenth Century. In: DONALDSON, G (ed) *Four Centuries: Edinburgh University Life, 1583-1983* Edinburgh University Press.

GRANT, Sir A 1884 *The Story of the University of Edinburgh during its first three hundred years* (2 vols) London, Longmans, Green.

HANS, N 1951 *New Trends in Education in the Eighteenth Century* London, Routledge & Kegan Paul.

HORN, D B 1967 *A Short History of the University of Edinburgh, 1556-1889* Edinburgh University Press.

HUME, David 1739 *A Treatise of Human Nature* 2 vols, 1739-40 London.

JONES REPORT 1967 *The Brain Drain, Report of the Working Party on Migration* Cmnd.3417 London, HMSO.

LIGHTHILL REPORT 1972 *Part I: Artificial Intelligence, General Survey* London, Science Research Council.

MACMILLAN 1983 *Dictionary of the History of Science* (ed Bynum, Browne and Porter) [DHS] London, Macmillan.

MORRELL, J B 1971 Individualism and the Structure of British Science in 1830. *Historical Studies in the Physical Sciences*, 3, 183-204.

MORRELL, J B 1983 Medicine and Science in the Eighteenth Century. In: DONALDSON, G (ed) *Four Centuries: Edinburgh University Life, 1583-1983* Edinburgh University Press.

ROBBINS REPORT 1963 *Higher Education* Cmnd.2154 London, HMSO.

RUSSELL, J L 1974 Cosmological Teaching in the Seventeenth Century Scottish Universities. *Journal for the History of Astronomy*, 5 (1974), 122-32 and 145-54.

SCOTLAND, J 1969 *The History of Scottish Education* (2 vols) University of London Press.

SCOTLAND'S CULTURAL HERITAGE Volume 5 1984 *The Royal Society of Edinburgh: Scientific and Engineering Fellows Elected 1784-1876* Edinburgh University, History of Medicine and Science Unit.

SCOTTISH UNIVERSITIES 1915 *The Universities (Scotland) Act, 1889, together with Ordinances of the Commissioners and University Court Ordinances, with an Appendix containing the Universities (Scotland) Act, 1858* Glasgow, James MacLehose & Sons.

SHEPHERD, Christine 1975 *Philosophy and Science in the Arts Curriculum of the Scottish Universities in the Seventeenth Century* Unpublished PhD thesis, University of Edinburgh.

STEWART, W A C 1989 *Higher Education in Postwar Britain* London, Macmillan.

TAYLOR, C J 1985 *Forestry and Natural Resources in the University of Edinburgh* Edinburgh University, Department of Forestry and Natural Resources.

TURNER, A Logan (ed) 1933 *History of the University of Edinburgh, 1883-1933* Edinburgh, Oliver & Boyd.

WEBSTER'S AMERICAN BIOGRAPHIES [WAB] 1984 Springfield, Mass., Merriam-Webster.

WHO'S WHO [WW] (annual publication) London, Adam & Charles Black.

WHO'S WHO IN SCIENCE IN EUROPE [WWISIE] 8ed, 1993 Harlow, Longman.
WHO'S WHO IN SCOTLAND [WWIS] 4ed, 1992-93 Irvine, Carrick Media.
WHO WAS WHO [WWW] 8 vols 1897-1990 London, Adam & Charles Black.
WYNNE, B 1977 *C G Barkla and the J-phenomenon; a case study in the sociology of physics*
     Unpublished MPhil thesis, University of Edinburgh.

SELECT BIBLIOGRAPHY

ANDERSON, R D 1983 repr 1989 *Education and Opportunity in Victorian Scotland* Edinburgh University Press.

ANDERSON, R D 1992 *Universities and Elites in Britain since 1800* London, Macmillan.

ANDERSON, R G W 1978 *The Playfair Collection and the Teaching of Chemistry at the University of Edinburgh 1713-1858* Edinburgh, the Royal Scottish Museum.

ANDERSON, R G W 1986 Industrial Enterprise and the Scottish Universities in the Eighteenth Century. In: CALDER, J (ed) *The Enterprising Scot* Edinburgh, the Royal Museum of Scotland.

BARTHOLOMEW M & MORRIS P 1991 Science in the Scottish Enlightenment. In: GOODMAN, D & RUSSELL, C A (eds) *The Rise of Scientific Europe 1500-1800* The Open University, Hodder & Stoughton.

BEVERIDGE, C and TURNBULL, R 1989 *The Eclipse of Scottish Culture* Edinburgh, Polygon.

BRÜCK, H A and BRÜCK, M T 1988 *The Peripatetic Astronomer* (Charles Piazzi Smyth) London, Institute of Physics.

BRYDEN, D J 1990 The Edinburgh Observatory 1736-1811: a story of failure. *Annals of Science*, 47, 445-74.

CHRISTIE, J 1974 The origins and development of the Scottish scientific community, 1680-1760. *History of Science*, 12, 122-141.

CHRISTIE, J R R 1975 The Rise and Fall of Scottish Science. In: CROSLAND, M (ed) *The Emergence of Science in Western Europe* London, Macmillan.

CUNNINGHAM, F 1990 *James David Forbes Pioneer Scottish Glaciologist* Edinburgh, Scottish Academic Press.

DEMPSTER, W J 1983 *Patrick Matthew and Natural Selection* Edinburgh, Paul Harris.

DONALDSON, G (ed) 1983 *Four Centuries: Edinburgh University Life, 1583-1983* Edinburgh University Press.

DONOVAN, A L 1975 *Philosophical Chemistry in the Scottish Enlightenment: the doctrines and discoveries of William Cullen and Joseph Black* Edinburgh University Press.

EDGE, D 1988 Twenty Years of Science Studies at Edinburgh. In: MAYER (ed) *Ordnung, Rationalisierung, Kontrolle* Proc of a Symposium, May 1987, Technische Hochschule Darmstadt.

EWING, A W 1939 *The Man of Room 40: the Life of Sir Alfred Ewing* London, Hutchinson.

FLETCHER, H R and BROWN, W H 1970 *The Royal Botanic Garden Edinburgh 1670-1970* Department of Agriculture and Fisheries for Scotland Edinburgh, HMSO.

FOOTMAN, R and YOUNG, B 1983 *Edinburgh University: an illustrated memoir* University of Edinburgh.

GOLDMAN, M 1983 *The Demon in the Aether: the story of James Clerk Maxwell* Edinburgh, Paul Harris.

GREEN, V H H 1969 *The Universities* (British Institutions series) London, Pelican Books.

KNOTT, C G 1911 *The Life and Scientific Work of Peter Guthrie Tait* Cambridge University Press.

MORGAN, A (ed) 1937 *University of Edinburgh: Charters, Statutes, and Acts of the Town Council and the Senatus 1583-1858* Edinburgh, Oliver & Boyd.

MORRELL, J B 1970 The University of Edinburgh in the late eighteenth century; its scientific eminence and academic structure. *Isis*, 62, 158-171.

MORRELL, J B 1976 The Patronage of Mid-Victorian Science in the University of Edinburgh. In: TURNER, G L'E (ed) *The Patronage of Science in the Nineteenth Century* Leyden, Noordhoff International.

MORRISON-LOW, A D and CHRISTIE, J R R (eds) 1984 *'Martyr of Science': Sir David Brewster 1781-1868* Proceedings of a Bicentenary Symposium, November 1981 Edinburgh, the Royal Scottish Museum.

MORTON, A G 1986 *John Hope 1725-1786: Scottish Botanist* Edinburgh, Botanic Garden (Sibbald) Trust

PHILLIPSON, N (ed) 1983 *Universities, Society, and the Future* Proceedings of a Conference held in the University of Edinburgh. Edinburgh University Press.

POOLE, J B and ANDREWS, Kay (eds) 1972 *The Government of Science in Britain* London, Weidenfeld and Nicolson.

RANKINE, W J Macquorn 1881 *Miscellaneous Scientific Papers* Ed by W J Millar, with a memoir of Rankine by P G Tait. London, Charles Griffin.

ROBERTSON, P 1984 Scottish Universities and Scottish Industry, 1860-1914. In: *Scottish Economic and Social History*, 4, 39-54.

ROBINSON, E & McKIE, D (eds) *Partners in Science: letters of James Watt and Joseph Black* London, Constable.

RODERICK, G W & STEPHENS, M D 1978 *Education and Industry in the Nineteenth Century* London, Longman.

ROYAL SCOTTISH MUSEUM 1968 *James Short and his Telescopes* Edinburgh, HMSO.

SANDERSON, M 1972 *The Universities and British Industry 1850-1970* London, Routledge & Kegan Paul.

SHEPHERD, Christine 1983 University Life in the Seventeenth Century. In: DONALDSON, G (ed) *Four Centuries: Edinburgh University Life, 1583-1983* Edinburgh University Press.

SIMPSON, A D C (ed) 1982 *Joseph Black 1728-1799: a Commemorative Symposium* Edinburgh, the Royal Scottish Museum.

STEVENSON, R L 1912 *Records of a Family of Engineers* London, Chatto & Windus.

STEVENSON, W S 1914 *Famous Edinburgh Students* Edinburgh, T N Foulis.

STEWART, Agnes G 1901 *The Academic Gregories* (Famous Scots series) Edinburgh, Oliphant Anderson & Ferrier.

SUTHERLAND, H B 1973 *Rankine, His Life and Times* London, Institution of Civil Engineers.

SWINTON, A A CAMPBELL 1930 *Autobiographical and other Writings* London, Longmans, Green.

THOMPSON, Ruth D'Arcy 1958 *D'Arcy Wentworth Thompson, the Scholar Naturalist, 1860-1948* Oxford University Press.

WOOD, P 1992 The Scientific Revolution in Scotland. In: PORTER, R and TEICH, M (eds) *The Scientific Revolution in National Context* Cambridge University Press.

NAME INDEX

NOTE: [a] = alumnus (ie studied with or without graduating), [s] = staff (academic, research or other), of the University of Edinburgh.

SUBJECT INDEX

EU - Edinburgh University